Contract and Domination

Contract and Domination

Carole Pateman and Charles W. Mills

polity

First published in 2007 by Polity Press
Reprinted 2007, 2008, 2010, 2012, 2013, 2014 (twice), 2015

Polity Press
65 Bridge Street
Cambridge CB2 1UR, UK

Polity Press
350 Main Street
Malden, MA 02148, USA

ISBN-13: 978-07456-4003-7
ISBN-13: 978-07456-4004-4 (pb)

A catalogue record for this book is available from the British Library.

Typeset in 10.5 on 12 pt Monotype Times
by Servis Filmsetting Ltd, Manchester
Printed and bound in USA by Courier Digital Solutions

The publisher has used its best endeavours to ensure that the URLs for external websites referred to in this book are correct and active at the time of going to press. However, the publisher has no responsibility for the websites and can make no guarantee that a site will remain live or that the content is or will remain appropriate.

Every effort has been made to trace all copyright holders, but if any have been inadvertently overlooked the publishers will be pleased to include the necessary credits in any subsequent reprint or edition.

For further information on Polity, visit our website: www.polity.co.uk

Contents

Acknowledgments

I should like, first, to thank Charles Mills for suggesting that we embark upon this book. It was a good idea and I have learnt a lot during the process, but it has taken far longer to complete than either of us ever anticipated. And it might not be finished now if it were not for support in very difficult times from the University of California, Los Angeles, my department, my colleagues and, above all, from my friends, for which I am very grateful to them all. I also thank the School of European Studies and Cardiff University for offering me the research position that, at last, has allowed me to put the final touches to my parts of our volume.

My thanks are due to Keith Wattenpaugh, Scott Hoaby, Mary McThomas, and Rebekah Sterling for their assistance at various points along the way with my chapter "The Settler Contract," which has a very long history. I am grateful to Peter Hoffenberg for his critical comments on an earlier version of this chapter, which also benefited from a seminar discussion at the London School of Economics, from the comments of Kirstie McClure and Anthony Pagden at a seminar in my department at UCLA, and from the responses of Mark Francis and David Boucher at a seminar at Cardiff University. I am grateful to Senator Martin Mansergh for his reply to a lecture presenting my ideas about the settler contract as part of the 150th anniversary celebrations of the School of Politics and International Relations, University College Dublin.

My response to my critics was presented to a seminar at Cardiff University and my arguments about the intersection of race and sex and the contract of mutual indifference to a seminar at the LSE. Mary McThomas and Rebekah Sterling gave me assistance with these chapters.

I should also like to thank Mary for her help during the years when I needed it the most.

Carole Pateman

Special thanks to begin with to my co-author Carole Pateman, whose work inspired my book *The Racial Contract*, and who has worked patiently with me over the years since the original conception of this project (too long ago to mention!) to its final completion here. Special appreciation also to Bernard Boxill, Howard McGary, and Iris Marion Young for their letters of support for my application for a University of Illinois at Chicago (UIC) internal fellowship at the Institute for the Humanities. The year-long fellowship (2003–4) was a great help in doing the background reading and starting the writing for the book, not to mention the stimulating atmosphere of the Institute itself under the leadership of Mary Beth Rose and Linda Vavra, and the critical feedback from my Institute fellows. I am also indebted as always to my department chair, Bill Hart, and executive assistants Charlotte Jackson and Valerie Brown, for their unfailing support. Christopher Marston did a fine job of turning my crude hand-drawn diagrams into the slick computer graphics of figures 1–4.

Material from this book has been presented in lectures at the following institutions and conferences, in chronological order through 2004–6: as a lecture to the Centre on Values and Ethics, Carleton University (2004); as one of the 2003–4 Seminars of the Fellows series, UIC Institute for the Humanities (2004); as a plenary presentation at the first annual meeting of the Caribbean Philosophical Association (2004); as a panel presentation at the annual meeting of the American Political Science Association (2004); as a lecture to the Graduate Association of Sociologists, Loyola University (2004); as a talk at a workshop of the Chicago Political Theory Group (2004); as the keynote address at the annual Graduate Student Philosophy Conference in Social-Political Thought and Value Theory, Michigan State University (2005); at a symposium memorial session for Susan Okin, American Philosophical Association Central Division annual meeting (2005); as the annual Sprague and Taylor Philosophy Lecture, Brooklyn College (2005); as a lecture at Vanderbilt University (2005); as a panel presentation at the Association for Political Theory conference (2005); as a lecture at Illinois State University (2005); as a talk at Haverford College (2006); as a lecture at Oakton Community College (2006); as a panel presentation at the third annual meeting of the Caribbean Philosophical Association (2006); and as a lecture sponsored by the Forum for Contemporary Thought, University of Virginia (2006).

I would like to thank the organizers for extending the invitations, and the campus and conference audiences at these presentations for their questions, criticisms, and general feedback.

Numerous people have either been very supportive of this project over the years, or have been critical of it in an intellectually stimulating way. I am indebted to Tommie Shelby for consistently pressing me to work out the implications of *The Racial Contract* for orthodox Rawlsian contract theory, and even if we disagree on those implications (see chapters 3, 4, and 8), I am grateful for his repeated prodding. Tony Bogues and Lewis Gordon have provided platforms on which to speak, and, from their different perspective on the black radical political tradition, principled criticisms that have forced me to think out the argument more carefully. Bernard Boxill and Howard McGary, already mentioned, as well as Bill Lawson and Lucius Outlaw, have been trailblazers in the field of black political and normative philosophy, as well as sources of solidarity and welcome beacons of an illuminating blackness at all too many otherwise dismayingly dark, all-white APA meetings.

Thanks also to Linda Martín Alcoff, who deserves particular mention as one of the earliest promoters of *The Racial Contract* manuscript, before it was even a book; to my former, now retired colleague Sandra Bartky for numerous discussions of race and gender; to Derrick Darby for many educational conversational brunches in Evanston; to my colleagues Samuel Fleischacker and Anthony Laden for their comments; to Dan Flory for single-handedly being responsible for sales of hundreds of copies of *The Racial Contract* to bemused students in Montana; to Paul Gomberg for his unwavering representation, touched neither by time nor circumstance, of an unreconstructed class-reductionist Marxism (for Paul, this is a compliment); and to Tyrone Forman, Amanda Lewis, and Eduardo Bonilla-Silva, both for their friendship and toward more joint interdisciplinary philosophy–sociology collaboration on race.

Brooke Ackerly, Alison Bailey, Lawrie Balfour, Meghan Burke, Ann Cudd, Jay Drydyk, Holly Graff, Kevin Graham, Sandra Harding, Sally Haslanger, Paget Henry, Alison Jaggar, Jane Kneller, Loren Lomasky, Emily Michael, Jerry Miller, Susan Moller Okin, Dan O'Neill, Diane Perpich, Drew Pierce, Nirmal Puwar, Neil Roberts, Rodney Roberts, Pauline Schloesser, Molly Shanley, Falguni Sheth, and Bill Wilkerson, have all, in different ways, assisted this project at one time or another. My thanks to all of you.

As we were going to press, Iris Marion Young – who had been fighting a courageous battle with cancer – died suddenly. She was a dear friend as well as an internationally known political theorist in the struggle for a genuinely racially and gender-inclusive social justice, and will be sadly missed both personally and professionally.

Finally, special appreciation to Bob Wolff (now an ex-white man – see his autobiographical account) for his unceasing enthusiasm and endorsements over the years.

Charles W. Mills

The authors and publishers gratefully acknowledge permission to reprint the following chapters:

"The Domination Contract" by Charles W. Mills is scheduled to appear, in a somewhat different version, as a chapter in the forthcoming *The Illusion of Consent: Essays after Carole Pateman* (Pennsylvania State University Press), edited by Iris Marion Young, Mary Lyndon Shanley, and Dan O'Neill.

"Contract of Breach: Repairing the Racial Contract" by Charles W. Mills is scheduled to appear, in a somewhat different version, as a chapter in the forthcoming *Reparations for African-Americans: Arguments For and Against* (Rowman & Littlefield), edited by Howard McGary.

We have been told that our struggle has loosened the bands of Government everywhere. . . . that Indians slighted their guardians and Negroes grew insolent to their Masters. But your letter was the first Intimation that another Tribe more numerous and powerfull than all the rest were grown discontented. . . . Depend upon it, we know better than to repeal our Masculine systems. . . . We have only the Name of Masters, and rather than give up this, which would compleatly subject Us to the Despotism of the Petticoat, I hope General Washington and all our brave Heroes would fight.

US Founding Father and President-to-be John Adams, in an
April 14, 1776 letter replying to his wife Abigail Adams's
declaration of her belief in universal natural rights

Introduction

Carole Pateman and Charles W. Mills

For some three decades feminist scholars have been re-examining and criticizing standard approaches and interpretations in political theory and political philosophy. On a smaller scale, a similar exercise by scholars of race has been underway for the last 20 years or so, although it has really only taken off in the last decade. In both cases, however, the general tendency has been for this body of work to be seen as marginal to proper theoretical endeavors and as appropriate only for gender, African-American, and ethnic studies departments. So the very basic challenges posed to the academic enterprise of political theory, whether in political science or political philosophy, have for the most part been bypassed.

Our two books, *The Sexual Contract* and *The Racial Contract*, published respectively in 1988 and 1997, were contributions to this revisionist political theory but they took a new direction by confronting mainstream contract theory, which had received little attention in the new critical scholarship on gender and race. The simplicity and attractiveness of the idea of a "social contract" have made it an immensely powerful, influential, and long-enduring political concept, with an impact far beyond political theory; even public figures sometimes refer to a social contract. As Pateman (1988: 1) wrote in the opening paragraph of her book: "The most famous and influential political story of modern times is found in the writings of the social contract theorists." Anyone with a standard liberal arts education will have encountered the concept in one course or another, and will have at least a passing familiarity with the names of Thomas Hobbes, John Locke, Jean-Jacques Rousseau, and Immanuel Kant. Precisely because of contract theory's centrality to the modern Western political and, more generally, humanist tradition, it cannot be ignored in the investigation of the issues of gender and race, especially since – with the publication of John Rawls's *A Theory of Justice* in 1971 – it has once again become extraordinarily widespread. But nobody had sought before to relate the numerous studies of sexism and racism either to classic theories of an original contract or to contemporary contract theory. This was Pateman's innovation for patriarchy, emulated a decade later for race and white supremacy by Mills.

In *The Sexual Contract*, Pateman reread the classic theorists of an original contract from a feminist perspective and argued that the standard commentaries on the texts provided only half the story. The social contract said to justify the government of the state was discussed and dissected but there was silence about the other dimension of the original contract – the sexual contract held to justify the government of women by men. She then explored two major institutions of modern society constituted by contract: marriage and employment. These singular contracts are about property in the person and create *relationships* – relationships of subordination. Contract is standardly seen as central to freedom, so her conclusion was that it was necessary to move beyond contract if there is to be a free social order.

Inspired by Pateman's book, Mills argued in *The Racial Contract* that European expansionism and the establishment of white/nonwhite relations of domination could be seen as similarly constituting "race" as a structure of exclusion. So rather than being genuinely egalitarian and inclusive, the social contract was predicated on regarding people of color (Native American and Australian "savages," African slaves, nonwhite colonial peoples) as less than equal, and so not worthy to be included as free individuals in the (white) polity.

Thus we both excavated the role of the classic theorists in justifying the patriarchal, racial, and imperial structures that have shaped the modern world, and examined the legacy of these structures in societies whose historical self-conception is so thoroughly, and misleadingly, informed by notions of individual freedom and equality. For three centuries there was no doubt that white women and nonwhites were deemed inferior to white men, were second-class citizens or outside citizenship altogether. The difficulty of writing about sexual and racial power today, especially in the rich countries, is that it exists in a context of formal equality, codified civil freedoms, and antidiscrimination legislation. People are thus encouraged to see any problems as a matter of discrete remnants of older discrimination or the outcome of unfortunate, backward individual attitudes. We tried to show how contract in the specific form of contracts about property in the person constitute relations of subordination, even when entry into the contracts is voluntary, and how the global racial contract underpins the stark disparities of the contemporary world.

Our pioneering efforts struck a chord and our books have been widely read and commented upon. Increasingly they are being taught together, not just in political theory and philosophy courses but also, for instance, in sociology, gender studies, ethnic and racial studies, anthropology, English literature, and postcolonial theory. A jointly authored book, then, seemed like a natural development. Not only would this enable us to develop our arguments further, answer our critics, and argue about the future of contract theory, but it would give us a chance to talk about the sexual and racial contracts in combination rather than in isolation. In the last chapter of her book, Pateman had stated that she had exaggerated when she had written of the sexual contract as (the missing) half of the story of the original contract. The story needed to be told again because the original contract was sealed by white men (Pateman 1988: 220–1). Similarly, Mills had conceded in a long endnote at the start (Mills 1997: 137–8 n3) that in making generalizations about whites and nonwhites he was abstracting away from gender relations of domination and subordination. So in a sense, the two contracts have been waiting to be brought together.

In chapters 5 and 6 we each bring them together and discuss their interaction or, at least, as much as is possible in two essays. The intertwined history of the sexual and racial contracts and how they have shaped the present is frequently forgotten. Or, to put this another way, that Britain, the United States, and globalization are the outcome of a long process of European expansion into the territories of "lesser" peoples, of colonialism, slavery, and the subjection of women, is not at the forefront of political argument. Yet it is virtually impossible to understand why certain patterns of deprivation, inequality, subordination, and violence persist at home and abroad without an appreciation of what has gone before and why it took so long (until the 1970s onward) and required such hard-fought battles before even formal equality was established.

Pateman argues in chapter 5 that the two contracts have been intimately connected since the early modern period when theorists of an original contract were at work. The modern notions of "race" (her argument is about the making of "race," not racism) and sexual difference emerged together, and the racial and sexual contracts shaped the institutional structures of states and the lives of individuals. The chapter focuses on the United States and Britain and on "black" (African) and "white." A modern racial structure of white supremacy was first established in the colony of Virginia and extended within a (patriarchal) state that likes to think of itself as the first truly civil order. Arguing that human reproduction, sex, and antimiscegenation are at the heart of the racial contract, and following her approach in *The Sexual Contract* and in chapter 2, Pateman works with historical examples to illustrate how even women fighting the sexual contract were entangled in the racial contract. The historical background also provides context for the final section of the chapter where she adopts Mills's global focus and turns to a more diffuse sense of "contract." What she calls the global sexual-racial contract is brought together, for the first time, with Norman Geras's contract of mutual indifference, and she argues that attention to the sexual contract helps to explain something about the persistence of widespread indifference to suffering at home and abroad.

Taking a more philosophical and conceptual perspective, Mills likewise proposes in chapter 6 that the sexual and racial contracts be integrated. With the help of a set of diagrams to illustrate the conceptual progression, he suggests that we start thinking in terms of "racial patriarchy," rather than the disjoined "patriarchy" and "white supremacy" which were the main theoretical frameworks of Pateman's and his original books. So if the sexual and racial contracts both relied on a simple opposition between, respectively, male/white contractors and female/nonwhite noncontractors, the racia-sexual contract introduces a more complicated set of "contractual" statuses, in which white women and nonwhite men get to be "subcontractors," and only nonwhite women are "noncontractors." By drawing on some of the vast recent literature on "intersectionality," Mills then tries to show how this modified contract framework better corresponds to the reality of race/gender interaction, where race is gendered and gender is raced.

Our contrasting approaches in these two chapters are indicative of some significant disagreements that we have about contract theory. We did not write a joint chapter or jointly authored book on the interrelationship of the racial contract and the sexual contract because it is doubtful that Mills's view that contract theory can be modified and used for emancipatory purposes and Pateman's view that contract theory should be abandoned can be reconciled. Pateman's "sexual contract" and Mills's "racial contract" are, in a sense, both descriptive and normative in that they characterize and condemn societies of gender and racial domination as unfree and unjust. But Mills, unlike Pateman, argues that contract theory can still be used normatively to help rectify racial and sexual injustice. The chapters, therefore, are written from our different positions to allow readers to see for themselves how these differences play out and to judge for themselves the merits or defects of contract theory.

We begin with a dialogue in which we try to thrash out some of our disagreements. We do not, of course, disagree about everything. We are in complete agreement that there are very serious problems with contemporary contract theory and that the Rawlsian approach, as it stands, cannot accommodate the questions about sexual and racial power with which we are concerned. Some large and very basic problems about justice lie outside the framework within which mainstream contract theorists ply their trade. Insofar as Rawls's difference principle raises questions about class, the original debate in the secondary literature did at least deal to some extent with issues of economic distribution. But with Rawls's shift to the more metatheoretical terrain of the 1980s essays, and *Political Liberalism* in 1993 (Rawls 1996), even this limited real-world connection has been lost, and there was never any great sensitivity to issues of gender and racial injustice in the first place. Rawls's methodological decision to focus on "ideal theory" and a "well-ordered society" has been of little help in addressing the problems of our non-ideal, ill-ordered, patriarchal and racist societies.

In addition, we both take the view that "masculinity," "femininity," and "race" are political constructs. Indeed, once all three dimensions of the original contract – the social, sexual, and racial – are part of the argument, their constructed, political character becomes clear, notwithstanding the classic theorists' use of the language of nature, and the construction is obvious within the framework of contemporary contract theory. But if there are similarities between the designation of sexual and racial differences, there are also differences. Race is, so to speak, a virtually pure construct, with none but the most superficial biological stratum, whereas the division between the childbearing and the non-childbearing halves of humankind is a natural fact, even if the gender differentiations that are taken naturally to follow from that division are not. Men and women also live together in separate households in the closest intimacy, which may make it even more difficult to eliminate oppressive patriarchal social structures than those founded on racial supremacy.

On the other hand, readers will notice that, drawing on her typology of traditional, classic, and modern patriarchy in *The Sexual Contract*, Pateman treats views about "masculinity" and "femininity" found in the classic texts as specifically modern. They form part of the sexual contract and part of a civil society constituted by contract, juridical freedom, equality, and "race." Mills argues that gender structures have a much longer history than race, which only comes into existence in the modern period. So for him the racial contract is distinctively modern, while the sexual contract can be conceptualized as having premodern incarnations. He sees the predominant form of gender ideology in notions of the complementarity of the sexes, notions that nicely obscure male supremacy.

We also both have sympathies with some general assumptions of classic left theory, albeit agreeing that it needs radical revision on issues of gender and race. In *The Sexual Contract*, Pateman criticized Marx's reliance on exploitation at the expense of subordination, and her wariness about any attempt to retrieve contract theory arises in part from the necessity of the idea of property in the person for the presentation of wage labor as unambiguously free labor. Mills, by contrast, thinks that this connection between contract, capitalist ideology, and property in the person is sufficiently attenuated in Kantian contract theory that it can be adapted for progressive ends.

Another point of differentiation is that Pateman's arguments remain more firmly within the tradition of the classic theorists of an original contract than Mills's, and her analyses, except for the final section of chapter 5, are confined to the development of structures of sexual and racial power in three Anglo-American countries. She explores the development of civil society (that is, "civil society" as the opposite of "the state of nature," not "civil society" in the sense popularized since the late 1980s to refer to associations that exist outside of and often in opposition to the state). The early modern theorists used the term to refer to the modern state, a political order that involved equality, freedom, rights, contract, and consent. The modern state is taken for granted by most contemporary political theorists and, in contract theory, is assumed to come pretty close to being a voluntary scheme. Present-day contract theory has forgotten that its predecessors began from the tricky position that their premise of individual freedom and equality threw the legitimacy of all authority structures into doubt. Its practitioners no longer notice the fancy theoretical footwork necessary to place the state and its sexual and racial power structures out of reach of critical scrutiny.

Mills's argument is in the more abstract tradition of Rawlsian analysis, and the racial contract was projected as being global in its scope. Without abandoning that wide viewpoint, he has more to say here about the United States. But he is using contract in what, in philosophical jargon, would be seen as a "thin" sense, as against the "thicker," more empirically informed sense used by Pateman.

Most fundamentally, despite the complementary character of *The Sexual Contract* and *The Racial Contract*, we disagree about the usefulness of contract theory. We part company on whether, in C. B. Macpherson's phrase, contract theory can be "retrieved" for political progressives so as to deal with male and white supremacy. Our divergence is about whether contract itself, and the theory which hinges on contract, is a major vehicle for the reproduction and perpetuation of central power structures. For both of us, contract is unnecessary to make the moral and political argument for a more just and free social order. But Pateman is more hostile because of the theoretical baggage it carries and because she sees contract as a central modern mechanism for the reproduction of sexual and racial hierarchies. Mills, on the other hand, thinks that contract theory can still be salvaged and put to egalitarian uses. One reason for his optimism is that his use of "contract" is looser and more metaphorical than Pateman's; he sees "contract" as basically just a figure for representing the human creation of sociopolitical relationships. Whether this difference contributes at least partially to our disagreement – whether in part we are presupposing different conceptions – is left for readers to decide.

In chapter 3, Mills develops the concept of a "domination contract," which has never been formally flagged as such. (Hobbes's contract is a domination contract in a different sense, in that it is domination freely agreed to, at least in his "commonwealth by institution.") He argues that we need to recognize Pateman as developing a strand of contract theory classically, if very schematically, initiated by Rousseau in *Discourse on the Origin of Inequality*: the exclusionary contract of domination. So in a sense, before the racial contract and the sexual contract, there was the class contract; Pateman discussed this aspect of Rousseau in *The Problem of Political Obligation*. Mills suggests that a distinctively feminist contract theory can be synthesized from the work of Jean Hampton, Susan Moller Okin, and Carole Pateman. He argues that this can be generalized to race and that his "racial contract" falls within this alternative strain of contract theory. The domination contract is meant as a "device of representation" for *non*-ideal theory. It maps not the ideally just society we want to attain, but the non-ideal unjust society we already have and want to get rid of. So the normative task here falls into the realm of corrective justice.

Chapter 4 follows up by attempting to show how this normative use of the domination contract is to be implemented. Mills takes as his example the highly controversial subject of reparations to African Americans, which has been surprisingly brought back to life in recent years (a discussion which complements Pateman's analysis in chapter 5). In a well-ordered society, reparations to blacks, or any other racial group, would not be necessary because no race would have been discriminated against in the first place. (Indeed, races would arguably not even have come into existence as social entities.) But how do we adjudicate such questions in societies like the United States which do have such a history? Mills argues that Rawls's apparatus of the veil of ignorance that blocks crucial knowledge from us can be adapted to the different task of determining rectificatory justice. In this revisionist Rawlsianism, the range of societies among which we must choose does not include societies with no history of racial injustice. So we are forced to make a selection, on self-interested grounds, not knowing our race, among a subset of possible social orders *all of which* have as their ancestor a white-supremacist state. Thus we must confront the possibility that we might end up as black in a society fundamentally shaped in its "basic structure" by systemic illicit white advantage. Mills argues that, once we face this reality, we will be prudentially moved to choose a society where reparations have been implemented as public policy, and that this is convergent with the moral judgment outside the veil that it is unjust for whites to benefit from, and blacks to be disadvantaged by, racial exploitation.

Mills's expansion of the sexual contract in chapter 3 is his contribution to the "other" contract, and in chapter 2 Pateman engages in the same exercise and develops the racial contract in another direction. She examines the doctrine of *terra nullius* and European expansion into North America and Australia. This embodied the claim found in early modern political theory and international law, and the opinions of colonists, that these territories were empty, uncultivated wilderness without property or government. Rather than proper political societies they were examples of actual states of nature.

Political theorists have recently reread Locke on America, and Pateman also considers Grotius, but the new scholarship gives insufficient weight to the fact that the idea of an original contract was central to the political theory of the period and says little about Australia – where *terra nullius* was, until 1992, part of the law of the land. Pateman argues that Europeans planted themselves and appropriated the lands designated as *terra nullius* to create new civil societies (modern states) to replace a state of nature and can thus be seen as making (it is as if they make) an original contract. The contract takes the form of a settler contract, which is also a racial contract. The Native peoples are excluded from it yet their lives and lands are governed by it. The leading jurisprudence, examined in the chapter, has now overthrown *terra nullius*, at least with respect to prior occupancy and native title. However, the question of sovereignty is carefully excluded from legal and political scrutiny. *Terra nullius* is now a politically and legally bankrupt concept, but this means that an unacknowledged question mark ultimately hangs over the legitimacy of the states created on what were claimed to be empty territories.

Finally, in chapters 7 and 8, we reply to the various criticisms that have been made over the years of *The Sexual Contract* and *The Racial Contract*, at the same time taking advantage of the opportunity to clarify our respective arguments and correct some of the many misreadings in the secondary literature of our respective positions. Nonetheless, even where we think we have been misinterpreted, we are both appreciative of and gratified by the attention both books have received, and we wish to thank our commentators for taking our work seriously enough to engage with it. We hope that this joint work will be of value both for fellow academics who may have been unclear about our views, for students encountering our work for the first time, and, who knows, perhaps even readers outside universities. Ideally, of course, we would like our books – *The Sexual Contract*, *The Racial Contract*, and this new work – to contribute to creating a world where both contracts have been consigned to the dustbin of history.

1

Contract and Social Change

A Dialogue between Carole Pateman and Charles W. Mills

Carole Pateman   Most people who know that the authors of this book are a white woman and a black man, both professors, will probably make an (implicit) assumption about our respective backgrounds. The white woman will be assumed to come from a better-off, or at least better educated, stratum of society than the black man. White women have made more inroads into academia in the past quarter-century than black men and professors tend to come from middle-class and professional households, so the assumption is not altogether unreasonable. In this case it is misplaced, but it serves to illustrate the complexities of race and sex. Carole Pateman's parents had only the education that could be acquired by the age of 14, and she left school herself at 16, entering into university later via Ruskin College, an adult education college in England. Charles Mills's father had degrees from the London School of Economics and Harvard, became a professor in Jamaica at the University of the West Indies, headed his department, and became Dean of the Faculty of Social Sciences. On the other hand, when either of them is going about their daily business in the United States, where both now live, they will be perceived and often treated differently. A middle-aged white woman, for example, runs no danger of facing a penalty for driving while black.

Charles Mills   The complexities of race, class, and sex, yes. It's so difficult to think them all together – like the many-body problem in mechanics – because they're all interacting with one another. My own case is interesting (to move to the personal level), since it's not just class, gender, and race, but nationality and ethnicity also, and how they affect the translation of these three across different national boundaries. In

Jamaica, as you rightly say, I was class-privileged by comparison to you in England: from the Jamaican middle class, my father a university professor, and going to what was then an elite high school, Jamaica College. I was also privileged by gender, obviously, and also to a certain extent by color. When I give talks on American college campuses, one of the things I always make a point of telling undergraduate audiences usually to the bewilderment of students with little sense of the contingency and relativity of race – is that I'm only black in the US. In Jamaica, with a different set of racial/color rules, I count as "brown" rather than "black," since blackness isn't determined by the "one-drop rule" (any black ancestry makes you black) as it is here. So browns constitute a recognized and relatively privileged social category of their own, intermediate between white and black, who especially after Jamaica's independence in 1962 become prominent in social and political spheres, though whites still have a lot of economic power.

And this has implications in terms of how you think about yourself, and how you see race. In Jamaica, as a middle-class brown kid, I wasn't very racially conscious, and would have thought of black Americans as puzzlingly obsessed with race.

CP   Becoming better acquainted with some of the literature both past and in the present on "the race question" has reinforced for me just how bizarre and arbitrary the racial classifications are – and just as the "woman question" should more accurately be termed "the man question," so this is, in the countries I have been writing about, "the white question." It is a deeply puzzling question exactly why skin color is so fervently held to signify various attributes, to be a mark of worth and a reason for hatred and homicide. Why should "one drop" outweigh all the other drops? Why is not the whole edifice seen to be ridiculous when, for example, in apartheid South Africa the Japanese were declared honorary whites? That, of course, is a rhetorical question; if I have learnt one thing from my interest in the history of feminism it is that rational argument does not go very far.

CM   On one level, racial classifications certainly are "bizarre and arbitrary," as you say. (One manifestation of this was that there was scholarly variation even on an issue as presumably basic as the number of races.) On another level, of course, left theorists in sociology would claim it's not arbitrary at all, but that the logic is sociopolitical, external, rather than intrinsic to the subject matter. Race is constructed according to particular political projects, and the lines of demarcation are drawn accordingly. So the one-drop rule, for example – which only applies to blacks, not other "races" (by its nature, it can't be generalized, for consistency reasons) – arose out of the need in the US to make sure that children of whites and blacks (and subsequent mixtures down the line) had the status of the "lower" race. Given the amount of white male/black female "miscegenation" that was taking place (outright rape and other kinds of coerced sexual relationships), it was important not to permit the growth of a class of "mixed" people with the same status as whites. So it's "rational" in the sense of being tied to the interests of privileged groups, and the reproduction of that privilege – instrumental political rationality if not scientific rationality.

CP   Of course, as you say, if the classifications are viewed from the perspective of those in power (who are determined to hang on to their power) then, say, for Japanese to be honorary whites can seem quite "rational." As I note in chapter 5, legislation was used in seventeenth-century Virginia to override the common law practice of patrilineal descent so that children of slave women inherited their mother's lifetime bondage and were "black" irrespective of their paternity. But all these stratagems, and the amount of effort required to implement them, sit very uneasily with the insistence that the subordinated naturally lack the capacities to govern themselves, hence the irrationality of it all is never very far from the surface. A good deal of denial and refusal to look and see what is going on is involved in maintaining both racial classifications and the subordination of women. Today, there is still much turning away but, after the successes of political movements over the past few decades, it is harder than it once was.

CM   Yes, it is harder, but unfortunately still possible. So progressive political theorists have to try to understand a complicated set of inter-relations of domination. In the process you make generalizations which have to be heavily qualified, and even then you often don't get it right. (Thereby vindicating postmodernists, or at least so they would claim.) In the old days, it was straightforward – to be "radical" meant being some variety of leftist, with Marxism as the most prestigious body of radical theory. And gender and race – the "woman question," the "Negro question," the "native question" – were an afterthought, if they were thought of at all. Now of course Marxism is dead, so nobody talks about class at all, despite the fact that here in the US the gap between rich and poor is now wider than it has been since the age of the Roaring Twenties. Second-wave feminism, both inside and outside the academy, was for a long time basically white feminism, with women of color being marginalized, and in the black, brown, and red antiracist movements of the 1960s and 1970s, gender usually took a back seat. So in a perverse sense, the Marxist model was emulated by other radical movements, with class/gender/race respectively being everything, or almost everything, and the others being sidelined. I know that that's another misleading generalization, of course, since socialist feminists were trying to combine the theorization of capitalism and patriarchy. But given the marginality of left theory in this country, they were always peripheral to mainstream feminism.

CP   Generalizations, even carefully qualified, have not been popular for some time in feminist theory (in the case of men and women, for example, you are accused of setting up "binaries" or believing that men and women are "naturally" antagonistic and so on). But without generalization structures of power tend to disappear into a sea of differences with few criteria to hand to decide which are the more important.

CM   Yes, "difference" rules – with commonality banished! But as someone who started out on the Marxist left, and retains many of those ideological sympathies, I completely agree that we need to be able to generalize and to develop abstractions, even if they're only approximately true. The challenge is how to do this, given the complexity of social reality.

CP   In *The Sexual Contract* I spent a good deal of effort trying to analyze the connections between the employment contract and the marriage contract. Employment and marriage are two of the central institutions of modern societies, and are also central to sex and class – and race. The "working class," and especially the aristocracy of labor, was the white male working class. The worker's wife, and the interrelationship between marriage and employment, were erased from the picture, as was the fact that the labor market was segmented according to race as well as sex. So there is a sense in which class was very much part of my book, but critics have paid little attention to my critique of employment. I am usually seen as writing about women – but to do that, or to write about race, is also to write about class since women and nonwhites are mostly found at the lower rungs of the occupational ladder, in casual and part-time jobs and in the ranks of the poor. But that raises a very important question: what does and can "class" mean in the first decade of the twenty-first century?

CM   In the US, nothing, since everybody is supposed to be middle-class, and pointing out the huge and growing wealth differentials is declaring class war (as against creating the differentials, which is class peace). At the same time the percentage of the work force that's unionized is down to 12 percent or so, the lowest in decades, with a crisis in the trade union movement, and rollbacks in pensions, health care benefits, and so forth. Certainly the material for left-wing analysis is there. But the problem is mapping a positive alternative, in a world where the left has been so thoroughly defeated and seemingly discredited.

CP A knotty problem indeed, not least because the grand utopian designs of the past do not have a good track record. However, we do still need to have as clear a sense as possible of the direction in which we want to move and some ideas about the institutional and other changes required. As far as political philosophy is concerned, some of the fashionable developments seem to me to be in tune with political and economic developments rather than offering a way to an alternative. Contract theory is a good example. Commodification is proceeding at an extraordinarily rapid rate; there is virtually nothing left now that is outside the reach of private property, contract, and alienation. This is one reason why I am much less happy than you with trying to salvage contract theory.

CM Yes, I know – this is something we need to talk about. In my work I'm operating with a significantly weaker and less loaded version of contract theory, pretty minimalist in its assumptions. It's certainly not tied to property in the person, as the specific Lockean contract is. Rather, it's a conception developed for utilization in a philosophical framework aimed at adjudicating matters of social justice, drawing normatively on central liberal-democratic ideals and factually on the simple insight that humans create the sociopolitical, and in the process themselves. In this weak sense, is "contract" really something you would object to? Surely not.

CP We have some important differences about contract theory. Neither of us, as you put it so nicely in your book, is working with ideal contract theory. But I am more critical than you of the whole enterprise. At the very broad level that you raise now, it is not so much your assumptions that I take issue with – my own work rests on the insight that humans create their own social and political structures and institutions; they are not "natural" – but the notion of "contract" itself. The question I am asking is why, say, social justice has to be discussed or adjudicated using the metaphor of contract.

The most common response is to argue that just or equitable democratic outcomes are most likely, or only likely, if the process through which they are arrived at is one of voluntary agreement, and "contract" captures what is required for such a process. My objection to that line of argument is that there is more than one form of free agreement and that these are not exhausted by contract. This is a point I made a long time ago in *The Problem of Political Obligation* (originally published in 1979). Although you use a minimalist version of contract theory, "contract" has to have some content. At a very general level that need not involve property in the person but, even without that, there is other baggage. On the one hand, in theories of original contracts – as Rousseau was well aware – the point of the social contract is that in the modern state individuals give up their right of self-government to another or a few others. And, as you and I are arguing, the original contract involves the sexual and racial contracts too.

On the other hand, if you start with a model of two individuals, the model requires that both are self-interested and only act if there is sufficient benefit to each of them taken separately. Now, you might reply that there can be an agreement without going along either of those paths. In that case, I go back to my question. Why introduce "contract" at all? Why not start by trying to move to another model of free agreement? It is very hard to get rid of the baggage, and most political theorists do not attempt to. Why not find other terms for "free agreement talk" that also convey the meaning of a voluntary mutual undertaking and offer some hope at least of moving away from all the associations and assumptions of "contract"? Contract has a valuable commercial place, but my argument is that it should be kept in that place. To see the whole of social and political life as no more than a series of contracts, to see individuals as packages of alienable property and to insist that "contract" is the metaphor for a free society is a very narrow view of humans and what they create. In short, my objection is that freedom has become identified with contract and I want to drive a wedge between the two. Freedom has other forms. Can "contract" be washed clean of the history of justification of subjection?

CM   A standard distinction drawn in at least some philosophical discussions is that between "contractarianism" and "contractualism." (Stephen Darwall, for example, has edited a book with just that title: *Contractarianism/Contractualism* (2003).) The former (paradigmatically Hobbes, and theorists inspired by him such as David Gauthier) see morality as conventionalist, as constrained and socially coordinated self-interest, so that the "contract" does really capture the idea of people bargaining with one another. But for the latter, morality is an objective set of other-regarding rules, and the "contract" is really (in Rawls's phrase) a "device of representation" for getting at what those rules are. So the contract is in fact quite dispensable, as various critics of Rawls pointed out fairly early on. (Similarly, Kant's hypothetical contractualism turns the contract into an "idea of reason," and as such a way of representing what is the really important underlying principle of ethics, viz. the categorical imperative.) You don't need Rawls's apparatus to get, say, the principle of equal liberties, or the difference principle – you can get them by arguing from basic considerations of how we should treat other people.

So for philosophers, the picture you paint above (self-interested individuals looking out for their own benefit) would really only apply to "contractarianism" (in this technical, term-of-art sense) not "contractualism." And relatedly, these philosophers would claim that the negative features you associate with contract (a commercial model of a "free" society as calculated self-seeking exchanges between individuals of the *homo economicus* species), while true of the Hobbesian-inspired versions, are not true of the Kantian-inspired versions.

Of course, one can then legitimately ask (as you do) why even use the language of "contract" at all, if this alternative conception is so remote from the original sense of the term? And why bother to go through all the elaborate stages of setting up the veil of ignorance, etc., if one can get the outcome far more straightforwardly and directly? The argument has been that it serves a useful heuristic purpose – it's a way of dramatizing the original social contract idea of humans choosing the principles that would regulate a just society. So it's a "contract" in that attenuated sense, and so (arguably anyway) still linked with the tradition.

I think a significant part of our disagreement on "contract" arises from divergent disciplinary perspectives (political science vs philosophy). As such, I'm not sure how much of our seeming disagreement is substantive and how much is merely terminological and in large part really just hinges on semantics – how we're using the term "contract," and what background disciplinary assumptions underlie this use.

CP   The fact that your career has been in philosophy and mine in political science no doubt has some bearing on how we approach contract theory, but there is more to it than that. First, perhaps I should say that I resisted becoming a philosopher (a path I was urged to follow) because I realized that my interests did not lie in purely philosophical problems. That said, I benefited enormously both from my undergraduate study of philosophy in the heyday of "Oxford philosophy" and from working as a graduate student with Brian Barry, one of the most eminent political philosophers working in the analytical tradition. I have always been keen on bringing together empirical evidence and theoretical argument, and more recently have used historical and legal scholarship. The label "political theorist" allows me to do that and to draw on analytical methods.

CM   Actually, though I did go into philosophy, and ended up as a philosopher, I had misgivings from the start, in part precisely because of concern about its remoteness from real-world issues. So I've always read extensively outside of philosophy texts, and this is manifested not just in my dissertation but in all three of my books, which are full of empirical stuff: history, sociology, political science, etc. (For purists, of course, this renders them suspect *as* philosophy.) But my belief has always been that if philosophy is to live up to its pretensions to illuminate the world, factually and normatively, it needs to know something *about* the world – not, one would think, an inherently absurd thesis.

CP   We do not disagree about that! Still, our differences are more than terminological. I take issue with both "contractarianism" and "contractualism." In *The Sexual Contract* I used "contractarianism" to refer to a specific tradition of argument, which, as you note, goes back to Hobbes. In the United States it is usually called libertarianism, but I rebranded it (as the saying now goes) in order to bring out the connection with contract theory and in order to explore the logic of the form of argument which (I argued) was crucial for an understanding of what was at stake in theories of original contracts and their successors. Contract is seen as the practice which exemplifies freedom, but to appreciate why and how that claim can be made it is necessary to grasp the vital place of the idea of property in the person. That becomes clear through an analysis of the logic of contractarianism.

The political fiction of property in the person is required in order to present major institutions such as traditional marriage and employment as constituted by free relations. Pieces of property in the person can (be said to) be freely contracted out without detriment to the person who owns them. Thus a worker who voluntarily enters an employment contract rents out not himself but his services or labor power, a piece of the property he owns in his person. However, the problem is that property in the person is a fiction. Property in the person cannot be contracted out in the absence of the owner. If the worker's services (property) are to be "employed" in the manner required by the employer, the worker has to go with them. The property is useful to the employer only if the worker acts as the employer demands and, therefore, entry into the contract means that the worker becomes a subordinate. The consequence of voluntary entry into a contract is not freedom but superiority and subordination.

The assumption is that no one enters a contract unless it is to their benefit; they can always refuse a particular contract. Implicitly, another assumption is also being made. This comes to the surface once the consequences and not just the fact of entry into a contract about property in the person are considered. Or, to put this another way, it becomes explicit when contracts about property in the person are put in the context of the institutions which they help constitute and are not seen as an endless series of acts between two parties. The individual is said to be contracting out use of labor power or a service, but what is also being assumed is that it is to the advantage of individuals to give up another piece of the property in their person, namely the "property" they have in their right of self-government or autonomy, a "property" which is necessary for them to participate in the practice of contract. The social contract depends on this assumption, as I argued in my book on political obligation, and so do the institutions of (traditional) marriage and employment.

Contractarians, or, at least, those who have the courage of their convictions, treat social life as nothing but contract all the way down, but contractarianism is rarely taken to its logical conclusion. The conclusion is that there are no limits on the property in the person that can be contracted out (no one would do it if it were not to their advantage), so that (uncoerced) slavery and "renting" of votes, for instance, become legitimate. David Ellerman, an economist, is one of the few scholars to have analyzed the logic of contractarianism and pointed this out. I drew on one such essay, which he wrote under the nom de plume of Philmore, in *The Sexual Contract*. (He revealed in 1995 that he was the author.)

CM   I had noticed that in *The Sexual Contract* you made that connection between Hobbesian contract theory and libertarianism, and I had wondered about it at the time. "Libertarianism" is used in different senses, of course, but in philosophy (I don't know about political science) the most important text would probably still be Robert Nozick's 1974 *Anarchy, State, and Utopia*. But the key theorist for Nozick isn't Hobbes, but Locke. It's Locke who claims that we have property rights, including the right of self-ownership, even in the state of nature.

For Hobbes, as you know, the state of nature is amoral, and though we have possessions, we don't have property rights there. The only right we have is the "right of nature," basically an unconstrained liberty to do whatever we deem necessary to survive. And this is quite different from Locke, where the state of nature is moralized, and our freedoms are limited by natural law, which requires respecting the rights of others. Moreover, the Lockean polity is supposed to be constrained in its architecture by natural law also, in that human civil laws cannot contravene natural law. The Lockean contract is not morally conventionalist in any deep sense, then, since there is an objective standard for what constitutes a good polity, including constitutional rights and freedoms, licit boundaries of state action, etc. So Nozick's libertarianism is neo-Lockean, demanding that we respect the rights people objectively have, including their property rights, which for him meant getting rid of the welfare state.

To the extent that self-ownership is crucial to your argument, then, I wonder if Hobbes can really be your presiding contract theorist spirit, since for him property rights are not basic but determined arbitrarily by the absolutist sovereign. (The Lockean sovereign, by contrast, has to respect pre-existing property rights.) So if he decided it worked better, he could decree socialist property rights tomorrow. So if self-ownership, private property rights, and property in the person are foundational to libertarianism, isn't that Locke rather than Hobbes? And if it is, then social life can't be "contract all the way down," since natural law provides a set of objective moral guidelines which cannot be transgressed. (Locke says explicitly in the *Second Treatise*, for example, that you *may not* sell yourself into slavery.) It seems to me, then, that you're working with a hybrid concept that's drawing on two different and conflicting strains of contract theory: property in the person as foundational, which is Lockean, and morally unconstrained freedom to make all kinds of property transactions, which is more Hobbesian. That's why I'm unsure that property in the person necessarily has all the pernicious consequences you're attributing to it.

But in any case, as I said, I am working (on the moral side) in the contractualist rather than the contractarian tradition, and so in the Kantian rather than Hobbesian strain. Kant is no socialist (though attempts have been made to argue for socialism from Kantian principles), but property in the person isn't really crucial to his theory. Rather personhood is, and our duty not to treat others as mere means. Correspondingly, the variety of contract theory advocated by Rawls and Thomas Scanlon is centered on what principles we should choose to regulate society given this overriding commitment to respecting others' personhood. I don't see why this kind of contract isn't perfectly defensible in principle as a set of moral guidelines, so I'm still trying to get clear on why you object to it.

I guess part of the reason is the link you're making between property in the person as self-ownership and "property as people's right of self-government or autonomy." So that would undercut the distinction I'm trying to draw between Lockean and Kantian contract theory (though I would still claim that insofar as objective moral principles are presupposed in both versions, they're both clearly distinct from Hobbesian theory). I did read your book in grad school, but that was, alas, a long time ago and I can no longer recall your argument. Refresh my memory: is the claim a factual one, that because of the way the world is, autonomy (self-government) requires property in the person, or is it a conceptual one?

CP I have developed my argument about autonomy much more recently, so you would not have read it in grad school. I am arguing that autonomy requires that the political fiction of property in the person is relinquished (Pateman 2002). But to understand how relations of subordination can be presented as free relations the conception of the individual as owner of property in the person is crucial. Individuals can then be seen as renting out a piece of property (a service), not their person. My claim is that we need to grasp the idea to understand the present but it has to be discarded to create a more democratic future.

One problem that I have with Kantian/Rawlsian "contractualism" is precisely that contract theory is now taken to be about morality and moral principles. Political philosophy has been turned into moral philosophy. But the examples I have just provided are not about morality (which is not to say that moral considerations are irrelevant), they are about social and political institutions and the political right of individual self-government. Moreover, theories of original contracts are not about moral reasoning either. To be sure, they are conventionalist, but they are about the creation and justification of specific forms of political order; they are about the creation of the modern state and structures of power, including sexual and racial power. To see Kant as an unqualified universalist and champion of individual autonomy is to ignore his writings about sexual and racial difference, part of his argument about politics not morals. He endorsed not just the social contract but also the sexual and racial contracts. Similarly, as Susan Okin demonstrated in detail, Rawls presupposed men's privileges within the family.

So I do not agree that "contract" is useful because it is a way of dramatizing that humans choose principles, just as they do in the classic theories of an original contract. In the latter theories, the parties to the original contract (are said to) choose – justifiably choose – the modern state and institutions of subordination. Contract, in particular contracts about property in the person, is the major mechanism through which these unfree institutions are perpetuated and presented as free institutions. Contemporary contract theory provides no help in either of its guises if we wish to create a more democratic and a more free society; we need an alternative political theory.

CM Re the "political philosophy as moral philosophy" and "political philosophy as the study of institutional power" distinction: of course, as we both agree, actual "social contracts" have not remotely conformed to any moral ideal. Political theory in the classic tradition dealt both with factual and normative issues, but you're right that mainstream Anglo-American political philosophy (which equals political philosophy simpliciter for mainstream Anglo-American types) now focuses, at least since Rawls revived it, just on normative matters. Particularly for the left tradition, though, the way things actually work is crucial. The late Jean Hampton, whom I've cited repeatedly in my work, was a feminist contract theorist who was critical of contemporary political philosophy's one-dimensionality. Hampton argued that the classic contract had both descriptive and normative aspirations. ("Descriptive" on a figural rather than literal level, of course.) I've picked up on and developed this theme by actually formally separating the descriptive and the normative aspects of the contract, as I discuss in my chapters in this book.

Rawls's contract is a normative contract, and one of a specific kind: a contract for an ideally just state. Your sexual contract and my racial contract are descriptive contracts of (manifestly) non-ideal states. So we're both using contract in a non-normative way to model oppressive societies. But I want to retain the normative side of contract theory by insisting that one can still then ask: in the light of these clearly *unjust* contracts (of sex and race), what does justice now "contractually" demand of us? So this is the normative contract rather than the descriptive contract. But by contrast with Rawls, this wouldn't be ideal moral theory, but non-ideal moral theory. An ideally just state is unattainable since that would be a state with no past history of injustice. So what we're trying to adjudicate is what corrective justice (by definition "non-ideal") now requires to eliminate or at least reduce past injustice. And my claim, as in my reparations chapter (chapter 4), is that a modified Rawlsianism can be adapted to that end.

I agree with you, of course, that Kant's vaunted universalism is actually limited to the white male population (or an even smaller subgroup thereof); indeed, I have published on this subject myself. (See my "Kant's *Untermenschen*" (Mills 2005b).) So when I said "Kantian contractualism," I was taking for granted that we are dealing with a sanitized Kantianism, washed clean of the sexism and racism. (If you see Kant as too deeply stained to grant him this titular status, then OK, choose some other term – deontology, or personhood theory. But that's a terminological rather than substantive point, since obviously the principle of respect for persons can be extended in a gender- and race-neutral way, whatever we choose to call it.)

Similarly, you cite Okin's justified critique in her book *Justice, Gender, and the Family* (1989) of Rawls's ignoring of gender privilege. But nonetheless Okin still went on in that book to argue that a Rawlsian apparatus can be used to go beyond Rawls himself; we can ask what gender justice in the family would require if one took into account the real-life family and the disadvantaging of girls and women in it. So Okin was in principle supportive of the "original position" conceptual framework, while critical of Rawls's own circumscribed use of it. And this is the model I'm following to theorize the correction of racial injustice. What would you choose behind the veil on prudential grounds (worried that you might turn out to be, say, black) if you knew your options were limited to non-ideal societies shaped by the legacy of white supremacy, and regulated respectively by corrective public policy measures ranging from non-existent to very strong? So what I'm not clear on is why you think Okin's adaptation of Rawls, and my attempt to emulate her on race, can't give us useful moral insights about what gender and racial justice demand to correct for the real-life sexual and racial contracts.

CP   Let me begin with your last point. Of course, I am not suggesting anything so absurd as that you or Susan Okin have no insights to offer. My question is how far those insights derive from the use of a (modified) Rawlsian approach. *Justice, Gender, and the Family*, for instance, contains an internal critique of Rawls et al. and an analysis of traditional marriage that uses empirical data. It seems to me that Okin's argument can be made without thinking about what we would choose if we had certain characteristics behind the veil of ignorance. I can see that such a thought experiment is an interesting philosophical exercise. But we are not behind the veil, we are right here, in circumstances that we have somehow to deal with. Thus the pertinent question for me is what policies might be feasible and have a reasonable chance of moving things in a more democratic direction. And that also requires an analysis of what is wrong at present, an analysis that we undertook in our two books. I prefer a more direct approach rather than asking what principles we might choose if we were in a hypothetical original position. Contractualism is not the only way of offering justifications for political starting points and policies.

Incidentally, in my chapter responding to my critics I quote Jean Hampton. She lets the cat out of the bag by admitting that in Rawlsian moral reasoning the contract metaphor does no real work. Reference to contract, she states, is not "in any sense foundational, or even necessary" (Hampton 2001: 357). Moral reasoning, that is, can be conducted without it – and, I would add, so can political analysis, criticism, and recommendations.

If I have understood it properly, I also balk at the normative/descriptive division. It seems to me reminiscent of old claims about the separation of facts and values which I criticized in my (unpublished) D. Phil.

thesis. You and I may both be writing about non-ideal contracts, but I would resist the notion that either *The Sexual Contract* or *The Racial Contract* is non-normative. The latter embodies a number of values and is politically normative; that is its point. And my criticisms of the sexual contract in my book have a number of normative implications about a more free and just society.

CM No, contract theory is not necessary to make a moral case for gender and racial justice, political democratization, and so forth. I'm not at all actually in disagreement with you on this score. Hampton's "letting the cat out of the bag," as you put it, is actually a familiar concession often made by contract theorists, at least the contemporary ones. Among the earliest criticisms of Rawls was that there were non-contractual routes to his moral conclusions, and he never denied this. So the claim has never been the strong claim that contract theory is the only way to go, but the weaker claim that it's the best – or, weaker still, one of the best – way(s) to go. And you're certainly correct that there are far more direct ways to go – for example through appealing directly to some schedule of rights, to ideals of self-realization, to human moral equality, and so forth.

From my own perspective, however, the overwhelming rationale for seeking to engage with contract theory is that it's already there, and hegemonic. In other words, it's not as if political philosophers today are starting from scratch, considering a range of alternatives, and then asking, how should we theorize about justice? Rather this approach has been established for decades as the most influential one. So if you're working on a marginal topic (race), as I am, then translating racial justice issues into a contract framework seems a natural route for mainstreaming topics not normally discussed in the literature. You're then challenging white contract theorists: if the actual "contract" that has established the present social order is so radically different from the sanitized version presupposed in your discourse, then shouldn't we be talking about the implications of that fact for justice? That doesn't mean they're going to listen, of course – certainly it's not remotely been the case that *The Racial Contract* has led to any rethinking of how contract theory is done in these circles! – but in theory at least you're raising a question which they should feel philosophically obligated to answer. As you know, the article on contract theory by Ann Cudd in the Stanford online encyclopedia of philosophy has us both listed there under the subsection of "subversive contractarianism" ("contractarianism" in the all-inclusive sense). The difference between us, then, is that I want to see subversive contract theory become mainstream contract theory, whereas you've written off contract theory altogether.

The fact/value descriptive/normative distinction can be formulated in different ways, and on different dimensions, some obviously vulnerable to criticisms, others less so. My usage of the contrast in this context, and in my other chapters, was not supposed to involve any particularly deep philosophical claim. It was just the obvious point (with which I think you would agree) that Rawls is employing the contract to map out a normatively ideal society, which does not exist, while you and I are using the contract to map out actual societies, which do exist. So in that respect we are both using the contract "descriptively" in a way that Rawls is not. At the same time, of course – and this was the point of our respective books – we are making implicit and explicit normative judgments about the sexism and racism of these societies. So in that sense (if that was your point) our characterizations are both descriptive and normative, factual and evaluative. But neither of us offered a detailed mapping of what gender or racial justice would require in the way of social transformation. So that's what I meant by saying we didn't use the contract normatively – we didn't explore within a contract framework what an ideally just gender and racial order would look like.

CP   Let me take up your earlier points about Hobbes, Locke, and contractarianism. My argument is that to understand the full logic of contract theory it is necessary to go back to Hobbes. My discussion of Hobbes drew on my analysis of his political theory in *The Problem of Political Obligation*. That book is also about theories of an original contract, but it is a criticism of the social contract in its standard interpretation.

Hobbes's state of nature is a mere collection of individuals with no natural connections (initially, entities in perpetual motion which are recomposed into individuals). Therefore, all relationships have to be created by these individuals and are thus all conventional, including family relations. Hobbes is a complete conventionalist. Contractarians also see individuals abstractly, in isolation from each other, and so they too must create all their own ties through contract (all the way down). You remark that in Hobbes's theory rights are not basic but depend on the will of the sovereign, so I should look rather to Locke than to Hobbes. But the logic is blurred in Locke; his state of nature is social, he sees individuals as part of God's workmanship and so on. Hobbes's radical individualism is crucial for understanding contractarianism.

In the state of nature Hobbes's individuals have the right to all things, and assess their position from a purely private (subjective) perspective. It is a very stark – and anthropologically unrealistic – conception, but is nonetheless a version of individual self-government. (Some severe coordination problems arise with this view of social life and I discussed the problems about covenants and Hobbes in my earlier book. I do not think that it is accidental that the most radical individualism is accompanied by Leviathan.) A contract, Hobbes tells us, is the mutual transfer of rights, a transfer that both parties judge is to their advantage. Thus I would argue that rights are also basic in Hobbes. In theories of original contracts, save for that of Rousseau, what happens in the social contract is that self-government is divided into two parts, private and political, and individuals give up their right of political self-government to representatives who decide for them. For Hobbes, political alienation is absolute, although even Leviathan has no sway over the right of self-preservation.

Of course, it is Locke, not Hobbes, who explicitly writes of property in the person, and my discussions of property in the person and self-ownership draw on Locke not Hobbes. And I should perhaps say explicitly that I introduced property in the person only in *The Sexual Contract*; it is not part of my earlier argument about political obligation. Nevertheless, consider Hobbes's individuals in the state of nature. They stand in the world with no ties to others except those they voluntarily forge through contract (and Hobbes treats coerced contracts as voluntary). Another way of looking at this portrayal is that such individuals, necessarily, own themselves. They are self-governing or autonomous in that sense. Hobbes's individuals own their rights, which can thus be seen as property along with their other attributes. Only the individual can judge when to contract out, or refrain from contracting out, some of that property owned in the person. In Hobbes's state of nature individuals decide that their political property (rights) should be relinquished to Leviathan. In civil society they still retain their right to make judgments about their private affairs. In principle, as you note, Leviathan could sweep away the latter right but Hobbes does not go that far.

As your reference to Nozick indicates, contractarians (i.e. libertarians) do not envisage Leviathan but a minimal state. However, they have a problem with institutions since they focus on contracts between individuals, abstractly conceived. Institutions fade away and this makes it easy to gloss over the subordination consequent upon entering into contracts about property in the person. I will not repeat my argument about that but I hope that I have said enough to show why I see Hobbes, and contractarianism, as central if the logic is to be appreciated.

Most contemporary contract theorists are far from being contractarians; they are contractualists. In other words, the logic of contract is dulled and sanitized in the Rawlsian approach so that, for example, the institution of employment can be put aside and taken for granted in an argument that claims that our social life is a voluntary cooperative scheme. If we only think about what we would choose behind the veil we can see that this is an acceptable description. Locke is important in this process of obfuscation, as is Kant. I do not think that Kant can be scrubbed clean and, in any case, in his bloodless version of the original contract the alienation of the right of political self-government (the institution of the modern state) becomes a necessary proposition in the creation of civilization. So I am back where I began; I do not agree we need contractualism to make the kind of case that you and I want to make for democratization.

CM   Your discussion of Hobbes and Locke really helps me to understand more clearly how you're viewing contract theory. For you, I now realize (I guess this was in your book), Hobbes is the paradigmatic contract theorist, and the others are only contract theorists in a Pickwickian sense, if that much. Contract theory for you is essentially predicated on the starting-point of individuals with no social or moral relations with one another, so that all their relationships are created, thus conventional, with contract extending "all the way down." Hence your judgment that Locke's alleged state of nature is really social, and that the logic of contract is blurred in Locke and Kant. So the contractarianism/contractualism distinction for you is in a sense bogus, insofar as both are wrongly being represented as falling under the genus of contract theory. Really, contractualism is a disingenuous attempt to avoid the unpalatable implications of contractarianism, which is actually coextensive with contract theory once its foundational assumptions are honestly faced. So that gives me a better sense of why you think the contract really can't be redeemed in any form.

I guess I'm not sure what response to make at this stage. You're offering what seems to me pretty clearly a revisionist view of the tradition (which doesn't make it wrong, of course), insofar as "contract theory" has traditionally been taken to include non-Hobbesian as well as Hobbesian approaches, with the former not viewed as bad-faith pretenders but legitimate alternatives. Histories of contract theory, such as those by J. W. Gough (1978) and Michael Lessnoff (1986), detail medieval antecedents whose assumptions about human interconnectedness are obviously antithetical to Hobbes's. But of course you could reply that by their very premodern character they can't serve as instantiations of contractarianism in the radically individualist sense that defines this new way of thinking about the sociopolitical. But even if you take individuals in the state of nature as your starting-point, why should the assumption that they have no moral relations with one another be assumed to demarcate the legitimate conceptual boundaries of the tradition? For moral objectivism, moral obligations to the entities in the moral universe (however defined) exist whether or not (focusing, say, just on humans) we have social relations with them. So even in the state of nature, before social or political relations have been established, there are moral constraints on what we may do.

Now one can simply stipulate, of course, that contract theory is to be understood as presupposing moral anti-objectivism, thus leaving Hobbes in triumphant sole possession of the field. But is this really a conceptual insight into the inner logic of contract theory, or is it just a semantic proclamation about how one intends to use terms? Why can't an opponent legitimately reply: "Individuals in the state of nature with no social relations with one another can be conceived of as having no moral ties (under the belief that morality is conventional) or as having moral ties (under the belief that morality is objective). In both cases, we can then ask: how and by what principles would they construct the sociopolitical order? The first variant generates Hobbesian social contract theory, the second variant generates non-Hobbesian social contract theory (Lockean-Kantian). But both are nonetheless examples of contract theory." I wonder, then, if the conceptual bottom line for you is not simply that contract theory presupposes moral conventionalism (i.e. morality as created by the contract), from which everything else follows. But if one rejects this assumption, or interpretation, then you get a different picture of what contract theory can include.

And I think this point is also pertinent for how we are respectively conceiving of rights. I was thinking of rights in the standard sense of norms which generate corresponding duties. So if A has a right to X, then B has a duty to respect A's right to X. Rights in this sense can be reciprocally coordinated with one another in a consistent normative system. Hobbes's "right of nature," by contrast, isn't a right in this sense, but an unconstrained liberty, since by its very character other Hobbesian individuals in the state of nature have no obligations to respect it. It's not possible to develop an internally consistent normative system of such rights, since everyone has the right to do whatever he judges necessary to survive, with no reciprocal duties on the part of others. So when I said rights were not basic for Hobbes, it's because I was thinking of rights thus conceived, which are the most important kind for normative political theory. To cite the standard philosophical judgment, equality for Hobbes is really equality of "threat advantage" (we can all threaten one another equally), not equality of moral status. So the foundation is really power, not normative entitlement (and thus rights in the standard sense).

Correspondingly, I don't see Hobbesian individuals in the state of nature as "owning themselves" if this is taken to mean (as I think it would be) having property rights over themselves. Property rights by definition (I don't think I'm begging the question here) are rights which others have duties to respect. But in the Hobbesian state of nature, as you point out yourself, everybody has the right to everything. So just as people have possessions rather than property (external or non-external goods to which they're morally entitled, and which others must respect), they possess rather than own themselves. Again, it's a question of power, not right. I have this dead deer in my hut that I've killed, in the process mixing my labor with it. But I have no Lockean right to it, and if you're stronger than I am and you take it, you're within your rights to do so – it's not "stealing." Similarly, if you decide that it's worth your while to enslave me and force me to work for you, I cannot complain that you're violating my right of self-ownership in doing so, since your right to everything makes your actions legitimate. Just as my right to everything makes it legitimate for me to throw off my chains one night and kill or try to enslave you in turn. So as I said: this kind of "right" can't be incorporated into a consistent normative system. It's not until the transfer of this peculiar "right" by the contract, and the accompanying constraints of obligation are thereby produced, that rights in the familiar normative sense appear. (And even then, as numerous commentators over the years have pointed out, the question remains of whether Hobbes can really claim we're now obliged to keep the agreement under circumstances where we can get away with breaking it.)

CP   I certainly did not intend to suggest either that Hobbes is the "paradigmatic contract theorist" or that contractarianism is "coextensive with contract theory." I do not subscribe to either argument. I have always seen Locke, Kant, Rousseau, etc. as part of the contract tradition, and still do – they are all theorists of an original contract, although Rousseau criticizes the version now taken as standard – and I have analyzed their political theories in that light. My argument in *The Sexual Contract*, as I stated earlier, is that if we want to understand why it is possible to see a central institution, such as employment, as free rather than based in subordination (why wage labor is put on the other side of a divide from unfree labor), then an appreciation of the logic of contract found in Hobbes, and running through contractarianism, is vital.

If you asked me which theorist is the "paradigmatic" theorist of an original contract my reply would be that it is Locke. This is because his state of nature is explicitly social and constrained by the laws of nature, and he makes a series of theoretical moves that cast relations that we now take for granted in (what appears as) an eminently reasonable form. For example, I teased out what he does with the separation between "paternal" and "political" (private and public) power and how that glosses over the subordination of wives. Contemporary contract theorists have ignored the latter because they see only the results of Locke's strategy, such as the division between private and public. The results fit in so well with existing intuitions, so they fail to scrutinize what he actually does and the effects of his maneuvers. As I wrote in my book "the classics are thus read in the light of the construction of modern civil society in the texts themselves" (Pateman 1988: 221).

The problem with which the classic theorists had to grapple, that the premise of individual freedom and equality threw all authority relations into question, and the theoretical paths they took to avoid the full implications of their own premise, are rarely discussed. Contemporary theorists (implicitly) draw back at similar points to their predecessors and so there is little sign that they want to confront the full significance of putting individual freedom and equality, or social life as a voluntary scheme, at the center of their arguments. As you put it, arguments such as ours raise questions they should feel "philosophically obligated to answer." But they do not. If they did, then questions about structural change would have been addressed long ago rather than attention being focused on the contours of moral reasoning and hypothetical agreements.

Incidentally, this is another reason why I disagree with you about non-ideal contract theory. The crucial question is how hegemony can be dislodged. As I commented at the beginning of our dialogue, spending some time thinking about the history of feminist political thought has brought me to the conclusion that even the most logical and compelling theoretical arguments will be shoved under the carpet if they are too inconvenient. From at least 1700, feminist thinkers have exposed the contradictions and evasions in theorists such as Locke. But who listened? Who changed their arguments because of it? The sharpest critic of Locke on natural freedom, Mary Astell (an absolutist), was completely lost from view and has only been discussed in very recent years. Of the famous philosophers, i.e. those routinely taught in universities, John Stuart Mill listened but his feminist arguments were regarded as an embarrassment until relatively recently; and how often are they now treated as an integral part of his work in standard commentaries? Quite apart from the fact that most people do not want to change a theoretical framework which they have claimed for their own, the hegemony is not just philosophical. The theoretical arguments have helped form institutions and power structures and it is hard to dislodge power by argument alone, which does not mean that we should not keep trying by a range of theoretical means – even reworked contract theory!

But to get back to Hobbes, let me reiterate that I am not suggesting that contract theory is really contractarianism. Contractarianism is but one form, albeit an especially revealing one, of contract theory. Therefore, I certainly do not want to argue that all contract theory has to begin by assuming that individuals are isolated atoms with no relations between them – that is anthropological and sociological nonsense and my book on political obligation was, in part, an extended argument against that view. However, it is necessary, I would insist, to look at the implications of such abstract individualism to appreciate the logic of a conception of society as nothing but contract, all the way down. Hobbes lays bare aspects of contract theory that are usually covered over. That is one reason that he is so important. The other is that he begins from the assumption that the sexes are equal in the state of nature; indeed, as mothers women are lords.

As far as Hobbes's state of nature is concerned, my interpretation of the laws of nature (morality), which are part of his picture, is that he cannot do without them. By this I mean that certain social and moral qualities that are imaginatively abstracted away from the "individual" nonetheless have to be presupposed or the transition to civil society is not possible. In order to conclude the original pact, individuals have to understand what "contracting" means or there could be no contract; that is, they have to understand Hobbes's third law of nature. Similarly, they have to understand "peace" and what the laws of nature mean or no morality or society would be possible at all.

Now, Hobbes says that in the state of nature the laws apply only *in foro interno*; this is necessarily the case given his portrayal of individuals and individual judgment. The laws cannot be acted upon with safety in the state of nature but nonetheless individuals understand them. The laws provide for mutual aid and forbearance, the fundamental conceptual requirement if "social" life is to exist. If there is no implicit understanding of the meaning of the laws (of what mutual aid and forbearance entails) then (civil) society is impossible. Another way of making this point is that a contract between two individuals is not possible without the practice of contract, albeit that the practice is only implicit in Hobbes's natural condition. Yet another formulation is that the noncontractual bases of contract are always taken for granted. So, in that sense, my reading of Hobbes is that morality and society both are and are not created by the original contract.

In my book on political obligation I drew a distinction between "ought" and "obligation" and argued that the laws of nature set out what we ought to do. In Hobbes's state of nature it would be virtually impossible for individuals to assume an obligation because it would always be to their disadvantage to "act second" (strictly, for Hobbes, a "contract," unlike a covenant, is a simultaneous exchange and so is possible). I would respond to the objection that you raise at the end of your previous remarks as follows: in civil society, as the laws of nature dictate, an obligation, if entered into, should be kept. The civil law can help enforce (some) obligations. The problem arises if individuals are seen in the manner of contractarianism and all relations are presumed to be constituted by contract. The end of each agreement will then always be as important as the beginning because something better may offer itself. In addition, the temptation will always be to break a contract if it appears advantageous and is likely to go unpunished. Thus, as theorists such as Hegel and Durkheim have taught us (a lesson ignored by neoliberals), a society modelled after the image of contract undercuts the conditions for its own existence and Leviathan thus always waits in the wings.

At a general level, I do not think we disagree very much about rights. I took your point about Hobbes and rights too literally, but the points I have just made can be extended to rights in Hobbes's state of nature. As you state, the right to all things is not a reciprocal right, but rights in the latter sense are embodied in his laws of nature. You are correct that, strictly, property cannot exist in Hobbes's natural condition (as he is well aware) so I have no quarrel at all with the formulation that in the state of nature individuals possess themselves. Indeed, that brings us back to C. B. Macpherson's famous characterization, the "possessive individual." Macpherson is not very fashionable today, but I learnt a great deal from his interpretation of Hobbes and Locke.

CM   Like Macpherson, we both have obvious sympathies with the left (or, as the joke has it, what's left of the left). So if you think of yourself as a political progressive today, what do you do? Well, one reaction is to aim at more realizable goals, given the prevailing climate. Though I don't use the phrase in *The Racial Contract*, I've been arguing in more recent work for a "non-white-supremacist capitalism." In other words, if capitalism limits our horizons, then at least let's have a capitalism that lives up to its "society open to talents" advertising. Obviously I'm making several assumptions here. One is that white supremacy can be conceptually and (more importantly) causally separated from capitalism. Another is that non-white-supremacist capitalism would be morally preferable to, more just than, white-supremacist capitalism. On the first, it's often pointed out to me by people on the left in campus or conference audiences where I'm speaking – or often claimed, I should say – that capitalism caused racism and white supremacy in the first place. And my response is that even if that's historically true (and I'm certainly sympathetic to the claim), it doesn't follow that in the present period sufficiently powerful material forces can't be marshalled to struggle for a nonracial capitalist order now. On the second, it's sometimes been argued to me that there'd be no difference. And I think that's just false – I think that racist capitalism has peculiar features, peculiar oppressions, of its own, and that eliminating them would represent real moral progress. Note that these objectors' position implies that the black civil rights struggles of the 1950s and 1960s would not have been worth supporting by the white left, since for the most part they weren't anticapitalist in character but antisegregation, anti-Jim Crow, anti-white-supremacy. They were struggles for equal inclusion in the polity and the capitalist economy.

So you'll recognize the position – it's basically the racial equivalent of the liberal feminist argument. That would be my first response to you, that while I agree completely that commodification has spread everywhere, to areas Marx would never have dreamed possible, isn't it still better in a market, property-dominated society to have property not distributed in such a racially inequitable way?

CP   I agree that it is better to have a racially equitable distribution of property, just as it would be better for women to have an equitable share of global property, wealth, and income. But why must we let (a certain form of) capitalism limit our horizons? In practice, a neoliberal form of capitalism has gained great power but I do not see why we should merely accept that power when we are doing political theory and thinking about "the good society." This is why I have been challenging the widespread assumption that the institution of employment, which, like David Ellerman, I have come to see as the lynchpin of capitalism, is a necessary part of democracy. Even in practice, prevailing economic doctrines are being challenged, especially in Latin America, and also by many grass-roots movements around the world. I agree that we should argue for a racially – and sexually – equitable property distribution but I disagree that this precludes keeping much broader goals in mind at the same time. There are different ways of working toward a change in the distribution of resources and some ways of going about it may be conducive to more than one political aim, as I have argued elsewhere, for example about a basic income for all citizens.

CM   You're right, of course, that one can be an activist, or a theorist (what "activism" comes to for most academics), on more than one front. In a classic left framework, that would have been negotiating the relationship between reform and revolution. So struggling for reforms within the system wouldn't necessarily rule out struggling against the system itself. But I guess for me the global defeat of the socialist project (in the Marxist sense) has been so overwhelming that I'm just pretty dubious about the current possibilities for antisystemic change of that kind. What's been happening in Latin America has indeed been inspiring, and I'm all for it. But that's social democracy, left-liberalism, not socialism in the classic sense of working-class ownership of the means of production. If that's what you mean by "socialism," then fine, I'm happy to support such redistributivist programs, and to endorse basic-income arguments. We certainly have a lot of models for that, for example in Western European social democracy. What we don't have are models for an economically functioning and politically attractive postcapitalist socioeconomic order.

As you know, there are many people formerly on the orthodox left who concluded that the collapse of state socialism did indeed vindicate the original criticisms of the Austrian school, i.e. that market mechanisms are crucial for informational reasons. Hence the work in recent years on trying to work out viable models of market socialism. But apart from the intrinsic problems of modeling such an alternative, there are also the extrinsic problems of trying to win over a population thoroughly socialized (at least in this country) to associate anything even slightly left with totalitarianism, the antichrist, etc. After all, "liberal" was successfully transformed by the right into a term of invective decades ago. So if people run scared of liberalism – milquetoast, boring, (once) respectable liberalism – how are you going to convince them to be socialists?

CP   If only I had an answer to your last question – although I'm doubtful that it is very fruitful to spend time arguing about the meaning of "socialism" and "liberalism" at this point. Concrete proposals and alternative theoretical directions are needed; the labels are less important. Prospects might look bleak but there is an enormous amount of questioning of and opposition to the neoliberal agenda, and more information is available about inequalities, injustices, and exploitation than ever before. One of the difficulties is that old-established parties and institutions in the rich countries are in decline and so the opposition remains diffuse. And since the "war on terror," time has to be devoted to defending some very basic requirements of democracy. Civil liberties are under threat – who would have thought that we would be in a position where the case has to be made against the use of torture, detention without due process and trial, and secret jails? – anti-Arab racism has been given a veneer of respectability, and accountability is in tatters. Mercenaries (aka private contractors), subject neither to military nor Iraqi law, are part of the occupation of Iraq, and they appeared on the streets of New Orleans after Hurricane Katrina.

My view is that if an alternative is to be developed some new ideas, and some old ideas brushed up and renewed, are called for about some very central matters, one reason that I am interested in basic income. For example, never has so much been heard about elections and democracy. But, given all the obvious problems with elections in the richest as well as poor countries, why not introduce experiments with decision-making bodies chosen by lot (proper random sample) instead of election? Again, political theorists have paid scant attention to the question of corporations, which are legal "persons" in the United States (another problem that needs tackling), and new thinking about ways to break down and democratize the rapidly expanding, vast reach of corporate power, including the corporatized media, is urgently needed. So much of vital importance is rarely touched on in democratic theory and, more generally in these dangerous times, political theory needs to be brought down to earth, away from the Higher Theory and focused on our present circumstances.

In *The Racial Contract* you wrote that we need to know "what went wrong in the past, is going wrong now, and is likely to *continue* to go wrong in the future if we do not guard against it" (p. 92). To raise the question of what went wrong in the past is not something that is always welcomed. Without much more knowledge of the history of the sexual and racial contracts than is commonly provided it is all the harder to map out potentially democratic paths for the future. We made a start on this in our two books, and two of my contributions to this volume try to take this further. All we can hope is that our new chapters make a contribution to the task of constructing an alternative.

CM   Well, whatever else we may disagree on, we can certainly agree on that.

2

The Settler Contract

Carole Pateman

> I like a plantation in a pure soil; that is, where people are not displaced to the end to plant in others. For else it is rather an extirpation than a plantation.
>
> Francis Bacon, On Plantations, 1625

> The Procreation, or Children of a Common-wealth, are those we call *Plantations*, or *Colonies*; which are numbers of men sent out . . . to inhabit a Forraign Country, either formerly voyd of Inhabitants, or made voyd then, by warre.
>
> Thomas Hobbes, Leviathan, 1651

In June 1992, the High Court of Australia ruled in the case of *Mabo v. the State of Queensland* that the country was not *terra nullius* when the first settlers arrived from England in 1788.[1] The political importance of the doctrine of *terra nullius* is that it provided an answer to one of the most fundamental questions of modernity. Why was it legitimate for Europeans to sail across oceans and "plant" settlers in (i.e. colonize) faraway territories? Why was it justified to turn these lands into New England, Nova Scotia, and New South Wales, and then into the modern states of the United States, Canada, and Australia (the three countries

The origin of this chapter goes back to the late 1970s when I became interested in citizenship and Aboriginal peoples in Australia, which led me to *terra nullius*. My interest was also stimulated by the publication of Henry Reynolds's *The Other Side of the Frontier* in 1982. I began to collect material about *terra nullius* all those years ago, but have not been in a position to write about it until now.

[1] 175 CLR 1, 1992. The case began in 1982 when five members of the Meriam people argued that their rights to their land in the Murray Islands (in the Torres Strait) were not extinguished on the annexation of the islands by Queensland in 1879. Three of the plaintiffs, including Eddie Mabo, died before the verdict of the High Court, and Mabo's own claim was denied. In *Mabo* (pp. 25–6), Justice Brennan stated that the propositions on which the defendant relied were not specific to the Murray Islands but were "advanced as general propositions of law applicable to all settled colonies," and thus to the whole continent of Australia. (Page references to legal cases are in the text.)

with which I am concerned here)? In the political theory and the law of nations of the seventeenth and eighteenth centuries it was argued that if land is *terra nullius* then it may rightfully be occupied.

The general principle underlying this argument, that if something is "empty" it is unowned and so open to claims of ownership, goes back to ancient times. Roman law included the concept of *res nullius*, an empty thing, or a thing that belongs to no one. An empty thing is common to all until it is put to use, and the person who puts the thing to use becomes its owner (Pagden 1995: 76–7). *Terra nullius* is a very capacious concept. To call a tract of land *terra nullius* has a range of meanings: the territory is empty, vacant, deserted, uninhabited, *vacuum domicilium*; it belongs to no one, is *terrritoire sans maître*; it is waste, uncultivated, virgin, desert, wilderness.

Blackstone writes of "sending colonies to find out new habitations," and states that "so long as it was confined to the stocking and cultivation of desert, uninhabited countries, it kept strictly within the limits of the law of nature" (1899: bk II, ch. 1, 7; also Intro. §4, 95). The problem was that lands without any inhabitants were very few indeed. The question of the justification for such stocking and cultivation in inhabited territories thus looms very large, or it did in the early modern period. Until very recently contemporary political theorists largely managed to ignore it, in part because discussions of the legitimacy of the modern state (always taken for granted) have said nothing about the land on which the state is created.

Defenders of colonization in North America, including political theorists, frequently invoked two senses of *terra nullius*: first, they claimed that the lands were uncultivated wilderness, and thus were open to appropriation by virtue of what I shall call the *right of husbandry*;[2] second, they argued that the inhabitants had no recognizable form of sovereign government. In short, North America was a state of nature (see section II). Settlers in Australia also used these arguments but Australia is of special interest because, in the eyes of the law, the continent was *terra nullius* in the sense of unoccupied or uninhabited in

---

[2] Virgin territories had to be tamed and subject to careful husbanding. As John Donne wrote in "To His Mistress Going to Bed" in 1669:

> License my roving hands, and let them go
> Before, behind, between, above, below.
> O my America! My new-found-land,
> My kingdom, safeliest when with one man manned,
> My mine of precious stones, my empery,
> How blest am I in this discovering thee!
> To enter in these bonds is to be free;
> Then where my hand is set, my seal shall be.

1788.[3] The *Mabo* judgment was necessary because in Australia *terra nullius* was part of the law of the land.

The legitimacy of the states created in North America and Australia is ultimately based on the claim that, in one or another sense of the term, they were created in a *terra nullius*. Therefore, the potential ramifications of *Mabo* are, to say the least, extremely far-reaching. However, legal judgments in North America and Australia have focused on the Native (Indigenous, Aboriginal) peoples' prior occupancy and right to title to land. They have carefully cordoned off sovereignty and legitimacy from consideration. The British Empire "saw itself as founded upon law" (McHugh 2004: 34). My conclusion is that ultimately, given leading legal judgments in all three countries, the question of legitimacy is impossible to avoid.

During the 1990s, political theorists began to look at justifications offered for European colonial expansion in early modern texts (see, e.g., Arneil 1996; Pagden 1995; Tuck 1999; Tully 1993b, 1994, 1995). Locke's arguments, in particular, have been scrutinized, and a Locke has emerged who is pivotal in the justification of English colonial expansion to North America. I shall have something to say about Locke, and also about Grotius who is the key figure in the development of international law (the law of nations). I have learnt a great deal from this valuable new scholarship, but from my perspective it has two limitations.

First, the focus is on the Americas and the right of husbandry; little is said about empty lands as uninhabited territory. To fully grasp the political significance of *terra nullius* it is necessary to look at the southern as well as northern New World. Australia was set apart from the rest of the British Empire in its colonial practice. Dispossession, extermination, and cruel and brutal treatment do not distinguish Australian history from that of North America,[4] or from other European colonies;

---

[3] Controversy surrounding *Mabo* and policies concerning Aboriginal peoples has extended to "*terra nullius*." For example, it has been argued that "it was not the legal doctrine behind the 18th-century occupation of Australia," that it "is not part of the common law" and was first introduced in Australia in a case in 1977 that referred to a judgment of the International Court of Justice (Connor 2003: 76, 77). *Terra nullius* was explicitly discussed in the ICJ report on the Western Sahara (see note 8 below) but does the apparent absence of the term itself from common law cases mean that it is irrelevant? Without it, it is hard to see how we are to refer to the legal argument and political theory which I discuss below about planting and land lacking cultivation, laws, property, or properly political institutions. Whether or not the term was explicitly used, the set of political elements to which it refers was much discussed; see section IV. (My thanks to my friend Louise Taylor for drawing Connor's argument to my attention.)

[4] In North America, the colonization of Canada was less bloody than in the United States; "the peculiar Canadian combination of economic integration, government

rather, Australia stands out in the lack of any recognition of Aboriginal peoples' lands or their forms of society and government. For the most part, colonial governments in the British Empire left local laws and customs relatively undisturbed, a policy exemplified by family law in Muslim and Hindu communities in the Indian subcontinent. In stark contrast, Aboriginal peoples were disregarded from the moment the settlers landed in Australia and proclaimed British sovereignty. For example, no treaties were ever entered into with them. Hundreds of treaties were concluded in North America, and the rest of the British Empire offers numerous examples, including the Treaty of Waitangi (1840) between Maori and Pakeha in New Zealand which forms the basis of the constitution.[5]

The second limitation of the new scholarship is that stories of an original contract are a major feature of the early modern texts, but *terra nullius* has not yet been placed within that context. This is my aim here. I shall begin to analyze the logic of the original contract in the form of *the settler contract*. In *The Racial Contract*, Charles Mills discusses an expropriation contract appropriate to "the white settler state," where "the establishment of society thus implies the denial that a society already existed" (1997: 24, 13; see also 49–50). The settler contract is a specific form of the expropriation contract and refers to the dispossession of, and rule over, Native inhabitants by British settlers in the two New Worlds. Colonialism in general subordinates, exploits, kills, rapes, and makes maximum use of the colonized and their resources and lands. When colonists are planted in a *terra nullius*, an empty state of nature, the aim is not merely to dominate, govern, and use but to create a civil society. Therefore, the settlers have to make an original – settler – contract.[6]

---

intervention, and treaty promises kept conflict to a minimum . . . . [T]he settler population found many means, typically short of armed conflict, of pushing the indigenous peoples to the margins of the emerging societies" (Coates: 1999: 143–4).

[5] The societies and cultures of the Maori and Aboriginal peoples and the histories of the two countries are very different. After the Treaty, a Native Rights Act and a Native Lands Act were passed in 1865, which recognized Maori rights in land and brought native title under the purview of the law of real property. A series of Maori Wars was fought between the government and the Maori peoples between 1856 and 1870. I should also note that the small population of settlers in Australia, the limited reach of the government, and the remoteness of many Aboriginal communities left some Aboriginal peoples to continue in traditional ways until well into the twentieth century.

[6] Strictly, it includes all three dimensions of the original contract, the social, sexual, and racial, but for analytical clarity I am leaving the sexual contract to one side in this chapter. I am also excluding a part of the racial contract, the slave contract, from discussion of North America (see chapter 5). The doctrine of manifest destiny, the invasion of Mexico in 1845, and the incorporation of Hawaii are also outside my scope here.

Colonial planting was more than cultivation and development of land. The seeds of new societies, governments, and states, i.e. new sovereignties, were planted in both New Worlds. States of nature – the wilderness and the wild woods of Locke's *Second Treatise* – were replaced by civil societies. The new colonies, and the texts of early modern political and legal theory, were part and parcel of the development of the international system of sovereign states, conventionally seen as beginning from the Peace of Westphalia in 1648. In the New Worlds, far away from the metropolis, *terra nullius* was at the heart of the creation of a new form of political organization. A modern state can have no competing sovereignties within its borders. Native peoples were not organized into states and were deemed insufficiently civilized to create one of their own, and so were forcibly incorporated into new state jurisdictions.[7]

The settler contract takes two forms. The first adheres to what I shall call the *strict logic* of the original contract; the second embodies a *tempered logic*. The two forms are illustrated respectively by Australia before the *Mabo* judgment and by North America.

Under the strict logic, the state of nature disappears as soon as the contract is concluded and is replaced by civil society. It is thus irrelevant whether or not a social order and a system of law were in existence in the state of nature (when the colonists first planted themselves). A new start has to be made, founded on the principles requisite to civil society, so no cognizance need be taken of what went before; the point of the enterprise is to leave it behind and create a civil society. But this means that the history and institutions of the state of nature (whether the conjectural histories to be found in the texts of political and legal theorists or the "natural" condition of the New Worlds) are obliterated. Once the (original) settler contract is concluded, the state of nature becomes a mere heuristic device; it acts as a threat and a warning of the disorder and nastiness that follow if the laws of the new state are not obeyed.

Under the tempered logic, aspects of the state of nature – preexisting social orders – can be recognized. However, they can be

---

[7] Or, as Hobbes notes (quoted in my epigraph), a territory can be emptied. Between 1967 and 1973 the British government removed the inhabitants from the Chagos Islands, and the "vacant" island of Diego Garcia was handed to the Americans to turn into a military base. In 2000, the High Court ruled that the islanders had the right to return, but in June 2004 the Foreign Office used Orders in Council to overturn the judgment, referring to the increased military needs of the USA. The base was used in both wars against Iraq, and reportedly houses prisoners of the "war on terror." In May 2006 the High Court again found in favor of the islanders, declaring the Orders in Council null and void, but the British government appealed the verdict and the United States opposed the islanders' return. A year later the government lost the appeal. The islanders can return – but not to Diego Garcia.

acknowledged only as, or must be recast into, forms appropriate to a civil society, a modern state in the making with its own jurisdiction and boundaries. But the very fact that Native peoples and their governments are recognized means that the question of the legitimacy of the settlers' creation of a civil society always remains in the background. It cannot be buried so thoroughly as under the strict logic of the settler contract.

Let me stress again that I am discussing only the two New Worlds. Appeals to *terra nullius* are not confined to English common law jurisdictions. A forerunner to the *Mabo* decision was handed down in 1975, when the International Court of Justice issued an Advisory Opinion on the Western Sahara. The Court's discussion of *terra nullius* is brief (§§79–83), but the judgment was that the territories of Rio de Oro and Sakiet El Hamra were not *terra nullius* when Spain declared a protectorate in 1884.[8]

The assumptions embodied in the idea of *terra nullius* can be found well beyond either theories of an original contract or the British Empire. Whether or not they used the term, *terra nullius* has been

---

[8] The impetus for an Advisory Opinion came from Morocco in 1974 after Spain, earlier in the same year, had proposed holding a referendum on independence under UN auspices. For a detailed analysis of the ICJ Opinion (including discussion of the historical background, the Algerian ambassador's view of *terra nullius*, and the suggestion that the territory was not *terra nullius* because it was part of an Islamic *civitas*, the Dar El-Islam) see Shaw (1978). Morocco immediately responded to the ICJ ruling with a "Green March" invasion of some 350,000 civilians, followed by its military, and Spain ceded the Western Sahara to be partitioned between Morocco and Mauritania. The Polisario front was formed in 1973 to begin a struggle for national self-determination. The Sahrawi Arab Democratic Republic was declared in 1976 (and recognized by South Africa in 2004). Mauritania was no match for the Sahrawi forces and withdrew in 1979, but Morocco took over its territory and has continued its occupation and repression ever since. It has constructed a fortified berm, 1,500 miles in length, through the country. A cease-fire was declared in 1991, the UN Security Council accepted a Settlement Plan and the UN sent a Mission to oversee the referendum (by then) scheduled for 1992. Morocco has obstructed all attempts to draw up the electoral roll for the referendum. In 1997 James Baker was nominated by the US as personal envoy for Kofi Annan, the UN Secretary-General, and in 2001 presented a Framework Agreement. This effectively eliminated Sahrawi self-determination, since the proposed electorate for the referendum was all full-time residents of one year or longer; i.e. settlers could vote on the future of the Western Sahara. Since then, all UN proposals have come to nothing and Baker resigned in 2005. The Sahrawi and their fishing, minerals, and potential oil and gas deposits are now caught up in corporate expansion and the "war on terror." As Toby Shelley notes, for Security Council members "the fate of a quarter of a million Sahrawis is a matter of supreme indifference except to the extent that it impinges on their economic and political ambitions" (2004: 200). For details of the history since 1975 see Shelley (2004), and on recent demonstrations, Finan (2006).

invoked by a variety of colonizers who declared that lands were empty of populations or were mere desert or uncultivated wilderness. In a striking example, Golda Meir (1969) stated in an interview: "There was no such thing as Palestinians. . . . It was not as though there was a Palestinian people in Palestine considering itself as a Palestinian people and we came and threw them out and took their country away from them. They did not exist." I am leaving open the question whether the idea of a settler contract has any wider relevance, either to British or other European colonialism outside of North America and Australia or to more recent plantings by non-Europeans in the territories of Indigenous peoples around the world.

I Occupation, Conquest, and Consent

"Occupation" is a term of art in international law that began to be developed in the early modern period. Sovereignty can be legitimately gained over a territory that is *terra nullius* through "occupation," or, in the language of the common law, "settlement." Colonies in Australia, like those in Canada, had legal status as settled colonies. Occupation (settlement) was one of four forms of legitimate territorial acquisition established by the European powers as part of efforts to regulate their expansion and avoid conflict over trading rights. The three others were cession, annexation (with neither of which I am concerned), and conquest: "It is only in our own times that it has become possible to argue that the right of conquest has ceased to be upheld by international law" (Korman 1996: 8).

The Spaniards led the expansion into the New World, and they were conquerors, *conquistadores*. They set sail under the authority of five Papal Bulls, issued in 1493 before they left Spain. The Pope made a grant of such land "as you have discovered or are about to discover" to the voyagers, by virtue of his temporal authority. Discovery was central to European colonialism, but what counted as "discovery"? According to Grotius (1983: 11–12), "to discover a thing is not only to seize it with the eyes but to take real possession thereof, . . . the act of discovery is sufficient to give a clear title of sovereignty only when it is accompanied by actual possession." In the late sixteenth century, the English agreed and argued that, although discovery was insufficient without "possession," it was unnecessary for possession that the whole of a claimed territory be occupied, an argument crucial in the settlement of Australia. The rule became that, if a territory had not already been claimed by a European power, then it came under the jurisdiction of the country that was first discoverer and occupier (for an example see Jennings 1971).

Neither the English nor the Dutch enjoyed the authority of Papal Bulls, so how were their colonies to be justified? By the latter part of the seventeenth century English settlement was in need of justification. Opinion had become unfavorable, especially since colonies were seen as an economic drain on resources (although Locke's patron, the Earl of Shaftesbury, was an eager proponent: see Arneil (1996: 90–4)). In North America, the legitimacy of settlement had already been questioned for some time.

Legitimacy followed conquest under the law of nations. In *The American Indian in Western Legal Thought* (1990), Robert Williams argues that English expansion into North America was based on "Discourses of Conquest" (his subtitle). As he points out, the English already had some practice in conquest and planting settlers; Queen Elizabeth had overseen the colonization of Ireland by force of arms in the latter part of the 1500s. Williams reads legal history after the American Revolution as a continuation of the British discourse of conquest. He takes one of Justice Marshall's famous judgments in the nineteenth century, *Johnson v. McIntosh* (1823), as authoritative. Williams's interpretation is that the case "provided Western legal thought and discourse with its single most important textual interpretation of the law governing the rights of indigenous tribal peoples in the territories they occupied." Marshall's acceptance of the "Doctrine of Discovery's discourse of conquest" encouraged further expansion, and "vested authority in a centralized sovereign to regulate the Indian's dispossession according to national interest" (Williams 1990: 289, 317).

The history on the ground is very hard to distinguish from conquest; in both America and Australia the settlers and the military used extensive violence to overcome the resistance of Native peoples and drive them off their land. Some of the settlers on both continents took the view that the land had been gained through conquest. So did Blackstone, who stated that "[o]ur American plantations" were obtained either by treaties (i.e. agreement) or "by right of conquest and driving out the natives (with what natural justice I shall not at present inquire)" (1899: Intro. §4, 96).

Grotius defended the right of conquest, arguing in *De Jure Belli ac Pacis* that all agreements enforced by victors in a formal war were valid; "they cannot be made void by reason of a fear unjustly inspired" (bk III, XIX, XI, §1; see also Forde 1998). But, even more importantly for colonial settlement, he provided a justification for conquest by corporations and colonists. In a *terra nullius* the settlers are in a state of nature, so the law of nature applies. Grotius was the first early modern theorist to argue, in *De Jure Praedae*, for what Locke (*Second Treatise* (henceforth II), §§8–9) later called the "very strange Doctrine" that each individual has a natural right to punish offenders.[9] Grotius writes that the power of the state derives from a "collective agreement" (an original contract) and so "it is evident that the right of chastisement was held by private persons before it was held by the state" (cited in Tuck 1999: 82). In *De Jure Belli* Grotius states that the law of nature allows anyone "of sound judgement who is not subject to vices of the same kind or of equal seriousness" to inflict punishment (bk II, XX, VII, §1), and only when families united together in a political order did specially appointed judges supersede this individual right (bk II, XX, VIII, §4).

Grotius justifies "private war" in *De Jure Belli*, an extension of the right of punishment of offenders by individuals or nonstate entities. He identifies three circumstances when private war is legitimate. First, if the danger is so great that there is no time to bring the matter before a judge. Second, where judicial institutions are unavailable "either in law or in fact." Institutions are unavailable in fact if the judge refuses to take cognizance, or "those who are subject to jurisdiction do not heed the judge." They are unavailable in law in "places without inhabitants, as on the sea, in a wilderness, or on vacant islands, or in any other places where there is no state" (bk I, III, II, §1). Thus judicial remedies cannot be obtained and the individual writ of punishment runs in "a wilderness," or "where there is no state"; that is to say, in a *terra nullius*.

Third, war can legitimately be waged against those who breach the law of nature, whether or not a king or his subjects is directly affected, and punishments can include loss of ownership (bk II, XXII, X, §§1, 2). In a discussion of the right of waging war against "sin against nature," Grotius emphasizes again that the right of punishment and war arises from "that law of nature which existed before states were organized," and that it is "even now enforced, in places where men live in family groups and *not in states*" (my emphasis) (bk II, XX, XL, §4). He comments that "the most just war is against savage beasts, the next against men who are like beasts" (bk II, XX, XL, §3).

By the early decades of the seventeenth century, Native peoples had already been placed in the category of men who are no more than beasts. Alberica Gentili (from 1587 Professor of Civil Law at Oxford University) had argued in *De Iure Belli* (revised edn 1598) that the Spanish were fighting a just war against Indians "who practiced abominable lewdness even with beasts, and who ate human flesh, . . . such sins

---

[9] This, Richard Tuck states, "must count as one of the most striking examples of intellectual convergence" (1999: 82). Locke could not have seen Grotius's text because it was in the part of *De Indis* (1609) – as Grotius called *De Jure Praedae* – only discovered in De Groot family papers in 1864. It then became clear that *Mare Liberum* was in fact a chapter of *De Jura Praedae* (*De Indis*); see Tuck (1999: 81). *De Jure Belli* (1625) owed a good deal to the earlier text.

are contrary to human nature, . . . against such men, as Isocrates says, war is made as against brutes" (Gentili 1933 [1612]: bk I, XXV, 122). In the first edition of *De Jure Belli ac Pacis* (omitted from the Kelsey translation of the 1646 edition which I am using) Grotius includes as people against whom war may justly be waged, "those who kill Strangers that come to dwell amongst them" (cited by Tuck 1999: 103).[10] Thus both international law and Grotius's arguments provide justification for the conquest of Native peoples.

However, a number of scholars (e.g., Tully 1994; Pagden 1995; Tuck 1999) reject Williams's argument that English claims were couched in terms of conquest. James Tully (1994: 172), for example, states that "conquest was never the doctrine of the Crown," and he takes a very different view of the Marshall cases from Williams. Tully reads the cases as the culmination of a long tradition of negotiation between Native nations, the Crown, and then the United States, to find "a constitutional association just to both parties" (1995: 118). He argues that, in *Worcester v. the State of Georgia* (1832), Marshall corrected and repudiated his previous judgment in *Johnson*, "thereby providing a response to later commentators who take this earlier decision as authoritative" (1994: 175). Anthony Pagden, too, argues that the British "increasingly came to regard conquest as unsustainable in fact, and morally undesirable in theory" (1995: 88).

There were two important pragmatic reasons for any justification of English planting to avoid a discourse of conquest. First, by the seventeenth century the British had dug a theoretical gulf between their colonial practice and that of their Spanish enemies and wanted to distance themselves from the atrocities that had accompanied the Spanish conquest – an English translation of Las Casas' *A Brief Narration of the Destruction of the Indies*, popularly known as *The Spanish Cruelties*, was published in 1583. And by the late eighteenth century even the Spanish had backed away from argument from conquest, at least as far as other European powers were concerned. They too acknowledged that if one power had already occupied a territory then another could take possession only if the first was willing to cede it to their rival.[11]

---

[10] Tuck (1999: 96 n39) draws attention to the fact that Grotius made some significant changes in the second edition of *De Jure Belli*, published in 1631. Little account has been taken of the differences between the first and later editions. Editions of the 1640s, on which modern editions of Grotius are based, largely follow the text of 1631.

[11] In 1788 (the year the First Fleet landed on the shore of Australia) the British and Spanish both claimed Nootka Sound. The Spanish did not appeal to the Papal Bulls of 1493, as they had in another dispute with the British over the Falkland Islands in the 1760s, but insisted that their explorer, Martinez, had discovered the Sound before Cook and his men. By 1790, the British had mobilized their ships and Spain "conceded

Second, justification in terms of conquest placed an awkward constraint on settlement. The British agreed with international lawyers that conquered peoples should retain their own customs and property. After all, it was insisted that the Norman Yoke imposed by William the Conqueror had not extinguished ancient Anglo-Saxon freedoms and the common law. Sir Matthew Hale wrote that it was "a hard and over-severe thing to impose presently upon the conquered a Change of their Customs, which long Use has made dear to them" (cited by Tully 1995: 150).

Moreover, the premises of theories of an original contract ruled out justification from conquest. The theories are based on the assumption of natural freedom – some settlers in America came to see the Native peoples and their societies as "exemplars of liberty" (the title of Grinde and Johansen 1991) – equality and rights. Therefore, all rule is illegitimate unless based on the agreement (contract, consent) of those who are governed. Natural rights include the right to private property; thus it follows that settlement is justified only with the consent of the Native owners. In the famous debates in the 1630s in Massachusetts, Roger Williams questioned the legal basis of the State Charter, and insisted that the Crown could not grant lands already owned by the Indians. Rights of usufruct only, he argued, could be acquired, but these must be gained through treaty (agreement). He compared the Indian lands to the great estates of England and argued that, just as "Noble men in England possessed great Parkes, and the King, great Forrests in England onely for their game, and no man might lawfully invade their Propriety: So might the Natives challenge the like Propriety of the Countrey here" (cited in Tuck 1999: 125).

On the other hand, even without recourse to the "strange doctrine" of individual punishment, the dividing line between contract, consent, submission, and conquest can be very porous indeed in the hands of theorists of an original contract. This is demonstrated by the frequency with which explicit consent makes way for hypothetical consent inferred from some action or sign (see Pateman 1985) and, most obviously, in Grotius's and Hobbes's insistence that my "consent" is still genuine even when obtained with the conqueror's sword at my throat. Slavery, too, as Grotius and Pufendorf illustrate, can be presented as consensual in origin. And Locke is ambiguous about both conquest and consent.

In chapter XVI of the *Second Treatise*, Locke distanced himself from doctrines of conquest and argued that it gives only circumscribed rights; even in a just war, for example, a conqueror has no right to the

---

Britain's right to settle the Nootka Sound region on the basis of prior discovery, negotiation with the Indians, and effective occupation" (Frost 1981: 518).

possessions or estates of the vanquished or their families (II, §§180–3). Locke states that

> *Conquest* is as far from setting up any Government, as demolishing an House is from building a new one in the place. Indeed it often makes way for a new Frame of a Common-wealth, by destroying the former; but, without the Consent of the people, can never erect a new one. (II, §175; 1988: 385)

As Tully has noted, this marks a shift from the tradition of continuity of old laws and customs under conquerors (1995: 150–1). And, given Locke's conception of "tacit" consent, the line between conquest and consent would be hard to maintain over time.[12]

In the *First Treatise* (henceforth I), Locke's criticism of Filmer's claim that all political power derives from Adam comes close to Grotius's argument about private war. Locke allows that, outside of "Politick Societies" (i.e. in a state of nature), masters of families have political power and can thus legitimately make war. One of his examples is a "Planter in the *West Indies*" who leads the men in his household "against the *Indians*, to seek Reparation upon any Injury received from them" (I, §130; 1988: 237). The state of war, he writes, does not consist in the numbers involved "but the enmity of the Parties, where they have no Superiour to appeal to" (I, §131; 1988: 238).

However, the settlers had a remarkable theoretical device at their disposal that bypassed the controversies over conquest and agreement. As used by English colonialists from the 1620s onward, the doctrine of *terra nullius* was an extremely powerful political fiction. Its brilliance was that it cut through all the problems of justification. In a *terra nullius* the settler contract could be concluded on a clean slate.

II Grotius, Locke, and the Right of Husbandry

Thomas More's *Utopia* (1516) is commonly cited as the first major statement of a right of occupation and plantation. More writes that if the population of Utopia grows too big, the inhabitants send "a certain number of people from each town to go and start a colony at the nearest point on the mainland where there's a large area that hasn't

---

[12] Tully states that Locke brings "his theories of conquest and appropriation into harmony" by arguing that waste land can be used by a conqueror in the state of nature (1993b: 155). Tully's argument has been challenged by Squadrito (2002: 110–11). Locke writes (II, §184; 1988: 392) that where there is "more *Land*, than the Inhabitants possess, and make use of, any one has liberty to make use of the waste: But there Conquerors take little care to possess themselves of the *Lands of the Vanquished*."

been cultivated by the local inhabitants." The Utopians produce enough for everyone, and if the local people are not satisfied with this arrangement they are expelled from the area. If they resist, "the Utopians declare war – for they consider war perfectly justifiable, when one country denied another its natural right to derive nourishment from any soil which the original owners are not using themselves. But are merely holding on to as a worthless piece of property" (More 1965: 79–80).

More thus offers a succinct statement of occupied but uncultivated land as "worthless," as waste, vacant, empty, virgin, wilderness – as *terra nullius* – that may rightfully be appropriated for productive use. In *The Rights of War and Peace*, Tuck argues that there is a direct line from *Utopia* to Grotius and Locke. He states that More's forthright declaration received little notice until Gentili "put the idea firmly in the minds of people engaged in constructing colonies in the New World" (1999: 50). Gentili writes that "True indeed, 'God did not create the world to be empty.' And therefore the seizure of vacant places is regarded as a law of nature" (1933: bk I, XVII, 80). Tuck reads Grotius as echoing the arguments of Gentili and suggests that, in the face of Pufendorf's (1934) criticisms, "much of [Locke's] *Second Treatise* can be read as a defence of Grotius's conclusions" (1999: 178).

Reading Locke's political theory as justifying the planting of settlers has its critics. William Uzgalis, for example, argues that "the point of [Locke's] comparison between Europe and America is not to provide a justification for European settlement, much less to justify the dispossession of Indian lands" (2002: 95). But the comparison is not only between Europe and America; it is, crucially, a contrast between a state of nature and the need to create a civil society. My argument does not depend on claims that Locke was a racist (discussed by Uzgalis (2002)), or that he or Grotius believed that Native peoples lacked reason.[13]

Both theorists were personally involved in the colonial enterprises of their own governments. Grotius wrote in defense of Dutch ventures in the East Indies, and his relatives were among the directors of the United East India Company. Locke was an investor in the Royal Africa

---

[13] For discussion and defense of Locke against this claim see, e.g., Squadrito (2002: 102–4) and Uzgalis (2002: 85–9). In setting out criteria for ownership, Grotius states that neither moral or religious virtue, nor great intellectual capacity, is required. But, he writes, it seems defensible to rule out "any peoples wholly deprived of the use of reason," though he "very much doubt[s]" that such people will be found. If they are, they cannot be owners, but charity prescribes that they should be provided with the necessities of life (bk II, XXII, X, §§1, 2). He adds that just as "universal common law" guarantees the maintenance of ownership for minors and the insane, so it does for "those peoples with whom there exists an interchange of agreements."

Company and in a company trading in the Bahamas. He was the first Landgrave (member of the nobility) in Carolina and was given land there. From 1668 to 1775 he worked as secretary to the Lords Proprietors of Carolina and helped draw up its constitution of 1669 (overthrown by the colonists in 1719); from 1672 to 1676 he worked for the Council on Trade, corresponding with settlers in America, and he was Commissioner for the Board of Trade and Plantations from 1695 until 1700.

Still, it is the theorists' use of the idea of *terra nullius* that is my concern. Arguments about the right of husbandry appear in their respective conjectural histories of the state of nature and the origin of private property, and they claim that Native territories are empty, waste lands. This is the reason why Grotius's arguments "started the seventeenth- and eighteenth-century Anglo-Dutch practice of justifying the seizure of aboriginal land on the grounds that the native peoples were not using it properly" (Tuck 1994: 167), and why Locke's "theory set the terms for many of the later theories that were used to justify the establishment of European property in America" (Tully 1994: 158).

Grotius argues that a thing that cannot be occupied cannot become property and remains open to the common use of everyone.[14] His conjectural history (with copious references to ancient sources) runs as follows. In the beginning, he writes in *Mare Liberum*, everything was held in common and could be used by all. The connection between the consumption of things and use shows that nature has pointed the way to the development of private property. Food, once consumed, cannot be used again, so "a certain kind of ownership is inseparable from use." Once use had been tied to ownership, the connection was extended to other things, such as "clothes and movables," and then to immovables, such as fields. The products of agriculture are necessary for future consumption, but there are not enough fields "for the use of everybody indiscriminately," and thus "the law of property was established to imitate nature." The system of individual property holding is called "occupation" and, once an individual has occupied a piece of property, the intention to maintain possession must be demonstrated. Moveables

---

[14] Part of Grotius's task was to separate property rights in land from any claims to the oceans. Free passage across the oceans was a major requirement for European colonialism, but it was generally held that states could exercise jurisdiction over the ocean as well as nearby waters. The sea, Grotius argues in *Mare Liberum*, cannot be owned in the same fashion as land. Neither the air nor the sea can be occupied and they are, therefore, naturally made for universal use. Grotius (1983: 67) states that "in the legal phraseology of the Law of Nations, the sea is called indifferently the property of no one (*res nullius*), or a common possession (*res communis*), or public property (*res publica*)." Tuck stresses the unrecognized "extreme originality of his view" (1999: 92).

have to be seized, and in the case of land the requirement is "the erection of buildings or some determination of boundaries, such as fencing in" (1983: 69–71).

Grotius's conjectures about the origins of property in *De Jure Belli Ac Pacis* are broadly similar to those in *Mare Liberum*, but he makes a significant enlargement of his argument. He extends it to cover the question of whether it is possible to have a right over things that are already owned. It is in this context that waste or deserted land, *terra nullius*, is introduced. In the earliest times, his argument runs, individuals took what they required for their use from the common stock. An individual had the right "to use things not claimed and consume them up to the limit of his needs, and anyone depriving him of that right would commit an unjust act" (bk I, II, I, §5). Such an arrangement required a very simple way of life, and this, Grotius states, is "exemplified in the community of property arising from extreme simplicity, [which] may be seen among certain tribes in America, which have lived for many generations in such a condition without inconvenience" (bk II, II, II, §1).

This simplicity no longer exists elsewhere; families ceased to be content to "feed on the spontaneous products of the earth,"[15] and men began to improve their condition and develop a division of labor (bk II, II, II, §4). "It is to be supposed" that, when communal ownership was abandoned, everyone agreed that existing possessions should become the property of their owners. Grotius argues that private property arose not by a deliberate act of will but by "a kind of agreement"; that is to say, an original contract (bk II, II, II, §5).[16] Occupation is now the primary means of acquisition and, he emphasizes, it has definite boundaries; things "are not divided until after they have become subject to private ownership" (bk II, II, III; see also Salter 2001: 539–46). Private property is created through an original contract and so is a civil arrangement, but communal property still exists in America which is thus a state of nature.

Grotius argues that the fact of ownership, in itself, does not entail the exclusion of others from access to, or even occupation of, property. He treats self-preservation as the fundamental natural right; thus "the right of necessity" applies in cases of dire need, and Grotius illustrates this

[15] On this concept see Hulme (1990).

[16] The agreement might be express, as in a division, or tacit, "as by occupation" (bk II, II, II, §§4, 5). Grotius remarks that acquisition by division took place "when the human race could assemble" (bk II, III, I). As Thomas Horne has noted, Grotius's argument is not as clear as it might be: "To what extent did agreement alone turn possessions into property?" He also notes that Pufendorf "virtually ignored the contractual element" in Grotius's theory (1990: 13–14).

by the example of the need to share provisions if they begin to run out during a voyage (bk II, II, VI–VIII).[17] He also postulates a right of "innocent use" of another's property. Property should be shared with another, if no inconvenience will be caused to an owner (bk II, II, XI). This is an example of "advantages [to others] which involve no detriment" to owners, such as the right to free passage over land or rivers, the right of temporary residence in a territory, or of permanent residence for foreigners seeking refuge (bk II, II, XV–XVI).

But foreigners have the right to do more than seek refuge and obtain sustenance; they also have rights over "desert places." Grotius states that

> if within the territory of a people there is any deserted and unproductive soil, this also ought to be granted to foreigners if they ask for it. Or it is right for foreigners even to take possession of such ground, for the reason that *uncultivated land ought not to be considered as occupied* except in respect to sovereignty, which remains unimpaired in favour of the original people. (my emphasis)

In support of this argument he notes that "the Latin aborigines" gave the Trojans 700 acres, and he quotes another ancient source: "they who bring under cultivation an untilled portion of the earth commit no wrong" (bk II, II, XVII). In short, Grotius argues that if lands are *terra nullius*, if they are uncultivated waste, they are open to rightful appropriation.[18] The right of husbandry is trumps.

Locke knew Grotius's arguments but, of course, he makes much more prominent use of the idea of an original contract. Locke's opponents were well aware that his assumption of an individual natural right to

---

[17] The right of necessity extends to the "acts" necessary to obtain that "without which life cannot be comfortably lived," although the consent of owners is required (bk II, II, XVIII–XXI).

[18] Some earlier remarks might seem to stand in tension with Grotius's argument about uncultivated land. He considers the case of land that has been "occupied as a whole" but is not yet parceled out into private property. He argues that "it ought not on that account to be considered as unoccupied property; for it remains subject to the ownership of the first occupant, whether a people or a king." He gives as examples "rivers, lakes, ponds, forests, and rugged mountains" (bk II, II, IV). Barbara Arneil argues that Grotius has in mind large tracts of territory claimed by a European power. Since the land will eventually be divided up into private allotments rival powers have no claim on it (1996: 52). But Grotius can also be read as making a general point about "ownership." The key is the intentions of the owners. In a case where the land will remain as unproductive waste, as *terra nullius*, like lands in North America, it is legitimately open for appropriation by foreigners (the nation that first discovers and occupies it). It is not open when the intention is that in due course the land will become private property.

property posed an obvious problem for English planting in North America. If settlement in the New World was to be justified, Locke had to find answers to two problems. First (the problem addressed in all the conjectural histories of the state of nature), how does communal property legitimately come to be divided up into private property; second, an explanation has to be provided, as Tully has emphasized (1993a, 1994), for the appropriation of land without consent. Locke explicitly states (II, §25; 1988: 286) that he will "endeavour to shew, how Men might come to have a *property* in several parts of that which God gave to Mankind in common, and that without any express Compact of all the Commoners."

Locke's arguments about appropriation have been discussed at length in the new scholarship (especially Tully 1993a, 1994, and Arneil 1996) and here I want only to emphasize three points. First, after his well-known claim that it is gathering or hunting, that is, the labor involved in appropriation, which creates property – God gave the world to "the use of the Industrious and Rational, (and *Labour* was to be *his Title* to it;)" (II, §34; 1988: 291) – Locke insists that the same line of reasoning applies to the appropriation of land. Although "the *chief matter of Property* being now not the Fruits of the Earth, and the Beasts that subsist on it, but the *Earth it self*; . . . I think it is plain, that *Property* in that too is acquired as the former" (II, §32; 1988: 290).

Second, he separates common land in England from that in America, a separation that relies on claims about stages of civilization. In England, a civil society, the commons are left unenclosed "by Compact, *i.e.* by the Law of the Land, which is not to be violated" (II, §35; 1988: 292). The common land belongs jointly to the members of a particular parish, and if some were to be enclosed it would not be as useful to the parishioners. In contrast, the whole of America is a commons in the sense that it is an example of "a Pattern of the first Ages in *Asia* and *Europe*" (II, §108; 1988: 339) – the pattern of a state of nature or a *terra nullius*. The condition of America is that of the first age of the world when it belongs to all mankind, a condition of "the beginning and the first peopling of the great Common of the World" where the "Law Man was under, was rather for *appropriating*" (II, §35; 1988: 292). America is still at the stage of history where it is nothing more than "wild woods and uncultivated wast . . . left to nature, without any improvement, tillage or husbandry" (II, §37; 1988: 294).

Third, Locke argues that enclosure is legitimate provided that good use is made of the land and nothing is left to spoil. Locke states that if fruit is planted but left on the tree to rot, "this part of the Earth, notwithstanding his Inclosure, was still to be looked on as Waste, and might be the Possession of any other" (II, §38; 1988: 295). Uzgalis asks "what follows from" this passage, and argues that it is irrelevant to the "Dispossession Interpretation" of Locke because he does not refer to waste "in terms of relative productivity" (2002: 93). Uzgalis, however, does not mention Locke's other famous argument about the consensual introduction of money.[19] To be sure, Locke bolsters his argument about the appropriation of land in a Thomas More-like fashion by stressing how much better off everyone is, English and Indians both, when land is turned into private property and used productively. "Land that is left wholly to Nature, that hath no improvement of Pasturage, Tillage, or Planting, is called, as indeed it is, *wast*; and we shall find the benefit of it amount to little more than nothing" (II, §42; and II, §41; 1988: 297). The point, however, is that money enables property owners to implement the right of husbandry and enlarge what they own, so that they can produce more than they need for their own use and trade the surplus.

The significance of money in a *terra nullius* is that it is central to the creation of a new civil society that includes an "economy." Locke writes of *"great Tracts of Ground"* that lie waste, where the inhabitants have not "joyned with the rest of Mankind, in the consent of the Use of their common Money" (II, §45; 1988: 299). That he has America in mind is clear three paragraphs later. He asks what is the worth to a man of a hundred thousand acres of cultivated, well stocked land isolated "in the middle of the in-land Parts of *America*," where there is no hope of commerce with the rest of the world "to draw *Money* to him by the Sale of the Product?" (II, §48; 1988: 301). The "in-land, vacant places of *America*" (II, §36; 1988: 293) must be brought into a system of states, and thus into a national and international trading system, before their worth can be realized.

By the mid-eighteenth century the line of argument found in Grotius and Locke culminated in the denial that Native peoples were "owners" at all. This view was enshrined as part of international law, notably by Vattel in his extremely influential *The Law of Nations* (1758). He insisted that the law of nature required all nations to cultivate their land. The Europeans had discovered lands where the population was so scanty that

---

[19] Uzgalis (2002: 95) also argues that another reason "to completely reject the idea that Locke wrote this section of the chapter 'Of Property' in order to justify English settlement" was that he did not "explicitly announce this as his project." It has been suggested that chapter 5, "On Property," was composed independently of Locke's *Second Treatise* and then inserted later. David Armitage (2004) has now found evidence to show that Locke was heavily involved in the revision of the Constitution for Carolina in 1682 when "On Property" was probably written. This explains why, even if he made no explicit statement, Locke was indeed very concerned with English settlement at the time and made many references to America in chapter 5.

vast acreages lay unoccupied and uncultivated and the population merely ranged over them. According to Vattel, the Native peoples' "unsettled habitation in those immense regions cannot be accounted a true and legal possession." He states that therefore land "of which savages stood in no particular need, and of which they made no actual and constant use" could lawfully be appropriated and colonized (bk I, XVIII, §209). He argued that settlement should not exceed just boundaries, but the logic of the settler contract meant the bounds were wide indeed.

III An Original Contract

The right of husbandry was not the only theoretical trump held by the settlers. The Native peoples, it was held, also lacked sovereignty. In *De Jure Belli ac Pacis*, Grotius distinguishes sovereignty (*imperium*), which is exercised over both people and territory, from ownership (*dominium*). Sovereignty and ownership, Grotius notes, are usually acquired together, but that they differ – although Edward Keene remarks that "Grotius did not make the point entirely clear" (2002: 57) – is illustrated by the ownership of land by foreigners as well as citizens (bk II, III, IV). Grotius's arguments about conquest, "innocent use," and the right of husbandry mean that *imperium* outside of Europe is a rather poor thing. And where there is no proper sovereignty the way is open for large-scale settlement.

In *Leviathan*, Hobbes states that people in many parts of America "have no government at all." They have only "the government of small Families, the concord whereof dependeth on naturall lust" (1996: ch. 13, 89). Locke does not go that far. He, like Grotius, recognizes that Native peoples have governments and monarchs but, he argues, they exercise only "a very moderate sovereignty" (II, §108; 1988: 340). The manner of government found among the Native peoples in America in this "Pattern of the first Ages" of the world is suited to their condition: "The equality of a simple poor way of liveing confineing their desires within the narrow bounds of each mans smal propertie made few controversies and so no need of many laws to decide them." The major requirement in such societies is "to secure themselves against foreign Force" (II, §107; 1988: 339). Thus,

> [T]he *Kings* of the *Indians* in *America* . . . are little more than *Generals of their Armies*; and though they command absolutely in War, yet at home and in time of Peace they exercise very little Dominion, and have but a very moderate Sovereignty, the Resolutions of Peace and War, being ordinarily either in the People, or in a Council. Though the War it self, which admits not of Plurality of Governours, naturally devolves the Command into the *King's sole Authority*. (II, §108; 1988: 339–40)

In a note to this paragraph Peter Laslett cites Locke's *Letters on Toleration*, where Locke writes in similar terms of "nations in the West Indies." They are organized only for defense against common enemies. During peace, neither the wartime commanders "nor any body else has any authority over any of the society."

That is to say, the Native peoples lack both proper sovereignty and a properly political government. Locke is very clear that a civil government is the only properly *political* form.[20] The purpose of civil government is the protection of (private) property,[21] and such a government must be constitutional, limited, and representative, acting within the rule of law as an "umpire" between conflicting societal interests. In America, a *terra nullius*, there is no private property, no husbandry, no money, and no real sovereignty – neither proper *dominium* nor *imperium* – therefore the settlers have found themselves in a state of nature.

A major contribution of the new scholarship on early modern political theory and European expansion is to show that in the texts of theorists of an original contract "the state of nature" is not merely a theoretical construct or heuristic device, as we were all taught, but is also portrayed as a historical condition. Theorists of an original contract used the idea of the state of nature both as a thought experiment and as descriptive of an actual stage of historical development. They draw on each element as needed in their arguments.

On the one hand, "the state of nature" and "civil society" are abstractions that presuppose and stand in contrast to each other. Political theorists ask their readers to imagine what society would be like if it were empty of the institutions of a modern state and if individuals lacked civil characteristics. Each political theorist draws the picture of the natural condition that is required to justify his particular account of civil society and government. The modern state is justified because it keeps the inconveniences or war of the state of nature at bay, whether it is the state of Leviathan or Locke's "umpire." But even as an heuristic device, "the state of nature" is not completely disconnected from the real world, from the English Civil War or 1688.

On the other hand, in Locke's evocative words, "in the beginning all the World was *America*" (II, §49; 1988: 301). Europeans have discovered a world that is in its first stage of history; a state of nature that exists in the seventeenth century. This (actual) state of nature *waits to be transformed*

---

[20] I discuss this conception of "political" in Pateman (1975). This view is not unique to Locke; for its association with "methodological Rawlsianism" see Pateman (2002: 39–40).

[21] For the connection between Locke's broader and narrower senses of "property" and his argument about America, see Arneil (1996: 133–4).

and developed, to be turned into a civil society. The settlers know what they have to build because they are familiar with the opposition between the "natural" and the "civil." The antinomy harks back to the ancient Roman division between barbarians and members of the *civitas* (see Pagden 1995: ch. 1). It has a variety of expressions, but one of the most telling is between the "savage" and the "civilized." Hobbes wrote of the "savage people in many places of *America*," who still "live at this day in that brutish manner" (1996: ch. 13, p. 89), and the language of the "savage" became part of international law. In 1893, Frederick Turner wrote of the frontier as the "meeting point between savagery and civilization" (1994: 32). Lacking all the attributes of a civil condition, savages cannot undertake the transformation of their lands. Or, at least, they cannot take the first step, although once they have begun to develop in the requisite manner some may be permitted to participate.[22]

The settlers did not go to North America with the intention of joining, say, Iroquois or Mohegan society or to Australia to become part of Pitjantjatjara or other Aboriginal communities. They could not become "savages." They planted themselves in the New Worlds to establish their own civil societies and could do so because they were English and so already "civilized" beings. As Blackstone states, the settlers "carry" law with them; "if an uninhabited country be discovered and planted by English subjects, all the English laws then in being, which are the birthright of every subject, are immediately there in force" (1899: Intro. §4, 107). They had both the capacities to enter an original contract and an understanding of the institutions of a modern state. Having journeyed, or, in 1788 been transported, to a *terra nullius* the settlers were, so to speak, the natural figures of the thought experiment in the texts of political theory come to life.

The "state of nature" and the "original contract" are powerful political fictions, and their power derives from the fact that they have had purchase on and have helped create the modern world. The colonization of the New Worlds took a long time; in a sense it can be seen as a series of origins, of settler contracts. But in both New Worlds there is an "original" moment that marks the Founding of the "United States," the Confederation of "Canada," or the Federation of "Australia." A striking characteristic of the United States is the mythical political status of this moment, with its concomitants of constitution and flag. Arendt, for example, makes a great deal of this founding act and argues that "remembrance of the event itself" generates "an atmosphere of

---

[22] It was widely believed that, in Condorcet's words, the inhabitants of colonized lands "seem to be waiting only to be civilized and to receive from us the means to be so" (quoted in Pagden 1995: 10).

reverent awe." This ensures that "the authority of the republic will be safe and intact as long as the act itself, the beginning as such, is remembered" (1973: 204).[23]

Thus, a civil society created out of a state of nature has (is understood to have) its origin in an original contract. In a *terra nullius* the original contract takes the form of a *settler contract*. The settlers alone (can be said to) conclude the original pact. It is a racial as well as a social contract. The Native peoples are not part of the settler contract – but they are henceforth subject to it, and their lives, lands, and nations are reordered by it.

The settler contract also excludes the Crown. Vattel writes that when "a nation takes possession of a distant country, and settles a colony there, that country, though separated from the principal establishment, or mother-country, naturally becomes part of the state, equally with its ancient possessions" (bk I, XVIII, §210). That may have been true *de jure*, or in the eyes of the metropolis, but the settler contract sets other political mechanisms in motion. Legal decisions made in London and Crown policies about colonization had to be implemented a very long way away, and settlers often had a very different view of what was required.[24] The settler contract sets up new (civil) political institutions (Tully's (1995) imperial constitution or empire of uniformity; see also McHugh 2004) that mark the beginnings of a new state that will in due course, in its own right, be part of an international commercial network and system of modern, sovereign states.

The Native peoples regarded themselves as nations, on a par with the European nations from which the settlers had come. By the early eighteenth century the Crown had acknowledged Indian sovereignty. In the 1690s, in "one of the most famous cases in colonial history" (Tully 1994: 171), the colony of Connecticut and the Mohegan nation went to law over Connecticut's claim to jurisdiction over Mohegan territory. In the face of arguments by Connecticut, that included appeals to *terra*

---

[23] She also discusses theories of an original contract, during the course of which she writes: "America should have presented to the social-contract theories that beginning of society and government which they had assumed to be . . . fictitious . . . if it were not for the undeniable . . . fact that these theories in the Old World proceeded without ever mentioning the actual realities in the New World" (1973: 172). While it is true that theorists of an original contract are silent about the activities of the settlers, they have plenty to say about America!

[24] The colony of Carolina provides an early example of divergence between London and colonists, which involved Locke. Together with Lord Shaftesbury, he had "assumed leadership" of the colony in 1669, with a plan to establish agricultural development. In 1672 Locke introduced a law prohibiting slavery of Indians. The colonists ignored it, and by 1680 "the fur trade and the sale of Indian slaves to the West Indies were the staples of Carolina's economy" (Tully 1993b: 143–4).

nullius, the Mohegans insisted that as a sovereign nation under the law of nations they would negotiate only with the Crown. The Privy Council found in favor of the Mohegans in 1705 and, on appeal, in 1743.[25] In 1764, the Indian Superintendent appointed by the Crown wrote that a boundary should be negotiated with the Iroquois Confederacy, which "never having been conquered, either by the English or the French, nor subject to their Laws, consider themselves as a free people" (quoted in R. Williams 1990: 240).[26]

By the mid-eighteenth century the British were in need of alliances with the Native nations because of the conflict with France. Indeed, a Proclamation in 1761 stated that the peace and security of the North American colonies depended on their friendship (Borrows 1997: 261 n39). This was followed by the crucial Royal Proclamation of 1763, issued at the end of the Seven Years' War.[27] John Borrows argues that the Proclamation together with the Treaty of Niagara in 1764 reaffirmed Native sovereignty. In itself, the Proclamation is ambiguous; it "uncomfortably straddled the contradictory aspirations of the Crown and First Nations." But it was also central to the Treaty negotiated between the Crown and about 25 Native nations, represented at Niagara by some 2,000 chiefs. The Treaty was sealed diplomatically by a two-row wampum belt signifying peace, friendship, and mutual non-interference in internal affairs; that is to say, the sovereignty of the Native parties was acknowledged. In the 1840s Native peoples in (what became) Canada still possessed copies of the Proclamation (Borrows 1997: 160).

The Crown had set in motion a process of colonization from which it did not withdraw. However, the colonists had different ideas about both *imperium* and *dominium*. In (what became) the United States the Royal Proclamation brought matters to a head. The British government was concerned about the settlers' continued territorial expansion and its implications for alliances with Native nations. The Secretary of State

[25] P. G. McHugh argues that to speak of "sovereignty" in this case is anachronistic. Premodern common law judgments were made in a context of "a feudal tributary system [rather] than a modernist model of sovereignty" (2004: 44; also 26). But either way, the point is that Native peoples' governments and political systems were recognized as "nations."

[26] The Iroquois Confederacy had itself conquered other nations in the Ohio country over whom they exercised sovereignty, recognized by their tributaries.

[27] Tully (1995: 118) states that the Proclamation was based on a review "of treaties since 1664, Royal Commissions on Indian Affairs since 1665, Royal Instructions to Colonial Administrators since 1670, the Board of Trade's Recognition of Aboriginal Sovereignty in 1696 (when Locke was a member) and in the case of the Mohegan nation . . . of 1705, and the advice of the Superintendent of Indian Affairs in North America." He sees the Proclamation as exemplifying consent as the policy of the Crown.

wrote that the principle informing British policy was that "invasion or occupation of [the Indians'] hunting lands" was to cease, and possession "is to be acquired by fair purchase only" (quoted in R. Williams 1990: 235).

The Proclamation reserved the lands beyond the eastern mountains to the Indian nations, and stated that

> it is just and reasonable, and essential to our interest and the security of our colonies, that the several nations or tribes of Indians with whom we are connected, and who live under our protection, should not be molested or disturbed in the possession of such parts of our dominions or territories as, not having been ceded to or purchased by us, are reserved to them, or any of them, as their hunting grounds.

Anyone who had "either willfully or inadvertently seated themselves" in the reserved lands was "forthwith to remove themselves from such settlements." The Proclamation further laid down that if Indians wished to sell land it was to be purchased "only for us, in our name [i.e., the Crown] at some public meeting or assembly of the said Indians, to be held for that purpose by the Governor or commander in chief of our colony" (reprinted in Commager 1968: 48–9). Such restrictions on expansion and appropriation of land were anathema to colonial elites and the Proclamation became a precipitating cause of the American Revolution.

Tenure had been granted to the settlers in a number of different forms depending, for example, whether a colony had been set up by a noble proprietor or through a corporate settlement agency. But most agencies and proprietors had tenure "as of the Manor of East Greenwich, in free and common socage," i.e. it was unencumbered, resembling allodial tenure (see Keene 2002: 62–76).[28] English land law after the Norman Conquest was based on the feudal fiction that all land was held as a derivative title granted by the Crown. The provision in the Proclamation that "vacant" land had to be purchased and held in the name of the Crown derived from the feudal fiction. Blackstone writes that "it became a fundamental maxim and necessary principle (though in reality a mere fiction) of our English tenures, 'that the king is the universal lord and original proprietor of all the lands in his kingdom'" (1899: bk II, ch. 4, p. 475). Or, as stated by Marshall in *Johnson v. Macintosh*, the British constitution held that "all vacant lands are vested in the crown, as representing the nation; and the exclusive power to grant them is admitted to reside in the crown, as a branch of the royal prerogative" (Marshall 1987: 274, 279).

[28] My thanks to Anthony Pagden for drawing my attention to the Manor of East Greenwich.

The colonists, including George Washington, were making large profits through land speculation and they were not inclined to limit the extent of settlement. One response to the Proclamation, not least by Thomas Jefferson, was a comparison with the English burdened by the Norman Yoke. The settlers maintained that the feudal fiction had no application in America. The English had brought Anglo-Saxon common law with them, including allodial tenure, and they should therefore be free to trade in land with the Indians. In a beautiful piece of colonial irony, the settlers turned to the principles of natural freedom and rights at the heart of theories of an original contract. These principles were now wielded in the interest of speculation and appropriation of territory. The Native peoples as the original occupiers, the settlers declared, had a natural right freely to dispose of their land to whom they pleased (see R. Williams 1990: chs 6, 7).

Nor were they inclined to let Crown acknowledgment of Native sovereignty stand in the way of the creation of a civil society from a *terra nullius*. The tempered logic of the settler contract is that any recognition of Native nations must be on the terms of the new *imperium*. Inside the territory of a modern state there can be only one sovereign power. Marshall's opinions are instructive. In *Johnson*, Marshall wrote that it has "never been contended that the Indian title amounted to nothing. Their right of possession has never been questioned" (1987: 285). However, the rights of the Native peoples are now "necessarily, to a considerable extent, impaired." They lack the power to dispose of their land as they please, and "their rights to complete sovereignty, as independent nations, were necessarily diminished" (p. 264). The Native peoples in America were "fierce savages," skilled in warfare. They fought the settlers to retain their independence, yet they could not be governed as a "distinct people." The "inevitable consequence" is the necessity to "resort to some new and different rule" (pp. 274–6).

In 1831 and 1832 in *Worcester* and *Cherokee Nation v. Georgia*, Marshall arrives at the formulation of the "new and different rule." In *Worcester* he states that the King purchased Indian lands, but "never coerced a surrender of them. . . . [Nor] intruded into the interior of their affairs, or interfered with their self-government" (p. 431). The Native peoples live in nations in the same sense as in Europe; they are "distinct, independent political communities, retaining their original natural rights" (pp. 444–5).[29] But, as he states in *Cherokee*, the relation between

---

[29] The reputed reaction of President Andrew Jackson, who had no time for talk of sovereignty and treaties, to Marshall's decision in *Worcester* was that "John Marshall has made his opinion, now let him enforce it." The Cherokee, Choctaw, Creek, Chickasaw, and Seminole peoples were forcibly removed from their lands and (those who survived) relocated hundreds of miles away.

the Native nations and the United States is "marked by peculiar and cardinal distinctions." They are part of the United States and under its protection, but under the law of nations they are still self-governing. It is in this case that he designates the Native nations as standing in a relation like that of ward to guardian, as "domestic dependent nations" (p. 414).

One commentator on *Mabo* sees Marshall's decisions as pragmatic, not founded upon any theory of fairness or justice, but the "only possible accommodation of the rights of settlers and aboriginal people" (Bartlett 1993: 182). No other accommodation was possible within the tempered logic of the settler contract. In a civil society Native peoples must be, at best, something less than sovereign and the "justice" of any arrangement with them is justice according to the new authority of the modern state. The United States prides itself on being a fully modern nation, so feudal fictions were eliminated; a modern state speaks the language of the national interest and regulates its borders accordingly.

In Canada, the Proclamation continues to have a prominent legal place but, again, the tempered logic of the settler contract was followed.[30] Many treaties were concluded from the 1750s onward, first negotiated by officials of the Crown and then, after the British North America Act (1867), the numbered treaties were negotiated by the government of the Dominion. They extinguished Native title in exchange for reserved lands for Native peoples to occupy and hunting and fishing rights. In a case in the Quebec Supreme Court in 1867 it was held that "existing Aboriginal laws were left in full force, and were in no way modified by the introduction of European law with regard to the civil rights of the natives" (Murphy 2001: 115). But *St. Catherine's Milling* (1888), in which the judgment rested on the feudal fiction, became authoritative.[31] Lord Watson stated that when the Indians surrendered

---

[30] The Canadian Charter of Rights and Freedoms, Section 25, part of the Constitution Act of 1982, states: "The guarantee in this Charter of certain rights and freedoms shall not be construed so as to abrogate or derogate from any aboriginal, treaty or other rights or freedoms that pertain to the aboriginal peoples of Canada including

  (a) any rights or freedoms that have been recognized by the Royal Proclamation of October 7, 1763."

[31] *St. Catherine's Milling and Lumber Company v. the Queen*, 14 AC 46 (PC) was decided by the Privy Council on appeal from the Supreme Court of Canada. The case in effect was between the governments of the Dominion and the province of Ontario over who had control of licensing of use of resources in the territory in question; the First Nations took no part (Kulchyski 1994: 22). The judgment stated that "[t]he treaty leaves the Indians no right whatever to the timber growing upon the lands which they gave up, which is now fully vested in the Crown, all revenues derivable from the sale of such portions of it as are situated within the boundaries of Ontario being the property of that Province" (reprinted in Kulchyski 1994: 30).

their lands through treaty (No. 3 in 1873) they were not owners in fee simple; rather, the "Crown has all along had a present proprietary estate in the land, upon which the Indian title was a mere burden." Public land was vested in the Crown and the right to beneficial use was lodged with the Provincial or Dominion government. Since 1763, the character of Indian interest in the lands in question was "a personal and usufructuary right, dependent upon the good will of the Sovereign. The lands reserved are expressly stated to be 'parts of Our dominions and territories'" (reprinted in Kulchyski 1994: 29, 27). The Native lands and inhabitants had become part of Canada, an expanding state and a self-governing Dominion within the British Empire.

In North America the logic of the settler contract was tempered and in the United States the Native peoples had their own jurisdictions, albeit mere remnants, within the bounds of the new state. In Australia the strict logic was followed. The doctrine of *terra nullius* was elevated to the law of the land and an entire continent was deemed uninhabited in the eyes of the law.

IV *Terra Nullius* Transported

When the settlers left England for North America they knew from the reports of earlier voyagers and visitors that they were going to an inhabited country.[32] But the First Fleet set sail south in 1787 to a continent which was virtually *terra incognita*.[33] That there were at least a few inhabitants had been established by William Dampier in his voyage of 1688 on the west coast of Australia, and by observations and encounters on the east coast in Captain Cook's first voyage in 1770. The botanist Joseph Banks gave evidence before government committees, including the Committee on Transportation, about the proposal for a colony. He stated that in 1770 he had seen "very few" inhabitants, and "did not think there were above Fifty in all the Neighbourhood, and

[32] Locke's library, for example, was well stocked with such accounts. Tully states that when the Europeans began to colonize the Americas they found "sovereign indigenous nations with complex forms of social and political organization and territorial jurisdictions that were older (3,000–30,000 years), more populous (60–80 million) and more variegated than Europe" (2000: 38). Contemporary estimates are that the Australian continent was occupied for some 60,000 to 120,000 years before the British settlers arrived, and that in 1788 the population was around 1 million people (Day 2001).

[33] After 1776 transportation to America was no longer possible. The proposal for a colony in Botany Bay was one of several made by Pitt's administration in 1783 (in the event it was a substitute for another in South West Africa). There were some other reasons to establish a colony in New South Wales besides setting up a new depository for convicts; see Day (2001: 25–8).

had Reason to believe the Country was very thinly peopled; those he saw were naked, treacherous, and armed with Lances, but extremely cowardly." In his journal from the voyage of the *Endeavour*, Banks conjectured that the "immense tract of [inland] country" was "totaly uninhabited." He drew this conclusion because he believed that if there were inhabitants there must be cultivation; even in North America, he noted, the Indians inland had sown maize. Agriculture would surely have spread to the coastal people, "otherwise their reason must be suppos'd to hold a rank little superior to that of monkies." He had seen no cultivation along the coast and assumed the people there lived from the sea (quoted in Reynolds (1987: 31–2), and (1996: 17–18)). In 1785 Banks reported that cession and purchase in the proposed colony were not possible "as there was nothing we could offer that [the Aborigines] would take except provisions and those we wanted ourselves" (quoted in R. King 1986: 76–7).

Dampier had set the tone for many subsequent portrayals of the Aboriginal peoples. He said that they were "the miserablest People in the World . . . setting aside their Humane Shape, they differ but little from Brutes. . . They all of them have the most unpleasant Looks and the worst Features of any People that I ever saw, tho I have seen a great variety of Savages" (quoted in G. Williams 1981: 500–1). Cook took a very different view in his journal, and different again from that of Banks. Cook wrote that the Aboriginal people

> are far more happier than we Europeans; being wholy unacquainted not only with the superfluous but the necessary Conveniences so much sought after in Europe, they are happy in not knowing the use of them. They live in a Tranquility which is not disturb'd by the Inequality of Condition. . . . they seem'd to set no Value upon any thing we gave them, nor would they ever part with any thing of their own for any one article we could offer them. (Quoted in G. Williams 1981: 499)[34]

The view of Aboriginal peoples as savages, or even lower than savages, was very persistent. Even in 1979 an opponent of land rights wrote in the manner of Gentili: "The aborigines' use of 'his' land is much closer to that of the wild beasts than that of other non-agricultural hunting

---

[34] But Cook's comments remained unknown until his journal was published in the late nineteenth century. Cook, Williams suggests, showed "a readiness to view a strange and primitive life style on its own terms," and he notes that in his *Life* of Cook, published in 1974, Beaglehole comments that "Cook bursts into a panegyric that almost persuades me that he had spent the voyage reading Rousseau" (G. Williams 1981: 509, 499). For a brief account of some Aboriginal stories of "Captain Cook" see Hunter (1996: 2–4).

and gathering people" (quoted in Reynolds 1987: 158; for other early examples see Banner 2005).

There were critics of the plan for a colony who worried about dispossession and killing of any Native peoples. Cook had been instructed that land was to be obtained only with the consent of the inhabitants and in 1788 Captain Phillip was charged by the King to "open an intercourse with the natives, and to conciliate their affections," and if any were "wantonly destroy[ed]" the offender was to be punished. Phillip reported that "the natives have ever been treated with the greatest humanity and attention," and he hoped to teach them "the advantages they will reap from cultivating the land" (quoted in R. King 1986: 80, 83–4). The local population around Port Jackson was estimated to be about 2,000, and it soon became clear that not only were other parts of the country inhabited but that Aboriginal peoples had their own mutually recognized territories. A mode of interaction was quickly established. The settlers decimated stocks of fish and game, and in 1789 smallpox killed about half the Native population (Day 2001: 42–3) discusses whether it was deliberately introduced). By 1804, the Aboriginal peoples were telling the Governor that "they did not like to be driven from the few places that were left on the banks of the [Nepean] river, where alone they could procure food. . . . If they could retain some places . . . they should be satisfied and would not trouble the white men" (quoted in R. King 1986: 84–6, 89).

In Australia, as in America, policies made in London were frequently ignored by settlers and their governments. When plans were made to colonize Tasmania at the beginning of the nineteenth century there was no doubt that it was inhabited. In 1828, Governor Arthur wrote to London that he intended "to allot and assign certain specified tracts of land, for [the Aborigines'] exclusive benefit, and continued occupation" (quoted in Reynolds 1996: 113). The settlers had other intentions, and reports of the unremitting slaughter in Tasmania, under martial law from 1828 to 1833, were a major impetus to formation of the British and Foreign Aborigines Protection Society (successor to the Society for the Abolition of the Slave Trade).

After his experience in Tasmania, Arthur offered advice to the Colonial Office about the colonization of South Australia, a venture undertaken by a private company with free settlers. In 1832 he wrote that the "fatal error" in Tasmania was that "a treaty was not entered into with the natives, of which savages well comprehend the nature" (quoted in Reynolds 1996: 115). In a communication to the Commission in charge of settlement the Colonial Office referred to "Tribes of People, whose Proprietary Title to the Soil, we have not the slightest ground for disputing" (quoted in Banner 2005: 120). However, the Commission and the settlers merely paid lip service to such instructions from officials in London and appropriated land in the new colony as they saw fit.[35]

In the *Mabo* judgment it is stated that *Cooper v. Stuart* (1889) was "seen as authoritatively establishing that the territory of New South Wales had, in 1788, been *terra nullius* not in the sense of unclaimed by any other European power, but in the sense of unoccupied or uninhabited for the purposes of the law" (p. 103).[36] This was one of two propositions that, Justices Deane and Gaudron write, "provided a legal basis for and justification of" dispossession. The second proposition was that "full legal and beneficial ownership of all the lands of the Colony [were] vested in the Crown, unaffected by any claims of the Aboriginal inhabitants" (p. 108). That is, the feudal fiction was held to apply as soon as the British set foot in Botany Bay and claimed sovereignty.

Cooper v. Stuart embodied the view that settled (occupied) colonies were without prior ownership of land. "There is a great difference between the case of a Colony acquired by conquest or cession, in which there is an established system of law, and that of a Colony which consisted of a tract of territory practically unoccupied, without settled inhabitants or settled law, at the time when it was peaceably annexed to the British dominions" (p. 291). A few paragraphs later Lord Watson stated that "[t]here was no land law or tenure existing in the Colony at the time of its annexation to the Crown" (p. 292). However, not everyone agreed that the New World was *terra nullius*. Some lawyers had presented dissenting views in cases (that concerned other legal matters) earlier in the nineteenth century.[37]

In 1827 (in *R. v. Lowe*), for example, one of the lawyers defending a soldier accused of murdering an Aboriginal man argued that the court had no jurisdiction because the manner in which the British had taken possession of the country was "repugnant to the law of nations"

---

[35] The South Australian Constitution Act had been drawn up by the company and referred to "waste and unoccupied lands." (For further details of the maneuverings by the Commission see Reynolds 1987: ch. 6; Banner 2005.) Reynolds writes that South Australia saw itself as "a child of the era of liberal reform, infused with the spirit of the Reform Bill and religious emancipation. What was discreetly dropped from the legacy was the powerful commitment to racial equality which ran through both the anti-slavery and Aboriginal protection movements" (1987: 121).

[36] 14 App Cas 1889; decided by the Privy Council on appeal from the Supreme Court of New South Wales. The case concerned a grant of land to a settler that contained a reservation about future public use. The government of New South Wales later resumed ten acres, and the action was challenged.

[37] The Privy Council would not have had access to two of the most relevant because the formal reports were only published after *Cooper v. Stuart* was decided. Indeed, "the scarcity of law reporting in early Australia" makes it difficult to determine when *terra nullius* was established in case law (Kercher 2002: 101).

(quoted in Banner 2005: 119). His colleague declared that there could be no "right of sovereignty over them [the Aboriginal peoples]; they are the free occupants of the demesne or soil, it belongs to them by law of nations, anterior to any laws which follow from human institutions" (quoted in McHugh 2004: 160). Two years later (in *R. v. Ballard*, another murder case) the judge argued that "although the notions of property may be very imperfect in the native[, the] Englishman has no right wantonly to deprive the savage of any property he possesses or assumes a dominion over" (quoted in Kercher 2002: 107).

But even those critical of the doctrine of *terra nullius* usually balked at the notion that the Aboriginal peoples should be recognized as owners. Instead they proposed the creation of reserves or compensation. However, such arguments appear to have been stifled by the mid-1830s. In 1834 the Chief Justice of New South Wales referred to "His Majesty's subjects settling an uninhabited country" (quoted in Banner 2005: 123). *R. v. Murrell* in 1836 "appears to be the founding case" in the legal consolidation of *terra nullius* (Kercher 2002: 108).[38] Interestingly, the existence and some rights of the Native peoples were acknowledged but, nonetheless, the judgment was that they were insufficiently civilized to exercise sovereignty. In his notes the judge stated that they merely wandered over the land which was thus open for appropriation. Kercher comments that *Murrell* was the only early case to be in the law reports and "was also the case most consistent with popular white views of the legal position" (2002: 114).

Two factors may help explain the judgment in *Cooper v. Stuart*, which was handed down well after Marshall had delivered his opinions and a year after the Privy Council had dealt with *St. Catherine's Milling*. By 1898 "the common law had industrialized" and the positivistic doctrine of undivided sovereignty held sway (McHugh 2004: 31). Moreover, modern ideas about "race" had reached their full development. The perception of the Aboriginal peoples was that they were lowest in the hierarchy of races. Late nineteenth-century international law was shaped by racial doctrines. For instance, in *Chapters on the Principles of International Law*, published in 1894, John Westlake discusses "civilization" in terms of a government that is able to stand against other European powers. No such government is to be found among the peoples of America or Africa: "Accordingly international law has to treat such natives as uncivilized." Thus "the first necessity is that a government should be furnished" by Europeans. In the absence of such a government, "the inflow of the white race cannot be stopped where

---

[38] This was another murder case but involving only Aborigines. Kercher's account is derived from newspaper and archival resources as well as a report published in 1896.

there is land to cultivate, ore to be mined, commerce to be developed, sport to enjoy, curiosity to be satisfied" (Westlake 1894: 142–3; see also Roberts-Wray's gloss (1966: 540)). The division of the world among themselves by the European colonial powers from the late nineteenth century presupposed that only "civilized" societies could become states (see Shaw 1986: 43–5).

"Strictly speaking," Robert van Krieken argues, there was only one legal precedent when *Mabo* was heard; only once had the law directly addressed the question of native title (2000: 66). The precedent was *Milirrpum v. Nabalco* (1971) in which Justice Blackburn reaffirmed *Cooper v. Stuart*.[39] Blackburn has been harshly criticized since *Mabo*. Hocking, for example, states of his judgment that "the law was misinterpreted and grievously wrong" (1993: 188). But Justice Dawson interpreted the law in a similar fashion in his sole dissenting opinion in *Mabo*. And Blackburn's judgment is significant for my argument because it follows the strict logic of the settler contract.

Blackburn agreed with *Cooper v. Stuart* that whether a colony was categorized as settled or not "is a matter of law," and that Australia "came into the category of a settled or occupied colony. This is established for New South Wales by an authority which is clear and, as far as this Court is concerned, binding: *Cooper v. Stuart*" (p. 242). In fact, the justices in *Mabo* did not disagree about this particular legal point. The crucial question was whether status as a settled colony entailed that, in law, it was uninhabited and without a system of land tenure.[40] The plaintiffs in *Milirrpum* argued that the "subject land" was inhabited in 1788 and enjoyed a system of law, so the question, in Blackburn's words, was "does there exist at common law a doctrine of native title" (p. 151). It was on this point that Blackburn and Dawson are at odds with the *Mabo* judgment.

One aspect of the question was whether the Rirratjingu and Gumatj peoples had enjoyed a system of law. Blackburn concluded that the evidence before him, which included Aboriginal witnesses and two anthropologists, showed that they did. He could not have been more emphatic

---

[39] 17 FLR 1971 141; the Gove Land Rights Case. The case concerned land of the Rirratjingu and Gumatj peoples in the Gove Peninsula, north-east Arnhem Land – very remote, but included in the land over which the British flag was hoisted on January 26, 1788; it is now part of the Northern Territory. Permanent settlement did not take place until the 1930s. In 1968 Nabalco was granted a mineral lease by the federal government to mine bauxite. The plaintiffs argued that under common law they had always had a proprietary right in the land, so the lease was unlawful.

[40] The High Court Justices argued that the legal claim that Australia was settled drew on a "restricted" concept of *terra nullius*. That it was settled and "practically unoccupied" involved an "expanded" notion. I do not think this distinction is necessary.

on this point. He stated that he was "suspicious about the truth of the assertions of the early settlers of New South Wales that the aboriginals had no ordered manner of community life" (p. 266). His opinion was that it was not possible to dismiss the plaintiffs' "social rules and customs" as "lying on the other side of an unbridgeable gulf."[41] Rather, what the evidence revealed was

> a subtle and elaborate system highly adapted to the country in which the people led their lives, which provided a stable order of society and was remarkably free from the vagaries of personal whim or influence. If ever a system could be called "a government of laws, and not of men," it is that shown in the evidence before me. (p. 267)

Blackburn's response to the evidence was that "the question is *one not of fact but of law*" (my emphasis). He continued that "[w]hether or not the Australian aboriginals living in any part of New South Wales had in 1788 a system of law which was beyond the powers of the settlers at that time to perceive or comprehend, it is beyond the power of this Court to decide otherwise than that New South Wales came into the category of a settled or occupied colony" (p. 244). The presumption being that, if settled, it therefore was in law without Native title.

Blackburn's legal argument is striking for the manner in which it tracks the strict logic of the settler contract. When the first settlers planted themselves on the shore of (what became) New South Wales and sovereignty was proclaimed they had to (it was as if they had to) conclude an original pact. An original contract simultaneously presupposes, extinguishes, and replaces a state of nature. A settled colony simultaneously presupposes and extinguishes a *terra nullius*. Settlers plant themselves in order to create a civil society out of a state of nature, an empty, vacant land, where there is no pre-existing title. All title is created by civil government. Thus, even though Blackburn explicitly stated that the Rirratjingu and Gumatj enjoyed the rule of law, this was beside the point. To be acknowledged, their "law" had to be recast (had been recast by the settler contract) in terms of the judicial system of a modern state.

---

[41] His reference is to a much-cited case, *In re Southern Rhodesia* (1919), in which it was held that some peoples were "so low in the scale of social organization that their usages and conceptions of rights and duties are not to be reconciled with the institutions or the legal ideas of civilized society. Such a gulf cannot be bridged" (cited, *Milirrpum*, p. 264; *Mabo*, p. 39). Blackburn's later reference to personal whims and influence also refers to this case; the peoples of Matabeleland were held to lack law because they were seen to be living entirely at the whim of their ruler, Lobengula. In addition to discussion of Australian cases in both *Milirrpum* and *Mabo*, cases from the United States, Canada, and other Imperial (later Commonwealth) countries were canvassed.

Thus Blackburn argues that Crown ownership of all land – the feudal fiction – had come into force with the proclamation of British sovereignty; "every square inch of territory in the colony became the property of the Crown. All titles, rights, and interests whatever in land which existed thereafter in subjects of the Crown were the direct consoquence of some grant from the Crown" (p. 245).[42] It followed, therefore, that if Native title existed it must do so not as a prior occupancy but as a title granted by the Crown. From his extensive survey of cases, Blackburn concluded that there was "no place" for a doctrine of native title in any jurisdiction where the common law had been introduced, unless it had been created by "express statutory provisions" and in Australia that had not happened (p. 244). After considering Australian legal history, Blackburn's conclusion is that, although there was an understanding that white occupation of the land "was ipso facto a deprivation of the aboriginals," there was no attempt to solve the problem by "the creation or application of law relating to title to land, which the aboriginals could invoke" (p. 256).[43]

Dawson, in *Mabo*, restates this legal view:

> The vesting of the radical title in the Crown upon the assumption of sovereign authority is, . . . incompatible with the continued existence in precisely the same form of any pre-existing rights. Necessarily the pre-existing rights were held of a former sovereign or in the absence of any sovereign at all. After the Crown has assumed sovereignty and acquired the radical title to the land, any pre-existing "title" must be held, if it is held at all, under the Crown. This new title is therefore not merely the continuation of a title previously held, notwithstanding that it may be identifiable by reference to the previous title. (p. 129)

Aboriginal title is thus occupancy permitted by the Crown, but in Australia the Crown "afforded no recognition to any form of native interest in the land" (p. 139). Dawson argues that the history of settlement shows that it was inconsistent with any such acknowledgment.

Given the number of cases from common law countries referred to in both *Milirrpum* and *Mabo* which included recognition of Native title, such a view can seem perverse. But Dawson's position follows the strict logic of the settler contract, not the tempered logic of the cases cited.

---

[42] In considering the plaintiffs' specific claim, Blackburn took the latter to mean that "property" existed as understood in non-Aboriginal law. "Property," he argued, included the rights of enjoyment and use, exclusion of others, and alienation. By that standard the plaintiffs had not shown that a "proprietary interest" existed (pp. 272–3).

[43] A "consistent feature" in Australia is that "the consciousness that a native land problem existed [went] together with the absence of even a proposal for a system of native title" (p. 259).

So in a settled colony the *terra nullius* vanishes; a civil society is developed as colonists plant themselves, husband the land, and create modern political institutions. In law, the original inhabitants and their societies are of no account and it is as if they no longer exist. They and their lands exist only if expressly recognized by the new state. However, the Australians "managed to evade law, to keep questions of indigenous interests in land out of law's reach" (van Krieken 2000: 74). In other words, they refused to follow the tempered logic of the settler contract and there was no recognition of Native peoples' prior occupancy within the common law.[44]

Mabo overturned *Cooper v. Stuart* and *Milirrpum.* Justice Brennan stated that there was a difference between accepting that in 1788 English law became the law of the new colony and accepting that "the theory which was advanced to support the introduction of the common law of England accords with our present knowledge and appreciation of the facts" (p. 38). He continued that:

> The facts as we know them today do not fit the "absence of law" or "barbarian" theory underpinning the colonial reception of the common law of England. That being so, there is no warrant for applying in these times rules of the English common law which were the product of that theory. It would be a curious doctrine to propound today that, when the benefit of the common law was first extended to Her Majesty's indigenous subjects in the Antipodes, its first fruits were to strip them of their right to occupy their ancestral lands. (p. 39)

Brennan argued that either the social and cultural level of the Merriam people would have to be investigated or "the Court can overrule the existing authorities, discarding the distinction between inhabited colonies that were *terra nullius* and those which were not" (p. 40). Of course, as Brennan notes, Blackburn was very well aware of the facts too. The question was the interpretation of the common law – and the logic of the settler contract. Once Blackburn's position is rejected and appeal is made to the "facts," the strict logic of the settler contract becomes untenable. The way was thus opened for the Court to

---

[44] There is an interesting comparison in the Reasons for Judgment of Chief Justice McEachern in the Supreme Court of British Columbia in *Delgamuukw.* He argues that the plaintiffs' ancestors had governed themselves in villages but could not be said to have "owned or governed such vast and almost inaccessible tracts of land in any sense that would be recognized by the law." Before the colony of British Columbia was formed there was a "legal and jurisdictional vacuum" and, after 1858, "aboriginal customs . . . ceased to have any force, as laws, within the colony." After the union with Canada in 1871 "there was no room for aboriginal jurisdiction or sovereignty which would be recognized by the law or the courts" (McEachern 1991: 222–4). My thanks to Jamie Baugh for a copy of the Reasons.

recognize Native title and for the tempered logic of the settler contract to be followed.

The judgment brought Australian jurisprudence closer to that of Canada following *St. Catherine's Milling*. In recent years, a series of Canadian Supreme Court cases has emphasized prior occupancy; "when the settlers came, the Indians were there, organized in societies and occupying the land as their forefathers had done for centuries. This is what Indian title means and it does not help . . . to call it a 'personal or usufructuary' right" (*Calder* (1973), reprinted in Kulchyski 1994: 69).[45] In 1982, the rights of the Native peoples were incorporated into the Constitution Act (§35.1), and in *Van der Peet* (1996, p. 548) these rights were characterized as "the means by which the Constitution recognizes the fact that prior to the arrival of Europeans in North America the land was already occupied by distinctive aboriginal societies."[46] This was echoed in *Delgamuukw* (1997): "aboriginal title arises out of prior occupation of the land by aboriginal peoples and out of the relationship between the common law and pre-existing systems of aboriginal law."[47]

But Australia before *Mabo* followed the strict logic of the settler contract and when *terra nullius* is at the center of the constitutional order a dark shadow is cast over the land. Aboriginal peoples were excluded from the new state with remarkable thoroughness. Under the common law doctrine of *jus soli*, they were, in principle, British subjects, having been born within the jurisdiction of the British Empire; "in reality they were dealt with as enemies of the state" (Markus 1994: 38). From the late nineteenth century through the first third of the twentieth century, "full blood" Aboriginals were commonly seen as a "dying race." The Aboriginal peoples were treated as politically non-existent. As I noted above, there were no official negotiations and no treaties were entered into with them.[48] The Commonwealth Constitution (1901) excluded

---

[45]   *Calder v. AGBC* (1973) SCR 313. The case was brought by the Nishga'a people claiming an unextinguished right to the occupation and use of their lands in (present-day) British Columbia. The case was lost but it began a new era of legal and political activity. On Canadian jurisprudence see also McNeil (1997).

[46]   *Van der Peet v. R* (1996) 70 DRL (4th) 385 (SCC). This case also originated in British Columbia and concerned the right to sell fish caught under a Native license.

[47]   *Delgamuukw v. British Columbia* (1997) 3 SCR 1010, at para. 145. The case, originating in 1987, was about the claim of the Gitskan and Wet'suweten peoples to some 22,000 square miles of territory as prior occupants who had never surrendered their land through conquest or treaty. The Supreme Court ordered a new trial on the grounds of defects in pleadings and errors of fact by the trial judge. The judgment confirmed that oral histories should be given due weight as evidence and stated that there was a duty of consultation with First Nations.

[48]   "Throughout Australia, Aboriginal people attempted to negotiate with those who first occupied their respective lands and although mutual compromises were sometimes

them from the census (§127), and from the federal power to "make laws for the peace, order, and good government of the Commonwealth" (§51, xxvi). In 1902 the Franchise Act excluded Aboriginal peoples from the national electorate. In subsequent legislation over the years they were denied citizenship benefits such as old age pensions, unemployment, and sickness benefits, widows' pensions, child endowments, and maternity allowances.[49] In the 1950s, the Australian government allowed the British government to test nuclear bombs in the deserts of South Australia, including Maralinga, which was sacred Aboriginal ground. Documents declassified in the 1980s showed that initially no "acceptable" radiation levels were even established for the Aboriginal populations who lived in the open. (See Milliken 1986 for the full story.)

The exclusions went hand-in-hand with the most detailed regulation. As John Chesterman and Brian Galligan (1997) have now documented, a vast and incredibly elaborate system of state and Commonwealth regulation was established that governed the most minute details of Aboriginal lives and movements, and included the removal of children from their parents.[50] By 1961, for instance, out of a population of some 17,000 people officially designated as Aborigines in the Northern Territory (under federal jurisdiction), all but 89 had been declared wards. Chesterman and Galligan comment that the "sheer amount of legislative ingenuity and administrative effort that went into devising and maintaining these discriminatory regimes is truly astonishing" (1997: 9). In *Mabo* the judges did not mince their words about this paradoxical

---

reached, these had no legal standing" (McGrath 1995: 14). In 1835 one of the first settlers in Victoria, John Batman, drew up deeds, made payment of blankets, flour, etc., and promised a yearly rent in goods to the Kulin people in return for 600,000 acres. The treaty was quickly declared void and the Crown's right upheld (see Broome 1995: 125–7).

[49] The very complex story is told by Chesterman and Galligan (1997). They discuss the contortions necessary to provide criteria to distinguish "aboriginal natives" from other nonwhites and from the rest of the population. In 1944 in Western Australia, legislation was enacted to enable Aboriginals to apply for a Certificate of Citizenship. The criteria centered on ability to live a "civilized life." If granted the dog tag (as the Aborigines called it) an individual was no longer regarded as a "native or aborigine." The Act also stated that the Certificate holder had all the rights and duties "of a native born or naturalized subject of His Majesty" – an interesting insight into *jus soli* and who actually counted as a British subject! Chesterman and Galligan comment that it "enabled the holder, who had been born in Australia, to travel freely within the country," but not to be included in the federal electorate (1997: 132–3). They state that "researching and documenting" their book "has taken years of painstaking work, even though our study is by no means comprehensive" (1997: 9).

[50] The present-day survivors have formed a movement of The Stolen Generations. The story of two little girls who escaped from their kidnappers was recently dramatized by Peter Weir in his film *Rabbit-Proof Fence*.

regime. For example, Justices Deane and Gaudron wrote of "the confla-
gration of oppression and conflict" across the continent, the effect of
which was "to dispossess, degrade and devastate the Aboriginal peoples
and leave a national legacy of unutterable shame" (p. 104); the dispossession justified by law constituted "the darkest aspect of the history of
this nation" (p. 109).

Although, in essence, as van Krieken (2000) has argued, *Mabo*
turned on a point of law, it has been called "the most radical piece of
judicial law-making in Australian history" (Chesterman and Galligan
1997: 206), and it caused a political uproar. There were wild declarations that no backyard was secure. The judgment was criticized as
political rather than judicial policy making (see, e.g., Lumb 1993 and
Moens 1993), the High Court was said to have become an "unelected
parliament," and echoes of old claims about savages were heard in
statements about stationary cultures and backwardness (see Markus
1996). Contention has continued and successive governments under
John Howard have been unsympathetic. The Native Title Act, passed
after *Mabo* in 1993, was curtailed in the Native Title Amendment Act
in 1998.[51]

The accusations of political judgments in *Mabo* had an element of
truth. By 1992 *terra nullius* had become politically untenable. It was
hardly surprising that all but one judge decided that historical facts now
had bearing on the interpretation of the law. By 1992 not only had the
Western Sahara case (cited in *Mabo*) been decided but a substantial
change in the legal and political position of the Aboriginal peoples had
taken place. They were enfranchised at the federal level in 1962, were
counted in the census after a referendum in 1967, and other legislative
reforms were made to end their exclusion from citizenship rights. From
the 1960s onward, Aboriginal organizations and voices raised the question of dispossession in a manner that made it harder to ignore, including a tent embassy set up outside Parliament in Canberra. In the late
1970s calls for a treaty, a Makaratta, between the Aboriginal peoples and
the Australian government, were made. Land rights began to be granted
in the 1970s, and by 1989 Aboriginal peoples held about a third of the
land in the Northern Territory and about a fifth in South Australia. In
1990 the Aboriginal and Torres Strait Islander Commission began its

---

[51] One question left open was whether pastoral leases, covering some 40 percent of the
country, had extinguished Aboriginal title. This was decided in *Wik Peoples v.
Commonwealth* (1996). The (narrow) majority judgment was that title survived and that
the Crown does not necessarily become beneficial owner when the lease expires. The
majority also held that pastoral leases were not leases in common law but bundles of
statutory rights so the terms of each lease become crucial (see F. Brennan 1998; Reynolds
1993).

work and in 1991 a Council for Aboriginal Reconciliation was set up. Internationally, too, by 1992 Indigenous peoples were established on the political stage.

Mabo also illustrates that once the strict logic of the settler contract is tempered the problem of sovereignty is never far away. If *terra nullius* is rejected, Native title is acknowledged and the "facts" (historical, anthropological, social) provide a basis for the law, the problem of legitimacy begins to surface. If, as laid down in *Mabo*, Australia was not *terra nullius* in 1788, if "distinct aboriginal societies" existed in Canada, and if "nations" existed in the United States, what made it legitimate for settlers to be planted and a modern state constructed? Why was the settler contract justified? This question still remains on the table.

V Past and Present

The process of decolonization and national self-determination that began after the Second World War has swept away all but tiny remnants of the colonies of the European powers, but the Native peoples of the two New Worlds, living within the boundaries of the states constructed from the plantation of settlers, have never been seen as candidates for sovereignty. From 1922 to 1924, the League of Nations refused to accept the Six Nations of the Iroquois Confederacy as members or to intervene on their behalf with the Canadian government, on the grounds that Canada's status as a sovereign state precluded recognition for peoples within its borders (Nichols 2005). The United Nations has followed in the footsteps of the League by supporting the maintenance of existing state boundaries and treating Indigenous peoples as national or cultural minorities, not nations or peoples. In other words, the sovereignty of states has been trumps. What effect the Draft UN Declaration on the Rights of Indigenous Peoples might have remains to be seen.[52]

However, we no longer live under the "sovereignty" of the Westphalian model. The inadequacy of the model in light of political developments over the past quarter-century, including the creation of the European Union, and the large economic and social changes gathered under the heading of globalization, has been much discussed. New political conceptions are being put forward to meet new circumstances; multilayered "sovereignty" and more flexible memberships would allow the sovereignty (autonomy) of the Indigenous peoples to be accommodated.

[52] For an argument that the Draft Declaration embodies the right of self-determination as a basic human right see Holder (2004).

A period of rapid change provides an opportunity to begin to refigure political relationships and remedy past injustice.

Jacob Levy has recently argued that the logic of the common law is incompatible with Aboriginal sovereignty and that the reasoning of Australian scholars who link *Mabo* to sovereignty is "fallacious" (2000; 170). He claims that it is only the logic of self-government, not the common law, that recognizes "a *lawmaker* in addition to, or instead of, *laws*. . . . Put another way, indigenous people are seen as having a right to give themselves laws rather than simply live according to their laws" (2000: 172). To refer to "living according to laws" sits easily with a view of Native peoples as cultural minorities. Talk of "giving themselves laws" raises the specter of self-governing nations. Levy's line of argument is a version of the tempered logic of the settler contract. Laws do not fall from heaven. When, under common law, Indigenous peoples are acknowledged as organized societies occupying their own territories, implicit acknowledgment is made not just of laws but lawmakers. To live according to laws means that life is lived under a system of government, which includes lawmakers (whether or not they operate in the same way as the lawmakers in a modern state). In recognizing Native title there is necessarily also recognition, albeit implicit, of a "people" that holds the title; that is, an organized self-governing society with laws that regulate social interaction (see Webber 2000).[53]

Levy comments that "land rights grounded in the self-government model . . . look more like political territory rather than like private property" (2000: 172). Indeed they do. The lands of Native peoples were not private property as justified in theories of original contracts or as understood by the settlers. That was, in part, why the lands were deemed *terra nullius*. Native lands belonged to peoples or nations, not private individuals or corporations. They were the equivalent of England, not of the landholdings of the Duke of Devonshire or John Doe. This is precisely why the question of the legitimacy of the settler contract – of sovereignty – arises.

The cases I have been citing have been concerned with *dominium*; *imperium* is always presupposed. As Borrows comments (referring to a statement in *Delgamuukw* that native title "crystallized" when sovereignty was proclaimed), sovereignty is "pretty powerful stuff. . . . simply conjuring sovereignty is enough to change an ancient peoples'

---

[53] "The tenure is 'collective' because the common law treats the land as the province of the community concerned; any internal allocation is left to the community" (Webber 2000: 70–1). He also points out that the Australian tendency to treat native title as if only recognition of proprietary rights were involved raises the dilemma that "if they do enforce an indigenous title like any other, they will, by that very act, displace the indigenous institutions on which the title depends" (2000: 73).

relationship to their land" (1999: 558). In *Mabo* it was held that Australian law had conflated sovereignty with ownership of land and so had clung to the view that Native title was extinguished on the declaration of sovereignty (see also Roberts-Wray 1966: 626, 631). Yet when sovereignty and ownership are separated and recognition of prior occupancy is granted, are there no implications for sovereignty?

The *Mabo* judgment explicitly stated (p. 32) that "the question whether a territory has been acquired by the Crown is not justiciable before municipal courts" (for an alternative view see Borrows 1999: 576–80). In Canada, in *Sparrow* (1990) the justices agreed that, while the Native peoples' right to land had been recognized since the Proclamation in 1763, "there was from the outset never any doubt that sovereignty and legislative power, and indeed the underlying title, to such lands vested in the Crown" (reprinted in Kulchyski 1994: 225).[54] This was recently reaffirmed in *Van der Peet* (p. 458); the Constitution is "the means by which prior occupancy is reconciled with the assertion of Crown sovereignty over Canadian territory."

For several reasons it might be objected that in the twenty-first century to raise the issue of sovereignty is a red herring. Use of the term "sovereignty," it could be argued, is misleading; most Native peoples are not seeking to set up their own states. They are realistic enough to recognize that in the decades to come the most powerful state in the world and two mid-sized powers are unlikely to wither away.[55] Moreover, as illustrated by the United States where Native peoples have long had their own jurisdictions, broad measures of self-government ("sovereignty") can be granted within existing states. Such rights of self-government have been used to open casinos on Indian lands. Recent developments in Australia and Canada reinforce this point. For example, in 1998 Canada entered into a treaty with the Nisga'a people under which they own their lands in fee simple, and Nunavut came into being in 1999, comprising around a fifth of Canadian territory. Again, it could be argued that, although manifest injustices occurred in the past, the damage was done long ago and non-Native inhabitants today are not to blame for those events. Any current injustices to Native peoples should be tackled, but that has nothing to do with original plantings and sovereignty.

This last objection raises a complex set of questions about the relationship between past and present. Everyone – including myself – who

[54] *R. v. Sparrow* (1990) 70 DRL (4th) 385 (SCC). The case was over fishing rights of the Musqueam Band in British Columbia and the size of a drift net. The Supreme Court also unanimously agreed "that 'existing' [rights] means 'unextinguished' rather than exercisable at a certain time in history" (reprinted in Kulchyski 1994: 219).

[55] Although challenges to sovereignty have been made. For Australia see *Coe v. the Commonwealth*, 1979; ALR, 24, 118.

lives in the two New Worlds is benefiting from the dispossession of the Native peoples. If remedies for present-day injustices are to be found, past and present cannot be so neatly separated as this line of argument suggests (see chapter 5 below). To understand why injustices today take particular forms is not possible without knowledge of the past. The fact, for example, that Native peoples score so poorly on all the standard social indicators – infant mortality, life expectancy, education, incidence of particular diseases, unemployment and so on – cannot be fully explained without reference to past events and attitudes, without reference to past relations between nations and peoples as well as to present policies.

Exactly how the connections between past and present are to be made is a controversial matter. Janna Thompson, for instance, has recently suggested some ways in which to think about this question, emphasizing that peoples and states are transgenerational entities. She points out that when a state enters into a treaty the supposition is that it will be honored by governments and citizens of the future. Similarly, today's governments and citizens have a responsibility, a historical obligation, to acknowledge and deal with past wrongs; whether or not they feel guilt or shame about the past is irrelevant to the responsibility they bear, as "national successors," for setting things to right (2002: 89). Reparation should take the form of just reconciliation; that is, the trust and mutual respect violated in the past should be reestablished.

There are no easy answers about how to do this. How best to rectify injustices of even the relatively recent past is an extremely fraught question, as shown by the debate and controversy surrounding various Truth and Justice Commissions, trials and amnesties of the last several years. There are also other complicated issues, such as whether the whole of the past is necessarily to be condemned (see Mulgan 1998) or about safeguarding human rights, especially those of women. And then, in addition to necessary policy changes, there is the issue of symbolic acts, such as demands for official apologies. Symbols can play an important role. The continued outright refusal of the Australian Prime Minister, John Howard, to make a public apology for dispossession and injustice hardly fosters mutual respect.[56] On the other hand, hundreds of thousands of citizens have signed "sorry books" and 250,000 people marched across Sydney Harbour Bridge in May 2000, accompanied by an aircraft writing "sorry" in the sky, in support of reconciliation.

The most fundamental symbolic act of all – and, given the political realities of a world of states and their military power, it will remain largely symbolic – is acknowledgment that the settler contract lacked justification, that, therefore, a question mark hangs over sovereignty.

---

[56] For a discussion of Howard's background and the refusal, see Marr (1999: ch. 2).

This is the action ruled out of court. While objections can be raised to talk of Native "sovereignty," no doubts are expressed about the legitimacy of the states constructed in the two New Worlds. Hobbes says at the conclusion of *Leviathan*, "there is scarce a Common-wealth in the world, whose beginning can in conscience be justified" (1996: 486). True though this is, a democratic state whose "beginning" is the settler contract requires the creation of a new political legitimacy, the building of a new settlement with Native peoples.

Political theorists have a part to play by bringing the question of legitimacy out of the shadows. A start has been made in recent discussions of the role of early modern theories in justifying European expansion and in debates about the rights of Indigenous peoples.[57] The problem is that most political theorists, including democratic theorists, take the modern state for granted. Tully has recently called attention to the way in which much contemporary political theory obliterates any discussion of embarrassing origins; argument proceeds from "an abstract starting point . . . that had nothing to do with the way these societies were founded" (2000: 44). The most prominent example of such an abstract starting point, contract theory as revived by John Rawls (1999h), is a direct successor to early modern theories of an original contract.

Rawlsian contract theory has become extraordinarily influential, but it takes no account of the actual origins of countries that, it is held, are best understood as if they were based on an agreement in an original position. Few traces can now be found of the settler contract and dispossession; contemporary contract theory is peopled by parties who are abstracted from social and political institutions and structures. The parties are provided with preferences, tastes, and a degree of risk aversion and are concerned with distributive justice rather than subordination or structural change. They are deprived of the knowledge that they systematically benefit from dispossession and the structures of racial privilege that constitute the modern democracies of the two New Worlds. For them to have such an understanding would require that the history and institutions so efficiently eliminated in contemporary

---

[57] The latter are to be found in political theory in the literature on multiculturalism, beginning from the mid-1990s (in particular in Kymlicka 1995; Tully 1995; and Levy 2000). The first problem is that "multiculturalism" is used to cover both the position of Native peoples and that of nonwhite groups (minorities) that have migrated to Europe and North America since the 1960s. Most discussions focus on the latter (and center round the same few examples) and have little to say about the connections between European colonialism and the more recent migrations. Second, as the term "multiculturalism" implies, the focus is on cultural differences, whereas many important questions, especially in the case of Indigenous peoples, are political.

contractual theorizing are put back in place, a very difficult task within the confines of Rawlsian theory.

The logic of theories of an original contract is that the "beginning," the creation of a new civil society, is made on a clean slate. Such a condition can be part of a thought experiment but it forms no part of the political world; the lands of the two New Worlds were not empty. *Terra nullius* is now a legally and politically bankrupt doctrine and questions about sovereignty and legitimacy will have to be tackled in the long run if a just accommodation and reconciliation is to be achieved. The three states where *terra nullius* was central to the justification of their creation pride themselves on their democratic credentials. The credentials will be more presentable once the settler contract is repudiated and a new democratic settlement is negotiated with the Native peoples.

3

The Domination Contract

Charles W. Mills

Carole Pateman's *The Sexual Contract* (1988) has become a classic text of second-wave feminism, and is widely and deservedly seen as constituting one of the most important challenges of the last 20 years to the frameworks and assumptions of "malestream" political theory. Moreover, its influence is not restricted to gender issues, since it was the inspiration for my own book, *The Racial Contract* (1997), which has also become quite successful in the parallel, if not as well-established, field of critical race theory. The impact of both books, of course, originates in part from their refusal respectively of "pink" and "black" theoretical ghettoization for a frontal conceptual engagement with a (male, white) intellectual apparatus, social contract theory, that has historically been central to the modern Western political tradition, and which has been spectacularly revived in the past three decades as a result of John Rawls's *A Theory of Justice* (1999h). Pateman and I are saying that the history of gender and racial subordination requires a rethinking of how we do political theory, that it cannot be a matter of some minor, largely cosmetic changes – a few "she's" sprinkled in where there were previously only "he's," a pro forma (if that much) deploring of the racism of Enlightenment theorists – before continuing basically as before. As such, the goal is a revisioning of the tradition that we both want the white male majority of practitioners in the field to accept and to incorporate into their own work.

What, though, is the specific nature of this challenge for contract theory in general, and Rawlsian normative theory in particular? As readers will have seen from our opening dialogue, Pateman is quite hostile to the project of trying to retrieve the contract for positive ends. So in this and the next chapter, I want to make a case for generalizing this revisionist version of the contract and turning it to the theorization of gender and racial justice. My claim will be that the concept of a "domination contract" can be fruitfully employed to overturn the misleading framework of assumptions of mainstream social contract theory, thereby better positioning us to tackle the pressing issues of "non-ideal theory" that, far from being marginal, in fact determine the fate of the *majority* of the population.

The "Contract" as Protean

Let me begin – in the "underlaborer" tradition of analytic philosophy – with some preliminary clarificatory distinctions. For if Pateman's book has been read in divergent and contradictory ways, as it has, then to a significant extent this interpretive variation goes with the conceptual territory. There are at least three major sources of the ambiguities in Pateman's revisionist contract: one endemic to the literature in general, even just the mainstream variety; one arising distinctively from her radical and unfamiliar non-mainstream use of the idea; and one generated by divergences in terminology.

The general problem is the astonishing range of the ways in which the idea of the "contract" has historically been employed, ironically – or then again, not ironically at all – coupled with the fact that in most cases it is actually doing no work, and is, in effect, otiose, a disposable part of the argument. (With only slight exaggeration, one could quip that in the long history of social contract theory, very few actual social contract theorists can be found.)

To begin with, there is the notion of the contract as in some sense, whether stronger or weaker, descriptive/factual. For example, the contract as ur-sociology or anthropology, providing us with a literal account of what actually happened. Or, more weakly, the contract as a plausible hypothetical reconstruction of what might have happened. Or, more weakly still, the contract as a useful way of thinking about what happened – the contract "as if" – though we know perfectly well it did *not* happen that way. Then within this "descriptive" sense, whether robustly or thinly conceived, there are additional differences (cross-cutting the above) of, so to speak, the object of the contract. Is it a contract to create society, or the state, or both? And, to introduce further complications within these categories, is society envisaged as an aggregate of individuals or a transformed collective community, and are rights alienated to the state or merely delegated to it? Then there is the contract as normative. For example, the contract as the outcome of a collective-bargaining agreement that brings morality into existence as a conventionalist set of principles. Or the contract as a way of elucidating and codifying pre-existing and objective moral principles, whether grounded in natural law or human interests. Or the contract as a thought-experiment, a device for generating moral intuitions about justice through the strategy of combining prudential motivation with ignorance of crucial features of the self.

[So the concept has been used in radically different ways – the contract as literal, metaphorical, historical, hypothetical, descriptive, prescriptive, prudential, moral, constitutional, civil, regulative ideal, device of representation.] It is no wonder then, that, as David Boucher and Paul Kelly conclude in an introductory overview of social contract theory: "The idea of the social contract when examined carefully is seen to have very few implications, and is used for all sorts of reasons, and generates quite contrary conclusions" (1994a: 2). Or as Will Kymlicka concurs in an encyclopedia essay: "In a sense, there is no contract tradition in ethics, only a contract *device* which many different traditions have used for many different reasons" (1991: 196).

Moreover, as if this bewildering array of distinctions were not enough, a further complication is that Pateman's peculiar use of the contract idea revives a strand of the contract tradition that has been so marginalized and ignored that it does not even have a name in the secondary literature: what I have called elsewhere the "domination contract" (Mills 2000). Though Pateman herself does not explicitly make the connection in *The Sexual Contract*, and though I have never seen them linked in discussions of her work, a case can be made that the sexual contract develops an idea whose nucleus is actually originally to be found in Rousseau's "class contract" of his 1755 *A Discourse on Inequality* (1984, 1997a). Seven years before publishing the *Social Contract* (1968, 1997d), Rousseau in his *Discourse on Inequality* (1997a) condemned and set out to explain the *non-natural* "political" inequalities of class society, which are the result of "a sort of convention," and that consist in "the different Privileges which some enjoy to the prejudice of the others, such as to be more wealthy, more honored, more Powerful than they" (p. 131). He offered a "hypothetical and conditional" (p. 132) history of technological progress in the state of nature, which eventually led to the development of nascent society, private property, growing divisions between rich and poor, and a state of war. In Rousseau's reconstruction, the wealthy, alarmed by this threat to their property and security, promised to the poor new social institutions that pretended to offer justice, peace, and impartial social rules for the mutual benefit of all. But in actuality these institutions

irreversibly destroyed natural freedom, forever fixed the Law of property and inequality, transformed a skillful usurpation into an irrevocable right, and for the profit of a few ambitious men henceforth subjugated the whole of Mankind to labor, servitude and misery. (p. 173)

Rousseau's contract is therefore a bogus contract, contract as scam – in the words of Patrick Riley (2001a: 4), "a kind of confidence trick on the part of the rich." In its uncompromising demystification of the consensual illusions of mainstream contract theory, it anticipates by a century Marx's later critique of supposedly egalitarian liberalism as a mask for the differential power of a capitalist ruling class. The later *Social Contract*, of course, would go on to outline an ideal contract that prescribed how society *should* be founded and what kinds of institutions would, through the "general will," be necessary to achieve genuine political egalitarianism. But in *Discourse on Inequality*, Rousseau is describing, if only in a "hypothetical and conditional" sense (1997a: 132), what might *actually* have happened.

The point is, then, that a clear precedent exists in the Western contract tradition for the idea of an exclusionary manipulative contract deployed by the powerful to subordinate others in society under the pretext of including them as equals. Yet whether because of the unacceptable radicalism of the idea, its polar incongruity with a mainstream conception for which, underneath all the variations listed above, a legitimizing consensuality is the crucial common factor, or the brevity of his treatment, Rousseau's first contract is hardly discussed in the secondary literature, whether on social contract theory in general or on Rousseau in particular. It is mentioned, for example, neither in David Boucher and Paul Kelly's (1994b) anthology on social contract theory, nor in Christopher Morris's (1999b) anthology, nor in Stephen Darwall's (2003) anthology, nor in three encyclopedia essays on the subject (Laslett 1967; Kymlicka 1991; Hampton 1993). Even *The Cambridge Companion to Rousseau* (Riley 2001b) devotes only a few paragraphs to it – not an entire essay, nor even a subsection of an essay.

So given this absence of any developed analysis in the literature, it is perhaps less surprising that the distinctive features of Pateman's "contract" should not have been recognized as homologous to Rousseau's, though centered on gender rather than class. For in *The Problem of Political Obligation*, whose subtitle is *A Critical Analysis of Liberal Theory*, Pateman gives a detailed discussion – indeed one of the most detailed in the secondary literature – of this "fraudulent" contract, which "has no basis in 'nature,'" but "is a result of a particular form of social development": "It is a contract that gives 'all to one side' and is based on inequality; its function is to maintain and foster that inequality by legitimizing political regulation by the liberal state" (1985: 148,

150). Her later "sexual contract" can be seen as extrapolating this demystificatory contract to the analysis of gender relations, though as I said she does not explicitly connect them herself in the later book. At any rate, I want to suggest that we formally recognize this use of social contract theory as a strategy for theorizing domination within a contract framework, since, as I will argue below, it provides a conceptual entry point for importing the concerns and aims of radical democratic political theory into a mainstream apparatus. And because the formal act of naming an entity helps to make it more real for us, incorporating it into our discursive universe, I move, as proposed (Mills 2000), that we call it the "domination contract."

Finally, the third factor accounting for ambiguities in Pateman's position is terminological. "Contractarianism" is usually taken in political theory to be coextensive with social contract theory in general, and as such to be a very broad umbrella covering many different variants (as illustrated above). In particular, as both Will Kymlicka (1991) and Jean Hampton (1993, 2001) point out in essays on the subject, the Hobbesian variety of contract theory, which derives morality from prudence as a conventionalist set of rules for coordinating the constrained advancing of our interests in a social framework, is radically different in its crucial assumptions from the Kantian variety, for which the contract is merely a regulative ideal, and morality inheres in the objective categorical imperative to respect others' personhood. The former kind leads to David Gauthier's *Morals by Agreement* (1986), the latter to John Rawls's *A Theory of Justice* (1999h), two books obviously quite different in their prescriptions for social justice despite their common contract identity. For this reason, some ethicists and political philosophers, such as T. M. Scanlon and Stephen Darwall, think the distinction is so crucial that it needs to be made explicit in our terminology, and they differentiate accordingly between *contractarianism* (the Hobbesian use of the contract idea) and *contractualism* (the Kantian use of the contract idea) (Darwall 2003). In this vocabulary, Gauthier would be a contractarian, but Rawls would then be a contractualist.

Now Pateman speaks generally about "contract theory" in the opening pages of *The Sexual Contract* (1988). But it turns out that she is using the term in a restricted sense, for she specifies that "property" is crucial to her argument, though this is not "property in the sense in which 'property' commonly enters into discussions of contract theory," as including material goods and civil freedom. Rather, "The subject of all the contracts with which I am concerned is a very special kind of property, the property that individuals are held to own in their persons" (p. 5). And she goes on to say:

> I shall refer to the [most radical form of contract doctrine], which has its classical expression in Hobbes' theory, as *contractarian* theory or *contractarianism* (in the United States it is usually called libertarianism . . .) . . . For contemporary contractarians . . . social life and relationships not only originate from a social contract but, properly, are seen as an endless series of discrete contracts. . . . From the standpoint of contract, in social life there are contracts all the way down. (pp. 14–15)

When Pateman uses the term *contractarianism*, then, it is really this restricted version of contract she has in mind (Hobbesian/libertarian), involving contracts "all the way down," not social contract theory in general. And obviously this would not be an accurate characterization of Kantian contract theory, for which the will is to be determined not by subjective inclination "all the way down" but rather objective universal moral law. For Kant, the normative bedrock of societal interaction is supposed to be the categorical imperative to respect others as ends in themselves. So when Pateman writes that in contract theory "universal freedom" is always "a political fiction," since "contract always generates political right in the form of relations of domination and subordination" (p. 8), one has to remember that her implicit reference is primarily to contract in the specific term-of-art sense she has previously stipulated. Clearly from our opening dialogue she is dubious about the "contractual" variety also. But given what various theorists have seen as the crucial differences between the two kinds, the extrapolation of her indictment to the Kantian version does not, to say the least, follow straightforwardly. At any rate, I will contend that more argument needs to be given to establish her case. I am going to proceed, then, on the assumption that the very strong statement made in the jacket copy on the paperback edition of *The Sexual Contract* – "One of the main targets of the book is those who try to turn contractarian theory to progressive use, and a major thesis of the book is that this is not possible" – is mistaken as a general characterization of contract theory, and try to demonstrate precisely the opposite: that social contract theory, including Pateman's sexual contract, *can* be so turned.

Hampton, Pateman, Okin: Toward a Theoretical Synthesis

So what I now want to do is to argue for a version of the sexual contract which does not preclude using contract theory to address issues of gender justice, and which can be seen as a particular instantiation of the domination contract. Since two of the most prominent feminist advocates of social contract theory were the late Jean Hampton and the late Susan Moller Okin, I will try to show that, suitably modified, Pateman's sexual contract is not at all in necessary theoretical opposition to their views, as is conventionally supposed. In fact I will claim that it can be thought of as *complementing* them, and should indeed be synthesized with them to produce a distinctively feminist contract theory that is all the more powerful *precisely for* its recognition of the historic (and ongoing) patriarchal restriction of the terms of the contract.

Consider first Jean Hampton. In her essays on contract, Hampton (1990, 1993, 2001) makes a crucial point that will be useful for us in developing the idea of the domination contract. She reminds us that unlike the contemporary Rawlsian contract, which is merely a normative thought-experiment, at least some of the classic contract theorists (though not Kant) "intended simultaneously to describe the nature of political societies, and to prescribe a new and more defensible form for such societies" (Hampton 1993: 382). So for them the contract was both descriptive and prescriptive. Moreover, Hampton believes that – suitably attenuated – this descriptive side of the contract should be revived. For once we realize that contract is basically a matter of "imagery," a "picture," we should recognize that it is not vulnerable to standard literalist objections (for example, that no promises are actually exchanged to support governmental structures), as it is essentially just expressing the insight that "authoritative political societies are human creations," "conventionally-generated" (1993: 379, 382–3).

So the first great virtue of contract theory for Hampton is its capturing of the crucial factual/descriptive truth that society and the polity are human-made – not organic "natural" growths or the product of divine creation. And this insight is, of course, distinctively modern, demarcating the conceptual universe of the modern period from that of antiquity and medievalism. Thus we get Hobbes's famous anti-Aristotelian characterization of the commonwealth as "an Artificiall Man; though of greater stature and strength than the Naturall" (1996: 9). The polis is not natural but constructed, artificial. Similarly, contemporary commentators such as Michael Walzer suggest that: "Perhaps the most significant claim of social contract theory is that political society is a human construct . . . and not an organic growth" (1995: 164). Banal as it may seem to us now, this insight was revolutionary in its own time, and I will argue below that indeed its full revolutionary significance has yet to be fully appreciated and exploited. For once we understand how far the "construction" extends, we will recognize that it can be shown to apply to gender and race also.

The second important truth captured by contract theory is, of course, the one that the contemporary contract *does* focus on: the moral equality of the contracting parties and its normative implications for sociopolitical structures. Here Hobbes is not the appropriate representative figure since, as noted above (Kymlicka 1991; Hampton 1993,

2001; Darwall 2003), commentators standardly differentiate between the Hobbesian and the Kantian contract. The first is rooted in the rough physical and mental (rather than moral) equality of the contractors in the state of nature, and leads to rational prudence rather than the altruistic regard for others for their own sake, as beings of intrinsic moral worth, that we associate with the second, that of Kant. Thus in the most famous contemporary version of the moral contract, John Rawls's thought-experiment to determine what "the principles that free and rational persons concerned to further their own interests would accept in an initial position of equality as defining the fundamental terms of their association" (1999h: 10), this scenario is set up to be not a process of bargaining, but rather, through the veil of ignorance, the modeling of an impartial other-regardingness.

Now it should be obvious that in this weak and minimal sense – contract as committed to society's being a human construct created by morally equal contractors, whose interests should be given equal weight in the sociopolitical institutions thereby established – there is nothing that anybody, including those wishing to theorize gender and racial subordination, should find objectionable about contract theory. Certainly it is not the case that feminists and critical race theorists want to argue, on the contrary, that sociopolitical institutions *are* natural rather than humanly created or that some humans *are* morally superior to others. At this highly abstract level of characterization, social contract theory is unexceptionable.

The problem really inheres, I suggest, in the assumptions that begin to be incorporated, the conceptual infrastructure that begins to be installed, at a *lower* level of abstraction, and the ways in which, whether explicitly or tacitly, they vitiate the accuracy of the descriptive mapping, obfuscate crucial social realities, embed certain tendentious conceptual partitionings (e.g., the private/public distinction), and thereby undercut the transformative normative egalitarian potential of the apparatus. So my claim is that our critical attention should really be directed at these "thicker" auxiliary shaping assumptions rather than the "thin" idea of the contract itself (in the minimal sense sketched above).

Start with the factual/descriptive side. While it is true that society and the state are human creations, it is obviously false, as mainstream contract theory classically implies, that all (adult) humans are equal contractors, have equal causal input into this process of creation, and freely give informed consent to the structures and institutions thereby established. The repudiation of this picture was, of course, the whole point of Rousseau's critique in his depiction of the "class contract." The wealthy have more power than the poor, and manipulate the rest of the population into accepting sociopolitical arrangements to which they would not actually consent were they aware of their real consequences. So the human equality of the state of nature becomes the unnatural "political" inequality of a class society ruled by the rich. But this plutocratic polity is not to be thought of as the outcome of free and informed choice among symmetrically positioned individuals. Rather it is the outcome of the collusion among themselves of *a social group* with far greater influence, who have their own self-seeking agenda. The real "contractors" (in the sense of those who are controlling things and know what is going on) are the rich. Similarly, in Pateman's sexual contract and my racial contract, men and whites, through a mixture of force and ideology, subordinate women and people of color under the banner of a supposedly consensual contract. So the latter are the victims, the objects, of the resulting "contract" rather than subjects, freely contracting parties, and are oppressed by the resulting sociopolitical institutions.

But note that there is no inconsistency at all between pointing out these usually unacknowledged facts of class, gender, and racial subordination and continuing to affirm the "weak" (arguably defining) contractual assertion of a humanly created society and polity. Contract theory in this minimal sense is not refuted by the actual history of social oppression and political exclusion since it is still true that it is humans (though a particular subset) who have been responsible for this history. The problem is that the *actual* "contracts" and their agents have been quite different from how they have been represented in the mainstream literature. But far from the subordinated being motivated as a result to want to *deny* the role of human agency in creating the resulting polity, surely this is all the more reason for them to want to affirm, indeed insist upon it! Class society, patriarchy, and white supremacy come into being not "naturally" but as the result of collective human causality – in which, however, some humans have a far greater causal role than others, and subsequently benefit far more from the sociopolitical and economic institutions thereby established. The social contract in its guise as the domination contract captures these crucial "descriptive" realities while simultaneously, by emphasizing their "artificial" genesis, bringing them across the conceptual border from the realm of the natural into the realm of the political. Class society, patriarchy, and white supremacy are themselves "unnatural," and are just as "political" and oppressive as the (formally and overtly political) white male absolutist rule (for example, as advocated by Sir Robert Filmer), predicated on white male hierarchy and moral inequality, that is the exclusive target of mainstream contract theorists, and which the contract apparatus prescribes abolishing.

Consider now the normative/prescriptive side. The problem is obviously not that moral egalitarianism among humans is an unattractive moral ideal, but rather that in these actual contracts moral egalitarianism was never realized. Pateman (1988) and numerous other feminist theorists over the past three decades (Clark and Lange 1979; Okin 1992; Pateman and Gross 1997) have documented the ways in which women have been seen as unequal by virtually all the male theorists of the classic canon, including (with the qualified and ambiguous exception of Hobbes) the very contract theorists who, as paradigmatic theorists of modernity, so loudly proclaimed human equality as their foundational assumption. Moreover, this inequality has been manifest in their drawing of the public/private distinction, their conceptions of marriage, and their view of the appropriate place of women in the sociopolitical institutions supposedly "contractually" established. Though the literature on race is less extensive, a comparable body of work is now emerging here also (Goldberg 1993, 2002; Outlaw 1996; Mills 1997, 1998a; Mehta 1999; Valls 2005). It argues similarly that people of color have generally been excluded from equal status in liberal thought, and have been seen (in my phrase) as "subpersons" rather than full persons, thereby justifying their subordination in the various racialized sociopolitical structures – Native American and Australian expropriation, African slavery, Third World colonization – imposed on non-Europeans by Europe in the modern epoch.

But obviously neither feminists nor critical race theorists are seeking to reject moral egalitarianism as such. Rather their complaint is that this egalitarianism has been *denied* to women and nonwhites both in theory and in practice, and that – at least for those of us still sympathetic to contract theory – a genuinely inclusive "contract" would need to recognize this legacy and prescribe appropriate corrective and transformational measures in the light of its historic injustice.

The real source of the problem should now have emerged clearly. The mainstream story of the contract builds on top of, or conflates with, the eminently reasonable *minimal* assumptions of human sociopolitical agency and human egalitarianism an *additional* set of assumptions that are quite false, radically untrue to the historical record. Only some humans had effective causal input; only some humans had their moral equality recognized. In this fashion, it completely mystifies the creation (in the ongoing rather than *ab initio* sense) of society, denying or obfuscating the various structures of domination that are either transformed (class, gender), or that come into existence (race), in the modern period. Thus when Christopher Morris, in his introduction to his social contract anthology, writes: "There may, however, be some explanatory import to the idea of states of nature and social contracts that should not be overlooked. . . . our political institutions and arrangements are, in some sense, our creations" (1999a: x), the obvious and classic retort is: Just who are this "we"? ("What do you mean *we*, white man?") Did women create patriarchy? Did nonwhites create white supremacy? Obviously not – these "institutions and arrangements" were created by *some* humans, not all. By its undifferentiated descriptive individualism, by its failure to advert to the existence of, and need to eliminate, "institutions and arrangements" of group domination, the mainstream version of the contract sabotages the radical potential of the apparatus.

And it is here, I would suggest, that Hampton's contract theory becomes deficient and needs supplementation. Normatively, Hampton (2001) endorses a feminist Kantian contractualism based on the intrinsic worth of all persons (as part, though not all, of a comprehensive ethic). Moreover, as noted at the start, she also argues for the revival of the descriptive dimension of contract theory. This proposal is in keeping with her emphasis elsewhere, for example in her book on political philosophy (1997: xiii–xv), that the subject should not be thought of as purely normative, but as extending to factual issues as well. The political philosopher, Hampton argues, should seek to understand the "political and social 'deep structure' which generates not only forms of interaction that make certain kinds of distributions [of resources] inevitable but also moral theories that justify those distributions." But she never brings these insights together, in the sense of asking how the revived descriptive contract she advocates would need to be rethought in the light of sexist exclusions, or how the descriptive and the normative sides of the contract would now need to be related given patriarchy as a "deep structure" with such a fundamental shaping influence on society (including, reflexively, the very moral theories generated about its founding). Instead, like Morris, she speaks of "political societies as conventionally-generated human creations" (Hampton 1993: 383) and, without asking who these "humans" and these "people" are, glosses the contract claim as equivalent to the assertion that:

> Certain institutions, practices and rules become conventionally entrenched (in a variety of ways) in a social system, and in so far as the people continue to support them, these conventions continue to prevail, and thus comprise the political and legal system in the country. (1993: 382)

Despite her feminism, then, Hampton does not press the further question of how we should think of this supposedly contract-equivalent "support" once the gender subordination of half the population is taken into account. Pateman's *sexual* contract fills this theoretical gap, making clear that a "contract" of gender domination would more accurately illuminate than the mainstream version not merely the "deep structure" of a society based on patriarchy, but also its justificatory moral theories and how they become "conventionally entrenched." We would then be better positioned theoretically not merely to apply, in a gender-inclusive way, the Kantian contractual theory Hampton endorses, but to understand, on the metatheoretical level, why its previous (male) application has been so systematically and structurally, not just contingently, exclusionary. For we would then be in a position to recognize gender *itself* as a political system established by the contract, and prescribing accordingly its own ground rules about the cartography of the social and the appropriate distribution of rights, privileges, and freedoms in the polity.[1]

The relation between the normative and descriptive aspects of the contract is thus necessarily more complicated in this revisionist contractualism than it is in mainstream contract theory. In the mainstream contract, a (supposedly) consensual founding establishes an egalitarian moral code. So this is a code we can (supposedly) be comfortable in endorsing. But once the contract is unmasked as really a contract of domination, the code itself needs to become an object of scrutiny for us. Under cover of egalitarianism, the domination contract generates norms, and stipulations about how to apply these norms, that will themselves reinforce domination, and so which need to be interrogated by those seeking to end their subordination by the contract. A greater degree of reflexivity, of self-conscious metatheoretical distancing from and questioning of concepts and values, is therefore required, insofar as the new normative contract has to take account of realities ignored or misdescribed by the terms of the old normative contract – certainly in its original form, but also later, even when nominally updated and purged of its original sexism and racism.

For even when the contemporary contract seems to drop the descriptive dimension, as in Rawls's thought-experiment, it continues tacitly to manifest itself, if only by default, in an underlying factual picture, a version of history, and a set of assumptions about society that continue to reproduce the inequities and obfuscations of the historic contract, and, correspondingly, an apparatus that retains many of its deficiencies. The famous early feminist critique of Rawls, of course, was that knowledge of gender was not one of the things listed as being stripped from

---

[1] By contrast, Hampton's apparent naivety about Kant is well illustrated when she writes at one point: "Kant also has opponents who, while agreeing that our value is noninstrumental and objective, reject the idea that all humans are of equal value – for example, those who think human beings of a certain gender or race or caste are higher in value (and so deserving of better treatment) than those of a different gender, race, or caste" (2001: 352). But of course *Kant himself* was a sexist and racist, for whom women could only be "passive citizens," while blacks and Native Americans were "natural slaves." (See Schröder 1997; Eze 1997a; Bernasconi 2001a, 2002; Mills 2005b.) The concepts of the sexual and racial contracts enable us to understand how these seemingly contradictory commitments are reconcilable, not merely in Kant but most other Enlightenment thinkers of the period, through the workings of white male moral psychologies and moral boundaries created by the exclusionary "particularistic universalism" of the domination contract.

us behind the veil. Nor was there any awareness, in the "general" social and historical facts we take with us there, of the historic subordination of half the human race – surely "general" enough to have made the cut! By assuming heads of households as the representative contractors, by taking the family as ideal, by not challenging the role of the public/private distinction, Rawls naturalized the family in the same way the classic contract theorists did.

Consider now the reclamatory work of Susan Moller Okin (1989). Okin's insight was to recognize that Rawls's moral contract apparatus had the potential to go beyond Rawls's own conclusions, once we admit a "veiled" knowledge of crucial non-ideal facts on gender:

> There is strikingly little indication, throughout most of *A Theory of Justice*, that the modern liberal society to which the principles of justice are to be applied is deeply and pervasively gender-structured. Thus an ambiguity runs throughout the work. . . . On the one hand, as I shall argue, a consistent and wholehearted application of Rawls's liberal principles of justice can lead us to challenge fundamentally the gender system of our society. On the other hand, in his own account of his theory, this challenge is barely hinted at, much less developed. . . . [This] potential critique of gender-structured social institutions . . . can be developed by taking seriously the fact that those formulating the principles of justice do not know their sex [behind the veil]. (1989: 89, 105)

Okin thus seeks to appropriate the contract for feminism, and in the closing chapter of her book shows how such a critique of a gender-structured social order can be developed from behind the veil. Correspondingly, in her review essay on *The Sexual Contract*, she criticizes Pateman for rejecting in principle (as Okin sees it) the attempt "to employ contractual thinking in the service of feminism" (1990: 659). But I would claim that there need be no principled opposition at all between their two approaches once we conceive of them as engaged in different tasks, with Pateman's view of the contract as intrinsically subordinating paradigmatically meant as a characterization of the Hobbesian/proprietarian contract in particular. Okin's skepticism about the sexual contract idea – she writes at one point "it is not clear to me what we gain in understanding by tracing [the forms of patriarchal power] to a supposed contract made by men" (1990: 660) – misses the value of a theoretical innovation that can provide the very knowledge behind the veil that Rawls's idealized contract avoids. The gender-structured social institutions Okin cites are precisely what are summarized in Pateman's non-ideal contract: the sexual contract.

So we can, I suggest, bring them together under a division of conceptual labor in a *common* enterprise: Pateman doing the actual non-ideal contract, Okin doing the ideal normative contract. As emphasized, the relation between the descriptive and normative sides of the contract becomes radically different in this alternative contract theory since the real-life contract is being conceptualized as a domination contract. Thus our aim becomes to dismantle rather than endorse it. As a "contractor" in the original position, one is now making a prudential choice informed by the possibility of ending up female in a society structured by the sexual contract. Gender subordination in its manifold dimensions and implications can thus become the object of normative critique, since these "general facts" are not ignored as in the mainstream contract. The full ramifications of patriarchy not just for the family but society in general (the state, the legal system, the differential status of men and women), as well as typical male moral psychology and dominant andro-centric ideology, can all now legitimately be considered within a "con-tractual" framework.

In this fashion, I claim, we can synthesize the crucial insights of Hampton, Pateman, and Okin to produce a feminist contractualism stronger than any of them individually: Hampton's *moral* Kantian con-tractualism, informed behind the veil by Pateman's *factual* Rousseauean contract, combined so as to generate an expanded variant of Okin's *non-ideal* version of Rawlsian contractualism, all deployed to achieve gender justice. From Hampton, the idea of contract as a descriptive metaphor capturing the key insight of society as a human creation, and the nor-mative endorsement of Kantian contractualism. From Pateman, the idea that the actual contract is an exclusionary sexual contract, not a gender-inclusive one, based on female inequality and inferiority, thereby shaping both society and, reflexively, our ideas about society. From Okin, the idea that a feminist agenda on justice can nonetheless still be promoted in a contractual framework by imagining oneself behind Rawls's veil with knowledge of these non-ideal gender realities. So if in the mainstream contract the circumstances of the creation of the sociopolitical sphere imply the moral endorsement of the institutions thereby created, in the radical use of the domination contract, this is inverted. The characteri-zation of the descriptive contract here serves to alert us to the structures of systemic institutional oppression, which need to be dismantled.

The Domination Contract

Let me now turn in greater detail to the illustration of the contrast between these two contracts, and the ways I think progressives can use the domination contract to address issues of gender justice, and social justice more generally. Consider the table, which summarizes what I see as the crucial differences. The key points are as follows:

MAINSTREAM CONTRACT	DOMINATION CONTRACT
Ethical Framework	
Ideal theory	Non-ideal theory
Starting-Point	
Ground zero (state of nature, original position)	Unjust stage of society
Role of History	
None presupposed	Historical account presupposed
Basic Agents	
People as presocial atomic individuals	People as members of social groups in relations of domination and subordination
Status Norm in Society	
Equality (ostensibly)	Inequality (explicitly)
Economic Transactions	
Typically mutually beneficial	Typically exploitative
Juridico-Political Sphere	
Egalitarian	Biased toward dominant groups
Human Divisions	
Class, race, and gender as natural	Class, race, and gender as artificial
Human Psychology	
Basically imported from nature	Fundamentally transformed by society (*amour de soi* → *amour-propre*)
Obstacles to Accurate Social Cognition	
Individual bias, "passions," "inclination," short-term self-interest	Dominant-group interests, dominant-group ideation
Locus of Problems	
Human nature	Corrupting social institutions
Goal of Contract	
To create a just society (laws, govt, etc.)	To reinforce and codify unjust institutions
Heuristic Purpose for Us	
Readers' endorsement of the contract as creating an ideally just society	Readers' condemnation of the contract, and corresponding awakening to systematic social injustice and the need for appropriate corrective measures to realize a just society

104-01

First, the overarching framework is non-ideal theory.[2] In the historic version of the mainstream contract, conceived of (though falsely) as consensual and inclusive, the way in which the polity is founded is supposed to confer on it a positive normative status. As such, the mainstream contract assumes ideal circumstances: society and government are brought into existence in a way that is fair, respecting the rights of those involved. By contrast, we know perfectly well from history that oppression of one kind or another has been the social norm since humanity left the hunting-and-gathering stage. The domination contract begins from this simple reality. Though the contemporary Rawlsian contract drops any historical claims, it nonetheless inherits this orientation in that Rawls sets out to ask what principles people *would* choose in ideally fair circumstances. Thus he makes clear throughout the book that his contract is an exercise in ideal theory, intended to work out "the principles of justice . . . defining a perfectly just society, given favorable conditions," and presuming "strict compliance" (1999h: 308–9). However, he claims that this starting-point is ultimately intended to illuminate the non-ideal: "If ideal theory is worthy of study, it must be because, as I have conjectured, it is the fundamental part of the theory of justice and essential for the nonideal part as well" (1999h: 343).

But a case can be made (and will be made in greater detail in later chapters) that such a starting-point handicaps his enterprise, and certainly the manifest failure in his own work, and in the thousands of articles it has inspired over the last 35 years, to apply his theory to the "nonideal" realities of gender and race does not encourage confidence in it. By definition, problems arise in non-ideal theory that do not arise in ideal theory, and one will need mapping concepts and data sets which cannot be readily extrapolated from those of ideal theory. So it raises the question of how useful, let alone "essential," it actually is. The mainstream contract – unsurprisingly given its conceptual ancestry – tends to abstract away from issues of social subordination, since historically it is really predicated on the experience of the bourgeois white male subject, that subsection of the population emancipated by modernity. By contrast, the revisionist contract, through utilizing the device of the domination contract, makes such issues its primary focus, since (following

---

[2] I am using the ideal theory/non-ideal theory distinction in the sense demarcated by Rawls. Both ideal and non-ideal theory involve the utilization of moral ideals, and the attempt to determine what justice requires in a particular situation, so the contrast is not that between moral and amoral approaches. The distinction is rather that ideal theory aims at mapping a perfectly just society, while non-ideal theory seeks to adjudicate what corrective or rectificatory justice would require in societies that are unjust. Rawls's focus is almost exclusively on the former.

Rousseau) it starts not from the state of nature but from an *already existing* unjust society, and then asks what measures of justice would be necessary to correct for them.

At the very least, then, Rawlsian ideal theory needs to be informed by the non-ideal. As just pointed out, to the extent that Rawls's method has been found useful in theorizing gender justice, most notably in Okin's (1989) work, it has been precisely through the *repudiation* of the key Rawlsian assumption of the ideal nature of the family, as a supposed paradigm of human interaction to be sharply contrasted with the interaction of strangers, and thus not requiring justice to regulate it. The disadvantaging of female children and women is only able to appear on the conceptual radar screen through the rethinking of the public/private boundary, and the unsentimental scrutiny of the actual, real-life family. In the case of racial justice, the non-ideal looms even more definitively, since measures of compensatory justice (affirmative action, reparations) presume by definition the need to correct for a history of *injustice* that Rawls's ideal-theory focus sidesteps. It is noteworthy that while in *The Cambridge Companion to Rawls* (Freeman 2003) there is at least a chapter by Martha Nussbaum (2003) on "Rawls and Feminism," there is no comparable chapter – indeed no section in *any* chapter – on race. And apart from the fact that the whiteness of the profession is even more overwhelming than its maleness, apart from the fact that most white political theorists, whether political scientists or political philosophers, take for granted what Rogers Smith describes as the misleading "anomaly" view of American racism (R. Smith 1997), the role of the ideal-theory framework itself must surely be a major contributory factor to this pattern of systematic omission and evasion. What has supposedly been intended to facilitate discussion of the remediation of injustice has served instead to obstruct it.

Relatedly, the domination contract is necessarily *historical*. Though contemporary poststructuralism is something of an exception, radical political theory, whether of class, gender, or race, traditionally emphasizes the importance of investigating the real history that has brought us to this point, and that explains who the major political players are and what are their agendas. Thus it seeks to contest both mystified histories and ahistorical naturalized accounts that deny *any* history, which simply sever the present from the past. Marx (to cite a very unfashionable figure) was famous for excoriating liberals and those he dubbed the "vulgar" economists for their timeless and decontextualized portrayal of the "free exchange" between capitalist and worker, without attention to the sequence of events (for example, the enclosures in Britain) that had reduced people who had previously been able to make a living from the land to workers with only their labor-power to sell. In the radical use of contract he pioneers, Rousseau establishes the precedent by giving an alternative narrative – naive by our standards, but expressing underlying truths nonetheless – of the origins of class inequality. Similarly, Pateman offers in her book (1988) an "as if" account of the origins of patriarchy, while I – comparatively advantaged by the fact that European expansionism takes place in the modern period, accompanied by a massive paper trail – was able to draw on actual events in describing how global white supremacy was established (Mills 1997). But in all three cases, the crucial point is that the non-ideal structure of domination in question, whether of class, gender, or race, is not "natural," not the outcome of the state of nature, but a sociohistorical product. The greater realism of radical contract theory as against mainstream contract theory is manifested in its recognition that the "contract" is really (à la Hampton) a way of talking about the human creation of sociopolitical institutions as the result of previous sociohistorical processes, not ex nihilo from the state of nature.

And this history is, of course, one of group domination and subordination rather than the classically individualist social ontology, and transactions among equal individuals, of the mainstream contract. I do not at all mean by this to endorse a communitarian position of the Sandelian variety (Sandel 1998), since, in agreement with many critics, I believe, contra Sandel, that people can and should gain a cognitive and normative distance from their socially assigned identities. My point rather is Rousseau's, and later Marx's, classic claim – now a political axiom among progressives – that society is most illuminatingly seen as a system of group domination rather than as a collection of individuals. So it is as members *of* social groups that individuals originally come to consciousness and agency, even if they later react against their socialization, and their differential status within the "contract" is tied to their group membership. The general facts of history and society that people take behind Rawls's veil apparently do not include the subordination of women or the subordination of nonwhites. (There is, of course, some sensitivity to class issues.) But we are certainly not bound by Rawls's ignorance. What makes radical contract theory better suited to make use of the device of the veil is its demystified, non-idealized view of recent human history as largely a history of social oppression, so that groups in interlocking patterns of domination constitute the real social ontology. The class, sexual, and racial contracts each capture particular aspects of social domination (while missing others), so that, whether singly or (ideally) in combination, they register the obvious fact that society is shaped by the powerful acting together, not individuals acting singly.

As such, the domination contract, which makes groups the key players, is obviously truer to the actual history of the world. If, as argued at the start, contract in the minimal sense does not specify who the crucial human actors are that create the sociopolitical world, then a group-based contract theory is not a contradiction in terms, and should be embraced by us as a more useful philosophical concept for political theory. The descriptive side of the contract is more accurately represented in the domination contract, and is certainly vastly more illuminating as a conceptual framework for orienting the prescriptive contract, since it points us toward the really important moral issues, viz., how do we dismantle these structures so as to achieve genuine egalitarianism. With such knowledge behind the veil, Rawlsian contractors would not be able to ignore gender and racial subordination as they currently do.

As a corollary, in understanding human motivation, one needs to take account of people's group membership, and how, whether privileged or subordinated, it shapes their psychology. Rousseau's famous critique of his social contract predecessors was that "They spoke of Savage Man and depicted Civil man" (1997a: 132). A healthy *amour de soi* had been socially corrupted into an unhealthy *amour propre*, which contractarians like Hobbes, not recognizing its social genesis, then took to be part of the human condition as such. Similarly, in Marx's critique of a specifically bourgeois vision of *homo economicus*, in feminist theorists' work on the production of "male" and "female" traits by gendered parental upbringing, in critical race theorists' analyses of "whiteness" and its psychological influence on its possessors, the conceptual door is opened to a much richer set of resources for theorizing actual human motivation and its social shaping than in the impoverished psychological framework of mainstream contract theory.

The relation between equality as a value and the contract also needs to be rethought. The mainstream contract is, of course, famous for its nominal egalitarianism, its emphasis that in the state of nature all men are equal, whether in physical and mental abilities, as in Hobbes, or in moral status, as in Locke and Kant. Hence the deep connection between social contract theory and conventional narratives of modernity, the promise of the American and French Revolutions. And this equality is then supposed to translate itself (in the societies created by these equal men) into a juridico-political equality, equality before the law and equality of citizenship, and in economic (and other) transactions that are non-exploitative in nature.

But however attractive this may be as an ideal, it obviously bears no correspondence with real life for the majority of the population, even in the modern period. Rousseau's concern is that the artificial class inequalities of society undermine this moral equality, and in Marx's more sophisticated treatment this is elaborated into the point that formal equality at the level of the relations of exchange is substantively undercut by economic compulsion at the level of the relations of production. But for gender and race, the situation is even worse. As feminists have long documented, in the case of gender, the "equality" was originally not even nominal, let alone substantive, since with the qualified exception of Hobbes, all the major contract theorists saw women as inferior to men, and so as appropriately to be regulated by male authority. Moreover, this theoretical inferiority was, of course, also manifest practically, in real life, in legal and political institutions. So the value that is perhaps most intimately associated with the social contract tradition – equality – was not at all meant to be extended to half the human race. Likewise, as various theorists of race and imperialism have pointed out, once one examines the representations ("savages," "barbarians") and the experiences of people of color in the modern period – expropriated and exterminated Native Americans and Australians, enslaved and later Jim-Crowed blacks, colonized non-Europeans – it becomes clear that both in theory and in practice, only white men were equal. Not merely as a matter of fact, but as a matter of proclaimed moral and legal norms, nonwhites had an inferior to non-existent schedule of rights – and were thus non-citizens or at best second-class citizens. How, then, can it make sense to conceptualize society as if, in the modern period, equality becomes the generally accepted norm, when in fact such a small section of the population were actually seen as equal?

In the domination contract, by contrast, this reality is frankly faced: *inequality* is the actual social norm obtaining for the majority. The evasive conceptual assimilation of the status of white women and non-whites to the status of white men that is embedded in the mainstream contract, thereby burying the distinctive problems the former groups face, is thus precluded. Correspondingly, the radical contract recognizes that the crucial juridico-political institutions are not egalitarian in their functioning either, but biased in various ways by class, gender, and racial privilege. The huge body of literature standardly ignored by contract theorists – the original left analyses of the workings of the state in capitalist society, the more recent work on the gendered and racial state (MacKinnon 1989; Anthony Marx 1998; Goldberg 2002), as well as all the biases in the legal system – can then legitimately enter here, rather than being conceptually blocked by the otherworldly and completely fanciful pictures of a neutral juridico-political realm assumed by the mainstream contract. And far from fair and reciprocal advantage being the norm – Rawls suggests, absurdly, that we think of society as *actually* (not just ideally) being "a cooperative venture for mutual advantage" (1999h: 4, 109) – exploitation of various kinds – of class, gender, and race – is the norm (Sample 2003a). Accordingly, one of the main aims of the normative contract will be the elimination of these structures of exploitation – unequal chances for the poor and working class, sexual exploitation, differential white advantage and corresponding wealth (Shipler 2004; K. Barry 1984; Oliver and Shapiro 1995) – that the individualist perspective of mainstream contract theory tends to obfuscate.[3]

In addition, the group interests of the privileged, and their resulting desire to maintain their privilege, will become both an ideational obstacle to achieving social transparency and a material obstacle to progressive change, which will need to be taken into account in theorizing the dynamics of social cognition and the possibilities for social transformation. For both the mainstream contract and the revisionist contract, accurate factual and moral cognition is crucial. But for the mainstream contract, the obstacles to attaining this desired objectivity are generally conceptualized in individualistic terms. For the domination contract, on the other hand, there is an additional category of cognitive obstacles that are generated by the vested interests in the established order of the dominant group, and their differential power over social ideation. So that whole set of problems that in the Marxist tradition is associated with the subject of *ideology* can enter here. If for mainstream contract theory social transparency is the ideal, here social opacity is the norm, and hegemonic conceptual and normative frameworks will have been shaped by the fact of group domination. So again, one will be equipped with a far more sophisticated and realistic view of the workings of the polity and its dominant illusory self-conceptions than in the mainstream contract. One will be beginning from the elementary political fact – and how could this be ignored by any serious political theory? – that dominant groups will in general want to preserve their hegemony, so that it is by no means just a matter of coming up with a more convincing picture of a just society.

Finally, apart from (I would claim anyway) all of these obvious merits, the domination contract has the great and overwhelming virtue of conceptualizing class, gender, and race *as themselves artificial*, not natural as in the mainstream contract. So it is not merely that society is seen as a complex of groups in dominance and subordination, but that the formation of the groups *themselves* is a product of the contract(s). The familiar claim of recent radical democratic theory that gender and race are "constructed" – not just the systems (patriarchy, white

---

[3] Rawls's left-liberal, social democratic contract is, of course, good on class – that is its main strength, from a radical point of view – though even here some on the political left argued that it did not go far enough, and was unrealistic or evasive about the implications for political power and people's social status of the economic inequalities it left intact. See, for example, Peffer (1990).

supremacy) organized around them, but what we take to be gender and race themselves – is thus perfectly accommodated.

Rousseau deserves the credit for this too, though, as noted, the lack of discussion in the secondary literature of his class contract, and his own notorious sexism, means that he has not been fully recognized for it. As underlined at the start, the social contract as it comes into its own in the modern period emphasizes the "artificiality" of society and the polity. These are human-made, not organic growths as in the discourse of antiquity, and the descriptive side of the contract expresses that insight. But Rousseau goes a startlingly radical step further: he suggests that in a sense humans themselves are artificial, human-created products. What to his predecessors were "natural" divisions of class he sees as a result of domination and convention. It is not merely that we make our institutions – we also make ourselves.

And the implications are that for the domination contract in general, dramatic social transformation, both good and bad, is pivotal. In this respect it contrasts with the more limited scope envisaged for changing ourselves in the mainstream contract. Hobbes sees humans as naturally self-seeking individuals who have to learn to constrain their propensity to maximization of short-term advantage for society to function. But this is not a radical metamorphosis. Nor are Lockean humans, who already largely obey natural law in the state of nature (though prone to bias in their own case), dramatically altered by their entry into society. And for Kant's Christian vision, of course, we are always characterized, as fallen humans, by our "radical evil," whether in society or not. But Rousseau differs from his fellow contract theorists in offering "a secular narrative of Fall" (Brooke 2001: 110), in which "a corrupt society is the cause and a debased human nature the effect" (Hulliung 2001: 67).

Extended from class to gender and race, this gives us the sexual and racial contracts, which in a dialectical relationship both consolidate in an oppositional relationship with one another the entities of men and women, whites and nonwhites, and create these groups themselves. So the (bad) contractual transformation of the non-ideal descriptive domination contract is far more thoroughgoing than in the mainstream descriptive contract. It is social institutions that form and corrupt us, an account "locating the origins of evil not in any original sin by the First Couple but in the consequences of the organization of human societies" (Brooke 2001: 111). And the implications for the (good) contractual transformation envisaged in the ideal prescriptive contract are, correspondingly, far more sweeping than in the mainstream version, since radical contract theory then points us toward the necessity not merely of dismantling these structures of domination, but *the contractors themselves* as intrinsically gendered and raced beings. As Marx envisaged a classless society, so the sexual and racial contracts, emphasizing the constructed nature of gender and race, open up for us the possibility and desirability of a genderless and raceless society.

Objections and Replies

I now want to consider some objections that might be made to this proposed revisionist contractualism.

(1)   The "domination contract" is an idle fifth wheel, not doing any work, and not necessary to theorize normatively about these issues.

The claim is not that it's necessary, but that it's helpful, in pointing us toward and highlighting certain important realities not usually discussed in this framework, and which the mainstream contract apparatus tends to obfuscate. So it's not a matter of logical implication but conceptual orientation, heuristic value, pointing us *there* rather than *here*. Besides, the "fifth wheel" accusation is standardly made about the Rawlsian contract also, so arguably the domination contract is no more vulnerable than it is.

(2)   "Contract" is just a metaphor, which doesn't explain anything, and that goes for a "domination contract" also; what we need is empirically informed sociopolitical theory about the actual causal mechanisms of oppression.

Many philosophers have long argued that metaphors do in fact do cognitive work. But in any case, the domination contract is no more meant to substitute for empirical sociopolitical investigation than the mainstream contract is. It's not competing with such work but complementing it, providing at the level of abstraction appropriate to political philosophy an intellectual framework that can be utilized by theorists with widely differing views on what the causes of social oppression are, while remaining agnostic and uncommitted about which of these accounts is most convincing. So theorists with quite divergent perspectives can at least get together on this common minimalist platform.

(3)   Whether the contract is one of "domination" or not, endorsing this apparatus ties one to a liberal framework.

I see this as a virtue, not a weakness – a way of mainstreaming issues typically discussed only in radical circles, piggybacking on to a respectable apparatus (isn't the goal of progressives to convert others and not just preach to the choir?). Besides, it's "liberal" only in terms of endorsing liberal values, not in its social ontology – it explicitly rejects liberalism's atomic individualism for an ontology of individuals *as* members of social groups. So it arguably retains the key insight of progressive theory, viz the oppressive role of class, gender, and racial structures.

(4)   Liberal values themselves are suspect.

What's the alternative? Besides, what's wrong with moral equality, autonomy, self-realization, equality before the law, due process, freedom of expression, freedom of association, voting rights, and so forth? Sounds pretty good to me. The real problem historically has been the restricted extension of these values to a limited population, or the emptying of nominal freedoms of any real substantive content by oppressive social structures. But the whole point of mapping a "domination contract" is to be able to track, and ultimately eliminate, these problems. Consider the alternatives: (i) Marxism: presently moribund in the absence of an attractive socialist project, historically weak on normative issues, and in any case arguably parasitic on liberal values for what little normative argumentation has been given in the tradition (for example, claims about liberal equality being undercut by class domination). (ii) Communitarianism: vulnerable to the charge of relativism, and in any case the backward-looking orientation of the dominant variety is particularly uncongenial for traditionally subordinated groups like women and racial minorities, for whom the "good old days" (coverture? slavery? colonialism?) were not so good at all, and are somewhat less likely to inspire nostalgia. (iii) Poststructuralism: famously better at deconstruction than positive reconstruction. Besides, if demands for gender and racial justice are conceptualized as just the will-to-power of the subordinated, how on earth will this legitimate them? (iv) Feminist ethic of "care": many feminists have moved away from their original strong endorsement of this alternative, conceding that even if (in some cases) we need more than justice, we do definitely need justice.

(5)   Insofar as no political theorist (today) would exclude white women and people of color, mainstream social contract theory already takes their concerns into account.

One needs to distinguish substantive from merely formal, nominal inclusion. The well-established feminist critique made by Okin and others shows that just-adding-women-and-stirring, alternating "he's" and "she's" in the manuscript, doesn't amount to a serious rethinking of the polity to achieve gender justice. Rawls's own original notorious assumption that the family can be treated as an "ideal" institution, and the general ignoring in mainstream male literature of the difference gender makes, demonstrates the continuing marginalization of these concerns. And the situation on race is even worse: there is next to no recognition in the work on justice by white political philosophers that the United States and the former colonial powers have historically been white-supremacist polities, and that racial *injustice* has been central to their history.

(6) The critique of mainstream social contract theory is misplaced, since it's not as if it's trying and failing to do what you want it to do, but that (as an exercise in ideal theory, as you recognize at the start) it's not trying to do what you want it to do *at all*.

If the task of political philosophy is to articulate ideals of a just society, then surely at some stage – even for ideal theory – the ultimate goal must be to bring these ideals into comparison with our own manifestly non-ideal society to see how to make it more just. (If this is *not* the intention, and these ideals are meant just for aesthetic contemplation, then this is a remarkable abdication of the historic role of ethical theory and its link with practical reason!) Rawls himself said that the point of starting with ideal theory was that it would give us a better grasp on the more pressing problems of non-ideal theory. But as pointed out at the start, 35 years later this promise remains largely unfulfilled. So it raises the question: are mainstream contract theorists really serious about social justice or not?

(7) The origins of social contract theory in white male bourgeois thought necessarily contaminate its theoretical assumptions and the structuring of its crucial concepts, for example the "individual" will, in effect, necessarily be conceived of as a male property owner, with a wife at home to do reproductive labor. So this apparatus cannot be reclaimed and turned to progressive ends.

We need to distinguish (ineluctable) logical implication from (weaker) theoretical bias. The history of the "contract" shows it is flexible enough to be radicalized and subjected to reconceptualization, as in Rousseau, as cited, or Okin's adaptation of Rawls as applied to the family. The task is to rethink (in the light of structures of domination) what would be necessary for the subordinated to realize their "individuality." But this does not require abandonment of the concept, just an expanded vision of pertinent social obstacles – which is precisely what the "domination contract" sets out to highlight.

(8) By your own concession, the appeal and continuing survival of social contract theory are owed in part to its very simplicity as an image and metaphor. But this simplicity is lost once you start fuzzifying things with not one contract but several interlocking "contracts." If all these complexities and epicycles are needed, isn't the original metaphor lost, and shouldn't the project just be abandoned?

Simplicity is undoubtedly a theoretical virtue, but not the only, or highest, one. More important is adequacy to the field of study. Society *is* complex, and while the original contract is easier to grasp, this comes at the cost of obfuscating and profoundly misrepresenting the actual social history, and blinding us to pressing issues of social justice. Arguably the central insights of social contract theory are the human-created character of society and the polity, and the commitment (if originally limited) to moral egalitarianism. These insights are retained in the domination contract, though put on a more sociologically informed foundation. So I would claim that more is gained by complicating the contract idea than is lost by the relinquishment of simplicity.

Appropriating the Contract

My recommendation, then, is that we – egalitarians, feminists, critical race theorists, and progressives in general in political theory who are concerned about real social justice issues – work toward a paradigm shift in contract theory, not conceding the contract to mainstream theorists, but seeking to appropriate it and turn it to emancipatory ends. According to the Kymlicka quote cited earlier, contract is really just a "*device* which many different traditions have used for many different reasons" (1991: 196). Rawls, similarly, sometimes refers to his updating of the contract (the veil, the original position) as an "expository device" (1999h: 19). So given this essentially instrumental identity of the contract, there is no principled barrier to developing it in a radical way: the domination contract as an "expository device" for non-ideal theory. Once one recognizes how protean the contract has historically been, and how politically pivotal is its insight of the human creation of society and of ourselves as social beings, one should be able to appreciate that its conservative deployment is a result not of its intrinsic features, but of its use by a privileged white male group hegemonic in political theory who have had no motivation to extrapolate its logic. Far from being a necessarily bourgeois or necessarily sexist or necessarily racist apparatus, contract theory has a radical potential barely tapped, and can serve as a vehicle for translating into conventional discourse most, if not all, of the crucial claims of radical democratic political theory.

The key conceptual move is simply to strip away the assumptions and corresponding conceptual infrastructure of an individualism once restricted to bourgeois white males and still shaping the contract's features today, and replace it with an ontology of groups (I. Young 1990). Rousseau's class contract, Pateman's sexual contract, my racial contract (ideally combined, of course), can all then be conceptualized as still being within the contract tradition in the minimal defining sense out-lined above, viz, the assertion of, indeed insistence upon, the historic role of human causality in shaping the polity, and the commitment to the substantive realization of moral egalitarianism in its necessary transformation. By contrast, the assumptions of the mainstream con-tract in its contemporary form, presuming universal inclusion and general input, handicap the apparatus in tackling the necessary task of corrective justice by, in a sense, assuming the very thing that needs to be substantively achieved. Once one adds women of all races, and male people of color (to say nothing of the white male working class), one is actually talking about the *majority* of the population's being excluded in one way or another from the historical contract, and its present descendant! A theoretical device whose classic pretensions are to repre-sent universal sociopolitical inclusion actually captures the experience of just a minority of the population, since inequality has not been the exception but the *norm* in modern societies.

Far from the domination contract representing "minority" concerns, then, it actually provides an accurate depiction of the situation for the majority. And far from being anti-Enlightenment, it has a much better claim to be carrying on the Enlightenment legacy. Getting the facts right is supposed to be an essential part of the Enlightenment mission, and in its mystified picture of the origins and workings of modern polis-ties, mainstream contract theory certainly does not do that. And if the Enlightenment is supposed to be committed to moral egalitarianism and a transformation of society to realize this imperative, then ignoring the ways in which class, gender, and race void nominal egalitarianism of substance is hardly the way to achieve such equality. Through the more accurate descriptive mapping of the domination contract, the emanci-patory reach of the egalitarianism of the prescriptive contract can then gain its full leveling scope rather than being, as at present, effectively confined to achieving the freedom and equality of a few.

In sum, a case can be made that radical contract theory, which deploys the domination contract as its descriptive mapping device, is, far from being a theoretical usurper, the *true heir* to the social contract tradition at its best, and it is mainstream contract theory that has betrayed its promise. If war is too important to be left to the generals, one could say that social contract theory is too important to be left to the social contract theorists. We should reclaim it.

4

Contract of Breach: Repairing the Racial Contract

Charles W. Mills

I want to turn now to the normative use, within this suggested alternative non-ideal contract theory, of the idea of the domination contract. I will focus on race, and use as my illustration the subject of reparations to African Americans.

After decades of virtually complete marginalization, black reparations as an issue has once again become topical. Its renewed life in the black American community, and the grudging acknowledgment it has begun to receive in at least some sections of the white community, can be attributed both to the untiring efforts of local activists and the increased global sensitivity in recent years to issues of atonement and apology for governmental wrongdoing. One anthology, for example, *When Sorry Isn't Enough* (Brooks 1999; see also Winbush 2003; Salzberger and Turck 2004; McGary, forthcoming), suggests that we are now living in an "age of apology," and has a planetary sweep, including sections on successful as well as so far unsuccessful demands for reparations to Jewish and Romani victims of Nazi atrocities during the Second World War, Korean "comfort women" kidnapped and subjected to gang rape by the Japanese military, Japanese Americans interned by the American government, expropriated Native Americans, black Americans suffering the legacy of slavery and Jim Crow, and South African victims of apartheid.

An outsider might expect that philosophy would be in the vanguard of such a movement, since it is political philosophers and ethicists who are by their calling supposed to be professionally concerned about matters of justice. But an outsider would be quite wrong. While a tiny handful of black philosophers, such as Bernard Boxill (1992) and Howard McGary (1999), have played a pioneering role for 30 years in trying to get the issue of reparations for racial injustice taken seriously by the profession, mainstream philosophical discussions of social justice have for the most part ignored it. The most obvious and revealing indicator of this pattern of exclusion is the silence on race in the Rawls industry. Rawls's *A Theory of Justice* (1999h) is widely credited with reviving Anglo-American political philosophy after the Second World War, and making it again possible, after the doldrums of meta-ethical noncognitivism, to do political theory in the old-fashioned grand style. Insofar as Rawls is tackling nothing less than what is required to make a society just, one would think that here is the ideal framework to discuss the legacy of racial injustice in the United States. But in Rawls's own writings, and in the literally thousands of articles his work has generated, the subject of race, and the history of American slavery and post-bellum Jim Crow, barely appear. Indeed, as mentioned in the previous chapter, in the recently published *Cambridge Companion to Rawls* (Freeman 2003), not one of the 14 essays has racial justice as a topic or even a subtopic. Nor is it discussed except in a passing sentence or two by any of the authors contributing to a special 2006 symposium on Rawls's legacy in *Perspectives on Politics*, the official journal of the American Political Science Association (Ackerley et al. 2006).

How is it possible for political philosophers in the United States, a country where racial *injustice* has been so flagrant, to be so indifferent to this issue? As with any complex social phenomenon, the causality involved is multiple, and for an answer, one would have to look both at the peculiar sociology of the profession itself (its overwhelming demographic whiteness, with its obvious implications for the shaping of experience, group interests, concerns, and priorities) and the de-racialized conceptions of the polity dominant in the culture at large (see, for example, R. Smith 1997). But apart from those factors, a significant contributory cause, I would claim, is the hegemony of "ideal theory" in political philosophy and the not unrelated adoption of a contractualism that abstracts away from embarrassing questions of corrective justice. As Rodney Roberts has recently observed, in the huge literature in Western philosophy on justice, surprisingly little attention has been paid "to questions of injustice and its rectification." Far from flowing smoothly, almost as a matter of logical implication, from the subject matter of justice, injustice as a normative topic has tended to be bracketed and sidelined, so that "a privileged perspective on justice" has been the outcome, with "questions regarding compensation which may be due to victims of injustice" being "well outside the 'central debate,'" and "relatively speaking, of little concern to philosophers" (R. Roberts 2002a: 1).

I have argued elsewhere (Mills 2005a) that this preference in the profession for "ideal theory" is not innocent, not a neutral methodological decision, but itself a deeply *ideological* one in the pejorative sense classically associated with left theory of the adoption of a set of ideas/values/approaches/framing assumptions that reflect and repro- duce the perspectives of the privileged (here, whites). Ideal theory has proven to be patently *non*-ideal for the theorizing of racial justice. For when racial oppression has been central rather than marginal — as has obviously been the case in the United States – it is absurd to utilize without modification a conceptual apparatus that presupposes race- neutral inclusion, color-blind universalism, and egalitarian political input as the actual dominant norms. If, in the terminology of Rogers Smith (1997), racism and white supremacy had been "anomalies" in a generally inclusivist and race-neutral polity, then conventional contract theory, classically predicated as it is on individualist egalitarianism, would be an apparatus appropriate to determining justice. If on the other hand racism and white supremacy have been norms in their own right, whether in tension with race-neutral liberalism as part of a complex of "multiple traditions" or, more ominously, as "symbiotic" with and rewriting liberalism in racialized terms, then a different theo- retical normative approach is required. Instead, we should start with the reality of *exclusion and inegalitarianism* as the norm, and a "contract" that theoretically registers that fact: a "contract of breach," in the sense that the very foundation of the contract is the breach of universalism and respect for all, so that oppression is normative. In this demystified framework – which corresponds to reality, unlike the mainstream one – injustice is located at center-stage, making impossible its marginaliza- tion. The normative task of contract theory within this alternative approach, then, would be to replace the domination contract, a "con- tract of breach," with a contract that repairs and corrects for that breach, thereby achieving racial justice – rather than the unhelpful and ultimately evasive abstracting away from questions of race altogether which has been the rule in white political philosophy.

In what follows, I will (1) argue for the unacknowledged "whiteness" of mainstream social contract theory; (2) demonstrate how the "domi- nation contract," in this case the racial contract, can serve as a useful tool for working in non-ideal theory; (3) show how to justify reparations within a modified Rawlsian contractual framework.

The "Whiteness" of the Contract

The enduring appeal of the contract idea inheres in large measure in its elaborating on a simple image, a picture, a metaphor, resonant with complex implications (Hampton 1993, 2001): that the sociopolitical order is created by morally equal human beings (descriptive claim) and as such the structure of the sociopolitical order should reflect that equality (normative claim).[1] The many and obvious criticisms that can be directed at the concept if taken too literally are in a sense irrelevant, defeated by the simple power of the idea of society as a human creation that should be morally bound by egalitarian norms.

Thus in his classic analysis of what he sees as the "political voluntarism" of social contract theory, Patrick Riley reminds us that "the central concept in social contract theory is will," thereby, in Michael Oakeshott's contrast, demarcating the modern political conceptual world of "will and artifice" from the "reason and nature" of antiquity (Riley 1982: vii–ix). From Hobbes's famous description in *Leviathan* of the commonwealth as "an Artificiall Man; though of greater stature and strength than the Naturall" (1996: 9), onward through the work of his successors Locke, Rousseau, and Kant, the emphasis is on the artificial, that is humanly created, character of the society and the polity. Similarly, though contemporary Rawls-inspired contractualism drops the historical claims, it is noteworthy that Rawls still begins *A Theory of Justice* with the suggestion that we think of society as "a cooperative venture for mutual advantage" (1999h: 4). So though the contemporary contract may have forsworn the robust explanatory pretensions of the original, the "thin" but still significant commitment to the shaping role of human causality remains.

The other – normative – commitment is, of course, not attenuated at all. In the non-Hobbesian mainstream of the tradition, it is manifested in Locke's assertions about equal rights in the state of nature and Kant's claims about the categorical imperative to respect our moral personhood. In the words of Murray Forsyth: "The emergence of the notion of the social contract is hence linked intimately with the emergence of the idea of the equality of human beings" (1994: 37). And in Rawls's updating, of course, it is manifested in the use of the contract idea to bring out "the principles that free and rational persons concerned to further their own interests would accept in an initial position of equality as defining the fundamental terms of their association" (1999h: 10). So the contemporary Rawlsian contract is a classic example of the moral contract: the mapping of a just order appropriate for a society of equals.

In what ways, then, can the contract be said to be "white," Eurocentric? After all, surely these two basic claims (society as a human creation, moral egalitarianism among humans) are perfectly reasonable ones, indeed (the latter in particular) to be applauded and highlighted by people of color seeking remedies for racial discrimination. My objection

---

[1] Hobbes is of course the notorious exception here.

is not, of course, to this foundation of the "contract" – I completely agree that these claims are to be endorsed. The "whiteness," I suggest, reveals itself in two ways. First, there is the historic fact, at least arguably, that the original contract theorists had overt or tacit racial restrictions on who counted as a full "person" with equal rights. Nonwhite "savages" and "barbarians" were generally seen as lesser beings covered by a different set of normative rules, as manifested both in the actually color-coded moral code obtaining and the racist sociopolitical institutions imposed on nonwhites by Europeans in the modern period. In other words, contra Forsyth, some humans were less human, and so less equal, than others. If moral egalitarianism is true, that does not mean that it was recognized to be true for the nonwhite population. I have made these arguments before (Mills 1997, 2006b) and will not repeat the evidence here.

Nonetheless, the obvious rejoinder to this criticism (even if its validity is conceded) is that these racial exclusions, deplorable as they were, can be simply eliminated from the theoretical apparatus, and are not a feature of the contemporary contract. If the contract was admittedly historically white, with equality limited to whites, it does not have to remain so. But this brings us to the second, deeper kind of "whiteness." My claim will be that – as with the corresponding feminist critique of the originally gendered contract (Pateman 1988; Okin 1989) – a genuine and substantive (as against merely nominal and verbal) rewriting of the "contract" to take account of the distinctive concerns of people of color *will require a fundamental rethinking of the depiction of the creation of society and what real egalitarianism now morally requires of us.* If the "political voluntarism" that defines social contract theory represents a "moral causality," as Riley argues, then this notion must necessarily be rethought for populations who, for racial reasons, have been denied – as moral inferiors – the equal capacity to will, and have been subjected instead to the immoral causal imposition of a racialized *white* will in the founding of the polity. So while it is true that humans create the sociopolitical order, they certainly do not all have an equal say in its shaping. The "will" involved is not the unanimous will of all, Riley's idealized "moral causality," but rather an *immoral* causality that reflects the differential power of whites.

A useful reference-point in this respect is an unwittingly revealing passage in a classic essay by David Gauthier, "The Social Contract as Ideology." Gauthier begins with the observation that "The conception of social relationships as contractual lies at the core of our ideology." But unlike most white contract theorists, he immediately goes on to ask "Who are 'we'?," and answers with commendable frankness: "In this essay, first-person plural references are intended to denote those persons who have inhabited Western Europe, who are descended from such inhabitants, or who live or have lived in social structures developed from those of Western Europe during the past three to four hundred years" (1997: 27).

Gauthier thus implicitly limits the "contract" to whites (in fact a subset of whites: the fully white Western European, so to speak, as against the off-white Eastern European (Jacobson 1998)) and those others living in the social structures created by whites in the period of Western modernity. In a way he anticipates, in an essay originally published in 1977, Rawls's shift from the 1971 *Theory of Justice* representation of the contract as a device with transhistorical, meta-ethical pretensions to the later more modest 1993 *Political Liberalism* representation of the contract as a political (not metaphysical) device for summarizing the "overlapping consensus" of ideas and values in ("our") modern liberal Western societies. As such, his judgment is both interestingly right and interestingly wrong. What makes it right is that he basically restricts the scope of contract ideas to his primary reference group of Europeans at home and abroad (to be fully accurate, of course, a further gender restriction would be necessary). It is really this population who, in the modern period, become free and equal "persons" who should have equal input into the creation of social structures and political institutions. Invaded and expropriated Native Americans, enslaved Africans, colonized Third Worlders, certainly had no such choice about the sociopolitical institutions imposed on them, so that the contract metaphor does not capture their political experience.

But what makes his judgment simultaneously wrong, of course, is that these oppressive social structures were also "developed from those of Western Europe during the past three to four hundred years," and imposed on people of color *by this very same population* of Europeans at home and abroad, so that while nonwhites lived (and – more often – died) within these social structures it was not as "contracting" citizens. As black and Third World political theorists have repeatedly and insistently pointed out: European imperialism, African slavery, and Aboriginal expropriation cannot licitly be conceptually Jim-Crowed in doing political theory, segregated from the standard triumphalist narrative that runs from Plato to Rawls, for they also are part of the modern political history of the West (Gilroy 1993; Mehta 1999).

The whiteness and Eurocentrism of the contract, then, do not inhere most fundamentally in the verbal and semantic exclusions, which can obviously be easily remedied with the stroke of a pen or a computer key. The whiteness and Eurocentrism of the contract inhere most fundamentally in the fact that this apparatus was originally designed for a population with a different history and facing a different set of problems.

The contract idea epitomized the birth of a European modernity that challenged patriarchalist and absolutist sociopolitical structures on a foundation of the moral equality of all (white) men. What it does not, of course, capture is the dark side of European modernity, the imposition of "absolutist" sociopolitical structures on morally inferior non-Europeans. So it is not the fact that nonwhite Aborigines, slaves, and the colonized were not included in the population of original "contractors" that makes the contract most deeply white, since this can nominally be corrected for. Rather, what marks the contract, even in its updated modern version, as white is that this contemporary inclusion *is* typically only nominal, that the history and legacy of Aboriginal expropriation, slavery, and colonialism are *not taken into account* in the conceptualization of the crucial issues and the framing of discussions of justice, so that nonwhites are simply conceptually assimilated to the white population. The mainstream contract takes moral equality as substantially recognized and achieved, and then asks what kind of polity would be voluntarily created by equal contractors. But the concerns of nonwhites are focused on what happens when a state is nonvoluntarily imposed upon them as *unequals* originally excluded from the contract, and what measures of justice would then be required *to correct for* that historic imposition of conquest, expropriation, and slavery. It is the deep theoretical orientation toward the first rather than the second set of problems that characterizes the contract as profoundly rather than merely superficially white.

Non-ideal Theory and the "Domination Contract"

The failure to deal with race, then, both in Rawls's own writings and in the huge secondary literature on Rawls, is a consequence not merely of the demographic whiteness of the American philosophical population, but of the methodological focus inherited from the original orientation of social contract theory.[2] In its incarnation as the moral contract, the apparatus – in keeping with the priorities of the population for whom it was originally designed – is aimed at working out what an ideally just social order would be assuming one is starting from ground zero, the state of nature for the classic contract, the original position for the Rawlsian updating. Thus *A Theory of Justice* (1999h) is, famously, an exercise in

---

[2] Obviously it can be argued – and I would indeed argue – that these two facts are sociologically, if not logically, connected. As the racially privileged population, whites do not suffer racial oppression themselves, and so do not have the same motivation to seek alternative methodologies as nonwhite philosophers have. There is, in other words, a "fit," an "elective affinity," between this community and this approach to issues of justice, since reparative justice is not a priority for them.

"ideal theory," aimed at elucidating "the principles of justice . . . defining a perfectly just society, given favorable conditions," and presuming "strict compliance" (pp. 308–9). But the issue of racial justice is, by definition, a matter of *non-ideal* theory, since it presupposes the need for corrective measures to remedy the legacy and ongoing practices of racial oppression. The Rawlsian contractors will presumably not choose a white-supremacist (or any other racially supremacist) society from behind the veil, since they do not know what race they will be when the veil is lifted. So the ideal Rawlsian society will not be a racist one, and its "basic structure" will not have been founded on racial exclusion, thereby reflecting "our" confidence that racial discrimination is unjust, indeed that "explicit racist doctrines . . . are irrational" (pp. 17, 129). In this framework, then, there is no need for affirmative action, reparations, or other measures of corrective racial justice because no racial group will have been discriminated against in the first place. But this will obviously be of scant comfort and little guidance to those members of groups who in the actual, non-ideal world *have* been discriminated against. Their starting-point is not ground zero and their justice priorities are understandably different, shaped by a different history and a different relationship to the orthodox contract.

Ideal theory is thus likely to seem evasive or just irrelevant. Simply put: in ideal theory, certain problems do not even arise in the first place; but given that in the non-ideal world, they *have* arisen, what should now be done to address them? If as a person of color I want to know what corrective justice demands in what has historically been a white-supremacist polity like the United States, of what value will it be to inform me that if the United States had been founded on Rawlsian principles, then there would have been no need for corrective justice? This is likely to seem a patent non sequitur. Yes, if it had been, there would not have been – but it wasn't, and so there is. (Cf. the classic retort: "And if your grandmother had had wheels, she would have been a bicycle.")

It seems to me that the proponents of ideal theory face a dilemma, which can be simply expressed as follows: either ideal theory is *not* ultimately intended to assist with the determination of justice in a non-ideal world, or it is so intended. If the former, then this, of course, would only confirm the worst suspicions of critics: ideal theory is an essentially onanistic exercise, divorced from any real intercourse with the world, and – in violation of the classic mission of ethical theory – severed from practical reason. If, on the other hand, the latter is the case and it *is* intended to be practically useful in this world, then surely ideal theorists owe us an account of why so little work has been produced in the thousands of articles over the past few decades on such an application (especially with respect to race), and also what the bridging concepts would be that are supposed to assist this application. Since Rawls himself formally endorsed the second position (pp. 8, 343), then if his authority carries any weight, this should indeed be the ultimate goal of ideal theorists. Are we not then entitled to ask why, up to the time of his death 30 years later, no progress from this "beginning" had yet been made, either in his own work or that of his followers?

For as noted at the start, it is a mistake to think that non-ideal theory is just the converse of ideal theory, to be addressed by simply flipping the crucial concepts over, as it were. When there has been injustice – when one is starting *not* from a moral ground zero, but from an already unjust situation – determining what remedial justice requires of us is more complicated than simple modus ponens or modus tollens. The righting of wrongs and the sketching of rights are two different enterprises. Prescriptions for remedial justice in a racist social order are not the same as prescriptions for ideal justice in a non-racist social order, nor can they be straightforwardly extracted from them by, say, the invocation of "justice as fairness," since the very question at issue, obviously, is exactly *what* fairness demands of us in the situation.

If this has not always been clearly seen, a contributing factor, I suggest, is the ambiguities in the term "ideal" itself (Mills 2005a). Determining what is ideally required for justice in an ideal situation is the task of ideal theory. Determining what is ideally required to redress injustice in a non-ideal situation is *not* the task of ideal theory, and ideal theory, contra Rawls, may not even be that useful in trying to adjudicate it. Reference to what would counterfactually, ideally have been the case may be simply irrelevant or unhelpful, for example because the ideal situation cannot be restored (as in the case of wrongful deaths during slavery, or the return of the Americas to Native Americans), or because we have to work with continuing non-ideal realities which Rawlsian concepts of an idealized polity or economy do little to illuminate. (For example, in trying to achieve proportional democratic representation in an electoral arena historically dominated by exclusionary white majoritarianism, or in giving people of color equal access to economic opportunities that encroach on what are seen as the legitimate entitlements, the racialized "property," of historically privileged whites.) (Corlett 2003; Guinier 1994; C. Harris 1993.)

Insofar as the normative use of the social contract idea has been oriented toward establishing the moral principles of an ideally just society, and thus to ideal theory, it is really focused on a different set of problems, and this is manifested in a conceptual array that is not well designed to map and clarify the actual non-ideal realities. Indeed, a case could be made that if ideal theory initially seems methodologically attractive, it is in part because "ideally just" as a term trades on the ambiguity between reference to a society with *no* history of injustice and reference to a society whose past history of injustice has been *corrected for*, so that the "ideal" represents a moral goal to be approached, if only asymptotically, thereby guiding our theory. Once it is realized that Rawls is actually talking about the former, not the latter, it will be appreciated that he is mapping an ideal of limited usefulness for tackling issues of racial justice, since by definition this involves the remediation of past injustice.

It might be thought, then, that a social contract framework is of little use, and that we should turn to some other approach. But as made clear in the previous chapter, I think that such a conclusion would be premature. Liberalism and the discourse of rights are globally triumphant, and contractualism is one of the best-established vehicles for expressing these normative commitments. So it remains of great value as a framework for establishing a dialogue with mainstream white theorists and translating the moral demands of people of color into a familiar language. What I will argue is that by drawing on the Rousseauean precedent – the only classic contract theorist to describe *two* contracts – we can reorient the tradition to address non-ideal matters.

Rousseau's famous contract is of course the second one, the agreement described in *The Social Contract* (1968, 1997d) to found a society based on the "general will." It is this contract that Rawls invokes as "definitive of the tradition" in *A Theory of Justice* (along with Locke's *Second Treatise* and Kant's writings) when he is sketching the genealogy of his own "contract" (Rawls 1999h: 10 n4). But as discussed in the previous chapter, in Rousseau's earlier *Discourse on Inequality* (1984, 1997a) he also describes, albeit very briefly, a fraudulent contract imposed on the poor by the rich under the pretext of guaranteeing the rights of all. Thus he is the only theorist in the classical tradition to expressly use the contract idea to map and theorize *injustice*. In Patrick Riley's assessment, he is, ironically, both "the purest social contract theorist of the eighteenth century (and simultaneously the deepest critic of contractarianism after Hume)" (2001a: 1).

The purpose of the *Discourse on Inequality* is to explain the origins of (class) inequality and to delegitimize conservative accounts that represent that inequality as natural. As such, it is clearly an exercise in *non-ideal* theory, in that he is expressly setting out to explain, demystify, and condemn the inequalities of an oppressive society, here class society. The "contract" is not the egalitarian inclusive contract of mainstream contract theory (though arguably, as noted, this contract is not really egalitarian and inclusive either!), but a contract of domination, that is hierarchical and exclusionary in character. Though the poor are conned into thinking that their rights will be respected (giving a whole new meaning to "con-tract"),[3] in reality the legal and political system established by the contract gives differential powers to the rich, and makes permanent, in the name of justice, the disadvantages of the poor.

One way of reading the two books, then, is as a linked account of what the major kind of social injustice is, how it ramifies through the sociopolitical order, and what measures would be necessary to avoid it. In Christopher Brooke's gloss:

> Rousseau's conjectural history of the emergence and the entrenchment of [inequality] in human society, presented in the *Discourse on the Origins of Inequality*, seeks to explain how humankind passed from an original state of contentment to one of degradation, corruption, and misery. . . . [F]or Rousseau it is . . . social existence that produces these bad effects in the first place, perverting natural *amour de soi* into awful *amour-propre*. . . . The democratic citizen republic of the *Social Contract* describes the institutions within which a people may live together without inflaming their *amour-propre*. The rough economic equality of citizens prevents the development of hierarchies and of certain forms of dependence and oppression. . . . Rousseau's politics deals with the collective moral transformation of an entire people. (2001: 110, 115–16)

So Rousseau's conceptual starting-point is the bad contract, the non-ideal domination (here class) contract, which then serves to guide his positive prescriptions for the good (general will) contract. The two are related in that the first serves as an antimodel for the second, and in that respect he is working within non-ideal theory. I want to follow Rousseau's precedent, but with a crucial difference (apart from my focus on race, that is). After introducing this innovation, Rousseau still – like Rawls – sets out to map an ideally just society, which is conceived of as separate from the first corrupt society. The additional innovation I am suggesting in this recommended shifting of contract justice away from ideal theory is to ask instead what would be necessary to transform the society *already* established by the first contract into a more just society, rather than, as he does, simply beginning anew with the second contract. (Obviously, this is not a realistic option for us.)

For the great virtue of the domination contract is that it identifies the ways in which an unjust basic structure affects not merely sociopolitical and economic institutions, but the psychology and the very nature of the human beings themselves enmeshed in these institutions and relations. It provides a "naturalized" account of the sociopolitical, as against the idealized account of Rawls, and thereby sensitizes us perceptually and

---

[3] I owe this wonderful line to my colleague Samuel Fleischacker, and wish I'd thought of it myself.

conceptually to what needs to be changed to make society more just. Rawls refers to his contract and the original position as an "expository device" (1999h: 19), a "device of representation" (1999d: 400), for ideal theory. I suggest that the domination contract can be thought of comparably as an "expository device/device of representation" in the realm of non-ideal theory for making vivid the extent to which the basic structure has been deformed by *injustice*, and orienting us to what corrective measures would be required to change it.

Rousseau's bad contract was, of course, one of class domination. I have argued in my work (Mills 1997, 1998a, 2003c) that race has been as central to the modern world as Rousseau claimed class was. And the implication, I contend, is that we need to change our contract apparatus. If racism was an "anomaly," then one can utilize the same conceptual framework endorsed by mainstream contract theorists (the United States as a raceless liberal democracy), since this framework is basically accurate. If, on the other hand, white racial domination/white supremacy was/is a well-established system in its own right, constitutive of the basic structure, then a new and distinct theorization of its logic will be required.

That this was in fact (and arguably still is) the case has been documented (outside of philosophy) by numerous theorists of race. Thus historian Leon Litwack points out: "America was founded on white supremacy and the notion of black inferiority and black unfreedom" (1998: xvi). Another historian, George Fredrickson, describes the United States as "a kind of *Herrenvolk* society in which people of color . . . are treated as permanent outsiders" (1981: xii). And political scientist Anthony Marx writes:

> Selective [racial] exclusion was not tangential to nation-state building, as liberals argue, but was instead central to how social order was maintained. . . . [B]y specifying to whom citizenship applies, states also define those outside the community of citizens, who then live within the state as objects of domination. . . . The original "deal" of a white coalition was made and remade, with outcomes varying to limit ongoing conflict. Indeed, such continued tensions kept alive the intrawhite dynamic refining racial domination in an ongoing process. (1998: 3, 5, 14)

Clearly, then, we need a philosophical concept adequate to this political picture: the founding and ongoing contract is better seen as a racial one, a "white coalition" which establishes white supremacy as the actual basic structure, and unfair white advantage as the norm. This reality is captured by the domination contract, which provides for us a corrective mapping of, an expository device for grasping, the *real* "basic structure." Not merely the obvious manifestations like educational and residential segregation, political majoritarianism, juridical bias, differentials in wealth, and racially coded occupations, but the very "construction" of whites and nonwhites out of previously unraced individuals, with all its implications for their typical moral psychologies, can also be seen as a consequence of the domination contract that likewise needs to be eliminated in the ideal contract. What are taken to be natural "racial" traits are products of the social order, as is race itself. But these traits do have a real influence on patterns of social interaction. Insofar as the achievement of justice requires the appropriate moral education of the citizens of the polity, this framework sensitizes us, in a way that Rawls's de-raced individualism does not, to the ways in which white domination will negatively affect whites' moral cognition, their capacities for transracial empathy, and their ability to relate justly to their fellow citizens of color.

So non-ideal theory then asks us to work out what would be required for the achievement of justice *against this background*. The deficiency of ideal theory is thus plainly brought to the fore: the problem does not inhere in the exploration of the ideal, since all moral theory necessarily deals with the ideal in some sense. The problem is the exploration of the ideal as an end in itself without ever turning to the question of what is morally required in the context of the radically deviant *non-ideal* actuality.

Repairing the Breach

Reparative racial justice as a matter of non-ideal theory, then, can be approached within the framework of repairing a "contract of breach." If the domination contract (in the case of race) is founded on a breach of respect for persons of color, a refusal to recognize them as full persons in the first place, then justice in reparations will require us to correct for this. Obviously, as just illustrated above, there will be many aspects to this "breach," and in fact I have argued elsewhere (Mills 2003f) that white racial domination/white supremacy has at least six dimensions: juridico-political, economic, cultural, somatic, cognitive-evaluative, and ontological. I will focus exclusively on the economic aspect here, but I would claim that these other dimensions of injustice can also be tackled via this approach.

The strategy is as follows. Rawls's great innovation of the "original position" and the "veil of ignorance" was designed to shift the traditionally controversial problem of moral choice, and what rationality required in that sphere, on to the less contested terrain (theoretically anyway) of prudential choice (not in general of course – just for the thought-experiment). The combination of self-interested motivation and ignorance of key features of oneself was supposed to provide a rough functional equivalent to other-regardingness. (In effect, you looked out for the other because you might be the other.) So the objectivity derives both from self-ignorance and social ignorance. People don't know whether they're white/nonwhite, male/female, rich/poor, ascetic/hedonistic, and so forth. They do "know the general facts about human society. They understand political affairs and the principles of economic theory; they know the basis of social organization and the laws of human psychology." But they "do not know the particular circumstances of their own society . . . its economic or political situation" (Rawls 1999h: 118–19). So they choose principles of justice self-interestedly on the basis of this ignorance and the fear that they might be disadvantaged in the resultant social order.

The alternative contractualism I am suggesting retains this key feature – self-ignorance – of the Rawlsian apparatus (cf. Okin 1989).[4] The crucial difference centers on the range of choices, and the extent of our *social* ignorance. We are not choosing an ideal "well-ordered" society, since that option is simply not open for us. Instead we are choosing, through a thinner veil (so our social ignorance is less), among various "ill-ordered" societies, all shaped to a greater or lesser extent by the legacy of white supremacy. The reason is, of course, that we are employing the veil to adjudicate matters of corrective justice. The point of retaining the descriptive contract – here as the "domination contract" – is then to model the sociopolitical reality that already exists. Ideal theory starts from ground zero; non-ideal theory starts from an already existing social order. So as with Rousseau, our starting-point is not the state of nature or its Rawlsian equivalent (the original position), but a particular social stage of an already-existing unjust society (the "later position"?).

The descriptive "racial contract" can then serve as a way of illustrating, dramatizing, and summarizing the non-ideal history involved (the actual workings of the state, the legal system, economic institutions, dominant white moral psychology, and so forth) that needs to be corrected for by the prescriptive normative contract. Precluded by the veil from knowing whether one is white or nonwhite, one would then have to choose prudentially among alternative societies evolving from that history, and based respectively on principles correcting strongly, weakly, or not at all, for its legacy. Such measures would not have been necessary in an ideal society because there would have been no discrimination to begin with. But here we are dealing with a non-ideal society, and

---

[4] So Tommie Shelby (2004: 1700 n10) gets me wrong when he claims that my critique of Rawls shows that I misunderstand the point of restrictions on self-knowledge behind the veil.

trying to make it better, as against (impossibly) constructing an ideal society from scratch. A "device of representation" appropriate for ideal theory needs to be altered to deal with non-ideal theory.

So what we are looking at here is patterns of economic distribution as they will have been affected by race. The debate about different patterns of economic distribution in Rawls is, of course, not at all new. Indeed it was central from the start to Rawls and the secondary literature on Rawls because "the principal economic and social arrangements" are among the "major institutions" that constitute the "basic structure of society" and "determine the division of advantages from social cooperation," thereby having a "profound" effect on people's life prospects (Rawls 1999h: 6–7). In particular, there are "especially deep inequalities" which are pervasive and "affect [people's] initial chances in life" (1999h: 7). Rawls's left-liberal/social-democratic concern about these inequalities is what motivates his difference principle and his radical "democratic" version of equality of opportunity, and in the original debate about *A Theory of Justice* (far less so for the more metatheoretically oriented *Political Liberalism* (1996)), the critique and defense of these claims was crucial. (In effect, this was one of the few concessions in the book to the "non-ideal": Rawls says explicitly that the difference principle, while "not the same as that of redress," "gives some weight to the considerations singled out by the principle of redress," and so "does achieve some of the intent of the latter principle" (1999h: 86–7).) In this respect, much of the secondary literature of the time could be plotted straightforwardly on a traditional left–right political spectrum of perspectives on class inequality, with Marxists and radical egalitarians arguing for greater equality while more traditional liberals, conservatives, and libertarians argued that Rawls's recommendations would illegitimately infringe on people's freedoms and property rights.

Now my suggestion is that with reference to the nontraditional (and hardly ever discussed) subject matter of *racial* economic inequalities, which obviously also have a very great and pervasive effect on people's life prospects, we can avoid most of these debates. The narrow focus on corrective racial justice, as against distributive justice in general, does *not* require us to take a stand on the wide range of positions in the secondary literature. Instead all we have to do, I claim, is to imagine ourselves behind the veil, but not in the original position of establishing an ideal society from ground zero, but rather of considering the possibility of ending up as a member of the subordinated races in a society whose basic structure *has already* been shaped by the racial contract.

So to repeat, an ideal non-racist society is not one of the available options. The choice is between various *non*-ideal options, and we have to make the best selection among them, given the reality of white supremacy as a common ancestral historic factor across all societal variants, and the motivation to eliminate or reduce as far as possible its legacy of racial economic disadvantage. (Not just for ourselves but for our children and grandchildren, since we represent "a continuing line of claims" (Rawls 1999h: 111). And if, for example, we turn out to be black, and the "one-drop rule" is retained, they will be black also.) For this limited purpose, and under the constraint of not violating the "overlapping consensus" of values and norms, I claim that (1) we would seek simply to eliminate illicit racial differentials; (2) we would need nothing more than a principle derivative from the weakest, least controversial sense of equality of opportunity – formal equality of opportunity – to achieve this goal.

(1)   To see how this case can be made, consider the following. Take three theories of distributive justice: egalitarian (E), Rawlsian justice-as-fairness (F), and libertarian (L), and assume that they are all non-racist theories. Now imagine as said that in a given society, there has been a history of racial injustice, so that one group, the R2s, have been systematically discriminated against by the R1s. Finally, let us suppose that the actual structuring of the society is neither according to E, nor F, nor L principles, but, as in the United States, an intermediate position I$_1$ that veers more toward the L model than the others, though with differential and inferior treatment for the R2s. So there are not only huge property differentials between classes,[5] but in addition huge property differentials between R1s and R2s, with R2s disproportionately concentrated at the bottom of the economic ladder.

What does corrective racial justice for the R2s require? Racial justice requires (analytically) the elimination of racial injustice. But the elimination of racial injustice does not require that the society be reorganized on E, F, or L principles, since that would take it out of the sphere of corrective justice to the different sphere of justice in general.[6] What racial justice requires is that people not be differentially and invidiously treated by race,[7] and that where such treatment has left a legacy, it

---

[5] Libertarians would, of course, deny that hugely unequal property differences follow from a free market situation, but the historical evidence is against them.

[6] Or at least it does not require it as a matter of logical necessity. I set aside here the interesting and important question of whether it might require such reorganization as a matter of social or political necessity, for example the traditional left claim that racism is functional for capitalism and so cannot be eliminated within a capitalist framework.

[7] It's necessary to include "invidiously," since where there has been racial injustice, corrective justice *will* require differential treatment by race.

should be corrected for. Assuming that E, F, and L are nondiscriminatory in their scope, meant to extend to the entire population, including
both R1s and R2s, then whatever their other differences as theories of
justice, they will agree on this. There is a core, a commonality of principle having to do with equal nonracist treatment, and it is this core that
is violated for all three theories by racial injustice, despite their wide
differences on other points. So racial justice will not require that distributive patterns be egalitarian, or Rawlsian, or libertarian (a nonpat-
tern, in this case), since advocates of the other two theories will
obviously contest this conception of justice. All it requires is that in the
new pattern, I_2, there not be invidious treatment of the R2s, and that
the legacy of past invidious treatment not be perpetuated.

In other words, the limited nature of racial justice must be appreciated. Racial justice is not supposed to be a comprehensive theory of
justice, capable of standing on its own. Racial justice is simply the correction of the differential and unfair treatment of an "inferior" race,
R2, *by the actual standards that prevailed in the polity* for the "superior"
race, R1. (The exception, of course, will be that subset of standards
themselves predicated on racial subordination, which now becomes
impermissible, for example the enslavement of others because of their
race.) These standards may well be unfair by other criteria and other
conceptions of justice, but that is not because of "racial" reasons, and
as such it is irrelevant to the debate. As Jules Coleman points out:

> [C]orrective or rectificatory justice is concerned with wrongful gains and
> losses. Rectification is, on this view, a matter of justice when it is necessary
> to protect a distribution of holdings (or entitlements) from distortions
> which arise from unjust enrichments or wrongful losses. The principle of
> corrective justice requires the annulment of both wrongful gains and
> losses. In order to invoke the principle of corrective justice . . . the distri-
> bution need not itself be just. (1983: 6)

The implication, then, is that a society could be racially just, but
unjust in other ways. Three societies organized on E, F, and L principles will respectively all be unjust for proponents of the other two conceptions of justice. But if they are nonracist societies, then egalitarians,
Rawlsians, and libertarians would be able to agree that they are all at
least *racially* just. Similarly, if a racially corrective I_2 reorganization of
the social order is brought about in the case posited above, then there
will still be huge property differentials between classes. So by egalitarian or Rawlsian standards, E or F, the society will still be grossly unjust.
But the point is that since there is now, say, proportional R1/R2 representation at all social levels, it is no longer *racially* unjust. An R2 capitalist whose business had been burned down by R1s in the I_1 order (as

actually happened to many black businesses in the early twentieth century, for example, in the famous 1921 Tulsa Riot, where the "Black Wall Street" was destroyed by white mobs (Hirsch 2002)) would deserve to be compensated for his loss. So in the new nonracial I_2 order, he would have his property restored, thereby becoming, by E standards, a member of the exploiting class that must be expropriated for social justice to be achieved. Yet, I would claim, an egalitarian committed to eliminating racial injustice – as part of transitional justice – would be morally bound to support this local restoration of private property, even if he would go on to argue globally – as a long-term ideal – that private property in the means of production should be eliminated.

So the debate about justice would continue, insofar as egalitarians and Rawlsians would challenge I_2 for its unfairness to the poor and the least advantaged. But these debates would not be about racial justice, since racial injustice (at least on this dimension) would have been eliminated. What may initially seem paradoxical and counterintuitive only appears so because we are thinking of racial justice in the same terms as egalitarian justice, Rawlsian justice, libertarian justice. Once it is appreciated that it is really in a different category, and its limited corrective nature is fully apprehended, the appearance of paradox should disappear. (Of course, the very fact that this conceptual separation is possible raises questions about Rawls's crucial claim that ideal theory "provides . . . the only basis for the systematic grasp of these more pressing problems [i.e. of non-ideal theory]" (1999h: 8), which is why we supposedly have to begin with it.)

(2)   Let us turn now to the second question of the principle of choice. Behind the veil, of course, one is choosing on prudential rather than moral grounds. Through a thinner veil than Rawls's, a veil that admits a knowledge more detailed than that of "general social facts," one makes a decision based on the possibility – the danger – of ending up as oneself (with one's heirs) a member (members) of the subordinated race, R2, in a range of societies all of which have R1-supremacy as their ancestor. So given the alternatives of no corrective measures, weak corrective measures, and strong corrective measures, one will presumably on self-interested grounds choose societies with stronger rather than weaker corrective measures, though weighed in some computation against the interests we would have if we ended up as R1s instead.

What, though, would this balance point be, and how would one uncontroversially determine it? (Remember here the general difficulties and wide spectrum of positions in normative rational choice theory, and the fierce debates about Rawls's claim in particular that one would use maximin (choosing the highest floor) as a principle of choice in his original position.) Moreover, the principles for rationally furthering one's interests chosen prudentially behind the veil need to converge, suitably translated, with principles of justice chosen morally outside of the veil. They should not be radically discrepant with a "reflective equilibrium" among what Rawls (1999b) would later characterize as an "overlapping consensus" of values in the Western democratic tradition. So the question is what principle would meet these criteria, especially given that the later Rawls (1999c) also argues that claims about justice must meet the test of "public reason," that is be capable of being put forward under conditions of pluralism, without assuming any "comprehensive doctrine," whether secular or religious. In other words, it is not merely a matter of finding a common liberal core among egalitarians, Rawlsians, and libertarians as liberals of a far-left, left, and right-wing variety. The normative core must be able to pass the test of meeting with the approval of nonliberals also (though excluding racists, obviously, and other proponents of "unreasonable" doctrines).

I suggest that for economic questions, which is our focus here, the principle that is indeed capable of meeting this test is "weak" formal equality of opportunity, and I will argue that once the realities mapped by the domination contract are taken into account, we will appreciate that in the context of white supremacy this seemingly innocuous principle has "strong," radical implications, and can in fact justify a case for reparations.

To make this argument, I need to begin by saying something about exploitation. Exploitation is, of course, antithetical to the Rawlsian ideal of society as "a cooperative venture for mutual advantage" among individual "persons" who for the most part recognize and act in accordance with fair principles of conduct (Rawls 1999h: 4). So one might expect that Rawls would provide an analysis of exploitation, if only as an illuminating antipode to be avoided. But in the 500+ pages of *A Theory of Justice*, his discussion is limited to a few sentences, couched in the language of neoclassical economic theory, about what happens when "factors of production" do not receive "their marginal products," so that "persons receive less than the value of their contribution." He concludes that "the notion of exploitation is out of place here," since that would imply "a deep injustice in the background system," which is precluded by his ideally just basic structure (1999h: 271–2).

Similarly, in his book *Exploitation*, Alan Wertheimer points out that liberal theorists have generally followed Rawls in his neglect and suggests three possible reasons for this lack of interest in the subject: the concept's historic associations with Marxism, contemporary liberalism's Rawls-inspired orientation toward ideal theory, and the fact that exploitation is typically a micro-level wrong while the focus of recent theorists on justice has been macro-issues of the fair distribution of rights and liberties, benefits and burdens, and resources (1996: ix, 8). But while I would completely agree with the first two, I would claim that the third is egregiously, question-beggingly wrong (except, perhaps, as a revelation of what mainstream white liberals like Wertheimer believe to be the case) and perfectly illustrates my point at the start about the sanitization by white political philosophers of the actual historical record. Clearly in the treatment of people of color, macro-level questions of unfairness *have* been involved, since in such economic practices as Aboriginal expropriation, slavery, and Jim Crow, rights, liberties, benefits, burdens, and resources have not been fairly distributed, and entire populations have been deprived of their just entitlements. Whites as a group have subordinated people of color as a group (Native Americans, blacks, Mexican-Americans, Asians) for unfair white advantage.

Obviously, then, the kind of economic transactions (if it makes sense to characterize Aboriginal expropriation and African slavery as "transactions") typical of the actual American polity in its founding and evolution do not remotely conform to the Rawlsian ideal of "a cooperative venture for mutual advantage." Rather, as I have argued in greater detail elsewhere (Mills 2004), these practices are more meaningfully thought of as part of a historic pattern of *racial exploitation*, predicated on and justified by the inferiority of nonwhites. To say that they are non-ideal "deviations" from the norm radically misconstrues the reality. They are guided by completely *different* norms (the norms of the domination contract), norms that take moral inequality and the legitimacy of the differential and inferior treatment of nonwhites for granted. So group rather than individual relations are the crucial ones. If, in Ruth Sample's (2003a) formulation, exploitation involves unfair benefit resulting from degrading treatment that does not recognize the other's personhood, then obviously the experience of people of color in the United States – as an inferior group seen as less than fully human – is a paradigm case of racial exploitation.

Now the important implication of this revisionist account is that one gets a picture very much like the Marxist portrayal of class society, in which group exploitation is central to society's workings, since Rawlsian primary goods like "rights, liberties, and opportunities, and income and wealth" (Rawls 1999h: 54) are continually being "transferred" from the subordinated to the privileged group rather than being distributed equitably. But the difference in this case, of course, is that the social groups in question are *races*, and the claim that the "basic structure" is unjust, resting on systemic exploitation and thereby reproducing illicit privilege and disadvantage at two poles, does *not* require controversial or discredited Marxist notions like the labor theory of value, but simply the consistent, "color-blind" application of *mainstream* norms. So once white supremacy is recognized as a system in itself, established by the racial contract, its condemnation by any "reasonable" conception of justice should be straightforward. Yet because of the idealized picture of US history hegemonic among mainstream normative theorists (wonderfully illustrated by the Wertheimer reference above), this pervasive pattern of racial exploitation has not even been acknowledged, let alone theorized as such in the literature.

Moreover, by contrast with the individualist focus of the mainstream contract, the domination contract points us toward resulting *group advantage*, the ways in which whites as a group are illicitly benefited by racial exploitation. Racial exploitation is unjust enrichment, a kind of racial *pleonexia* – in Rawls's gloss of Aristotle, "gaining some advantage for oneself by seizing what belongs to another . . . or by denying a person that which is due to him" (Rawls 1999h: 9). Through various mechanisms that have only recently begun to be adequately documented by sociologists and economists – slavery, the denial to the freedmen of their promised 40 acres and a mule, Jim Crow, debt peonage, land theft, trade union exclusion, the restriction of job opportunities and the imposition of ceilings on promotions in those jobs permitted, the blocking through housing segregation of an equal chance to build wealth, the refusal of bank loans, the outright destruction by white mobs of black businesses, unequal allocation of educational resources with the corresponding limitation on possibilities for building human capital, inequitable transfer payments by the state, market discrimination in goods and services, relocation of jobs and industries on the basis of a racialized geography, and many others – blacks have been denied an equal chance to succeed, and whites have benefited from this (America 1990; Massey and Denton 1993; Oliver and Shapiro 1995; Lipsitz 1998; Conley 1999; L. Williams 2003; T. Shapiro 2004; Katznelson 2005).

Charles Tilly has coined the useful phrase "opportunity hoarding" to describe this situation, when "members of a group acquire and monopolize access to valuable resources or privileges" (cited in M. Brown et al. 2003: 17). The virtue of this concept is that it takes discrimination out of an individualist paradigm and makes the causal link between black failure and white success: the "diverging fates of black and white Americans" are conceptualized within the "same analytic framework":

> Discussions of racial inequality commonly dwell on only one side of the color line. We talk about *black* poverty, *black* unemployment, *black* crime, and public policies for *blacks*. We rarely, however, talk about the gains

whites receive from the troubles experienced by blacks. . . . In our view, the persistence of racial inequality stems from the long-term effects of labor market discrimination and institutional practices that have created cumulative inequalities by race. The result is a durable pattern of racial stratification. Whites have gained or *accumulated* opportunities, while African Americans and other racial groups have lost opportunities – they suffer from *disaccumulation* of the accoutrements of economic opportunity. (M. Brown et al. 2003: 22)

Similarly, in their important and prizewinning book *Black Wealth/ White Wealth*, Melvin Oliver and Thomas Shapiro conclude that: "Just as blacks have had 'cumulative disadvantages,' whites have had 'cumulative advantages.' Practically, every circumstance of bias and discrimination against blacks has produced a circumstance and opportunity of positive gain for whites. . . . [A] focus on job opportunity is not sufficient to the task of eradicating racial disadvantage in America." Instead what is necessary is "to close the wealth gap" (1995: 51, 177).

For perhaps the clearest manifestation of this history of exploitation is differentials in wealth. At the time of the 1863 Emancipation Proclamation, blacks owned only 0.5 percent of US wealth, unsurprising considering that most blacks were slaves. But by 1990 – more than a century later, after all the civil rights legislation of the 1950s and 1960s, and the seeming dramatic progress in blacks' national status – this figure had only risen to 1 percent, though black Americans make up more than 12 percent of the US population (Conley 1999: 25). Or, looking at it another way: according to the most recent available figures (2004), the median white household has a net worth (assets minus debts) that is a startling ten times the figure for the median black household. Moreover the white-to-black ratio for median financial wealth (liquid and semi-liquid assets, including mutual funds and pensions) is even more remarkable: more than *100 to 1* (Mishel et al. 2006: 258–9). And the overall implication of this huge differential in wealth – along, of course, with continuing segregation, inferior education, and discrimination – is that white life-chances of getting good jobs and opportunities will be significantly greater than black life-chances.

Against this background, let us now examine how Rawls partitions his discussion of equality of opportunity. He distinguishes three ways in which people may lack equal opportunity: they are discriminated against by law and/or custom;[8] they come from a disadvantaged class background and so do not get an equal educational chance to develop their natural talents; they are born with a thinner bundle of natural

---

[8] Actually, Rawls does not mention custom, but this is a standard extension of the formulation to which I assume he would not object.

talents in the first place (1999h: 62–73). Correspondingly, he demarcates three varieties of equality of opportunity: formal (no discrimination: people have "the same legal rights of access to all advantaged social positions" (1999h: 62); fair (no discrimination + compensatory measures for class disadvantage: "those with similar abilities and skills should have similar life chances" (1999h: 63); and democratic (fair equality of opportunity + the difference principle: "the distribution of income and wealth" should not "be settled by the distribution of natural assets" (1999h: 64). He himself endorses the third of these, which requires compensatory measures not merely for disadvantaged class positions but also for natural deficiencies, and this of course is what makes his position a radically redistributivist one condemned as unjust both by more traditional liberals and libertarians. But my point is that we do not have to take such a controversial position to achieve the correction of racial injustice. Focused on ideal theory, and in any case intellectually blinded by the analysis of the United States through traditional European class categories, Rawls does not see how his cartography needs to be revised once white supremacy and the reality of systemic racial exploitation are taken into account.

I suggest that the non-ideal reality mapped by the domination contract and the concept of racial exploitation requires a partitioning of inequality of opportunity into at least *four* categories. Obviously the differential opportunity disadvantage suffered by R2s and their children is not (except for racists) due to their inherently inferior natural abilities, so this is not an example of Rawls's third category. But it needs to be appreciated that it is not an example of his second category either. Rawls's implicit reference group here is really the white working class. But while for Marxists, class disadvantage may be the result of exploitation, this is not conceded in a mainstream liberal framework. White working-class children will be poorer, and thus handicapped, but assuming there has been neither force nor fraud, this disadvantage is fair given the standard liberal picture of individual market competition, and an outcome of winners and losers, the former of whom can then legitimately pass on differential advantages to their children. So because the poor have lost fairly (by mainstream standards), it is *unfortunate*, but not *unjust*, that their children should be socially handicapped. (I am not endorsing this view myself, merely emphasizing that racial disadvantage is conceptually different.) Entitlement to our natural assets, and to the proceeds of those assets, trumps needs-based claims; the property rights of the winners override demands for equalization of opportunity. So not only "democratic" but also "fair" equality of opportunity would be opposed by theorists to the right of Rawls's social-democratic left-liberalism, who would only recognize as legitimate the first – "formal" – kind of equality of opportunity. (Indeed some far-right figures, like Richard Epstein, would repudiate even this variety.)

In the case under consideration here, though, R2s and their children inherit a disadvantaged position that, as argued above, is *not* the result of fair market competition, *but of discriminatory practices wrong by mainstream standards, and their cumulative outcome over decades.* So this kind of inequality of opportunity is not the result of subordinate class membership in the colorless sociopolitical systems of white social contract theory, but of subordinate *racial* membership in a polity of a white-supremacist kind which is not conceptually recognized, let alone theorized, by mainstream contract theory. The children of the R2s have *not* lost fairly by mainstream liberal standards – they have lost because of practices that in a (de-racialized) liberal framework are unjust. So if they inherit a disadvantaged position (their parents have fewer resources, they get inferior schooling, they live in the ghetto far from the better jobs, and so forth) then this should count as a denial of equal opportunity on *weak* and uncontroversial rather than strong and controversial grounds. But their situation is not covered by Rawls's first category in its unmodified form, since the likelihood is that as a result of these negative factors, their credentials *will* be inferior. So even if formal equality of opportunity is implemented they will often not be competitive with R1s. In other words, though equally qualified candidates will, given this policy, have the same employment chances, independently of race, many R2s will continue to lose through having weaker credentials that are themselves the result of earlier discrimination against their parents. The R2 candidate loses out to the R1 candidate apparently "fairly," under conditions of formal equality of opportunity, because the R1 candidate's credentials are better. But the reason for this edge (in most cases) is *the history of inherited advantages that come from systemic and intergenerational racial exploitation.*

What this shows, then, is that we need a fourth category to cover these cases of "opportunity hoarding," where whites have an illicit advantage that comes about through the inherited legacy of past discriminatory practices sanctioned by law and/or custom. And such a category is extendable, I would claim, from *weak* formal equality of opportunity, once this uncontroversial mainstream value is applied to circumstances that Rawls himself, because of his ideal theory focus, did not envisage. The first kind of formal equality of opportunity, which is the only one Rawls recognizes, proscribes discrimination by law or custom at the point of assessment of candidates' credentials (R1s and R2s). The second – derivative – kind that I am arguing for would proscribe in addition the admission of R1s' differential and superior credentials when they arise illicitly out of that history of discrimination against R2s by law or custom. (And note, to repeat, that this is conceptually distinct from class inequalities in a colorless capitalist economy, and Rawls's "fair" equality of opportunity as a corrective left-liberal measure.)

In practice, of course, we would not be able to make this determination on an individual basis; the point is rather to establish the conceptual groundwork for justifying on the macro-level the corrective public policy measures that would be required to make the "basic structure" less unjust once the history and long-term effects of white supremacy are conceded. Since Rawls himself admits that "the distribution resulting from voluntary market transactions will not in general be fair unless the antecedent distribution of income and wealth and the structure of the market are fair" (1999e: 257), this extrapolation should be completely consonant with his own principles. Formal equality of opportunity in a racial polity needs to be thought of as having two dimensions.

The case for reparations, then, can be based on at least two (linked) grounds: (a) the ending of present racial exploitation, and the redistribution of the unjust proceeds of past racial exploitation (since the Rawlsian society is supposed to be a non-exploitative "cooperative venture for mutual advantage"); (b) the achievement in both its aspects of formal equality of opportunity – the least controversial kind of equality of opportunity, which should be endorsed by public reason as a common principle in all "reasonable" views, and which requires no "comprehensive doctrines" for its justification.

Thus, Oliver and Shapiro end *Black Wealth/White Wealth* with the conclusion that to eliminate the "artificial head start accorded to practically all whites," racial reparations are a possible "practical and moral approach," though it should be just "the first step in a collective journey to racial equality" (1995: 188–9). Similarly, in *Being Black, Living in the Red*, Dalton Conley points out that antidiscrimination measures against *present-day* discrimination will not be sufficient to eliminate illicit white advantage. He goes on to argue that the cycle of continuing black disadvantage is no longer primarily, or at all, a result of continuing market discrimination, but rather the product of the fact that median black assets are such a small fraction of median white assets, which is the result of *past* discrimination:

> What these results indicate is that merely creating equal opportunity in the housing, securities, and credit markets will not do to rectify the racial imbalance because parental asset levels (which were presumably fixed in the past) engender advantages and disadvantages that are very important for the next generation. . . . [M]erely eliminating remaining discrimination – be it individual or institutional – will do little to alleviate the wealth gap, which has already been set into intergenerational motion. Only a

radical, progressive, wealth-based policy will redress the issue. . . . While young African Americans may have the *opportunity* to obtain the same education, income, and wealth as whites, in actuality they are on a slippery slope, for the discrimination their parents faced in the housing and credit markets sets the stage for perpetual economic disadvantage. (1999: 53, 152)

And he too concludes by considering reparations as one appropriate policy option.

What I have tried to show, then, is that social contract theory can indeed be helpful in theorizing issues of racial justice, but that the conventional approach needs to be modified. Racial justice is pre-eminently a matter of non-ideal theory, and correspondingly requires a modification of the orthodox contractual apparatus, producing a "device of representation" – the racial contract – that accurately maps the non-ideal realities in question rather than unhelpfully abstracting away from them. Behind the veil, it would no longer be a matter of choosing self-interestedly, under conditions of ignorance of one's race, an ideal polity, for obviously a nondiscriminatory polity will be the preferred choice. But as argued, this is not enough to guide us in determining what corrective justice now requires in a polity whose basic structure *has* been founded on systemic discrimination and racial exploitation. The thought-experiment here would be to imagine what one would prudentially choose to correct for the disadvantage of being born a member of the subordinated race in such a polity.

I have argued that because of the peculiar nature of racial justice, such a correction requires only a derivative form of the weakest kind of equality of opportunity, the kind that in theory should be unobjectionable across the political spectrum. So paradoxically, in one sense the prescriptions are far less radical than Rawls's own, since one is only asking that formal equality of opportunity be implemented (not the difference principle, or even the less extreme "fair" equality of opportunity), and the legacy of its lack be corrected for. But from this seemingly weak requirement, very strong and dramatic conclusions follow, since a case can then be made that reparations in the form of the transfer of wealth are morally required for justice and the realization of genuine formal equality of opportunity for the racially subordinated.

Moreover, whereas Rawls's response against centrist and right-wing criticisms had to take the form of a controversial repudiation of any role for desert, a violation of strong Lockean property rights, and a metaphysics of the self that some critics have found incompatible with his original ostensible commitment to robust Kantian personhood, corrective justice in this modified contractualism needs no such assumptions.

Rather, property rights *are* being respected – indeed with far greater seriousness than in contemporary right-wing discussions, insofar as illicitly acquired property based on racial exploitation would then be returned to its owners or their heirs (Boxill 2003) – while desert and Kantian personhood need not be modified for the argument to go through, since normatively it depends just on a weak equality of opportunity accepted across the board by all "reasonable" views. The key premises are really the factual ones that assert the historic reality and continuing legacy in its many different manifestations of white supremacy. If white political philosophers are serious about social justice, then it is time for them to begin to acquaint themselves with these facts and to swear off the addictive evasions of ideal theory.

POSTSCRIPT: The Difference Principle and Race

I want to address the objection that (assuming equal liberties to be guaranteed by the antidiscriminatory first principle) the difference principle is all that is needed to deal with issues of racial justice, so my recommended modifications are not in fact necessary. (I thank George Klosko of the University of Virginia for pressing me on this point.) My response would be that the difference principle cannot do the job because (1) it is too strong; (2) it is too weak; (3) it is conceptually and normatively inappropriate.

   (1) Even if the difference principle could handle the issue, its assumptions (the moral arbitrariness of our natural assets and consequent irrelevance of "desert") are far too strong. As earlier argued, the desideratum for a principle of racial justice is that it be acceptable across the political spectrum of "reasonable" (nonracist) views. But only those on the left-liberal end of the spectrum accept Rawls's position; traditional liberals, centrists, and the right reject it. It should not be a prerequisite for endorsing racial (corrective) justice that one has to endorse a left-liberal position on distributive justice. Rather, what we want is an uncontroversial, more minimalist position that can be accepted by all committed to redressing racial inequities. The difference principle cannot fulfill this role. (Though less extreme, "fair" equality of opportunity is also controversial for the political right.)

   (2) But in any case, the difference principle cannot handle the issue because it is too weak. It is targeted at the "least advantaged" (Rawls 1999h: 266), and as such, will not extend to middle-class blacks who are better off than their "underclass" brothers and sisters, but who nonetheless are worse off than they would have been without the legacy of racial discrimination against their ancestors. Their situation may not be as urgent as those lower down the socioeconomic ladder, but, as Bernard

Boxill (1992) has emphasized, they are entitled to racial justice nonetheless.

(3) Finally, and perhaps most importantly, the difference principle is simply conceptually and normatively inappropriate. Rawls is quite clear that "the difference principle is not of course the principle of redress" (1999h: 86). But redress is precisely what is called for here. "Redress" is *rectificatory/reparative* justice, the measures called for when a wrong has been committed which needs to be corrected, and as such a part of *non-ideal* theory. The difference principle is a principle for *distributive* justice under *ideal* theory, where there has been no past history of wrongdoing. (Cf. Roberts 2002a.) Someone born physically handicapped and someone born into a socially stigmatized and oppressed race are both disadvantaged, but the nature of the disadvantage is very different. To conceptually assimilate them because in both cases justice might require a transfer of resources is to conflate heterogeneous cases that need to be clearly distinguished. Rawls points out that "[t]he natural distribution is neither just nor unjust. . . . These are simply natural facts" (1999h: 87). The situation of blacks, by contrast, is a *social* fact, and an obviously unjust one, resulting from a history of past discrimination. Moreover, full rectificatory justice would arguably require measures additional to a material transfer of resources, such as an official apology for slavery from the United States government (Roberts 2002a), rewritings of national narratives (McCarthy 2002, 2004), and transformations of white moral psychology to end the social "dissin' " of blacks in the national moral economy. None of these issues arise for ideal theory because, to repeat, ideal theory is focused on a perfectly just society. So when Rawls later writes in his unfinished *Justice as Fairness* that "distinctions of . . . race give rise to further relevant positions to which a special form of the difference principle applies" (2001: 66), I would have to say that, absent further details, this is either a contradiction of his original statement, or a gesture towards a *revision* of the difference principle ("a special form") for specific application in non-ideal theory. But if the latter is the case, my point still holds, since I was referring to the difference principle in its familiar, ideal-theory version, not a difference principle modified to deal with redress. Rawls's remark would then be an intriguing theoretical promissory note that unfortunately, because of his death, will never be redeemed.

5

Race, Sex, and Indifference

Carole Pateman

Voters in Alabama were asked in 2000 to vote on a constitutional amendment to eliminate a provision prohibiting interracial marriage. This had remained on the books although in 1967 the US Supreme Court, in *Loving v. Virginia*, had finally declared such laws to be unconstitutional and a Federal District Court judge had told Alabama in 1970 that the provision could not be enforced. The amendment passed, with 40 percent of voters against it.

In December 2003, Essie Mae Washington-Williams revealed at the age of 78 that she was the daughter of Strom Thurmond who had died in June, aged 100. Thurmond, a member of the United States Senate for 48 years, was for most of his life one of the most prominent supporters of racial segregation. Washington-Williams's mother, Carrie Butler, was the Thurmond family's black maidservant and only 16 when she gave birth. Thurmond never publicly acknowledged the existence of his daughter.

About 1,200 Danish couples were living in Malmo in Sweden in 2004 because they were partners in "mixed" marriages. In early 2006 about 60 couples were moving there each month. Changes to Danish immigration law in 2002 included requirements about housing, finance and family reunion that make it very difficult for interracial partners to remain in Denmark.

The sexual and racial contracts have been intimately connected since modern states (civil societies) began to be created in the seventeenth century and the three dimensions of the original contract – social, sexual, and racial – have cut across and reinforced each other. The state has upheld laws and policies that have consolidated structures of racial and sexual power, the sexual contract has been refracted through race, the racial contract has shaped sexual relations, and both contracts have structured citizenship. Modern civil societies developed as patriarchal "racial states" (Goldberg 2002). It not possible fully to understand or analyze either the major institutions of modern civil societies or the construction of the world system of modern states without reference to both race and sex. The idea of "race" and the conviction that women must be governed by men became interwoven social and political forces that were at the heart of structures of power and subordination and molded the beliefs and lives of individuals.

My analysis in *The Sexual Contract* (and chapter 2 of this volume on the settler contract) are tied more closely to early modern theories of an original contract than is Charles Mills's conception of the racial contract. I confined my argument to Britain, the United States, and Australia, societies that can plausibly be seen as contractual "civil societies" (the modern political order created to replace "the state of nature"). Mills ranges much more widely: "the Racial Contract is *global*." I agree, but part company with him when he writes of the application of "the social contract" to "non-Europe, where it becomes the Racial Contract" (Mills 1997: 20, 42). My argument is not that the "social contract" becomes the racial contract, or that the latter has separately to be applied. The racial contract is one dimension of the original contract and shapes Britain as well as British colonies, although in a different fashion. Most colonies were not seen as *terra nullius* and transformed wholesale in the manner of (what became) the United States, Canada, or Australia (see chapter 2 above). Rather, British rulers made enough changes to allow power and control to be exercised and wealth extracted. Thus, I agree with Mills that economic exploitation is central to the racial contract, but I do not see it as "the *most* salient" aspect (Mills 1997: 32). Sexual difference is just as important for the racial contract.

My approach here is, for the most part, similar to my book. I use selected historical illustrations – this time from Britain and the United States – to show connections between the sexual and racial contracts and to provide a context to consider the relationship today. I refer to "illustrations" because an adequate discussion of the extraordinarily complex interrelationship between the sexual and racial contracts cannot possibly be undertaken in a single chapter. In section IV I broaden my discussion to include economic exploitation, move to the present and to a more diffuse sense of "contract", and draw on Norman Geras's (1998) argument about the contract of mutual indifference.

The concepts of race and racism are often conflated but my discussion here is not about racism. My interest is in the development of the idea of race as part of the structure of a modern state. "Race" is necessary for and breeds racism, which remains a major problem, anti-Arab racism being one of its most prominent recent manifestations; the UN World Conference Against Racism in 2001 was surrounded by clamor and controversy.

"Race" developed differently in the United States and Britain and this further complicates any discussion. In the United States, founded in slavery and the forcible seizure of the territory of Native peoples, racial segregation was enforced by law until the 1960s. British racial conceptions and practices were played out in the context of a vast, diverse empire (initially including the American colonies) in which, as Linda Colley (2002) has recently stressed, the British rulers were a small minority.[1] There was also a metropolitan black population; by the late eighteenth century there were at least 10,000 blacks in London, including a small middle class.[2]

I "Race" and Reproduction

From the early modern period onward, "race" became the vehicle through which certain groups of humans were deemed to be inferior, to be at the margins of humankind or even outside of humanity altogether. Accounts of differences between groups of people and between men and women have a long history but familiar, modern conceptions of "sex" and "race" began to be developed in the seventeenth and eighteenth centuries, together with theories about the stages of "civilization." Indeed, theorists of an original contract played an important part in the emergence of modern ideas about racial and sexual differences and hierarchies, albeit that their theories were couched in the subversive language of universal freedom and equality.

Kant's arguments are of particular interest. In *The Sexual Contract* I discussed his endorsement of the subordination of women, and Robert Bernasconi (2001a, 2002) has argued that he was the first philosopher to develop a concept of race, in the sense of a clearly defined notion

[1] Colley argues that in "all sorts of ways" the British Empire "remains an unknown quantity" and that anyone interested in the Empire needs to understand "Britain itself, the ways in which it was once powerful, but also the ways in which its power overseas was always constrained and sometimes faltered" (2002: 374, 375). It is also worth noting that the first act of the new Australian federal parliament in 1901 was to create immigration restrictions to maintain "white Australia."

[2] One of its best-known members was Olaudah Equiano; another was Ignatius Sancho, born a slave and brought to Britain as a child, who argued against slavery, became a writer, a shopkeeper, correspondent of Laurence Sterne and was painted by Gainsborough (see King et al. 1997).

with scientific status (see also Eze 1997a).[3] Kant upheld both the sexual and racial contracts, but now that attention has been drawn to embarrassing aspects of his arguments, two common responses are to detach the offending parts from his major principles and arguments or to explain them away.[4] But these strategies ignore his characterization of women and Africans and that he lectured and published on the subject of race for several decades (see: Kant 1965, 1978, 2000, 2001).

For Kant, the concept of race, like the Idea of marriage, is necessary; it is dictated by reason from "the viewpoint of natural history." This viewpoint deals with the "natural science of origins" and so is much more than a description of nature (Kant 2001: 40; see also Kant 2000: 13 n1). The crucial racial differences are permanent and they arise from reproduction and descent. Kant argued that there were "original seeds of the human line of descent" and, together with hereditary predispositions, these were implanted for the purpose of peopling the earth (2001: 42). The seeds and predispositions produced the different races of humans (in "Of the Different Human Races" he distinguishes four).[5] In principle, the assumption about innate seeds implies nothing about the worth of the human races to which they give rise; all seeds could produce races of equal value despite some fundamental variations among them. Kant, however, makes it clear that white men are the only individuals who possess the capacities required to grasp the universal principles fundamental to civil society and thus the capacities to govern others.[6] The natural attributes of nonwhite races and women were widely seen in similar terms; in particular, both were seen to lack or have a lesser capacity for reason and self-government. By the late eighteenth century, questions about such issues as why Africans were black, whether or not humans all descended from one original couple as laid down in the

---

[3] Bernasconi (2001a: 15) notes that this argument was first put forward in the 1920s. The relation between Kant's arguments about race and the *Critique of Judgment* has been acknowledged by some scholars, including one of his contemporaries; Bernasconi provides some references (2001a: 27 n84). He also states that "a great deal more work needs to be done, both to establish the context of Kant's discussion of race with reference to his sources and to clarify the various aspects of Kant's theory of race that have been treated largely in isolation from each other" (2001a: 15).

[4] See, e.g., Hill and Boxill (2000) for an example of the first response, and Ladd (1999) for an example of the second.

[5] The role of climate in the development of races was much discussed, and one claim was that different environments were the cause of racial differences. Kant argues for the differential development of the seeds over long periods through lines of descent in hot, cold, etc., climates.

[6] Kant is not entirely consistent. He criticized the doctrine of *terra nullius* but left doors open for the justification of colonization, and his view of slavery was ambiguous.

Bible (monogenesis vs polygenesis), and how human beings were to be classified had become matters of extensive debate and controversy. "Races" began to be seen as distinct human groupings, recognizable by such markers as skin color, hair texture, skulls, facial features, and specific dispositions and attributes.

The early eighteenth century, and the development of slavery as a condition suffered only by Africans, marked a turning point. From the beginning of the seventeenth century significant numbers of Britons had been captured by corsairs from Barbary and sometimes enslaved, which made it hard to see slavery in racial terms. But in 1672, the Royal Africa Company was established in Britain with a government monopoly to supply African labor to the colonies, and "after the 1730s, slavery became rhetorically established as a polar opposite to Britishness" (Colley 2002: 64). Or, in other words, freedom became signified by a white skin.

The *blackness* of (sub-Saharan) Africans became perceived, in itself, as a mark of lesser humanity. Europeans came to believe that they were *white* and hence superior. "Black" Africans were decisively marked out from "white" Europeans and the civilization and freedom of whites. By the early eighteen century, lifetime servitude was established for black, but not white, indentured laborers in Virginia (see section II). As Europeans seized more overseas territories and imposed colonial rule, the belief in white superiority fostered a consciousness among other "races" that they were "nonwhite." My historical illustrations are drawn from "white" and "black" since this antinomy – and Africa – lies at the heart of the construction of the political fiction of race. Other developments in the United States, such as the prohibition of Chinese immigration from 1882 until 1944, the expulsion of nearly half a million Mexican American citizens and Mexican nationals across the border between 1931 and 1935, and the internment of most Japanese American citizens in camps during the Second World War, were an outgrowth of the initial creation of a racial order of "whites" who ruled over "blacks."

In the late nineteenth and early twentieth century, fairs, ethnological exhibitions, and "human zoos" (Bancel et al. 2000) provided a graphic portrayal of white beliefs about "race." Various displays were prompted by the Crystal Palace exhibition in London in 1851. In the United States, 100 million people attended the world fairs held between 1876 and 1916 (D. King 2005: 39).[7] By the early twentieth century, "the world on view at the fairs had been anthropologized and racialized according

---

[7] At the Columbian Exposition in Chicago in 1893 black Americans were included in the exhibits. Six African-American women spoke at the World's Congress of Representative Women, part of the Exposition but, Hazel Carby argues, this was not from "concern to provide a black political presence but part of a discourse of exoticism that pervaded the fair" (1987: 5).

to social Darwinian taxonomies provided by leading lights of the anthropology profession" (Rydell 2002: 224). Exhibitions of humans included reconstructions of colonial victories. In France the stocking of displays before the First World War followed overseas conquests: "Tuaregs were exhibited in Paris after the French conquest of Timbuktu in 1894, and the first Malagasies appeared a year after the occupation of Madagascar. The exhibition of Amazons from Abomey followed the defeat of King Behanzin in Dahomey" (Bancel et al. 2000: 9). Nor have echoes of such exhibitions entirely died away. In 2005 there was an outcry in Germany after Augsburg Zoo put on a show of African culture and featured a dance display next to a cage containing baboons (Pancevski 2005).

Human racial exhibitions were also sexual curiosities. The most (in)famous example is that of Saartjie Baartman, labeled the "Hottentot Venus," who was a member of the Khoisan people from the Cape of South Africa. She, and particularly her large buttocks and genitalia, was displayed in London and Paris from 1810; doctors and anthropologists examined her. Robert Wedderburn, a Jamaican abolitionist, was instrumental in a case being brought against her exhibition in London on the grounds that it was indecent and tantamount to slavery, but the court rejected the claim, ruling that she had freely entered a contract. Baartman died aged 25, and after her death she was dissected and her remains put on display until 1976 in the Musée de l'Homme in Paris. Nelson Mandela finally succeeded in obtaining her return to South Africa after he became President.

A good deal of effort and some remarkable contortions were required to fit people into a tidy racial classification. Who counted as "white," and thus privileged, was the most difficult problem. Perhaps the best-known proclamation of whiteness is when Japanese in South Africa under apartheid were deemed honorary whites for economic reasons. The whiteness of immigrants to the United States from Ireland and Southern and Eastern Europe was in question for a long time.[8] In 1790, shortly after ratification of the United States constitution, Congress limited naturalization to "free white persons." From the 1870s a series of cases was brought to decide which applicants for naturalization counted as white.[9] Naturalization and citizenship involved both the racial and sexual contracts. On the one hand, if a woman was not

[8] Charles Kingsley, a Briton, put the Irish on a lower level in a different fashion. He wrote to his wife of a visit to Ireland, "I am haunted by the human chimpanzees I saw . . . to see white chimpanzees is dreadful; if they were black, one would not feel it so much" (quoted in McClintock 1995: 216).

[9] Haney López (1996) discusses the numerous cases; see especially *Ozawa v. United States* 260 U.S. 178 (1922) and *United States v. Thind* 261 U.S. 204 (1923).

"white" and so ineligible for naturalization she did not, despite coverture, take on the citizenship of an American husband. On the other hand, even if eligible she could not be naturalized if her husband was ineligible (see also Cott 2000: 165).

John Stuart Mill remarked in his *Subjection of Women* (1989 [1869]) that the elaborate social and political stratagems and intimidation required to keep women in their place demonstrated that there was nothing natural about subjection. In one sense, the belief that women's subordination springs directly from biology is more plausible than analogous claims about racial differences. A basic fact about humans is that women, not men, become pregnant and give birth. Human reproduction provides a biological thread running through sexual difference. But it is a very thin thread indeed and is far too slender to bear the weight placed upon it by patriarchal conceptions of sexual difference, views of proper relations between the sexes and women's place in the world. These are not entailed by biology but matters of culture, politics, and power. That is to say, as Mill saw (and as I argued in *The Sexual Contract*), "masculinity" and "femininity" are political constructs.

"Race" is also a political construct, and more completely so than alleged sexual difference. Like an original contract, it is a political fiction, a "rational absurdity" (Gilroy 2000: 14; see also Appiah 2000). Race has no natural or scientific basis. The "science" of race, which reached its peak in the racial classifications of the nineteenth century, was challenged as soon as it began to be developed – Herder, for example, took a different position from Kant – and has been largely discredited since the Second World War; UNESCO rejected a biological basis for race in 1948. A further blow has come from recent advances in genetics which show that variations between human populations are not much greater than genetic variation within those same populations (which is not to deny that some humans are, for example, more genetically susceptible to certain diseases than others). And people are, so to speak, voting with their feet in increasing numbers by forming interracial partnerships.[10]

---

[10] In the United States a movement has begun for the recognition of a "mixed race" category for official purposes (Hollinger 2005). About 12 percent of young people fall into this category, and by 2050 perhaps 10 percent of whites and blacks and over half of Latinos, Asians, and American Indians will marry outside their "race" (Hochschild 2005: 76). Census Bureau projections indicate that whether or not whites remain a numerical majority depends on whether Latinos who identify as "white" on the Census are so counted. If they are not, by 2050 whites are likely to be a numerical minority (Haney López 2005: 43; on Census categories see also Prewitt 2005). One British survey found that, of respondents who had a partner, half of the British Caribbean men and a fifth of British Indian men had a white partner and so did a third of the British Caribbean women (Modood 1998: 387).

Nonetheless, race is popularly seen in biological terms as a matter of "blood." Blood was used in law to classify individuals according to race in the United States. As recently as 1974 the Supreme Court of Louisiana upheld the view that anyone with 1/32 of African blood was black (Allen 1994: 27–8). Now, bloodlines are lines of descent – and here is the point at which human reproduction enters and sex and race come inextricably together. If the idea of race is to have social and political purchase, then populations perceived in racial terms have to maintain themselves over time. Women must have babies if a population is to continue; or, at least, the "right" women must do so and they must reproduce with the "right" men if the population (its bloodline) and its culture are to remain pure. Race is about reproduction and sexual relations, about purity, degeneration, and the right human stock.

II Race and Miscegenation

To create societies in which race was an ordering principle demanded a great deal of theoretical, social, political, and cultural work – and much violence. Individuals had to learn to see themselves as members of races and to believe that one race was superior to another. This change in consciousness demanded a particular form of life in politics, law, the economy, and in everyday behavior and sexual relations.

A racial order was established in the first stages of settlement in the colony of Virginia. The "white race" – that is, a social category based on skin color whose members exercised power over, and enjoyed superior standing to, all those with black skins – came into being in the early part of the eighteenth century (Allen 1997). The seeds for the creation of a racial power structure were sown in the seventeenth century. Theodore Allen remarks that initially there was little point in landowners setting up a dual system of service, limited term for whites and lifetime servitude for Africans, because "the death rate was so high for several decades that there would have been no practical advantage for employers in such a distinction" (1997: 178). From the 1620s it became common practice for tenants to be transferred from one landowner to another without their consent and, through a variety of means, the term of service of indentured laborers, both African and white, was lengthened.[11] By the 1640s there were indications that lifetime servitude was

---

[11] This broke with the Statute of Artificers (1563) under which specified wages had to be paid and laborers bound by the year were allowed to terminate their employment with due notice. It was forbidden to punish an apprentice by extending the term of his service.

to be reserved for Africans and that an aristocracy of skin color was to be created. Nevertheless, until late into the seventeenth century some Africans owned land, engaged in commercial transactions, and even made use of white laborers.

The establishment of a modern racial system meant that "race" had become widely understood. Moreover, once race became an ordering principle in social life everyone was caught up in it, irrespective of their individual beliefs. Indentured Africans were turned into property and measures were taken to deprive free Africans of rights and exclude them from various trades. Conversely, "white" men became legal "persons" merely because they were white. Married white women were not legal persons but, despite their subordination to their husbands under coverture, they shared in the power and privileges of the white-skinned. "Whites" from the highest to lowest social stratum, both men and women, conscious that they were not "black," took part, actively or passively, in the maintenance of the new power structure or were forced to struggle against it. On the other side, Africans had to bear all the manifold burdens that now accompanied the designation of "black," even if they were not slaves.

"Race" required purity of the bloodline and so fashioned the sexual contract. In a racial order only some women were deemed worthy of "protection" by white men. The women of the ruling race, who continued the racial bloodline and were held to have the attributes of true womanliness ("the fair sex"; see Schloesser 2002), were protected (governed) by the men who shared their skin color. The interrelationship between the sexual and racial contracts meant that the sexuality of whites and blacks was seen quite differently. African sexuality was viewed as untrammeled and degenerate. Black women could never be "pure" like white women and African-American men were greatly feared as a standing threat to white womanhood. Nonwhites were for white people, at one and the same time, objects of desire, revulsion, curiosity, and prurient speculation.

The "white race" was safeguarded through prohibitions, both formal and informal, against interracial sexual relations. Or, rather, the prohibitions were first and foremost directed against relations between white women and black men. This provided some assurance that the white bloodline would not be polluted.[12] For white men, the prohibition came

[12] Elizabethan drama suggests that opposition to interracial sexual relations between white women and nonwhite men was itself produced along with modern conceptions of race. Sexual liaisons between white women and black men were portrayed as the "ultimate romantic-transgressive model of erotic love" (Boose 1994: 41). But once "race" began its course any connection between white women and nonwhite men became the most feared and the most viciously punished relationship.

into play against *marriage* with nonwhite women. Nonwhite women were not "protected" so, outside of marriage, white men demanded sexual access, coerced if necessary, to black women.

In *The Sexual Contract* marriage has a central place. I argued, first, that the marriage contract provided for legitimate, orderly access for each man to a woman of his own. But under the racial contract men's choice of a wife had to be limited if racial bloodlines and racial power were to be maintained. Maryland enacted the first criminal law in 1664, and this was aimed at "freeborn English women" who had made "shamefull Matches" with African slaves (Cott 2000: 44). Six of the original American colonies prohibited marriage between a white and black or mulatto and three of the thirteen banned inter-racial sex outside marriage. Nancy Cott states that "the English colonies stand out as the first secular authorities to nullify and crim-inalize intermarriage on the basis of race or color designations" (2000: 41).[13]

Second, I emphasized the interconnections between marriage, employment, and citizenship in *The Sexual Contract* but under the racial contract the connections were severed for African Americans in the aftermath of slavery. Slaves were prohibited from marrying, thus underlining their exclusion from civil law, but after emancipation the federal government took steps to ensure that as many of the freed slaves' unions as possible were regularized. The Freedmen's Bureau took care to enforce the sexual contract, and the labor contracts it pro-moted upheld coverture (see Cott 2000; also L. Edwards 1996 and Stanley 1996).[14] However, the power that free black husbands gained over their wives did not translate into political standing. The civil rights of black men and women alike were severely limited and, especially in the Southern States, their political rights denied. In the twentieth

---

[13] "[T]here seems to be no historical precedent for the sexualization of race in the United States, that is, no earlier cultural example of the assignment of a debased form of sexuality to an hereditary caste, over generations" (Zack 1997a: 148). During the 1860s more states passed antimiscegenation legislation and some Southern states introduced new bans after the Civil War (the Oxford English Dictionary records the first use of "miscegenation" in the United States in 1864); "[i]n Mississippi the penalty was life imprisonment" (Cott 2000: 41). The Civil Rights Act (1866) excluded these laws on the grounds that they applied equally to black and white, and all chal-lenges brought after the 14th Amendment (1868) were rejected by the Supreme Court. The California Supreme Court led the way in 1948 in striking down antimis-cegenation laws; the federal Court (as noted at the start of the chapter) finally acted in 1967.

[14] The major function of the Bureau – its official title was the Bureau of Refugees, Freedmen, and Abandoned Lands – was to turn "ex-slaves into wage workers" (Cott 2000: 85).

century, major social policies, such as Mothers' Pensions and Aid to Dependent Children, largely excluded African-American women, and the GI Bill after the Second World War did not benefit black servicemen in the same way as their white counterparts.[15]

White men were husbands, "persons," and citizens and, as I have stressed, their extramarital choice of women was unconstrained, especially if they were slave masters. Slaves were property; that is, they were mere factors of production to be used in the plantations and great houses. They were factors that could be replaced or increased by breeding but, unlike the breeding of livestock, the slave masters themselves could participate directly in their reproduction. Indeed, the paradox of slavery, which I highlighted in *The Sexual Contract*, is perhaps most evident in the case of female slaves. They were property, but it was their humanity that made their reproduction possible and made them sexually attractive to white masters.

Initially, the slave master's part in breeding led to a problem. On the one hand, children of slave mothers were property at the disposal of the master/father who could sell them at will. On the other hand, descent was patrilineal under common law. Race trumped patriarchy to solve the difficulty. In Virginia in 1662 it was decreed that slave mothers would pass their lifetime bondage onto their children. The ruling also meant that, notwithstanding their paternity, all such children were to be treated as "black." In my book (Pateman 1988: 122) I noted Mary Chesnut's comment that, in *Uncle Tom's Cabin*, "Mrs. Stowe did not hit the sorest spot. She makes Legree a bachelor." Wives of slave-owners exercised power over slaves but they had to pretend not to see their husbands' other offspring.[16]

Law, social sanctions, and a great deal of violence were used to regulate interracial sexual relations and prevent African Americans from exercising their newly acquired rights. The most violent forms of intimidation were the lynching of black men and the rape of black women; Hazel Carby argues that the rapes were "political terror," "an

---

[15] Southern politicians were determined to maintain very low wages for their workforce and they opposed the 1935 Social Security legislation. Agricultural, domestic, educational, and hospital workers were not covered, thus excluding most nonwhite and women workers. Vagrancy laws were used to compel black individuals into employment (see Kerber 1998: ch. 2).

[16] See also the comment about a member of Congress who had fathered six children by one of his slaves in Harriet Jacobs's memoir of her life as a slave (1969 [1861]: 215). Jacobs's book was edited by a white women, L. Maria Child, and Jacobs used the name Linda Brent, necessary protection given that she wrote about her sexual history. She refused Harriet Beecher Stowe's offer to incorporate her memoir into *The Key to Uncle Tom's Cabin*.

institutionalized weapon of oppression" that was the equivalent of lynching (1987: 18, 39).[17] Few could escape from the taint of such a racial order.

One telling example is the exchange over lynching between Ida Wells and Frances Willard, two remarkable and very politically astute women. Willard, a white woman, was the leader of the Women's Christian Temperance Union, the biggest women's organization in the United States in the late nineteenth century, which not only campaigned against alcohol but was the organizational mainstay of the suffrage movement (this was true too in Australia and New Zealand, though not in Britain). Wells's parents were slaves; she obtained an education, but lost her job as a schoolteacher because she drew attention to the second-class treatment of black children. She then became a journalist and co-owner of the weekly *Memphis Free Speech*.

In 1892 Wells wrote an editorial after the lynching of three black shop-owners, her friends (the paper was then attacked and the business destroyed). Wells wrote that most of the recent lynchings had been prompted by "the same old racket – the new alarm about raping white women," and she warned that Southern white men might "overreach themselves and public sentiment will have a reaction" (Wells-Barnett 2002: 29; she married in 1895). Wells saw the murder of her three friends as an example of the use of lynching to prevent black men becoming economically successful and competing with white businesses, but she used the phrase "new alarm" because, following Frederick Douglass, she argued that three different claims had been made about lynching. The first, immediately after the end of the Civil War, was that lynching was necessary to prevent race riots and insurrections. From the early 1870s lynching was said to prevent Negro domination at the ballot box. By the 1890s, when lynchings were at their peak, it was claimed that the atrocities resulted from the propensity of sexually depraved black men to rape white women.[18]

---

[17] The victims of lynching were predominantly male and black. Lynching began in the 1830s (the term was first used then) and before the Civil War most lynchings took place in California. It has a long history; there were lynchings still in the 1940s. In the 1890s, crowds numbering in the thousands, including whole families, often witnessed the dreadful killings of black men and mementoes were collected and disseminated to friends and relatives.

[18] Wells also noted that during the Civil War the slave master had safely left his wife and children with his slaves when away fighting. And at the end of the Civil War many white women came from the North as teachers to the freed slaves and for more than a quarter of a century they had worked without any fear. As Pauline Hopkins wrote, "[t]he men who created the mulatto race" continued to fill its ranks "year after year by the very means which they invoked lynch law to suppress, bewailing the sorrows of violated womanhood" (quoted in Carby 1987: 141).

Wells then embarked on an extraordinarily courageous campaign against lynching. One of her aims was to "[t]ell the world the facts" and to demand that accused black men should have a fair trial (Wells-Barnett 2002: 151). She emphasized one crucial fact: that only about a third of the victims were actually alleged to be rapists.

Before Ida Wells's campaign and the anti-lynching movement in Britain (the first Anti-Lynching Committee was formed in Britain in 1894), the WCTU had never condemned lynching and had no black members in the Southern states. Willard attacked Wells in an address to the WTCU in Cleveland after Wells pointed out that in many cases of lynching where rape was alleged it was known at the time and "indisputably proven after the victim's death" that the relationship was consensual, although clandestine. A charge of assault would have been thrown out in a courtroom. Wells asked the question

> what the white man means when he charges the black man with rape. Does he mean the crime which the statutes of the civilized states describe as such? Not by any means. With the Southern white man, any mesalliance existing between a white woman and a colored man is sufficient foundation for the charge of rape. The Southern white man says that it is impossible for a voluntary alliance to exist between a white woman and a colored man, and therefore, the fact of an alliance is a proof of force. (Wells-Barnett 2002: 61)

Willard refused to acknowledge that white women could, and sometimes did, enter voluntarily into sexual relations with black men. She leapt to the defense of white womanhood and insisted that Wells's arguments put an unjust and unfounded "imputation upon half the white race in this country" (2002: 130). Wells replied in a letter, published while both women were campaigning in Britain.[19] She reproduced some earlier remarks of Willard's on the need for "safeguards" against illiterate aliens and Negroes voting and on the "problem" facing white Southerners. "The colored race," Willard had written, "multiplies like the locusts of Egypt. The grog-shop is its center of power" and the safety of women and children was threatened (quoted in Wells-Barnett 2002: 131–3). After the publication of an interview with Willard, conducted in Britain by one Lady Henry Somerset, Wells had to publish another letter in her own defense. Willard never entirely retracted her attack on Wells.

During Wells's first visit to Britain in 1893 she was involved in a very curious incident. She had been invited through the initiative of Isabella

---

[19] Wells was one of a number of black women and men activists from the United States who visited Britain in the nineteenth century.

Mayo and her friend Catherine Impey.[20] Mayo took in nonwhite lodgers as part of her philanthropic activities, one of whom was George Ferdinands, a student from Ceylon. Shortly after the three women departed on Wells's tour, Impey wrote to Ferdinands proposing that they marry. Ferdinands forwarded the letter to Mayo who was scandalized and called Impey a nymphomaniac and a disgrace. Vron Ware writes that "[i]t is hard to believe that Catherine would have made the proposal without any encouragement, and the whole episode remains a mystery" (1992: 191).

Mayo showed the letter to Wells and demanded that Wells turn her back on Impey, but Wells refused. Mayo sent letters to America criticizing them both and continued her attack during Wells's second visit to Britain. She published an article in which she referred to the "diseased imaginations" of "women who will 'fancy' anything which will give them a sensation." In some states of the United States, she wrote, this imagination "would mean *the death of the man*," and "[i]f the women in the South were all 'pure in heart and sound in head,' we should hear of fewer lynchings" (quoted in Ware 1992: 195–6). Willard's reaction to Wells and this strange episode illuminate the complex ways in which the racial and sexual contracts played out, even in circles where one or the other, or both, were challenged.

III White Women, Black Women

Through the nineteenth century and into the first decades of the twentieth, women in both Britain and the United States were very politically active, both inside and outside conventional political arenas and in a wide range of women's organizations. They used arguments about rights and equality but stress was also laid on (white) women's particular affinity for morality and much "civilization work" was undertaken, both at home and abroad (Newman 1999). One observer wrote in 1900 of the Hull House settlement in Chicago that it was "a colony planted in a strange land by immigrants from a superior civilization" (quoted in Newman 1999: 23). The London Missionary Society had begun to recruit single women in 1875 and by 1899 women missionaries

---

[20] Impey ran a monthly paper, *Anti-Caste*, which in its final issues stated as its aim that "the dark races of Mankind [should have] equal right to protection, personal liberty, equality of opportunity and human fellowship" (quoted in Ware 1992: 190) She was acquainted with a number of leading black American activists and was especially concerned with racial justice. She was involved in other radical causes, supporting "the abolition of the alcohol traffic, an end to militarism, a respect for the environment and the humane treatment of animals – she was also a strict vegetarian" (Ware 1992: 187).

outnumbered men (Haggis 2003). The women's foreign mission movement was the largest women's movement in the United States by 1915 (Newman 1999: 53).

White women who attacked the sexual contract could still compare their position favorably to that of the women of lesser races. Female slaves, wives in polygamous marriages, inhabitants of harems or victims of suttee were frequently invoked. For white women to see black women as political equals was very difficult in a context of "race" and colonialism. Their ambiguous attitude is nicely illustrated by the image adopted by British women anti-slavery activists in 1828. They modified a famous cameo, first produced by Josiah Wedgwood in 1787, to portray a female slave, with the words "Am I not a woman and a sister?" But, like her earlier male counterpart, the slave was on her knees, a supplicant before a standing white woman.

The sexual and racial contracts reached into the anti-slavery movement. Black campaigners rarely had an equal place, even though the genesis of the anti-slavery movement lay in the activities and writings of blacks in Britain in the 1760s. The Anti-Slavery Society was founded in 1823 but it was not until the 1850s that the first steps were taken to include women in national committees. In 1840, the British organizers of the World Anti-Slavery Convention in London refused to accept women delegates from the Garrisonian wing of the American abolitionist movement, and the question of women's rights was thus thrust in front of the British movement.[21] But British women did not take part in the debate at the Convention; they could attend only as visitors.

Yet (middle class) women were at the heart of the British anti-slavery movement. They had begun a campaign against the slave trade (abolished in 1807) in the 1780s, they organized a boycott of sugar from the West Indian plantations from 1791 and, after the British ended slavery in 1833, turned their attention to the United States. From 1825 women developed their own extensive network of independent anti-slavery organizations and engaged in a wide variety of extraparliamentary activities, some of which they pioneered. British anti-slavery organizations initially supported gradual emancipation and it was a pamphlet by a woman, Elizabeth Heyrick's *Immediate, not Gradual Emancipation* (1824), and the women's associations that changed this. Heyrick's arguments were grounded in the principle that freedom was a "sacred

---

[21] In the United States "women's discontent with their position was as much cause as effect of their involvement in the antislavery movement. What American women learned from abolitionism was less that they were oppressed than what to do with that perception, how to turn it into a political movement" (DuBois 1978: 32).

unalienable right." She saw gradualism as "puerile cant" and slave insurrections as self-defense again appalling oppression.[22]

But Heyrick was unusual among women anti-slavery activists, who more resembled missionaries than revolutionaries. They commonly came to the movement out of Christian duty, and focused on the plight of women slaves, the tearing apart of slave families and education. Their Christianity meant that the humanity and spiritual equality of the slave was emphasized, a radical position. But this was counteracted by a general sense of cultural superiority. Most women in the movement, however benevolent and opposed to slavery they might be, failed to see blacks as other than in tutelage, waiting to be assisted by their white mother. It was not until Sarah Remond, an African American, arrived in 1859–61 that a (very short-lived) anti-slavery organization had black committee members. The case of Mary Prince, a slave brought to London from Antigua by her owners, Mr and Mrs Wood, who refused to emancipate her, is instructive. In 1831 she published her autobiography, *The History of Mary Prince: a West Indian Slave*, widely used by the Anti-Slavery Society in its publicity.[23] Clare Midgley summarizes Prince's position. She was treated "not as a fellow-activist but rather as a victim of slavery, as a possibly unreliable individual whose account needed authentication, and a working-class servant. Given this, it is hardly surprising that they did not think to recruit her as a member of one of their ladies' anti-slavery associations" (1992: 91).

The racial order permeated the women's movement in the United States. The enormous suffrage movement, for instance, was largely segregated. A difficult political dilemma arose with the Fifteenth Amendment; should suffragists support the enfranchisement of the freed male slaves despite the fact that black women continued to be excluded from the ballot box? The two most prominent white leaders, Elizabeth Cady Stanton and Susan Anthony, opposed the Amendment

[22] Heyrick believed that everyone was implicated in slavery and called on the population to act themselves through mass abstention from slave-produced goods (Midgley 1992: 104–8; see also M. Ferguson 1992: 253–8). In 1804 Maria Edgeworth wrote in her tale "The Grateful Negro" of the benevolent slave-master Mr Edwards: "He wished that there was no such thing as slavery in the world; but he was convinced, by the arguments of those who have the best means of obtaining information, that the sudden emancipation of the negroes would rather encrease than diminish their miseries. His benevolence therefore confined itself within the bounds of reason" (2003 [1804]: 49).

[23] The book was dictated to and edited by a white woman and included a lengthy supplement and appendices to authenticate it. "[T]here are times when Prince's voice seems more discernable than at others" (Salih 2000: xiii). The editor, Susanna Strickland, excised Prince's sexual history but this was revealed in Wood's libel action against Thomas Pringle, the Secretary of the Anti-Slavery Society (see Prince 2000: app. 3).

and the controversy split the movement for a generation. By the 1890s, white suffragists, who had already campaigned for decades and were desperate for any political opening, began to attack votes for ignorant, unwashed men, whether African American or immigrant, and entered into extremely unsavory alliances with racist Southern politicians.

Another example: one of Frances Willard's campaigning slogans was "a white life for two." By this she meant that the sexual double standard should be abolished and that sexual equality would be lived out in a tee-total and monogamous life, with chastity for both partners before marriage. But how should the metaphor of a "white life" be interpreted? Did it mean a pure life for all or was it a life suited to a racially superior population? Again, should Charlotte Perkins Gilman's many references to "the race" – in her day she was the most famous feminist writer in the United States – be read as referring to the human race or to the white race? Such uncertainties were well suited to a society that by the 1890s was in the grip of Social Darwinism (derived from Herbert Spencer) and in which popular acceptance of eugenics was growing.[24]

Gilman provides a fascinating illustration of how feminism (rejection of the sexual contract) and race (acceptance of the racial contract) were interwoven. In modern societies, she argued in 1898, there was too great a differentiation between the sexes; it was "carried to such a degree as to be disadvantageous to our progress as individuals and as a race" (1966: 33). Women traded on their sexual attractiveness, not their talents, and one result was "pathological maternity" (1966: 169).[25] Women, she insisted, had a "racial duty of right selection" of a father for their children (1966: 201). Prospective mothers, not fathers, should be responsible for selecting suitable mates to ensure sturdy offspring. But if women were to exercise this responsibility they had to be educated, independent, and men's equals. The human race would thus become fitter, but it is clear that Gilman had whites in mind as the model for progress.

In 1908 she published an essay, "A Suggestion on the Negro Problem." She notes that, as a result of contact with "our more advanced stage of evolution," many Negroes had rapidly become "self-supporting and well behaved" but most had not (1908: 80). To improve

---

[24] Francis Galton invented the term "eugenics" in 1883, but his interest in the subject had begun in the 1860s. He devoted a chapter of *Hereditary Genius* in 1869 to "The Comparative Worth of Different Races" and was explicit that the white race contained the most advanced humans (Galton 1978 [1869]).

[25] Wives were nothing more than house servants and one saw all around "innumerable weak and little women, with the aspirations of an affectionate guinea pig" (Gilman 1966: 168). She advocated radical reform of marriage and the home, which she saw as a relic from an earlier era.

and civilize them Gilman suggested that they should be formed into a labor army. This would have its own uniforms, music, and insignia and include all ages, with schools for children. The army would provide its own food and clothing and there would be training in domestic service, but its major task would be in agriculture and in developing the South. Gilman declared that this plan was "not enslavement, but enlistment"; once individuals were deemed capable of working on their own initiative they would graduate "with honor." The army would be "compulsory at the bottom, perfectly free at the top" (1908: 81, 82).

"[C]oncern with eugenics was characteristic of nearly all feminists of the late nineteenth century" (Gordon 1990: 110). The sociologist Edward Ross was one influence on Gilman, and he coined the term "race suicide," popularized by President Theodore Roosevelt. This could mean either that the least fit were breeding too fast and thus endangering the human race, or that the falling birthrate among whites and rapid growth in the nonwhite population was leading to the end of white civilization.[26] Either way, *some* women (not even all white women) were required to have more babies. The eugenic argument was that only the better specimens of their kind should be allowed to reproduce.

By the early twentieth century, prevailing opinion across the political spectrum was that a modern society should take scientific steps to ensure that its population was of the requisite quantity and quality.[27] Leaders of the birth control movement, such as Margaret Sanger in the United States and Marie Stopes in Britain, joined in the efforts to limit the reproduction of the least fit human beings.[28] In principle, examples of poor quality could occur anywhere in the population but, in practice, the "undesirables" were found in certain groups. The criteria hinged on such features as social inadequacy, fecklessness, feeble-mindedness, and sexual indicators, all of which overlapped with the characteristics typically attributed to the poor in general, poor women in particular, and nonwhites.

[26] "Race suicide" was a major issue in Australia as well as the United States. Ironically, in the United States between 1870 and 1910 the black birthrate seems to have been declining at a faster rate than that of whites (Gordon 1990: 150–1, and note, 151).
[27] Reference was made to "Bolshevik eugenics." J. B. S. Haldane wrote in 1938 in Britain that questions about eugenics spanned the conventional political divisions: "For example, the English National Council of Labour Women had recently passed a resolution in favour of the sterilization of defectives, and this operation is legal in Denmark and other countries considerably to the 'left' of Britain in their politics" (quoted in Paul 1984: 570–1).
[28] The movement in the United States had begun as agitation for "voluntary motherhood," part of the campaign for women's rights and reform of marriage law, but in the twentieth century became a professionalized part of population control (Gordon 1990).

By 1904 Galton was arguing that eugenics "must be introduced into the national conscience, like a new religion" (2000 [1909]: 83). In the United States and Europe it became very big business, funded by major foundations and supported by many of the most prominent and progressive figures on both sides of the Atlantic.[29] By the end of the 1930s the Birth Control Federation was singling out African Americans, arguing that their numbers were increasing from births among the least fit. Between 1919 and 1964 at least 30 states had eugenics legislation to allow involuntary sterilizations. Huge numbers of women were sterilized, whether voluntarily or not. One estimate is that in 1972 alone the federal government had funded over 100,000 sterilizations, many on black women; in North Carolina the majority of sterilizations were carried out on black women from 1933 onward. Sometimes the operation was performed on girls as young as 12. In Puerto Rico, after legislation in the late 1930s, over 35 percent of women of childbearing age had been sterilized by the 1970s (Davis 2003). Nonwhite women, mostly poor Puerto Ricans and Chicanas, were also used, respectively, to test the birth control pill and the IUD (Gordon 1990: 421–4).

One of the charges made against the women's movement by nonwhite women in the United States soon after its revival in the late 1960s was that, while the right to abortion was vigorously advocated, little was said about involuntary sterilization.[30] This was an example, they argued, of their exclusion from the movement and the failure to see that their interests frequently differed from those of white women. There were differences, too, over feminist critiques of the family and the oppression of women (see, e.g., Joseph and Lewis 1981) and over paid employment. The majority of African-American women had always had no choice but to be in paid work. When welfare measures were introduced in the 1930s, black women with children, unlike white women, were seen as "employable mothers" (Kerber 1998: ch. 2).

[29] Eugenics, of course, took its most extreme form in Nazi Germany, where American developments had been eagerly followed. In Sweden and other Nordic countries it was an integral part of the welfare state. A National Commission in Sweden in 1997 drew attention to the scale of eugenic activities there. A National Institute for Race Biology had been established in 1922, and by the time the legislation was eliminated in 1975 over 60,000 sterilizations had taken place, 90 percent of them on women.

[30] This remains a pressing issue. In 2002, for example, a report from investigators appointed by the Health Ministry in Peru stated that over 330,000 women, mostly poor Amerindian women, had been sterilized between 1995 and 2001. The report stressed that "they were blackmailed, threatened, or bribed with food; none was properly informed" (Barthélemy 2004: 8). Pharmaceutical corporations also carry out clinical trials in Africa without the ethical safeguards required in the West, a matter dramatized in the movie *The Constant Gardener*.

Many nonwhite women today still see feminism as relevant only to middle-class white women, a perception no doubt reinforced when women's organizations remained silent about the welfare reform legislation in 1996 that abolished Aid to Families with Dependent Children. The beneficiaries of the program were mostly mothers from minority groups, particularly African Americans, caring for children on their own. To be sure, by 1996 most mothers, from choice or necessity, were in the paid labor force and only "welfare mothers" received assistance to be at home with their children. Yet many Americans saw black mothers as moral failures, as lazy and unwilling to help themselves (Gilens 1999). This was why the figure of the undeserving, African-American "welfare queen" was able to haunt the popular political imagination.

The complexities of the position of black women, and the corrosive effects of the sexual and racial contracts, were highlighted when Anita Hill, a former employee of Clarence Thomas at the Equal Employment Opportunity Commission, accused him of sexual harassment during his nomination for the Supreme Court.[31] The hearings of the Senate Judiciary Committee became a major public spectacle after Hill's accusation. The Chair of the Committee ruled that the burden of proof lay with Hill, and the Senators apparently found it difficult to believe that sexual harassment was commonplace in workplaces. The hearings and media coverage turned not on Thomas's conduct but on Hill's truthfulness, another episode in the very long history of distrust in women's ability to tell the truth in court combined with an even greater disbelief in black women's veracity.[32] Many African Americans saw the charge of sexual harassment as part of a white feminist agenda that operated to the detriment of black men and so as casting doubt on Hill (Burnham 1992: 311–13). They also saw Hill as violating a code in her own community. She had criticized a fellow African American in public and raised the question of the treatment of black women by black men. The breach, Hill said, "damned me in the eyes of many Blacks whose

---

[31] Thomas was nominated by President George H. Bush in 1991, despite the fact that the American Bar Association had found him only marginally qualified and his performance as Chair of the Equal Employment Opportunity Commission had been poor. He seemed unwilling to enforce antidiscrimination law (see Burnham 1992; Swain 1992). Resnick (1995) gives an account of the judicial background to the hearings and discusses the procedure. Thomas's nomination was narrowly confirmed.

[32] Thomas even famously claimed that he was the victim of a "high-tech lynching." In contrast, Hill was seen as having "betrayed the man who had done me a favor by hiring me" (A. Hill 1995: 275). Moreover, she was a single woman and this gave rise to insinuations that she was attacking Thomas because she had been spurned by a black man married to a white woman.

profound experiences of racism have led them to ignore within our own community what we find intolerable when committed by others against us" (A. Hill 1995: 284).

IV Home and Abroad

It might be objected that my historical illustrations are drawn from a completely different context than my two examples from the 1990s. After all, I argued in *The Sexual Contract* that the heyday of modern patriarchy in Britain was between 1840 and the late 1970s; by then its props had begun to crumble and conventional understandings of "masculinity" and "femininity" were under challenge. In addition, the legal underpinnings of racial power in the United States had been dismantled, and almost all colonies had become self-governing.[33] Further changes have taken place since the late 1970s; for instance, multiculturalism is now public policy. But although the context has changed, the social and economic legacy of old forms of women's subordination and racial superiority linger on, and newer forms have emerged.[34]

Some insight into the persistence of these patterns of power can be gained by bringing economic exploitation, emphasized by Charles Mills, to the fore and by bringing the racial and sexual contracts – or what, in the wider focus of this section, might be called the global sexual-racial contract – together with Norman Geras's contract of mutual indifference (1998). The latter (and the global sexual-racial contract) are "contracts" in a broader sense than my usage in *The Sexual Contract*, more akin to Mills's conception of the racial contract.

Geras distinguishes the contract of mutual indifference from theories of an original contract. It is not, he argues, about origins or justifying government; nor does it involve a state of nature. Rather, the contract of mutual indifference is "imputed," it "can be read from the realities of our time" (1998: 28). But early modern theories, with their pictures of the state of nature and justification of a particular form of government, also owed a good deal to the realities, as each theorist interpreted them,

---

[33] I cannot discuss here the contribution made by women to the liberation movements and how they were then typically relegated to lesser citizenship in the new states. There is now a growing literature on nationalism and gender; for two early examples see Yuval-Davis (1997) and McClintock (1995: ch. 10).

[34] In Western countries race "persistently correlates with statistically overwhelming significance in wage levels, unemployment levels, poverty levels, and the likelihood of incarceration" (Alcoff 2002: 15). In the United States, African-American men are arrested and imprisoned in extraordinarily large numbers. Brian Barry writes of the "black gulag" in the United States and he notes that a similar trend is occurring in Britain with young black men (2005: ch. 7).

of their present. The crucial question is precisely how we are to read these realities. Not everyone sees Geras's contract, or the sexual or racial contracts, in our past or present circumstances.

The contract of mutual indifference reflects a world in which, in general, people remain unmoved by large-scale atrocities, mass deprivation and distress. Geras does not deny that there are people and groups who are motivated by humanitarianism and make efforts, sometimes very heroic efforts, to assist others in torment or distress, but most people, most of the time, do not do so. The contract reflects *general* not *universal* relations of mutual indifference. The contract of mutual indifference, Geras argues, is a model of our world that is "exaggerated – or, better perhaps, reduced – by omission of such mutually assisting behaviour in dire misfortune as there is" (1998: 29). That is to say, the contract takes the form of a pact that I do not come to your aid in an emergency and I do not expect you to come to mine. Geras's central argument is that we lack a social morality of mutual aid and so feel under no obligation to come to the assistance of others, even in the most extreme circumstances. We are governed by mutual indifference.

Humanitarianism – a concern for the well-being of people unknown to, and often far distant from, ourselves – was created, Thomas Haskell has argued, in an early stage of capitalism in the late eighteenth century. A major change in moral sensibility occurred when individuals began interacting in a capitalist market; ideas of moral responsibility broadened and individuals became "men of principle" (1985: 560).[35] Haskell, however, remarked that the later stages of capitalism might provide much less support for humanitarianism. This is the import, too, of Geras's comment that in societies such as Britain and the United States the norm of "collective existence" is for the wealth of some to be accumulated from the poverty of others. Poverty and its deprivations, though often deplored, are accepted as part of the social order and so "to all intents and purposes" the sufferings of the poor "are of little consequence" (1998: 59). That is, we remain indifferent to them.

During the past quarter-century, capitalism, and so Geras's norm of collective existence, has extended across the world and into most areas of social life. Even Marx might be surprised by its scope. The expansion has been accompanied by a marked increase in economic inequality and insecurity, both within the United States and Britain and between rich (mostly white) and poor (mostly nonwhite) countries. The "Overview"

---

[35] Haskell's main example of humanitarianism is the anti-slavery movement but he overlooks both the prominence of women in the movement and that, by the late eighteenth century, capitalism was being constructed as an arena for men. Middle-class women were supposed to confine themselves to the home. How, then, did they become women of principle?

in the 2005 *Human Development Report* (UNDP 2005) provides a summary of the extent of global inequality. Some countries and regions have prospered, but many have not – some African countries have gone backwards – and there are large disparities between urban and rural populations. At present it looks unlikely that the UN Millennium Development Goals will be met by 2015. Income inequalities have increased in countries inhabited by over 80 percent of the world's population; 2.5 billion people live on less than $2 a day and have 5 percent of global income (more than 1 billion live on less than $1), while the richest 10 percent enjoy 54 percent of global income.

Africa was at the heart of the construction of the modern concept of "race" and now the image of the starving, about-to-die African infant symbolizes the suffering of the global poor. Predatory, brutal, and corrupt leaders and elites share responsibility for destitution in Africa, as do companies engaged in the latest round of plunder of the continent's riches, but as Thomas Pogge (2002) has recently argued, the structure and policies of global economic institutions have contributed too.[36] These institutions are part of the changes now called globalization (for data, see Held et al. 1999). In one sense, globalization is hardly new. It was part and parcel of early modern European expansion and formed the context in which political theorists formulated theories of original contracts. But the present phase is wider, is moving with greater speed (see T. Brennan 2003), and has been driven by neoliberal doctrines of structural adjustment, deregulation and privatization, touted with the same fervor as the old colonial mission.

The extraction of resources from poor countries is now, for the most part, less dependent on the gun and the lash than it was during the colonial period; bodies such as the International Monetary Fund and the World Trade Organization, and agreements such as the North American Free Trade Agreement have taken center stage.[37] But, in the last analysis, just as military force upheld colonialism, neoliberal policies and the power and reach of Western corporations are underwritten by the overwhelming military strength of the United States (demonstrated most vividly by the orders for the complete privatization of occupied Iraq drawn up by the Provisional Coalition Authority under Paul Bremer, which received remarkably little publicity). Few poor countries have escaped the imposition of structural adjustment, the creation of labor

[36] Policy for Africa in both the United States and Britain is geared towards privatization and big corporations through the Corporate Council on Africa in the US and the Investment Climate Facility in Britain (Monbiot 2005).
[37] Thankfully, King Leopold's Congo is a thing of the past; but, for example, few questions were asked for a long time about "blood diamonds" and oil companies have been accused of complicity in major human rights violations in more than one country.

markets, the entry of Western corporations and the consequent transformation of their economic life and cultures. Their borders must be
opened to corporate capital and their social services and resources,
including water, handed over to private buyers; their agriculture must
be focused on crops for export (though they face tariffs) and compete
with imports from the rich countries (subsidized at the level of $2 billion
per week); farmers must cease to save seeds and buy them from corporations each season.[38] The poor even sell their vital organs, particularly
kidneys, to the rich through thriving illicit global markets.

This is the context in which the contract of mutual indifference reinforces, and is reinforced by, the global sexual-racial contract.

If "poverty" were defined as living on 60 percent of median income,
23.8 percent of the population in the United States would have been
living in poverty in 2000.[39] The richest two-fifths have almost three-
quarters of the national income (B. Barry 2005: 175). In Britain
inequalities have increased to the point where the poorest 20 percent of
the population have an income that is comparable to that of their counterparts in a much poorer country, the Czech Republic (UNDP 2005:
56). In 2002, the poorest 10 percent received 3 percent of the national
income and the richest 10 percent received over a quarter (B. Barry
2005: 175). Income inequality is also correlated with other important
social indicators such as education, health, and longevity.[40]

These inequalities are fueled by the sexual and racial contracts. In
both countries women and nonwhites are overrepresented among the
poor.[41] Statistics about wealth are particularly telling; disparities are
much greater than for income. In the United States, 80 percent of the
population received only 9 percent of gain in marketable wealth
between 1983 and 1998; in Britain, the poorer half of the population
received only 7 percent of the increase in marketable wealth between
1982 and 1996 (B. Barry 2005: 188). Of households in the United States

---

[38] Thousands of farmers in Andhra Pradesh in India have committed suicide since the
early 1990s when their livelihood began to fail as market reforms were introduced. In
2003 the Department of Justice was investigating 120 slavery cases, many involving
migrant farm workers in the fields of the United States (Bowe 2003: 38).

[39] The Luxembourg Income Study, at www.lisproject.org/keyfigures/povertytable.htm.
A level of 50% or 60% of median income is a common measure of poverty in Europe
and in cross-national studies. In the United States poverty is measured by the income
required to buy a bundle of basic goods, a measure virtually unchanged since the 1960s.
This gives a threshold of around 40% of median income.

[40] In Washington, DC, the infant mortality rate among African Americans is higher
than in Kerala in India (UNDP 2005: 58).

[41] See, for example, for figures for Britain, DWP 2004: ch. 3, and for the United States
the website of the US Census Bureau, at http://pubdb3.census.gov/macro/032005/
pov/new01_100_01.htm.

with less than $5,000 net worth in 2000, 45 percent were headed by non-whites (although nonwhite households were only 24 percent of all households). The median net worth of (non-Latino) white households in their highest quintile was $208,023 compared with $65,141 in the highest quintile of black households. In the lowest quintiles, the median net worth of white households was $24,000 – and in black households it was $57 (L. Williams 2004: 684).

These figures go a long way to explain why it was predominantly African Americans who had no means to leave New Orleans – one of the poorest cities in the United States – during Hurricane Katrina in 2005 and were herded into an unsanitary, ill-equipped stadium. In an interesting insight into the workings of the contract of mutual indifference at home, the then head of the Federal Emergency Management Agency is reported to have remarked that "we are seeing people we didn't know exist."

The consequences of the global sexual-racial contract are even starker; the poor and destitute of the world are overwhelmingly non-white and the worst-off are likely to be female. Women's plight is summed up in the well-known statement that women do two-thirds of the world's work, earn 10 percent of the income, and own less than 1 percent of the property. Most of the world's refugees and displaced persons are women and their children. Girls and women are likely to be less literate, less well nourished, and to receive less medical care than men and boys; they are also less likely to survive. Amartya Sen (1990) calculated that over 100 million women are "missing" in South Asia and China, cultures where girls have little value.

Increasing inequality has weighed very heavily upon women (and their children) everywhere, but especially in poor countries. The survival of families depends on the work of women, and the reduction, privatization, or elimination of public services means that they now carry extra burdens. An illustration of the global sexual-racial contract is the emigration of many women, who send home remittances to support their children and other family members, to work as maids and nannies. There is now "a global transfer of the services associated with a wife's traditional role . . . from poor countries to rich ones" (Ehrenreich and Hochschild 2002: 4). Domestic servants largely disappeared after the Second World War in the United States and Britain but demand is now rising. One reason is that although the majority of women are in the paid workforce they are, typically, still responsible for domestic caring work; men refuse to do their fair share. Thus employing a maid avoids marital conflict – and allows men to continue to free-ride – and maids are increasingly likely to be imported. Maids move from Southeast Asia to the Middle and Far East, from the former Soviet bloc and Africa to

Western Europe, and from south to north in the Americas (see the maps in Ehrenreich and Hochschild 2002: 276–9, and in Seager 2003: 72–3).

The sex industry and sexual violence are two other graphic illustrations of the global sexual-racial contract. The growth of the sex trade – the demand by men for the sale of women's bodies as a commodity in the market – has expanded apace since I wrote my book. Women emigrate to work in the industry and are also tricked and forced into it; numerous well-organized criminal organizations have women and girls as one of their products. The trade is fueled by women's impoverishment (including in Russia and the former Soviet bloc countries) and by the wars and population displacement of the last two decades.[42] Women and young girls in refugee camps and conflict zones may have to provide sex to their "protectors" in the form of UN peacekeepers and aid workers for the means of survival.[43] The global flows of women into the sex industry are well defined enough to be mapped and reflect men's racial preferences (Seager 2003: 56–7, map 20).

In addition to the violence involved in the sex trade, other forms of violence against women continue unabated. In November 2005, the World Health Organization issued a report on domestic violence showing that it is a global problem, occurring in rich and poor countries alike, something that feminist scholars and activists have been aware of for some time. Men kill women every day.[44] Rape is endemic worldwide (contributing to the spread of HIV), committed by men with virtual impunity. Women have always been seen as one of the spoils of war and rape is also used on a mass scale as a weapon of war. Many recent wars have involved (what is now called) ethnic cleansing. Here again the sexual and racial contracts are interwoven. Rape has been used not only to humiliate enemy men by violating, shaming and

---

[42] The "shock" introduction of capitalism and privatization in Russia has impoverished much of the population while creating the new class of ostentatious millionaires. The poorest 20% receive 6% of the national income, 27% of the population (officially) is below the poverty level (unofficially it is around 40%), and pensions are around 20% of subsistence level; welfare expenditure has remained stagnant since 2000 and public health expenditure is 0.2% of GDP (Clément 2003: 10). In 2004, seven members of Putin's entourage controlled 40% of the GNP (Clément and Paillard 2005: 6).

[43] When troops and a variety of civilians arrived in Kosovo in 1999 the sex trade increased enormously; "the international presence . . . initially made up some 80 per cent of the clients." Women are now trafficked from all over the Balkans and Eastern Europe to Kosovo to be sold onward (Vulliamy 2005: 14–15; see also the Amnesty International report of May 2004). In 2005 there was another such scandal about the Congo. But such predations are not new; over a decade ago, for instance, UN forces sent to Mozambique were reported to be utilizing child prostitutes.

[44] In the town of Ciudad Juarez, over the border from El Paso, Texas, for example, over 300 women have been murdered since 1993. In Guatemala more than 1,600 women have been killed since 2001 (Asturias and del Águilas 2005).

degrading "their" women and girls, but as a way of "diluting" the bloodline of the enemy community through forced impregnation.[45]

At this point it might be objected that, while my examples show that there is still work to be done, the task of eliminating global inequality and the sexual-racial contract is well underway. And, far from being indifferent, people respond very generously to major appeals for help and numerous organizations provide assistance. I do not want to deny that much is being done or to dismiss the generosity; indifference, as Geras argues, is general not universal. However, the problem is not only that problems persist but that not all cases of distress receive the same response.

For example, generosity is generally greater for natural disasters than in the case of man-made catastrophes or deeply entrenched problems. It is, of course, very much easier, at least in the first stages of a natural disaster, to see how a difference could be made than to see what can be done in the face of endemic, grinding poverty or wars which destroy not just numerous communities but whole countries.[46] Seeing what might be done has become harder, too, because citizens in the United States and Britain have little exposure now to criticism of prevailing economic dogmas. We are encouraged to believe that there is only one "natural" way to organize economic production across the globe and to believe that everything must be on sale in markets.

Besides such obstacles, response and lack of response to distress is refracted through the contract of mutual indifference and the global sexual-racial contract. Many problems have been acknowledged only very recently; violations of women's rights began to receive attention as breaches of *human* rights only during the 1990s and it has taken until the twenty-first century for rape to be prosecuted as a war crime. Rape during war began to receive major publicity only when it happened in the early 1990s in Europe. Little was heard about the quarter to half a million women, almost all Tutsi, raped in 1994 during the genocide in Rwanda. There is still indifference to the enormous number of victims in the conflicts in the Congo. A great deal of attention was paid to killings in the Balkans, unlike the genocide in Rwanda or the indifference for a quarter of a century to the death toll and atrocities in East Timor

---

[45] Raped women, and any consequent children, may be shunned by their communities. For a discussion of rape as a central weapon in genocide see MacKinnon (2005).

[46] It is especially difficult when we are told that wars arise from primordial ties or are fought by peoples much more prone to violence than ourselves. This neatly diverts attention both from the desire for power and control of resources by elites and from sales of small arms – some 640 million in existence worldwide – and torture equipment from Western and other companies (leaving aside the matériel available on the black market).

after it was invaded and annexed by Indonesia.[47] Indifference continues to the Russian blitzkrieg and violations in Chechnya. There has been little concern about the fate of the 4 million souls who have perished in war and its consequences in the Congo. Indifference persists to the Israeli occupation of Palestine, the destruction of infrastructure, agriculture, and homes, and the killing and maiming of Palestinians (or the construction of roads for the use of Jews only; even South Africa did not go that far).

In 2006, it is relatively easy to find out about these examples and about many other tragic cases. Occasionally they are in the news, and the United Nations, the World Bank and a plethora of nongovernmental organizations issue reports, major international conferences have been held on women's rights, and war crimes tribunals are hearing cases from a number of conflicts. Information is available on the internet. The question is why people prefer not to know about, make no effort to find out about, ignore, remain unmoved by or turn away from deprivation and distress, even extreme torment. This is a very difficult question to answer (and my remarks do not address the politics of governmental and international inaction; why, for example, the World Food Agency announced at the end of April 2006 that it was halving rations being distributed to the traumatized, displaced people of Darfur because donors had supplied only a third of funds needed). But consideration of the past history and present realities of the sexual and racial contracts can make a small contribution to understanding the widespread phenomenon of indifference, of turning a blind eye to suffering.

That, at the beginning of *States of Denial*, Stanley Cohen can list 27 expressions related to "hearing what we want to hear," "not believing that this is happening" and so on, shows how adept we are at avoidance (2001: 1–2). As Geras points out, it is not easy to learn about and think about past or present horrors; indeed, it can be unbearable to dwell on them. It is much less disturbing and a great deal easier to remain as indifferent bystanders, or to adopt the position where "we know and don't know at the same time" (Cohen 2001: 5; see ch. 6 for bystanders). Yet it is easier for some rather than others to maintain "willful ignorance" (Frye 1983). Part of being in power or being privileged is that a choice is available about what is seen or listened to. The powerful can ignore or be shielded from anything that might threaten their position

---

[47] Documents declassified in late 2001 confirmed that President Ford and Henry Kissinger, Secretary of State, had assured Suharto that the United States would not object to action against East Timor. Aceh has been in the news and a peace settlement has now been reached only because of the total devastation caused by the tsunami in 2004 and the influx of foreign news media and personnel from the UN and nongovernment organizations. West Papua is still ignored.

and their comforts. Frequently they lie about what is going on. On the other hand, their underlings, too, can prefer "to know and not to know" if speaking out would undermine their security or bring down sanctions on their heads. Cohen (2001) discusses such mechanisms in detail.[48]

Knowing but not knowing occurs in the context of the global sexual-racial contract. It is easier to be indifferent to the misery of others if those involved are seen as having brought their distress upon themselves, or are perceived as very different, as alien, as worth less, as inferior, as barely human or as another "race." Their sufferings can then be seen as of little or no account. Charles Mills argues that the racial contract requires that the distress of whites count for a great deal more than that of nonwhites. The sexual contract plays just as large a role in fostering indifference. Prevailing conceptions of masculinity and femininity cultivate and sustain indifference. The lesson that little girls and women are worth less than little boys and men (that women exist *for* them) is conveyed in a multitude of ways, beginning in the home. No emergency or "war on terror" has ever been declared because of the scale of violence against women. Everyday violence by "our" men against "our" women continues remorselessly but we turn away our eyes. We do not want to know about the violence inflicted on "their" women.

Geras's argument is about our response to dire emergencies and extreme suffering, but lack of mutual aid, indifference, and knowing but not knowing are found in less dire circumstances. They are part of everyday life. Indeed, indifference at home helps explain at least something about indifference to the fate of those far away. Perhaps the most common objection to arguments for universal mutual aid is that our natural inclination, and our first obligation, is to care for those closest to us. The most common response to this objection is that, even if this is the case, there is no reason why it should preclude assistance to others abroad. What is usually overlooked is that it is not true that all those closest to us receive assistance. There is a hierarchy of worth at home and abroad. The interrelationship between the sexual and racial contracts encourages turning a blind eye, corroding everyday life at home and fostering indifference to destitution and suffering abroad.

V Concluding Observations

Part of present economic orthodoxy is that there must be unfettered movement of capital, goods and services – but no free movement of

---

[48] For a novel in which a whole country "knows and not knows" (and which raises some questions touched on here about a different problem) see Ishiguru (2005).

poor, nonwhite people. The European Union (EU) has expanded east, where skins are mostly not so dark, but at the same time it has become "fortress Europe" against the nonwhite poor outside. Far-right, racist parties are gaining ground and in Britain resistance to the entry of refugees has been growing amid hysteria about "asylum seekers." Immigrant communities – labeled "immigrant" even if large numbers are citizens by birth – tend to be on the margins of society, concentrated in poor areas, their members working in low-level jobs or unemployed. A large part of immigration into Europe has been, as it were, the return of the repressed colonial past.[49] But the connection between the population flows of the past 50 years and the European expansion that began in the early modern period has largely been erased from the popular political imagination. This is why the history of the sexual and racial contracts is so crucial; it is not possible to understand present-day patterns of global inequality, sexual and racial subordination, and indifference to distress without some understanding of their historical development.

For example, shades of old debates about civilization and lesser races, and of previous claims about the poor treatment of women in colonial possessions compared to the position of women at home, hang over controversies about immigration. Much popular attention is now directed to the oppression of women in immigrant communities. In several European countries the *hijab* and other female Islamic dress has become a battleground for the defense of "European culture." Albeit that all this is a backhanded compliment to the influence of the women's movement, much of the concern appears to have less to do with women than to be a way of presenting the communities concerned as alien. It is reminiscent of the cynical use made by the United States government of the extreme subordination of women in Afghanistan under the Taliban. During the years that the Taliban were forming and after they seized power in Afghanistan little or nothing was said at official levels about the position of women, but when bombing was imminent it was claimed that war on Afghanistan would liberate women, a claim accepted by some prominent feminist spokeswomen.

---

[49]   This has now been replaced in Britain by large inflows from the East European countries newly part of the EU; estimates in the latter part of 2006 were that around half a million had immigrated, mostly from Poland. A high rate of immigration into the United States continues, but nonwhite illegal immigration, especially from Mexico and Central America, is now a controversial political matter and since 9/11 the southern border continues to be fortified. Hypocrisy is the order of the day. In California the economy, especially the service and agricultural sectors, depends on cheap immigrant labor but in 2005 and 2006 growers were complaining that because of crackdowns on entry they did not have enough workers to harvest their crops.

Two final comments: toward the end of *The Racial Contract* Charles Mills notes that it is not only whites who are implicated in a racial contract and he mentions Japan and World War II (1997: 127–8). There are many current examples of states governed by a particular racial or ethnic group that exploit, ill-treat, or wage war against members of their own population, often in the name of maintaining the unity and borders of the state. It is not only Europeans who see people unlike themselves as backward and unfit to be self-governing. Nor is imperialism a uniquely European phenomenon. The expansions of the Han Chinese into Tibet or the Javanese across the Indonesian archipelago are examples. The strategic and economic importance of numerous countries to the United States and other Western countries means that the global racial contract is now enmeshed in a range of lesser racial contracts. Local rulers and elites support the interests of Western governments and corporations, and are supported by them, assisting the transfer of resources from the global South to the North.

Conceptions of racial and sexual difference are political constructs and both can, and do, change. The possibility is open that "race" could be eliminated and that what it means to be a "man" or a "woman" could alter radically. The racial and sexual contracts could, therefore, become mere historical curiosities. But, as this chapter is designed to show, both are deeply embedded in social and political institutions, national and international, and in individuals' sense of themselves. A great deal has to change, including the neglect of the history I have illustrated, before the global sexual-racial contract withers away.

Paul Gilroy has recently argued that there is a "crisis" in which the idea of race "has lost much of its common-sense credibility, because the elaborate cultural and ideological work that goes into producing and reproducing it is more visible than ever before, because it has been stripped of its moral and intellectual integrity, and because there is a chance to prevent its rehabilitation" (2000: 28–9). That Charles Mills and I have written this book is, in a sense, a testament to that very crisis. But there can be no certainty whether, or about the manner in which, it might be resolved. In our current global circumstances and the "war on terror" it would be foolhardy to make a prediction about the future of mutual indifference and the sexual and racial contracts.

6

Intersecting Contracts

Charles W. Mills

Following Carole Pateman, I too now turn to the crucial question of race/gender intersection, of when and where (or if and how) women of color enter the social contract universe.

In 1886, Anna Julia Cooper announced: "Only the BLACK WOMAN can say 'when and where I enter . . . then and there the whole *Negro race enters with me*' " (1998: 63). This proclamation has long been a trumpet call for black American women, providing the title of Paula Giddings's pioneering black feminist text, *When and Where I Enter* (1984), and inspiring other feminists of color increasingly insistent over the last two to three decades that neither white feminism nor nonwhite male antiracism can speak adequately for them. So if the original challenge to a bogus universalism was "What do you mean *we*, white man?" the more recent variants have become "What do you mean *we*, white woman?" and, more recently still, "What do you mean *we*, black man?" A book jointly written by two of these new (non-usual) suspects, a white woman and a black man, must therefore be particularly self-conscious about not simply reproducing such past exclusions, especially given that Pateman's original "sexual contract" had little to say about race while my "racial contract" had little to say about gender. Indeed, taken together they might seem perfectly to exemplify the indictment of another classic 1980s text of black feminism, *All the Women Are White, All the Blacks Are Men, But Some of Us Are Brave* (Hull et al. 1982). As Laura Brace comments, perhaps a bit unkindly:

> The racial and sexual contracts are difficult to put together because they stand rather stiffly beside one another without ever really engaging. . . . They work together Pateman and Mills, they do a double act on the

conference circuit,[1] and they're writing a book together called *The Domination Contract*, but she does gender and he does race. I suspect that it's partly using the social contract as their explanatory device that allows them to carry on dis-engaging like that. (2004: 3)

So the obvious question is whether an engagement – and indeed a marriage – can be arranged between these stiff and distant parties, or whether the contract framework itself inhibits any such matrimonial get-together (or would make it, perhaps, no more than a marriage of convenience, never to be consummated). In the previous chapter, Pateman gave her political scientist's reply to this question; here I will offer my more abstract philosophical one.

Women of Color and Philosophy

Why bother, though? If it's difficult enough to think race and gender together (let alone in combination with other factors), as the huge and ever multiplying literature on "difference" and "intersectionality" shows, why exacerbate these problems by trying to formulate them within the somewhat awkward and artificial additional framework of a "contract"? Obviously, the claim – the hope – has to be that the theoretical payoff will make it worthwhile. Political philosophy has been spectacularly revived over the last three decades, generating a vast outpouring of articles, books, series, introductory texts, and reference companions. But a vanishingly small proportion of this material addresses the distinctive problems of women of color. There is, in fact, an almost complete disconnection between two huge bodies of literature, the writings on race/class/gender intersectionality in feminism, sociology, history, legal theory, cultural studies, and so forth, on the one hand, and the writings on social justice in philosophy on the other. A highly regarded black feminist text of ten years ago like Dorothy Roberts's 1997 *Killing the Black Body*, which seeks to "confront racial injustice in America" by tackling the "assault on Black women's procreative freedom" (Roberts 1999: 4), will not through the most powerful Hubble telescope appear in the universe of discourse of the Rawlsian secondary literature. These are in effect two parallel non-intersecting universes. But wasn't the original point of resurrecting contract theory to adjudicate what would be a just social order? Wasn't the point of starting with

[1] Actually, this is untrue. We've only ever appeared together once, at the 1999 American Political Science Association meetings. Nor, apart from the present book, have we ever worked together. I was inspired by Pateman's book in writing my own, but I never consulted with her on it, and only met her for the first time (after it had been published) at that same panel.

ideal theory to be able to eventually move on, better equipped, to non-ideal theory? Yet the response of most white male political philosophers to the growing irrelevance of their apparatus to the real world (and the concerns of the majority of the population) seems to be not, as it should be, "So much the worse for this apparatus," but, remarkably, "So much the worse for the real world (and the concerns of the majority of the population)."

The point of the project, then, is to contribute toward ending this ludicrous situation by helping to create a possible theoretical space, an opening in this area of philosophy, for women of color interested in the field – and, for that matter, for all ethicists interested in making their prescriptions truly general. (It is not, of course, that social justice issues *have* to be discussed in a contract framework. But given the continuing hegemony of Rawlsian approaches, a conceptual intervention here is likely to have more impact than elsewhere.) At present, by contrast, as Naomi Zack points out in the introduction to her edited volume *Women of Color and Philosophy*, the overwhelming demographic whiteness of the profession and the hostile conceptual terrain interact in a disastrous positive feedback loop to repel nonwhite women in particular. They are likely to be seen "as having doubly benefited from affirmative action hiring policies," to have "scholarly interests [that] are marginal in the field," and thus to be multiply "atypical" figures as philosophers, with at least "initial failures of credibility with colleagues, as well as students" (2000: 7).

In the introduction to *The Racial Contract*, written a decade ago, I commented on the paucity of African-American philosophers in the profession, only about 1 percent of the North American total (Mills 1997: 2). In the ten years since then, that figure has not changed, proportionally. What I did not single out for special mention, and perhaps should have, is how few of these were women. Even today, there are not more than thirty or so black women in philosophy. And black women, pathetic as their numbers are, actually represent the *largest* nonwhite female group. The figures for Latina and Asian-American philosophers are even lower (moreover, some Latinas self-identify as racially white), while with Native Americans, it's not more than five or six people in the entire United States. All nonwhite female philosophers put together constitute perhaps half of one percent of the North American total.[2]

So if women of color have emerged as a global force, as Cherríe Moraga, the co-editor of *This Bridge Called My Back*, one of the most famous women of color anthologies, boasts in her foreword to the latest edition (Moraga and Anzaldúa 2002: xvi), they barely make up a block

[2] In 2000, Zack estimated the number at no more than 30 (Zack 2000: 5).

committee in the white male world of professional philosophy. In Nirmal Puwar's striking phrase, they are "space invaders," "trespassers" marked by both race and gender as doubly "out of place" in a discipline whose pretensions are paradigmatically to the universal, the world of disembodied mind – and which for that very reason cannot accommodate those whose "dissonant bodies" putatively link them so ineluctably to the particular, the physical, the *non*-universal, the *non*-representative: "the exclusionary some body in the no body of [philosophical] theory that proclaims to include every body" (2004: 8, 11, 57, 141). Indeed, it is noteworthy that the most famous woman of color with a philosophy background, Angela Davis, does not teach in a philosophy department, or generally publish in philosophy journals, though her book *Women, Race, and Class* (1981) is one of the pioneering texts in the "intersectionality" literature.

Uma Narayan recounts the experience she, an Asian American, and an African-American woman had at a meeting of the American Philosophical Association in New York when they were both fellow philosophy graduate students, colorful walking anomalies:

> We had both been subjected to an unbelievable amount of staring by fellow professionals, which made us feel like exotic wildlife, and she had had to deal with requests for assistance by several philosophers who, despite her APA name tag, assumed she was on the hotel staff! In anger and frustration, she burst out, asking, "Why should I have to be the one to integrate the bus?" I am sorry to say that this remains a question for women of color in the profession more than a decade later, and it is one to which I have no better answer than I had earlier, which was "What choice do we have?" . . . If there is one thing I would like to see before I retire, it is philosophy becoming a profession where a generation of women of color do not feel these huge institutional burdens of integrating the academic and philosophical bus. (2003: 92)

But how is this integration to be accomplished? In his classic collection of interviews, *African-American Philosophers: 17 Conversations*, which can be seen as a kind of black oral history of the profession, editor George Yancy interviews Adrian Piper, the first black woman philosopher to be tenured in the United States. Yancy asks: "How can we get more Black women in the profession of philosophy?" And Piper replies frankly: "I think about this a great deal and I think the problem about getting Black women into the profession is that if you tell them what it is really like, no rational Black woman would want to go into it" (1998: 59). Similarly Anita Allen, with the advantage of a J.D. from Harvard Law School as well as a Ph.D. from the University of Michigan, exited philosophy departments (as her primary appointment) long ago for law

school positions. She comments that black women have done "[e]xtra-
ordinarily badly" in the field:

> With all due respect, what does philosophy have to offer to Black women?
> It's not obvious to me that philosophy has *anything* special to offer Black
> women today. I make this provocative claim to shift the burden to the dis-
> cipline to explain why it is good enough for us; we should be tired of
> always having to explain how and prove that we are good enough for the
> discipline. . . . Any Black woman who has the smarts to do philosophy
> could do law, medicine, and politics with greater self-esteem, greater
> financial reward, greater visibility, and greater influence. Why bother with
> philosophy when there [are] so many other fields of endeavor where one
> can do better, more easily? This is the question that must be answered.
> (Yancy 1998: 172)

My hope, then, is that putting my and Pateman's contracts together
may be one useful way of creating a conceptual space in social and
political philosophy to address nonwhite women's distinctive concerns,
thereby helping to make it somewhat more welcoming terrain than it
currently is.

Rethinking and Renaming the Basic Structure: Racial Patriarchy

The natural starting-point is a rethinking and renaming of the system,
the "basic structure," involved. Pateman and I are both sympathetic to
social-structural accounts, and so in our respective books we both found
it natural to conceptualize domination in terms of a system, *patriarchy*
for her, *white supremacy* for me. Obviously, then, the thing to do is to
combine them, and in fact many feminists of color (largely outside of
philosophy, of course) have long been doing precisely that, speaking var
iously of *racial patriarchy*, *racist patriarchy*, *white supremacist patriarchy*, and so forth.[3] So it is important to be clear on the fact that *outside*
of academic philosophy, these concepts have a long history, generated
by the creative work and theoretical innovations of progressives in the
activist movements of the 1960s and afterwards. The first question is
whether such a structural approach is useful. Mary Maynard argues
against postmodernist objections in terms of "difference," suggesting

---

[3] I don't know who deserves credit for the first formulation of the term. Barbara
Omolade (1995) speaks of "racial patriarchy" in her 1983 essay "Hearts of Darkness."
Audre Lorde (2002) refers to "racist patriarchy" in her famous 1979 talk at Barnard
College, "The Master's Tools Will Never Dismantle the Master's House." The
Combahee River Collective's pioneering 1977 "A Black Feminist Statement" implicitly
draws on such a composite concept (though including, as well, "capitalism and imperi-
alism"), but does not actually name it.

that they elide questions of power and material advantage, not to mention foreclosing any broader global understanding of the socio-political order:

> So many forms of difference are created that it becomes impossible to analyoo thom in terms of inequality or power. ... The possibility of offering more structured socio-political explanations disappears, except in a localized sense, because these, necessarily, must be rooted in generaliza-tions which cannot be made. There is, therefore, the danger of being unable to offer any interpretations that reach beyond the circumstances of the particular. ... The deconstruction of categories such as race and gender may make visible the contradictions, mystifications, silences and hidden possibilities of which they are made up. But this is not the same as destroying or transcending the categories themselves, which clearly still play significant roles in how the social world is organized on a global scale. (2001: 129)

I share Maynard's misgivings about postmodernism, and endorse her conclusions. So let us proceed under the assumption that, duly quali-fied, structural generalizations about the intersection of race and gender can be justified. The question now is whether they can be trans-lated into a contract framework, and whether, even if they can, it con-tributes at all to the debate.

Pauline Schloesser is one political theorist who thinks they can, and that it does. In her book, *The Fair Sex*, about three leading female intel-lectuals of the early American revolutionary period (Mercy Otis Warren, Abigail Smith Adams, and Judith Sargent Murray), Schloesser comments, like Brace, that in Pateman and myself: "The study of male supremacy and white supremacy as two separate systems has led to awkward universals" about "male" and "racial" privilege, which obvi-ously have to be qualified to register the realities of intersecting racial and gender subordination (2002: 49–50). However Schloesser expressly sets out to remedy this situation by trying to integrate our contracts, and to theorize racial patriarchy in contractual terms, and in effect I want to follow her lead.

Refer now to the set of accompanying diagrams, which I think will assist the discussion by graphically representing the progression of the idea. In figure 1 we have the classic social contract (idealized, of course), in which all (adult) persons are contractors, symmetrically positioned with respect to one another, agreeing to establish an inclusive liberal democratic polity. So in the official narrative, as Pateman pointed out in her book (1988: ch. 1), the old world of inherited ascribed status is supposed to be replaced by the new world of egalitarian individual agreement.

| Persons (Contractors) | The (idealized) social contract establishes the inclusive liberal democratic polity |

Figure 1

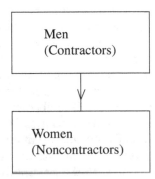

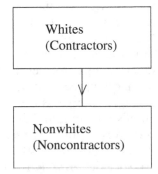

The (actual, non-idealized) sexual contract establishes the patriarchal polity

The (actual, non-idealized) racial contract establishes the white-supremacist polity

Figure 2

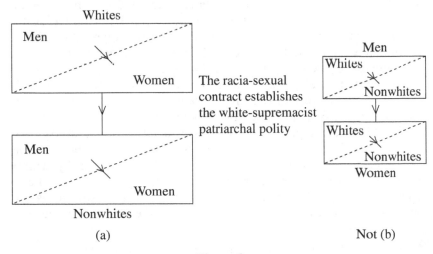

The racia-sexual contract establishes the white-supremacist patriarchal polity

(a)

Not (b)

Figure 3

But of course it wasn't. The contemporary idealized model, however pedagogically useful, retroactively sanitizes the gender and racial exclusions both in the classic social contract theorists and in the modern polities their work rationalized. The ancient inferior status of women, seemingly a paradigmatic candidate for elimination by the promise of modernity, is recodified under the new system of "fraternal patriarchy," while a new structure of superiority and inferiority, race, emerges to displace the (formal) class estates of the feudal epoch.[4] Hence, in figure 2, the more accurate modeling proposed respectively by Pateman's sexual contract and my racial contract. In these *non*-idealized representations, the real contractors are now revealed as a subset of the adult human population rather than being coextensive with it. Men and whites, whose superior status locates them asymmetrically, in relations of domination rather than reciprocity, over the noncontracting class of women and nonwhites, emerge as the real players. The sexual and racial contracts establish the patriarchal and white-supremacist polities.

Thus far, thus familiar. The sexual and racial contracts do undeniably capture some important truths about gender and racial subordination in modern societies, especially when compared with the nominally genderless and raceless social contract that was our polemical target. But as Brace and Schloesser point out, no interaction between them is described. However, once racial patriarchy has been established (and this is a specific historical development, not a transhistorical formation), the interlocking nature of the systems means that one cannot speak of the "contracts" in isolation, since they rewrite each other. Or, perhaps better (since patriarchy predates white supremacy, and the sexual contract – assuming a premodern incarnation – precedes the racial contract), the racial contract is written on patriarchal terms, and the sexual contract is rewritten on racial terms. As Maynard concludes: "It thus does not make sense to analyse 'race' and gender issues as if they constitute discrete systems of power" (2001: 131).

On then to figure 3, and the attempt to combine them. Here we have what I am going to call the *racia-sexual* contract (corresponding to "racial patriarchy"), in which pre-existing patriarchal structures are modified by the emergent new structure of racial domination. My claim is that though gender subordination predates racial subordination, once racial subordination has been established, it generally trumps gender. (As I will document later.) So the interaction of the two contracts does not produce a symmetry of race and gender subordination, but a pattern of *internal* asymmetries within the larger asymmetry of

---

[4] But for a challenge to the view that race and racism are a product of the modern period, see the recent work of the German scholar Wulf Hund (2006).

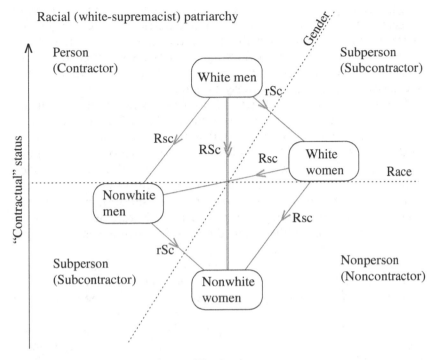

Figure 4

social domination. Whites as a group dominate nonwhites as a group, while within these racial groups men generally dominate women (figure 3a). If you think this picture is wrong, just contemplate the alternative, figure 3b. Here men as a group dominate women as a group, with whites positioned over nonwhites in each sexual group. Ask yourself: does this model match up with, say, the historical experience of Native American and Australian expropriation, African slavery, European colonialism, South African apartheid, American Jim Crow? Do nonwhite men dominate white women in any of these situations? Obviously, the answer is "No." So figure 3a gets it right and figure 3b gets it wrong. If the sexual contract establishes patriarchy, and the racial contract establishes white supremacy, the racia-sexual contract establishes the white-supremacist patriarchal polity.

Turn now to figure 4, which could be regarded as a kind of "blow-up" of figure 3a. In Pateman's and my one-dimensional contracts, we had two status positions, one relation of domination (men over women, whites over nonwhites), and one set of contractors (men, whites). So in both cases, a simple dyadic relation – privileged at one end, oppressive at the other – obtained. The contractors, in the sense of the active agents, are respectively men and whites. Women and nonwhites are the objects of the contract rather than active participants (except in some coerced or ideologically socialized way that undermines the standard liberal norm of informed voluntary consent). So though the overall picture was more complex than the idealized, internally homogeneous social contract, it was still a fairly simple one.

In the racia-sexual contract, by contrast, a far more complicated topography is generated. As the asymmetrical diamond of figure 4 illustrates, we now have *four* contractual status positions with *six* relations of domination linking them. The four locations denote one position of unqualified privilege (white men, privileged by both race and gender), two hybrid intermediate positions involving both privilege and subordination (white women, privileged by race but subordinated by gender, and nonwhite men, privileged by gender but subordinated by race), and one position of unqualified subordination (nonwhite women, subordinated by both race and gender).[5]

The way to think of this set of relationships in "contractual" terms is then, I suggest, as follows. White men are located at the top of the diamond, as full persons, positioned superior to everybody else. They are thus the only full contractors of the composite racia-sexual contract, and so dominate all three other groups. White women and nonwhite men, by contrast, should be thought of as *subcontractors*, a term meant to indicate that (by contrast with the generic "women" and "nonwhites"

---

[5] One of the manuscript reviewers pointed out the danger of a "static" modeling of racial and gender domination, reminding me that some theorists have claimed – as manifested for example in differential educational attainment and employment rates – that black women in some countries (Britain, the United States) are now positioned above black men. The cautionary word is well taken. But even if such shifts have recently taken place in some countries (and the claim is contested by others), the diagram still seems to me to be at least roughly accurate as a representation of *most* of the several hundred years of the modern period. So in contrast to the clearly wrong inclusive social contract of modernity (figure 1), and the partially right but clearly one-sided and one-dimensional sexual and racial contracts (figure 2), this picture provides a good corrective starting-point, and one that arguably still applies to most of the former colonized world, where it is certainly not the case that women of color are generally privileged over men of color. One must remember that where race, gender, and contract theory are concerned, philosophy's owl of Minerva is not taking off at dusk, but the next morning, or is indeed still asleep. It is not the case that *in contract theory* there is an already-existent extensive literature on these matters that I am failing to take into account. Rather, as emphasized at the start of the chapter, there is next to none. What I am trying to do is to translate the insights of the intersectionality literature into a contract discourse. So the first priority has to be correcting the grossly misleading picture currently presumed by this discourse. I would claim that figure 4 provides such a heuristic corrective, if only as a useful starting-point for subsequent development and debate.

of figure 2) they do have real, though inferior, power. They have a subordinate role in the global racia-sexual contract, typically being more active participants in one dimension of it than the other. (I signal this by the respective upper-case/lower-case, R/r and S/s, formulations of RSC, the racia-sexual contract, on the different intergroup axes.) White women, being on the wrong side of the (diagonal) gender line, are subordinated by white men through the sexual side of the racia-sexual contract, and are to that extent subpersons. But being on the right side of the (horizontal) racial line, they are located above both nonwhite men and nonwhite women, and so are in a position to dominate both. So the intermediate pair of white women and nonwhite men are *not* (I claim) symmetrically located with respect to each other – note the "tilt" of the diamond – since race lifts white women above nonwhite men. It is a mistake, then, to think that their "common" oppression by white men puts them in the same situation. White women are subcontractors of the racia-sexual contract to the extent that they assist in the racial subordination of people of color. Nonwhite men are also subcontractors, since they are participants in the sexual dimension of the racia-sexual contract. However, this will generally only be possible in connection with nonwhite women, at least in the contract's classic stage, when racial subordination is overt and *de jure*. Finally, nonwhite women are at the bottom of the structure, dominated by all three groups: by white men through the racia-sexual contract in both its aspects, by white women through the racia-sexual contract (primarily) in its racial aspect, and by nonwhite men through the racia-sexual contract (primarily) in its gender aspect. If white men are full persons and full contractors, while white women and nonwhite men are subpersons and subcontractors, then nonwhite women are nonpersons and noncontractors.

The Racia-Sexual Contract: Key Positions

The preceding discussion has necessarily been somewhat abstract and schematic. Let me now try to illustrate its applicability with concrete examples from the vast literature on intersectionality earlier mentioned.

(1) *Mainstream liberal color-blindness and gender-blindness as simple blindness* First, a general framing point. In the original classic social contract, as Pateman and I tried to demonstrate in our respective books, white males come together in the modern period under the self-description of "men" (or, occasionally, "persons") to create (what I will now term) racial patriarchies. Contemporary contract theory retroactively sanitizes this history of exclusion and represents itself as universalist, the "men" (or "persons") supposedly now (and then) including

everybody. But insofar as the conceptions of the polity in the contract abstract away from this history of gender and racial subordination, they only contribute to its perpetuation. Susan Moller Okin (1989) famously pointed out the illusoriness of a political gender neutrality that is merely terminological. The contractors behind Rawls's veil are supposed to be sexless heads of households, but in the range of problems they consider, and – more important – do not consider, they reveal themselves as actually male. Even more obviously, it can be argued, they reveal themselves as white, since they have no concern about such issues as affirmative action, reparations, land claims, the legacy (and continuing subtler incarnations) of white supremacy, and so forth.

So what is represented as simple innocuous philosophical abstraction per se, a standard and necessary tool of the discipline – the gender- and race-neutral language of "men" or "persons" – is actually an abstraction of a particular sort. It is an *idealizing* abstraction that in ignoring the effects of gender and race differentiation abstracts away from the concrete specifics of social oppression (O'Neill 1993; Mills 2005a). But the solution is not, in frustration, to reject abstraction itself as problematic, but rather to reject evasive abstractions – that obfuscate the crucial social realities that need to be mapped – in favor of non-idealizing abstractions – that reveal them. The racia-sexual contract, building on the racial and sexual contracts, does this by explicitly recognizing how race and gender position people differently, in complex asymmetrical interrelations, rather than pretending that we are featureless atomic individuals in egalitarian contractual relations with one another.

Judith Shklar points out that the reality in the United States, in opposition to the myth of a liberally all-inclusive polity, is that citizenship has crucially hinged on "social standing," and that political theorists who ignore this history, especially "the part that slavery has played in our history," "stand in acute danger of theorizing about nothing at all" (2001: 2, 9). (Think of the implications of this point for the "ideal theory" of Rawls's *Theory of Justice* (1999h) – a book written by an American with no mention in its 500+ pages of the history of slavery in the United States and its legacy in the present.) In particular, the standing of white males as citizens was defined "very negatively, by distinguishing themselves from their inferiors, especially from slaves and occasionally from women" (Shklar 2001: 15). Indeed "black chattel slavery stood at the opposite social pole from full citizenship and so defined it" (2001: 16). Similarly, Evelyn Nakato Glenn argues that "the citizen and noncitizen were not just different; they were interdependent constructions. Rhetorically, the 'citizen' was defined and therefore gained meaning through its contrast with the oppositional concept of the 'noncitizen' (the alien, the slave, the woman)" (2002: 20).

So the actual civic interrelations of individuals in the United States – and, I would claim, elsewhere – are not the symmetrical and harmonious ones of idealized contract theory, but relations of domination and subordination. Apart from global gender differentiations, the moral status equality achieved in theory for males in general in contract theory is obviously hopelessly inappropriate as a characterization of the American polity, given its founding on a basis of racial hierarchy as a white settler state. Nor is it an accurate modeling of a tacitly intra-European liberal modernity that raises white Europeans everywhere, at home and abroad, above inferior nonwhite non-Europeans (Mehta 1999). Insofar as contract theory ignores this history, it is simply entrenching a hierarchy that, in more subtle forms, still exists today. By marginalizing the distinctive problems associated with gender and race, the mainstream contract – in effect, if not in self-description – is taking the white male as the paradigm contractor, and limiting its social justice prescriptions to his concerns. In contrast, the racia-sexual contract makes this status hierarchy explicit in its very apparatus, thereby pre-empting the theoretical evasion of these issues. By formally demarcating different subject positions, with their attendant privilege or disadvantage (or both), this non-ideal contract forces us to confront the question of what would be necessary to achieve ideality, rather than starting *from* that ideality. Louise Michele Newman condemns American liberalism's typical "purposeful overlooking – a not-seeing – of difference, even when the consequences of such not-seeing lead to the maintenance of structures of oppression":

> The national romance with colorblindness, and its corollary, gender sameness, is a fundamentally misguided strategy (metaphorically, a two-headed ostrich with both heads in the sand) – an ineffective way to address the real discursive effects of social hierarchies intricately structured along the multiple axes of race, class, gender. . . . [P]eople of different races, classes, and genders are always already situated differently. To assert "sameness" is to purposefully ignore the material and ideological effects that race (gender, class, sexuality) have had in creating oppression, inequity, and injustice. (1999: 20)

But while I completely agree with the spirit of this indictment, I disagree with Newman's implication that "egalitarian liberalism" is itself the problem. Rather the problem lies in a gender- and race-evasive liberalism which, in assuming sameness of status, has *not* been egalitarian, presupposing as long since accomplished an egalitarian goal that has yet to be achieved, thereby conceptually eliding the ongoing barriers to its realization. The racia-sexual contract confronts these problems by acknowledging the difference race and gender make, rather than pretending that they make no difference.

Moreover, it overcomes the dichotomization of Pateman's and my partitioned contractual discourse. The sexual and racial contracts represented an advance on the nominally genderless and raceless social contract by recognizing the differential and inferior status within the contract of women and nonwhites. But in treating gender and race separately, the sexual and racial contracts generalize in a way that can be misleading. As Glenn puts it: "In studies of 'race,' men of color stood as the universal racial subject, while in studies of 'gender,' white women were positioned as the universal gendered subject" (2002: 6). Once racial patriarchy has been established, however, race and gender become intertwined, so that one has to speak of gendered race and racialized gender. What is true of white men is not necessarily true of whites as a group, or of men as a group; what is true of white women is not necessarily true of women as a group. I used a vocabulary of white persons and nonwhite subpersons, while Pateman described fraternally linked male patriarchs denying civil equality to inferior women. But white women whose legal personality is subsumed into their husbands' by the doctrine of coverture can hardly be accurately characterized as full persons, nor under white supremacy does male fraternity extend across the color line to permit nonwhite rule over white women (Pateman 1988: 220–1), nor does either formulation explain the distinctive situation of women of color. The racia-sexual contract formally recognizes this more complex reality (while abstracting away, of course, from further complications) by overtly demarcating four contractual subject positions. Thus it pre-empts unqualified generalizations about "men" and "women," "whites" and "nonwhites," forcing us in each case to ask the question of what actually does hold true for the group in question, given their specific location in the composite multidimensional "contract."

(2)   *White men as full persons and full contractors* I will have the least to say about white men, since in a sense they were the primary topic of Pateman's and my books, so that this has all been said already, if not within this revised framework. Located at the top of the diamond, privileged by both gender and race (albeit in some cases disadvantaged by other memberships, such as class or sexual orientation), they occupy the premier status position of the racia-sexual contract. As full persons, they are the paradigm contractors of mainstream social contract theory, originally overtly and *de jure*, now covertly and *de facto* through the assimilation of other subject positions to their status – which does not in the least make nonwhites and white women actually equal to them, of course, but only serves to obfuscate the latter groups' continuing disadvantages. They are in a superior power relation to white women, nonwhite men, and nonwhite women, and the beneficiaries of

the gender and/or racial exploitation of all three groups. Thus they will for that very reason be most susceptible to the delusions of race and gender ideology, since they have the greatest stake in maintaining the structure of illicit benefit and exploitation.

(3)   *White women as both subpersons and subcontractors*   The racia-sexual contract self-consciously breaks up the undifferentiated category of "women," making it explicit that race as a structure of domination lifts white women into a category that is generally privileged with respect to their nonwhite sisters. Thus it registers in its apparatus the central, crucial accusation repeatedly made by women of color over the last three decades since the "second-wave" revival of feminist theory (as well as echoing earlier nineteenth-century "first-wave" grievances): that there is no "natural" sisterhood between the white plantation owner's white wife and his black female slaves, between white settler women and the women of the Amerindian or Australian Aboriginal peoples being displaced, between the female white colonist in the European empires and the female nonwhite colonized, between Jane Crow and the Jane Crow-ed, between the white suburban housewife and her black or Latina domestic. It forces white women to recognize that white supremacy exists as well as gender domination, and that their subject location and contractual status are different from that of women subordinated by both.

As such, it challenges what Vicki Ruiz and Ellen DuBois call the "uniracial" model, in which "White women appear 'raceless,' their historical experiences determined solely by gender" (2000a: xi). Rather, in the words of Pauline Schloesser, white women are both "subjects" and "subjected" (2002: 8), "a racialized sex group," "ambiguously positioned in the hierarchy of gender and race relative to white men and nonwhite persons of both sexes," or, perhaps better, "doubly positioned, as subordinate others with respect to white men and as superior subjects with respect to nonwhites" (2002: 53). Contradictorily located, they are subpersons with respect to the white male, but are nonetheless superior to the different variety of nonwhite male subpersons, and certainly to the nonwhite female nonpersons. So while they may be objects for the subjecthood of the white male contractor, they are nonetheless subjects and subcontractors in their own right with respect to nonwhite men and women. Thus the theoretical challenge is to grasp, to somehow think simultaneously, *both* of these aspects of the contract, instead of letting one simply displace the other, so that white women are seen only as victims or only as oppressors.

In the early stages of second-wave Western feminism, the constant complaint by women of color was the condescension or outright racism of white feminists, so that it was white women's subcontractual role that required highlighting given their self-positioning solely as victims. bell hooks writes about the US experience: "[White women] did not see us as equals. They did not treat us as equals. . . . From the time the women's liberation movement began, individual black women went to groups. Many never returned after a first meeting" (2000: 141). Similarly, in her history of what she calls "separate roads to feminism" in the United States, Benita Roth argues that standard histories of the second wave "have erased the early and substantial activism of feminists of color embedded in these movements" (2004: 2), an activism necessitated by the fact that "racism within the (white) feminist movement was an inescapable issue, and racial division among feminists was the subject of many discussions and workshops" (2004: xi). (See also Breines 2006.) In Britain, likewise, Valerie Amos and Pratibha Parmar talk about the need to challenge the "imperial feminism" of the time: a "white, mainstream feminist theory, be it from the socialist feminist or radical feminist perspective, [which] does not speak to the experiences of Black women and where it attempts to do so it is often from a racist perspective and reasoning" (2001: 17). Thus for black women ("black" here including Afro-Caribbeans and Asians) the women's movement in Britain, claiming to analyze and seeking to end oppression, was itself seen as "oppressive . . . both in terms of its practice and the theories which have sought to explain the nature of women's oppression."

From the structural perspective earlier adumbrated, of course, the point is that this is not just a matter of subjective attitudes and values but rather an outlook rooted in the *objectively differentiated* position of white women in the social order. In Roth's account:

> White women became the reference group for feminists of color, such that white feminists, as white women, were a group to be challenged for unfair advantages, just as white men were . . . based on an understanding of structural inequality. . . . African American and Chicana feminists . . . did not see [white women] as natural allies in the struggle for gender, racial/ethnic, and economic justice. . . . For feminists of color, structural inequalities among women mattered more than those between women and men within the racial/ethnic community. (2004: 44–6)

Moreover, as various accounts of the history of the women's movement have documented, this differential positioning, with its resultant peculiar blindness and self-serving politics, goes back to the nineteenth or even eighteenth century and the "first wave." Amos and Parmar point out that "the movement for female emancipation in Britain was closely linked to theories of racial superiority and Empire" (2001: 19). Similarly, Vron Ware argues that in imperial Britain "the ideology of white womanhood, structured by class and race, embraced women in all their familial roles":

> Whether as Mothers of the Empire or Britannia's Daughters, women were able to symbolize the idea of moral strength that bound the great imperial family together. . . . Faced by this ideological burden, the writings of many feminists . . . show a fundamental tension in their attitudes to the idea of Empire. They might challenge or contest reactionary images of womanhood on which the imperialist project depended for support, but in doing so they expressed a lack of patriotism. Or they could adhere to their feminist principles, and effectively condone racist and imperialist policies which suppressed the freedom and independence of other people. . . . What was lacking was a vision of liberatory politics that connected the struggle against masculinist ideology and power with the struggle against racist domination in the colonies. (1992: 162–3)

So if the experience of gender subordination opened their eyes to feminist consciousness, the experience of racial privilege blinded them to the oppression of white supremacy.

But the implications of this lack of vision go deeper, affecting the very concepts central to white feminist theorizing. For both first- and second-wave white feminist theory, centered on the white woman's experience, the family and the separation into private and public spheres are at the heart of women's oppression. Patriarchy is the overarching theoretical concept that is supposed to cover the subordination of all women in its many different forms. However, with the establishment by global white supremacy of racial patriarchy as a distinct historical formation, the family will no longer be primary, even if it originally was, in the oppression of nonwhite women. Rather, it is their subordination through conquest, land expropriation, slavery, regimes of colonial forced labor, segregation, racialized occupational positions in the job marketplace, the sex industry, the modern sweatshop, and so forth, that becomes far more salient. Nor can it be said that women as a group are oppressed by being excluded from the public sphere, since it will often be the case that (as just cited) nonwhite women *are* in the public sphere, whether as slaves working in plantation economies, colonial laborers, domestics forced to seek employment in white households, or workers in racially and gender differentiated occupations.

Thus a far more complicated political geography than the simple Aristotelian dichotomization of (male) public polis/(female) private household is generated, so that the familiar white feminist cartographies inspired by this ancient partitioning, and its modern variant, will have to be redrawn. The subordination of nonwhite women will often be most manifest in racialized public sphere regimes of work and differential racia-gender exploitation (see, for example: Glenn 2002; Ehrenreich and Hochschild 2002), not in nonracial domestic gender exploitation by a nonwhite patriarch who confines one to one's home. It is not that patriarchy is not manifest, but that racial patriarchy largely displaces power to whites as a group. The "patriarch" is, in a sense, the collective white population, with white men as the full contractors and white women as the subcontractors.

So in this revisionist picture, in opposition to white feminist orthodoxy, (white) women become active agents, if only on the subcontractual level, of (racial) patriarchy, insofar as they are complicit in the differential and inferior treatment both of nonwhite men and of their nonwhite sisters in systems of racial and gender subordination. In the racia-sexual contract, *white women get to be patriarchs too*, at least with respect to nonwhites. And in a sense, especially in the colonial world, nonwhite women in the *public* sphere are in the *private* sphere of the white patriarch, as minors subject to their paternal rule. The white "family" needs to be reconceptualized as writ large, on a national scale, with white women simultaneously subordinated individually in their private families and privileged collectively as co-rulers of the "national" or "international" public family. Antoinette Burton refers to the "maternal imperialism" of the period, involving "the white woman's burden" (1992: 144), and Mary Procida, in her article on British imperialism in India as a "family business," points out that for the Anglo-Indian rulers:

> Husband and wife, together, embodied status and authority. . . . Their family business, therefore, was literally the business of empire in all its practical and ideological manifestations. . . . In the British Raj, Anglo-Indian women's political power stemmed not from their position as citizens in a democratic polity (which the British empire obviously was not), but rather from their personal, social, and marital connections with imperial officials. As the wives of imperial officials and as members of the ruling race themselves, Anglo-Indian women . . . actively participated in the ongoing discourses of imperial politics. . . . They were married not only to their husbands; Anglo-Indian women were also married to the Raj itself. For women, therefore, their roles as wives allowed them not only to create their own biological families, but also to construct roles for themselves in the greater imperial family of British India and in the family business of empire. (2002: 168–9)

And within this extended "family," "the colonized peoples of India took on, in the eyes of their British 'guardians,' the role of adopted children in the imperial family of the British empire," if more as "troublesome stepchildren of the Raj than as the legitimate heirs to the family business of empire," since because of race they "stood outside [its] genealogy and reproductive biology" (2002: 177). White wives as a collective *memsahib* assisted in the ruling of a "household" of inferior nonwhites that was national in scope.

Similarly, Schloesser's (2002) book is an analysis of how, in the United States, Mercy Otis Warren, Abigail Smith Adams, and Judith Sargent Murray, leading female intellectuals in the revolutionary period, all ended up – whatever their initial liberalism – by acquiescing to the terms of racial patriarchy. Through the endorsement of "fair sex" ideology, which differentiated them as white women from all males and from nonwhite females (black slaves, Native American "savages"), white women in the United States embraced a vision of themselves as a group possessing distinctive virtues and a particular civilizing mission in the early days of the republic. White female "subjectivity and agency," then, were likely to manifest themselves in a severely qualified and restricted "feminism":

[A] white woman concerned mainly with gender issues would attempt to view issues of sexual inequality in isolation from race and class issues, such that women of color, uneducated, or poor women would be largely invisible or irrelevant to her critical or reformist vision. In other words, a "feminist" would attempt to challenge the sexual contract while leaving intact the racial contract. . . . This strategy is basically an attempt to maximize one's own power as a white woman by equalizing the opportunities between white men and white women without giving up racial privileges. (Schloesser 2002: 80–2)

In the new vocabulary I am suggesting, the racia-sexual contract recognizes, in its overt demarcation of four separate subject positions, with their accompanying dominant ideational tendencies and political options, an ideologico-political terrain more complex than that mapped by the sexual or racial contracts individually. So if *The Racial Contract* sketched a one-dimensional white blindness, an epistemology of racial ignorance afflicting undifferentiated white "contractors," here one has simultaneous insight and sightlessness, the racia-gendered cognitive interplay of oppression and privilege. From the beginning, white women are so positioned in the diamond structure that a subcontractual role is open to them, making it not just possible but very likely that resistance to their gender subordination will coincide with their signing on to general nonwhite subordination. Very few white feminists took a principled stand against *both* aspects of the contract.

Thus Louise Newman's book, *White Women's Rights* (1999), explicitly subtitled *The Racial Origins of Feminism in the United States*, documents the conviction of most white women in the largely segregated feminist movements of the 1850s–1920s that they, as members of the superior race, should be "the primary definer and beneficiary of women's rights," and that this struggle was quite separate from issues of racial justice:

> In the decades from 1870 to 1920 . . . despite moments of interracial cooperation, the woman's movement remained largely segregated. Many white leaders dismissed the concerns of black women – such as miscegenation, interracial rape, lynching, and their admittance to the all-women cars on the Pullman trains – as "race questions," irrelevant to the woman movement's foremost goal of "political equality of women.". . . .
> [W]hite activists had a heightened racial consciousness of themselves as civilized women. . . . Shared racial inheritance meant that men and women of the same race had more in common with one another than they did with the same sex of different races. (1999: 6, 7, 134)

As I claimed at the start, then, race generally trumped gender. Thus the primary concern for most white American feminists of the period was the achievement of gender equality with white men (joining the *Herrengeschlecht* of the *Herrenvolk* at the top of the diamond, and turning it, perhaps, into a simple rectangle), certainly not the ending of racial inequality. They were contesting the sexual dimension of the racia-sexual contract, but were quite happy to maintain its racial dimension, hoping, one could say, to move from the status of subcontractors to full contractors. In Newman's uncompromising summary of her book's thesis:

> This book . . . rejects the premise that [white] feminism, in any of its late nineteenth- or early twentieth-century incarnations, was an egalitarian movement. . . . [F]eminism was part and parcel of the [United States's] attempt to assimilate those peoples whom white elites designated as their racial inferiors. . . . Increased political power and freedom for white women was, in a material as well as ideological sense, dependent on asserting the racial inferiority and perpetuating the political subordination of nonwhite others. . . . In other words, racism was not just an unfortunate sideshow in the performances of feminist theory. Rather it was center stage: an integral, constitutive element in feminism's overall understanding of citizenship, democracy, political self-possession, and equality. (1999: 181–3)

This demystified account provides the historical background for appreciating the deficiencies of second-wave feminism, making clear its continuity with the exclusionary political agendas and corollary distinctive blindnesses of the past, whether in the colonial world or in white settler states like the United States. If progress has been made recently in developing a less monochromatic, more democratic and inclusive feminism, it is because of the insights and criticisms of women of color, who were able from their vantage point to recognize in a way that most white feminists were not the racial dimension of mainstream feminism – that it was a specifically *white* feminism. By bringing race and gender together in the same framework, the racia-sexual contract acknowledges the conflicted coexistence of subordination and privilege in the situation of white women, and the corresponding need to theorize both on the multiple axes of cognition, exploitation, cultural representation, and political ideology and strategy.

(4)   *Nonwhite men as both subpersons and subcontractors*   We turn now to the other intermediate position in the diamond: nonwhite men. Like white women, they are both subpersons and subcontractors, but as I have emphasized, and tried to illustrate graphically in the tilt of the diamond, this is not an equivalence. Because race generally trumps gender in racial patriarchy, white women are originally positioned as superior not merely to nonwhite women but also to nonwhite men, though admittedly in a later more liberal period of the formation, this might change. White women are, after all, an integral part of the white family, the white household, in a way that nonwhites – slaves, savages, colonial populations – are not. (When domestic black slaves were part of the white household, it was obviously not on the same terms as white women.) The distinctive gender ideology of (white) complementarity, though undeniably demeaning and oppressive for women in its denial to them of full civic and political rights, does nonetheless link them with the superior white male apex of the diamond in a way that, say, racial ideologies of nonwhites as bestial, subhuman, in some cases exterminable, in most cases noncomplementary, do not. Thus if white women and nonwhite men are both – in the terminology I have suggested – subpersons, they are not subpersons of the same type and moral/civic standing, since the racia-sexual connection with the full personhood of the white male underwrites white women's status in a virtual way that has no equivalent for nonwhite men.

Moreover, and relatedly, the patriarchal relation between nonwhite men and nonwhite women should not be seen as equivalent to, or a black-faced version of, the patriarchal relation between white men and white women. Displacing the racial and sexual contracts with the composite racia-sexual contract requires us to rethink gender relations even when they are white-on-white and nonwhite-on-nonwhite. Male–female relations in the Europe and the Africa of, say, 1000 CE are (given the conventional periodization of the emergence of racism, and of race as a category) unaffected by race. So to describe them as white-on-white or black-on-black would be mistaken, since these categories and realities have no existence then. Once white supremacy is established, though (whether as racial slavery, nonwhite expropriation, or European colonial rule), and with it racial patriarchy, gender relations are changed since one is now interacting with someone of the opposite sex *within* a particular racial structure. Margaret Strobel emphasizes that: "Colonization trans formed not only the material lives of colonized people, but also their sense of what it meant to be female and male" (2002: 57), and Chandra Talpade Mohanty refers to "the effects of colonial institutions and policies in transforming indigenous patriarchies" (1991: 15). Thus patriarchal relations even between people of (what are now categorized as) the same nonwhite "race" in, say, pre-invasion Native America and Australasia, or precolonial Africa and Asia, are necessarily going to be altered by the overarching reality in its different manifestations of white domination.

To begin with the obvious point: the shaping of the public sphere by "men," so ideologically crucial to white feminist theory's analyses of the causes of female subordination, will not generally be within the power of nonwhite men under racial patriarchy – as slaves, expropriated and reservation-confined aborigines, colonial populations, marginalized racial minorities – to accomplish. Rather, the public sphere, with its distinctive patterning of the functioning of the state, the legal system, the market, civil society, will be a *white* male creation, or a *white* male transformation of the pre-existing polity. Thus nonwhite males are originally in no position to play the kind of public patriarchal role, as powerful global arbiters of the topography of the sociopolitical, attributed simply to "males" in much of white feminist theory. Paula Giddings points out that under slavery, "slave women maintained their authority over the domestic domain – as women have traditionally done – while Black men had no authority over the traditional male spheres of influence" (1984: 58). Likewise, Hazel Carby, in a classic critique of white feminism, asserts, "It bears repetition that black men have not held the same patriarchal positions of power that the white males have established. . . . There are very obvious power structures in both colonial and slave social formations and they are predominantly patriarchal. However, the historically specific forms of racism force us to modify or alter the application of the term 'patriarchy' to black men" (1996: 67–8). Similarly, in criticizing Kate Millett's generalization in her famous white feminist text *Sexual Politics* that "the military, industry, technology, universities, science, political office, and finance – in short, every avenue of power within the society, including the coercive force of the police, is entirely in male hands," Elizabeth Spelman raises the obvious objection: "But surely that is white male supremacy. Since when did Black males have such institutionally based power, in what Millett calls 'our culture'?" (2001: 77). Or consider coverture, another key concept in understanding white female subordination. Schloesser argues that "one's status in slavery nullified the protections of coverture; if either husband or wife was enslaved, the owner retained his or her right to treat his or her slave as property. Thus, patriarchal power of husbands over wives would have been disrupted at best. . . . These conditions suggest the primacy of the racial contract over the sexual contract" (2002: 33).

Understandably, then, nonwhite men have generally been seen by nonwhite women more as fellow oppressed than oppressors. The prime movers and shakers of the social order are not men as such but men of a particular race. And since race has generally trumped gender, as illustrated above, the dominant political tendency within nonwhite communities of all kinds has been the affirmation of racial solidarity over against the white oppressor (both male and female). Giddings writes that in the United States of the 1840s and 1850s, "All Black women abolitionists . . . were feminists. But when it came to a question of priorities, race, for most of them, came first" (1984: 55). Nor had this changed by the early twentieth century, in the years following the First World War: "[R]acial concerns overwhelmed those of sex. . . . [One Black feminist wrote]: 'feminist efforts are directed chiefly toward the realization of the equality of the races, the sex struggle assuming a subordinate place'" (Giddings 1984: 183). And obviously in the anticolonial struggles and national liberation movements of the twentieth century, it was the white colonizing power and the European settler population who were seen as the primary enemies, not nonwhite men. Indeed, even for postcolonial, post-1960s second-wave feminism, Benita Roth suggests that in the United States: "[Feminists of color] rejected the idea that their relationships with the men in their communities were, or should be, equivalent to those that existed between white women and white men. . . . [C]ommunity as such was conceptualized as the entire racial/ethnic community in battle against white America's domination" (2004: 43, 70).

Appreciating the realities of the racia-sexual contract, and the way it differentiates gender relations for the dominant and the subordinate races, thus helps us to understand what many white feminists of the time found quite mystifying: the refusal of many women of color to classify nonwhite men as part of the male "enemy." The overarching racial domination by whites invests the nonwhite male–female relationship with a dimension of joint transgender solidarity against oppression that will necessarily be absent in the gender relations of the privileged race.

Correspondingly, the nonwhite family and home will often be seen in terms quite different from those of white feminist theory. Under the terms of the racia-sexual contract, it is white supremacy that is crucially responsible for the subordinate status of nonwhite women, whether as white expropriation, slavery, colonial rule, or segregation. Usually the nonwhite family will be a refuge from the oppression of white supremacy, even if patriarchal relations obtain there. So the relation of the white woman and the nonwhite woman to the family will not be equivalent. If under racial patriarchy, as suggested, the public sphere for nonwhites can be thought of as being under the private rule of the collective white patriarch, the nonwhite private sphere will sometimes be the locus, or nucleus, of an incipient counterpublic sphere, the only place where nonwhites can exercise their limited freedoms and seek to challenge white rule. Hazel Carby points out that "during slavery, periods of colonialism, and under the present authoritarian state [in 1980s Britain], the black family has been a site of political and cultural resistance to racism" (1996: 64). It is a mistake, then, to see the family as the main source, transracially, of gender oppression, since for nonwhite women it may also be the place where opposition to the "patriarchal" rule of the global White Father and Mother is nurtured. So the classic white feminist slogan of the personal as the political acquires an alternative significance here, reflecting this more complex topography. If the public political sphere can for nonwhites in certain regimes be conceptualized as also being part of the white personal familial sphere, then the nonwhite personal sphere can sometimes serve as the virtual location of the beginnings of the oppositional nonwhite political sphere.

But these very structural realities, of course, can also facilitate the subcontractual role of nonwhite men in the racia-sexual contract. For both intermediate groups, white women and nonwhite men, the racia-sexual contract offers the option, which will be both ideologically dominant and politically most appealing, of a partitioned struggle against one aspect of the contract that meanwhile maintains the other. Subcontracting will always seem more attractive than fighting for the tearing up of the contract altogether. The racialization of all gender relations – not merely interracial gender relations – means that nonwhite men will benefit from, and be cognitively influenced by, the status positioning of nonwhite women at the bottom of the diamond. So if most white feminists sought gender equality within white racial superiority, most nonwhite male antiracist activists sought the restoration of traditional male privilege unqualified by race.

Thus the struggle for black "manhood" – think of the celebrated placard carried by black demonstrators in the United States in the 1950s and 1960s, "I AM A MAN" – usually meant, inter alia, the struggle for the restoration of the full range of nonwhite masculine gender privileges taken away by racial patriarchy, an end to the racial subordination of black men as mere subcontractors rather than fully and equally privileged male contractors. Activist Pauli Murray wrote in 1970:

> The black militant's cry for the retrieval of black manhood suggests . . . an association of masculinity with male dominance. . . . Reading through much of the current literature on the black revolution, one is left with the impression that for all the rhetoric about self-determination, the main thrust of black militancy is a bid of black males to share power with white males in a continuing patriarchal society in which both black and white females are relegated to a secondary status. . . . [T]he restoration of the black male to his lost manhood must take precedence over the claims of black women to equalitarian status. (1995: 187–90)

Similarly, in her mordant memoir of the "revolutionary" 1960s and 1970s, Michele Wallace recalls the gender-restricted nature of the "struggle" of the time:

> It took me three years to . . . understand that the countless speeches that all began "the black man. . ." did not include me. I learned. I mingled more and more with a black crowd, attended the conferences and rallies and parties and talked with some of the most loquacious of my brothers in blackness, and as I pieced together the ideal that was being presented for me to emulate, I discovered my newfound freedoms being stripped from me, one after another. No, I wasn't to wear makeup, but yes, I had to wear long skirts that I could barely walk in. No, I wasn't to go to the beauty parlor, but yes, I was to spend hours cornrolling my hair. No, I wasn't to flirt with or take shit off white men, but yes, I was to sleep with and take unending shit off black men . . . [T]he "new blackness" was fast becoming the new slavery for sisters. (1995: 221–3)

So nonwhite men were generally opposed to a racia-sexual contract that denied them male equality and gave white men access to "their" women. But the dominant response was not (and is still not) a demand for the outright leveling of the diamond structure, but rather for the clearing of a space for them at its apex. In *The Sexual Contract* (1988), Pateman describes the gender transition from feudal status to modernity in terms of the replacement of paternal patriarchy by fraternal patriarchy. Here the analogous goal is the replacement of racial patriarchy by transracial patriarchy, of the white-imposed racia-sexual contract by the raceless sexual contract. The trumping of gender by race in the structure of privilege can then be exploited by nonwhite men to demand of women of color a transgender solidarity against white racist oppression

that denies nonwhite men's subcontractual role in the racia-sexual contract, and represents any alliance with white feminists as a kind of
treachery. In the words of former Black Panther party leader Elaine
Brown: "A woman attempting the role of leadership was, to my proud
black Brothers, making an alliance with the 'counter-revolutionary,
man hating, lesbian, feminist white bitches' " (cited in Breines 2006: 57).

In her 1982 introduction to the first edition of *Home Girls: A Black
Feminist Anthology*, Barbara Smith listed various "myths" devised by
"Black men . . . to divert Black women from our own freedom," including the claims that "Racism is the primary (or only) oppression Black
women have to confront," "Feminism is nothing but man-hating," and
"Women's issues are narrow, apolitical concerns. People of color need
to deal with the 'larger struggle' " (2000a: xxviii–xxxi). Nearly 20 years
later, in her 1999 preface to a new edition, she laments how little has
changed outside the academy: "To this day most Black women are
unwilling to jeopardize their racial credibility (as defined by Black men)
to address the reality of sexism. . . . [I]t has been extremely difficult to
convince most in the Black community to take Black women's oppression seriously" (2000b: xiv–xv). She quotes Jill Nelson: "To be concerned with any gender issue is, by and large, still dismissed as a 'white
woman's thing'. . . . Even when lip service is given to sexism as a valid
concern, it is at best a secondary issue. First and foremost is racism and
the ways it impacts black men" (Nelson 1997: 156).

In effect, then, continuing nonwhite male benefit from racial patriarchy is denied, and the role of nonwhite men as subcontractual signatories is obscured. An overcoming of both of the contract's dimensions
will require a demystified confrontation with the fact that, like white
women, nonwhite men do gain something from the terms of the contract, and that if sex is racially differentiated, race is gender differentiated. Nonwhite men, like white women, are subcontractual subjects
and agents as well as oppressed victims. Gloria Anzaldúa writes about
Chicano machismo:

["M]achismo" is an adaptation to oppression and poverty and low self-
esteem. It is the result of hierarchical male dominance. . . . The loss of a
sense of dignity and respect in the macho breeds a false machismo which
leads him to put down women and even to brutalize them. . . . Though we
"understand" the root causes of male hatred and fear, and the subsequent
wounding of women, we do not excuse, we do not condone, and we will
no longer put up with it. . . . As long as woman is put down, the Indian
and the Black in all of us is put down. (2001: 99)

So in this revisionist picture, nonwhite men who resist the struggles
for equality of nonwhite women are in effect subcontractually complicit

with the role of white racism in confining them to the bottom of the social structure. In the racia-sexual contract, *nonwhite men get to be white supremacists too*, at least with respect to nonwhite women.

(5) *Nonwhite women as nonpersons and noncontractors* We come now to our primary subject of concern: nonwhite women. Originally located at the bottom of the diamond, disadvantaged by both gender and race, they do not even attain the qualified status and limited benefits of the two intermediate groups. So if the latter are at least subcontractors, if not full contractors, and subpersons, if not full persons, nonwhite women could be said to start off as noncontractors and nonpersons, subordinated by white men, nonwhite men, and white women.

The positioning of all three other groups gives them a greater or lesser material interest in blinding themselves to pertinent social realities. White men's ignorance will be greatest and most systematic, but white women and nonwhite men will have their particular blinders also. Only nonwhite women will have no vested interest in privilege, which does not, of course, mean that their cognitions will automatically be veridical, but means that they will have no group interest, as others do, in getting things wrong. It should be unsurprising, then, that from the start it is nonwhite women who have been the intellectual pioneers of this "intersectionalist" perspective, a feat all the more impressive considering that precisely because of their status they will usually have been the ones with the least access to education, and the ones facing the greatest epistemic barriers to their credibility. So they will find it more difficult to speak in the first place, and more difficult to be taken seriously even when they are heard (if they are).

Anna Julia Cooper pointed out that "[The colored woman] is confronted by both a woman question and a race problem, and is as yet an unknown or unacknowledged factor in both" (1998: 112–13). Sojourner Truth complained in 1867: "There is a great stir about colored men getting their rights, but not a word about the colored women; and if colored men get their rights, and not colored women get theirs, there will be a bad time about it" (Truth 1995: 37). In effect, women of color have had to fight on multiple fronts, against the racism of their own sex and the sexism of their own race. They have experienced the racia-sexual contract in full unmitigated force and from all directions at once (see figure 4). Thus it has been clearer to them than to others that what has variously been called "a single-axis framework" (Crenshaw 2000: 208), "a monist politics" (King 1995: 299), is necessarily going to be inadequate. Different metaphors have been used to express the complex intersectionality of their experience, but one of the most popular is Deborah King's insistence that nonwhite women do not experience race and gender as "additive," but as "multiplicative." Thus in what is seen as a classic 1988 paper, she rejects earlier models of "double" or even "triple" jeopardy:

> The experience of black women is apparently assumed, though never explicitly stated, to be synonymous with that of either black males or white females . . . It is mistakenly granted that either there is no difference in being black and female from being generically black (i.e., male) or generically female (i.e., white). . . . [T]he concepts of double and triple jeopardy have been overly simplistic in assuming that the relationships among the various discriminations are merely additive. . . . An interactive model, which I have termed multiple jeopardy, better captures those processes. The modifier "multiple" refers not only to several, simultaneous oppressions but to the multiplicative relationships among them as well. (King 1995: 295–7)

Obviously, then, neither the sexual nor the racial contracts, whether individually or additively, will succeed in mapping this reality. Instead, nonwhite women will fall between theoretical stools (refer back to figure 2: think of this as a literal graphic representation of the theoretical alternatives). Insofar as the sexual contract takes white women's experience as normative, insofar as the racial contract takes nonwhite men's experience as normative, nonwhite women will be squeezed out. As Kimberlé Crenshaw writes: "[Because of] the tendency to treat race and gender as mutually exclusive categories of experience and analysis . . . Black women are theoretically erased" (2000: 208). Similarly, Elizabeth Spelman (2001) refers to "the ampersand problem in feminist thought," the difficult challenge of thinking race and gender together. Kum-Kum Bhavnani suggests that in effect women of color will either be rendered "invisible" or appear as "merely an 'add-on'" (2001a: 4). Likewise, Angela Harris describes what she calls the "nuance theory," where one starts from white women as "the norm, or pure, essential Woman," and then makes generalizations about "all women" with "qualifying statements, often in footnotes": "the result is that black women become white women, only more so" (2000: 162). The ways in which race modifies gender and gender modifies race will not be part of the theoretical apparatus: appropriate concepts, narratives, "multiplicative" realities, will be missing. Instead the cognitive tendency will be to try to assimilate the experience of nonwhite women to one or the other of the two conceptual frameworks: women (nominally colorless, but tacitly white) and nonwhites (nominally genderless, but tacitly male).

But as the Combahee River Collective announced in their famous pioneering black feminist statement: "[T]he major systems of oppression are interlocking. The synthesis of these oppressions creates the conditions of our lives. . . . We know that there is such a thing as racial-sexual oppression which is neither solely racial nor solely sexual" (2000: 261, 264). In the "contractual" translation of these claims that I am advocating, the racia-sexual contract registers this interlocking and multiplicity, recognizing that nonwhite women have a distinct location in the diamond, one that is separate from both nonwhite men and white women, with peculiar "contractual" features of its own. Thus the formal partitioning of the different subject positions requires us to think through how these different aspects of the contract will impact nonwhite women. In the absence of such differentiation, one will fall back on concepts and tropes that are insensitive to the peculiarities of their position, assimilating it to one or the other of the terms of the sexual or racial contracts on their own.

To begin with, by virtue (vice?) of being nonwhite, women of color, like men of color, fall on the wrong side of the racial line that, with the establishment of global white supremacy, demarcates the civilized from the primitive and savage. Thus the nonwhite woman is immediately differentiated from the white woman by her racial inferiority, and as such is necessarily located in a different category, which is why any conceptual apparatus presupposing a homogeneous gender status is going to be wrong from the start.

Moreover, white women were not merely civilized but, as we saw earlier in the discussion of Louise Newman, agents of civilization, having a "unique role" "as civilizers of racially inferior peoples," "civilization-workers" exercising "cultural authority over those they conceived as their evolutionary and racial inferiors" (1999: 21, 53). In the iconography of the West, the white woman, in keeping with her contradictory location, has been glorified as well as degraded, chosen in paintings, sculpture, statuary, and monuments as an appropriate figure to represent Civilization, Progress, Culture, Europe, Justice, Liberty, and so on. For the woman of color, on the other hand, *non*contradictorily, *un*equivocally, located at the bottom of the diamond, it has been simple degradation without glorification. The Statue of Liberty, so emblematic of the United States, is not merely a woman – certainly not a generic woman – but a *white* woman. Can one imagine a black or Native American woman as the Statue of Liberty? Rather, the black woman's contrasting status in the national iconography is summed up by a 1920s proposal by the Daughters of the Confederacy (fortunately not implemented) "to erect a statue in Washington, D.C., in memory of 'Black Mammies'" (Giddings 1984: 184). Where women of color appear, it is as the Savagery, Backwardness, Nature, Africa/Asia/Aboriginal America, Bondage that need to be enlightened and liberated, the Servility that smilingly accepts its subordinate place, or the illicit Carnality that threatens the white family.

Morally, then, nonwhite women's location at the bottom of the racia-sexual contract lowers them normatively beneath the subpersonhood of white women, who were, after all, when all is said and done, the mothers, wives, sisters, daughters, of white men. While some white women might have fallen short of the (original) virginal ideal, nonwhite women as a *class* – especially black women – were seen as unchaste, nat-urally promiscuous, likely to be infected with sexually transmitted diseases of various kinds. Antoinette Burton points out that women of India were, in the "feminist-imperial hierarchy" of the nine-teenth century's "Orientalist" views of female sexuality, judged to be "inherently licentious and immoral" (1992: 143). Chandra Talpade Mohanty quotes from a US Exclusion Act which, based on the 1870 hearings on Chinese prostitution, "assumed that all 'Oriental women' wanting to emigrate would engage in 'criminal and demoralizing acts' " (1991: 25). Paula Giddings cites an English slave trader's description of black women as "hot constitution'd ladies," possessed of a "lascivious temper" (1984: 35). Indeed, this was "scientifically" backed up (in different ways) by the eighteenth- and nineteenth-century racial science of theorists like George Buffon and J. J. Virey, who singled out black women in particular as embodied epitomes of a primitive and bestial sexuality (Gilman 1986). Similarly, Kimberlé Crenshaw cites a 1918 law court characterization of blacks as a "race that is largely immoral," and a 1902 commentator's view that "the idea [of a virtuous Negro woman] is . . . absolutely inconceivable to me" (2000: 234 n48), the corollary being that, by contrast with white women, "there has been absolutely no [white] institutional effort to regulate Black female chastity" (2000: 223). If some white women were fallen, no black woman was capable of rising to a level from which she could fall. There is a sense, indeed, in which black women's genitalia were not "private parts" but "public parts," open by their very nature to the scrutiny and access of the inquir-ing white gaze, as illustrated by the horrific story of Sarah (Saartjie) Baartman, the so-called Hottentot Venus (Holmes 2007). The racia-sexual contract deprives nonwhite women as a group of the protections that at least some white women had, making them carnality incarnate, whereas in the case of white women, as Richard Dyer (1997) argues, whiteness is so linked to the spiritual, to the disembodied, that sexual-ity can be combined with, redeemed by, the disincarnating spirit of white racial metacorporeality. So whites, but not blacks, get to have it both ways. Not Civilization, Progress, Culture, but National Mammy, Transnational Pudendum – such were the defining images of the black woman.

The racia-sexual contract therefore shapes conceptions of sexuality and femininity aesthetically as well as morally. The nonwhite woman, especially the darker nonwhite woman, is uglier as well as lower. The fetishization of the white female body extends, of course, beyond the symbolic and metaphoric to the libidinal. In his study of somaesthetic whiteness, Richard Dyer points out that "In [the] Western tradition, white is beautiful because it is the color of virtue," so that, in a 1950s ad for Lux toilet soap, illustrated by a white movie star, "cultural symbol (classical antiquity), product and effect are all linked by the idea of whiteness as, in [Jackie] Stacey's words, 'purity, cleanliness, beauty and civilized culture' and by the attainment of ideal (therefore implicitly white) feminine beauty" (1997: 72, 78). So even if this ethereal ideal is out of reach for the average white woman, she is at least visually categorized within the same somatotype, as against the woman of color whose features disqualify her from the start.

In reviewing the work of black women writers, Mary Helen Washington points out that a recurrent theme is "the intimidation of color," and she cites her introduction to an edited short story collection of black women writers, *Black-Eyed Susans*: "In almost every novel or autobiography written by a black woman, there is at least one incident in which the dark-skinned girl wishes to be either white or light-skinned with 'good' hair" (1982: 210). Across the black diaspora, from the Caribbean to Latin America and the United States, norms of "good" and "bad" hair, "nice" and not-so-nice complexions, derived from what Harmannus Hoetink (1967) calls the "white somatic norm," influence aesthetic judgments about self and other for women in particular. Angela Gilliam cites a Brazilian proverb: "Preta p'ra trabalhar, branca p'ra casar, e mulata p'ra fornicar" ("A black woman to work, a white woman to marry, and a brown-skinned woman to screw") (1991: 227, 233 n10). But it's not just blacks. On the other side of the world, Tricia Capistrano (2006) describes how, in her native Philippines, "skin-whitening products fly off the pharmacy shelves," and how as a child she was told to stay out of the sun lest she get even darker, and urged "to pinch the bridge [of her nose] daily so that the arch would be higher."

Thus Angela Harris's (2000) critique of Catharine MacKinnon's analysis of beauty standards argues that she misses the point that "a black woman's pain at not being considered fully feminine is different qualitatively, not merely quantitatively, from the pain MacKinnon describes. It is qualitatively different because the ideology of beauty concerns not only gender but race." She goes on to cite the fate of Pecola Breedlove, the protagonist of Toni Morrison's *The Bluest Eye*:

> Her story ends in despair . . . not because she's even further away from
> ideal beauty than white women are, but because Beauty *itself* is white, and

she is not and can never be. . . . There is a difference between the hope that the next makeup kit or haircut or diet will bring you salvation and the knowledge that nothing can. The relation of black women to the ideal of white beauty is not a more intense form of white women's frustration: It is something other, a complex mingling of racial and gender hatred from without, self-hatred from within. (Harris 2000: 163)

The internalization of a racist somatic norm means that the white body is perpetually hovering as an unquiet corporeal ghost, a haunting and mocking spirit never to be exorcised from the house of one's inferior flesh.[6]

So there is a sense in which white women's complaint about their sexual objectification, though of course completely justified, is itself a luxury of the intermediate status they occupy in the racia-sexual contract. As the distaff side of the master race, they benefit by being the complementary sexual and romantic objects of their co-racial subjects, who control the iconography of the social order. Insofar as white aesthetic standards, and their link with sexuality and romance, are propagated through the media as hegemonic for the whole society (indeed for the planet) rather than being relativized to race, white women's situation is necessarily different from those women of color too dark and non-Caucasoid ever to achieve desirable femininity. In her recent exploration of the causes for the failure to develop "a racially integrated women's liberation movement in the United States," Winnifred Breines points out that black women's resentment over "interracial liaisons between black men and white women" was an important if rarely publicly discussed contributory factor: "The continuity of this painful issue is striking as is its power to divide black and white women. It came up repeatedly as a source of bitterness" (2006: 6, 61). The hoped-for global sisterhood, already divided by class and race, is also split by differential handicapping in the sexual competition.

Black women's resistance, accordingly, to being "endlessly caricatured as grotesque and ugly in popular representations in the dominant culture" has centered on "subverting dominant standards of beauty" (Glenn 2002: 131). Donna Hope writes about Jamaican dancehall that the body becomes "a representative canvas that is adorned and accessorized with regalia (clothing, jewellery, hairstyles and hair colours)" affirming a "daring, aggressive, loud and demanding [identity]," which in its "presentation of black, lower-class and grassroots femininity and eroticism in a public arena gives legitimacy and a sense of personhood" to women stigmatized by the color hierarchy of Jamaican society (2006:

[6] For a detailed philosophical analysis of Pecola's plight from a Foucauldian perspective, see George Yancy (2004b).

126, 76). Differently located in the racia-sexual contract, black women originally (and still presently) had (have) to affirm black aesthetic worth rather than protest its fetishization and commodification.

Cognitively, then, the positioning of nonwhite women, with its intersecting oppressions, has the epistemic virtue of fostering a far greater realism about the actual nature of the social order. Unlike white women, nonwhite women will generally be more likely to be conscious of both aspects of the racia-sexual contract since they are subordinated by both. White women, by contrast, being elevated rather than subordinated by race, and the beneficiaries of a racialized gender ideology less straightforwardly oppressive than that applying to nonwhite women, will be more susceptible to illusions about their situation. Thus the very fact that white women had to "discover" that they were oppressed, that (in Betty Friedan's famous formulation) they were haunted by "the problem that had no name," was itself the clearest manifestation of their comparative privilege over their darker sisters. As Ruth Frankenberg (1993) shows in her interviews, white women are generally clueless about their own racial advantages, seeing themselves simply as "women" without realizing, or being willing to admit, the extent to which their location as *white* women shapes their lives and empowers them. bell hooks comments: "To [black women] it was just another indication of the privileged living conditions of middle- and upper-class white women that they would need a theory to inform them that they were 'oppressed' " (2000: 140). For women of color subordinated not just by gender but by white supremacy, whether in the form of aboriginal expropriation, slavery, Jim Crow, or European colonial rule, there was no problem in identifying "the problem," and it definitely *did* have a name: "white people"! So as emphasized at the start, the standpoint of nonwhite women at the bottom of the diamond tendentially produces the greatest cognitive clarity, unlike all three of the other subject positions, which are influenced to a greater or lesser extent by the epistemology of ignorance, the cognitive adaptation to privilege and corresponding shaping of epistemic norms.

And this leads back, of course, to the conceptual consequence discussed at the start. Because of the comparative social advantage of the two intermediate locations, both white women and nonwhite men have a set of concepts tailored to their own experience that between them occlude the distinctive features of the nonwhite woman's experience. So as famously illustrated by the 1991 Senate hearings on the confirmation of Clarence Thomas for the US Supreme Court, nonwhite women may end up being cognitively erased. Kimberlé Crenshaw points out that dominant competing narratives of what had or had not happened between Thomas and Anita Hill were polarized "into separate and competing political camps," "blacks and women" (1992: 403). There was a "lack of available and widely comprehended narratives to communicate the reality of her experience as a black woman to the world," one that was "intersectional" (1992: 404). The rape narrative went with (white) feminism's history of patriarchal subordination by men; the lynching narrative (high-tech or not) went with the history of black (male) subordination by whites. Neither a white woman nor a black man, Hill was caught between two dominant stories, neither of which fit her situation: as a supposed victim of sexual subordination (but as a nonwhite member of a class traditionally categorized as naturally promiscuous, and so not harmable in this way); and making the kind of possibly mendacious sexual accusations about a black man that had traditionally been used to justify lynching (but not when the victim was herself black). So in a sense, Crenshaw suggests, there was no conceptual location for Hill, no readily available cognitive apparatus to make sense of her: "the simultaneity of Hill's race and gender identity was essentially denied" (1992: 406). The *partial* insights into the racia-sexual contract's oppressive historical workings that had attained at least some acceptability because of the *partial* success of the feminist and civil rights struggles did not in conjunction add up to an illuminating *whole*, but rather extinguished each other. For each insight had as its blind side a complementary darkness about the *full* dimensions of the contract as it affected those at the bottom that jointly overshadowed Hill's testimony, discrediting her in advance.

Moreover, Crenshaw and other critical race feminists (Wing 2003) have argued that this exclusionary dichotomization manifests itself not merely in the absence of appropriate narratives for nonwhite women, but in their problematic juridical status as well. Models of discrimination, and corresponding formulations of antidiscrimination law, are based respectively on race *or* gender, where, as before, the paradigmatic experience of gender discrimination is that of the white woman and the paradigmatic experience of racial discrimination is that of the nonwhite man. Once again, then, black women, rather than being accommodated by the combination of the two, end up as debarred by both. Crenshaw suggests that a "single-axis framework" ends up excluding black women since "[race] discrimination tends to be viewed in terms of sex- or class-privileged Blacks [while] in sex discrimination cases, the focus is on race- and class-privileged women" (2000: 208–9). By examining a series of cases where black women were the plaintiffs, she demonstrates through the varying problematic court judgments a general underlying pattern of assuming that black women's "claims of exclusion must be unidirectional" (2000: 216). But in actuality "Black women can experience discrimination in ways that are both similar to and different from those experienced by white women and Black men" (2000: 217). This greater degree of complexity of inter- and intragroup domination is recognized in figure 4, the graphic representation of the racia-sexual contract, thereby providing us with a more accurate picture, both morally and juridically, of the functioning of racial patriarchy and its distinctively variegated subject positions.

The mainstream social contract mystifies these realities by presenting a white male fairyland, a Walt Disneyfied picture of the present and recent past, complete with magic rides and wishing-makes-it-so idealizing wands. In proposing the racia-sexual contract as a superior modeling of the world, I am trying to build on the insights of women of color in the activist movements of the past few decades, attempting to break down this whitewashing and masculating of reality, facing the truths obfuscated and ignored in the idealized orthodox contract. Ignorance "is not a passive state," but "creat[es] the conditions which ensure its continuance," writes antiracist white feminist Marilyn Frye (1983: 118, 120). "The dominant white culture is killing us slowly with its ignorance," says *mestiza* Gloria Anzaldúa (2001: 102). "Certain absences are so stressed, so ornate, so planned, they call attention to themselves," suggests black writer Toni Morrison (2000b: 34), thus raising the questions: "What are the strategies of escape from knowledge? Of willful oblivion?" The theory of the racia-sexual contract tries to overcome this strategic ignorance, this willed obliviousness, by inciting the "invasion" of the "dissonant bodies" of women of color (Puwar 2004) into the cloistered, (ostensibly) monastic, and Jim-Crowed white male conceptual space of the classic contract, thereby exposing its own nonrepresentative, denied and disavowed, white corporeal particularity. Thus it attempts to fulfill the normative mission which that contract has in effect abandoned: contributing to the creation of a society that would realize the egalitarian ideals of liberalism for the whole population, and not just the white male subsection of it.

7

On Critics and Contract

Carole Pateman

The thread that has run though all my work is an interest in democratic theory and a concern with democratization; that is, with changes required for the creation of a more democratic society. *The Sexual Contract* (1988) was not couched in terms of democratic theory, but I see it as part of my contribution to this area of scholarship.[1] I have a long-standing interest in early modern theories of an original contract. My first critical study of the subject was *The Problem of Political Obligation*, originally published in 1979 when a major revival of contract theory was already underway in the wake of John Rawls's *A Theory of Justice*, first published in 1971. My two books on contract theory have not often been considered together, but my analysis in *The Problem of Political Obligation* informs my argument about the sexual contract. In 1979, together with Teresa Brennan, I also published " 'Mere Auxiliaries to the Commonwealth,' " my first feminist reading of Hobbes and Locke.

---

[1] I have been very gratified over the years by the large number of scholars from many different disciplinary backgrounds and intellectual persuasions who have read, commented on, criticized, and made use of *The Sexual Contract*. One of the most pleasing developments has been that scholars working in very different cultural milieus have found something of value in my book. Despite the fact that I made clear that my argument was specifically about Anglo-American political theory and societies, scholars of the Middle East have told me that they have found *The Sexual Contract* a valuable source, a Korean translation was published in 2001, it has been used in a paper on Nepal (Tamang 2002), and I recently learnt that it appears in a study of drama in colonial India. It has been read by scholars in disciplines that range from political theory and women's studies, to law, history, literature, French studies, postcolonial studies, and art theory. I have made other responses to critics in, e.g., Pateman (1990a, 1990b), and on a different note (1996); see also Pateman (1997).

Reading critics of my work over the years has made me aware that *The Sexual Contract* is much more complex and contains a much denser argument than I appreciated when I was writing it. I have always been a rigorous editor of my own work, and I have thought for some time now that perhaps my argument was expressed rather too concisely for its own good. As critics have noted, some aspects could have benefited from further explication, and if it had been more leisurely perhaps some of the more bizarre accounts of my argument might have been avoided. Yet I doubt that would have been sufficient to deter critics who try to stuff my book into boxes labeled with conventional classifications in feminism and political theory. I was unlucky, too, that it got caught up in various trends in feminist theory, such as the vogue for hunting out essentialism, an attack on feminism for complicity in the sins of the fathers, and a preoccupation with individual differences and experiences at the expense of institutions and structures of power. Attention thus got distracted from the full scope of my argument and from the concepts around which it was framed. Few commentators have discussed my notions of civil subordination, civil slavery, or my use of the paradox of slavery. Little has been said about my analysis of the employment contract and my argument about subordination and exploitation. Property in the person is mentioned more often, but seldom the reason why I regard it as so important.

The Sexual Contract began from a simple enough starting-point. After Teresa Brennan and I wrote our article, I decided to take a more extensive look at early modern theories of an original contract. I wanted to reassess a major claim of contemporary political theorists: that if we think of our (Anglo-American) society as if it were based on an original contract or, alternatively, if we formulate principles that would be agreed to if we were in the original position, we can see that our major institutions are structured by free relationships in a system of voluntary cooperation.

In *The Problem of Political Obligation* my criticism of this claim was directed at citizenship in the liberal democratic state, one of the three institutions that lie at the heart of modern societies. In *The Sexual Contract* my analysis focused on the other two institutions – marriage and employment. I looked in some detail at the creation of, and relationship between, modern marriage (under coverture) and employment from the seventeenth and eighteenth centuries to the end of their patriarchal heyday, which in Britain covered the period from around 1840 to the end of the 1970s. I was also concerned with the connections between marriage and women's standing, or lack of standing, as citizens.

From *Participation and Democratic Theory* (1970) onward, my primary concern in reading the classic texts of political theory has been with what we can learn about how we have arrived at where we are today. My use of historical material in *The Sexual Contract* serves a similar purpose. We need theoretical and historical understanding in order to provide insights into how best to move forward to a more democratic future. My interpretation of the early modern theorists of an original contract was thus undertaken in a spirit similar to Moira Gatens's view of genealogy; I was asking "what form of life has been supported . . . by a particular narrative about the origins of a body politic" (Gatens 1996: 30).[2] But Gatens and other critics deny that I was undertaking this form of inquiry. In one of the more peculiar readings of my book, they insist that I was concocting a history of origins (see section III).

Instead of engaging in such a quixotic quest, I investigated the logic of contract theory, or, more exactly, I tried to unravel a number of different aspects of that logic. At the most general level I explored how, once the logic of stories of an original contract is appreciated, it becomes possible to see something of the way in which the sexual contract – the view that men have justified right of government over women in the modern state – has been, so to speak, built into major social institutions.[3] I was concerned too with the logic of stories of an original contract. A very small part of this was the discovery of two logical gaps that I filled with conjectures: first, Hobbes's lack of any explanation of how free and equal women in the state of nature become subject to their husbands in civil society; and, second, the absence of any account of the genesis of the sons over whom fathers rule.

I analyzed the logic of the structural connections between the institutions of marriage, employment, and citizenship in the modern state. I should note here that my approach differs in two crucial respects from Hegel's use of the trilogy of state, civil society, and family. First, my argument is about the institution of marriage, not about the family (see section IV). Second, theorists of an original contract used the term

---

[2] Gatens (1996: 42) argues that I offer "an incomplete genealogy," so that *The Sexual Contract* "performs" what Nietzsche called a genealogy "of the English kind." Wendy Brown (1995: 138) also wants to turn my historical argument "in the direction of genealogy." Genealogy and Nietzsche have been all the rage for some time, but Jacqueline Stevens has recently argued that the view that genealogy derives from Nietzsche is mistaken, propagated through Gilles Deleuze by a misreading on the part of Michel Foucault. Nietzsche "mocked genealogists and their enterprise"; his objection was to history "used to proffer moralizing, self-righteous, functionalist justifications of the status quo" (Stevens 2003: 559, 560).

[3] Brown argues that my focus on contract involves a "fetish" since "an imaginary social contract" is no longer required to legitimate a "liberal" political order (1995: 137). I want to move away from contract, but the "social contract" is commonly invoked not only by political philosophers but in popular political rhetoric and discussion, so it is necessary to investigate the logic and power of this political fiction.

"civil society" to refer to political society, the modern state (that includes marriage) created through an original contract. Hegel's "civil society" marks out only part of this social order; in particular, it refers to "the market." But the crucial market in modern states is the labor market, without which there can be no institution of employment.

The political fiction of property in the person (the commodity of labor power is one example) is central to another aspect of my argument, in which I teased out the logic of the process through which subordination can be presented as an exemplification of freedom. My analysis was designed to help an understanding of how certain concepts and ideas allow an institution of subordination (say, employment) to be seen as constituted by free relations. Wage labor can then be placed at the opposite pole from unfree labor and treated as an essential part of democratization. This logic demands an appreciation of what, following Hegel, I called the standpoint of contract or contractarianism, the rigorously consistent form of contract theory. An analysis of contractarianism, a form of political argument that, unusually, does not flinch from the view that there are contracts all the way down, shows how subordination can be generated through contract. Let me emphasize that I was concerned with *voluntary* contracts (about property in the person) and the problem of how it is that a contract can be freely entered into, result in (civil) subordination, and yet be seen as creating free relations (see also Ellerman 2005).

My investigation of the classic stories of an original contract is relevant to two widespread misunderstandings of my argument. The first is that my book is about "social contract theory." I have indeed written a book about social contract theory – about the justification of the authority of the modern state over its citizens – but it is not *The Sexual Contract*. I left the social contract to one side in the latter because it was the subject of *The Problem of Political Obligation*.[4] It was not until some years after I had written *The Problem of Political Obligation* that I came to appreciate that the social contract was only *one* dimension of the original contract and that there was another dimension, the sexual contract, to be explicated.[5] Standard interpretations of the texts present the

---

[4] Not because "solutions to the problem of male competition don't rivet the interest of females": (Caton 1990: 67).

[5] Joanne Wright argues that "[i]t appears that Pateman develops the concept of the sexual contract . . . in the abstract, drawing on a variety of sources including Freud's primal scene narrative, and subsequently applies it, unsuccessfully in my view, to the individual social contract theorists" (2004: 116). I am unclear how I could have possibly arrived at the idea of a sexual contract "in the abstract." It occurred to me after a long process of reading the early modern theorists and thinking about them in relation to feminist and socialist political argument.

creation of civil society as a story of the government of the state. Nothing is said about *men's* claim to political right or about the creation of other social institutions, such as marriage. The implicit assumption seems to be that these are "natural," but the logic of an original contract, the creation of a new social order that then *stands in contrast* to the state of nature, is that all institutions must be "civil" (i.e. conventional or created through contract).

Unfortunately, the habit of treating theories of an original contract as if they were merely one-dimensional and so calling them "social contract theories" still persists among political theorists and political philosophers.[6] This characterization neatly obscures both the sexual and racial contracts and so buries the stories of domination embodied in the original contract. "Social contract theory" can thus continue to be told as a story of freedom, usually embellished today with arguments about distribution and exploitation, and there seems to be nothing at stake about domination and subordination.

This terminological habit is relevant to the second misunderstanding of my argument. Numerous commentators state that I see the sexual contract as prior to the "social contract," i.e. the original contract. The conflation of the original contract with the social contract helps explain why this mistake is made so frequently. If the social contract *is* the original contract then it inevitably appears that I must be claiming that the sexual contract came first. But that is not my argument. Rather, my retelling of the story and analysis of the logic of contract theory entails that the two contracts come into being simultaneously. There is only one original contract, although each theorist provides his own version of the story, and the sexual and social (and racial) contracts come into being together, two (three) dimensions of a single pact that creates civil society.

There are two other misconceptions about my book. Many critics assume that my argument is about liberalism. The enormous influence of Rawls has no doubt contributed to the way in which contract theory disappears into liberalism, but theories of original contracts and the

---

[6] Rousseau's famous book is, of course, called *The Social Contract*, but that is not sufficient reason, especially in light of his other work, to continue the practice. Paul Hegarty (1999: 293) claims that Rousseau "eludes" my criticism in *The Sexual Contract*, but flattered though I am to have Rousseau read through the lens of my book, the reason that Hegarty reads my argument in this way, if I have understood him correctly, is that he is concerned with the social contract and the origin of "society" as such. He argues that my earlier recognition, i.e. in *The Problem of Political Obligation*, that Rousseau differed from the other theorists has disappeared. But Rousseau's criticism of his fellows is over the *social* contract; he concurs with them on the *sexual* contract.

standpoint of contract are distinct traditions of argument that have little in common with some other theories also called "liberal." The terms "liberalism" and "liberal" are now so overused, and cover such a wide array of theories from Hobbes to Rawls and beyond, that more often than not they are a hindrance rather than a help to theoretical clarity. Second, it is also often assumed that I was writing about consent, but my argument rests on a distinction, which I first drew in *The Problem of Political Obligation*, between contract and consent. Unlike consent, the practice of contract brings something new into being. The original agreement is a contract of creation; it is not consent. A new political order, a civil society, is (said to be) created through the original pact.

I The Original Contract, Contracts, and Institutions

Critics have raised a number of questions about the connection in *The Sexual Contract* between my interpretation of theories of an original contract and actual contracts and about the relationship between contracts and institutions.

Nancy Fraser (1997a) charges that I reduce institutions to a series of "dyadic relations" between a master and subject in which an individual superior commands an individual subordinate. It follows, she argues, that I cannot account for "gendered constraints on women's lives" that involve "processes in which the actions of many people are abstractly or impersonally mediated" (1997a: 227). In a marriage there are two individuals, and, similarly, each worker is subject to a boss, but my interest was not in these "dyads." Rather, my focus was on what it meant, in law and society, to be a "husband" or "wife," "worker" or "employer." Power was exercised by "husbands" within the (patriarchal) institution of marriage, but whether any particular husband availed himself of the power available to him was not the point, as John Stuart Mill recognized.[7] Fraser complains that I overlook workers' varied experiences in

---

[7] Fraser argues that in my alleged reductionist approach I am following in a line of feminist thinkers beginning with Mary Wollstonecraft and John Stuart Mill. While I am delighted to be placed in such an illustrious lineage, Fraser has misread them too. Neither theorist works with a model of a dyadic power relation; both are concerned with marriage and employment as institutions, although, of course, Mill has a great deal more to say about the latter institution than Wollstonecraft. The statement that Mill composed before his marriage to Harriet Taylor, declaring that he would never use the powers he was about to acquire as a husband, illustrates my point. Mill could not legally divest himself of his power because, in entering into the marriage contract, he did not merely become a member of a "dyad" but a participant in an institution governed by law as well as social mores. I discuss Mill in *The Sexual Contract*, and Wollstonecraft in Pateman (2003).

employment. Within the institution of employment, an institution that manifestly involves processes of abstract or impersonal mediation of individuals' actions, bosses and workers can behave in many different ways, but my interest was not in these varied experiences (that would have been an entirely different book) but in the fact that to be a "boss" is to have power over subordinates.

That is, I was interested in the authority structures within which power is exercised, in the historical importance of mastery and the ways in which its legacy still lingers. Individuals enter into contracts about property in the person and the consequence is that they become "wives" or "workers," "husbands" or "employers," superiors and subordinates, precisely because they then interact within an *institution*. The institution is maintained through these contracts, which create relationships that reproduce "wives," etc. and thus uphold structures. Far from setting up "a binary" of contract and institutions (Gatens 1996: 34), my argument is based on the mutual interaction (dialectic) between contracts and structures.

I have also been criticized for failing to separate contract and institutions. Donna Dickenson argues that contract is "not itself inimical to women's interests" (1997: 64).[8] Her insistence that feminists should embrace contract relies on the assumption that the practice of contract is always politically neutral. She argues that it is not the "mechanism" of contract itself that gives rise to the problems with which I am concerned but the "content" of the contract; namely, that what is at issue is a (sexual) contract about women's bodies (1997: 67). Elizabeth Anderson (1990: 1806–7) offers a similar criticism, arguing that the problem is "patriarchal norms" embedded in the noncontractual basis of contract, not contract as such.

In this line of argument, contract is, once again, being seen as the means to defeat patriarchy – a restatement of the view that I was criticizing in my book. Contract is separated from social relations and institutions and seen as a neutral mechanism, waiting to be filled by content. I emphasized (1988: 57–9) that contracts about property in the person were peculiar in that they do not involve an exchange, or at least do so only in a very special sense. To repeat, these contracts create *relationships* (of subordination) within institutions. The specific form of contract that I analyzed is not an abstract mechanism but inseparable from its relational and institutional context.[9]

---

[8] For examples of feminist use of contract argument see, e.g., Hirshman and Larson (1998) and Ertman (2001).

[9] Compare my discussion of the separation of rules from social practices, with reference to promising, in *The Problem of Political Obligation* (1985: 26–30).

Another criticism is that I did not adequately account for the connection I drew between early modern political theories and the institutions of marriage and employment. I have been criticized, for example, for "textual essentialism," and "[assuming] a straightforward identity among political philosophy, juridical discourse and practice, and domestic and work relations" (Dean 1992: 130, 127).[10] Gatens argues that "*The Sexual Contract* is a confusing text because Pateman does not convincingly manage to link its two parts: that which concerns the repressed of social contract stories . . . with that which concerns the character of contemporary social institutions" (1996: 42).

The connection I was making seemed unremarkable to me at the time, both in light of the revival of contract theory and the secondary literature which assumes that "the social contract" is relevant for an understanding of our social and political institutions.[11] My argument rests on the belief that the ideas embodied in the classic texts of political theory, including the stories of an original contract, have helped shape our major institutions. Without the ideas of ("natural") individual freedom and equality, modern practices of contract, citizenship, and democracy could not have developed. However, the relationship between texts, ideas, social relations, and institutions is hardly straightforward.

To call upon "freedom" or "equality" without further specification only goes so far. General, abstract ideas have to be given a more detailed interpretation if they are to be politically useful. The interpretations are often bitterly contested and so feed into different institutional structures. Declarations of individual freedom and equality have helped shape the social order since the seventeenth century – but they have shaped both subordination and freedom. Thus I noted that the abolitionists called upon natural freedom to denounce slavery and that another conception of the "individual" and his "freedom" was used to justify civil slavery (Pateman 1988: 65–6). "Freedom" helps emancipate and subordinate.

"All men are born free" is a theoretical premise that has revolutionary implications. The justification of all structures of authority is thrown open to question and (logically) only one basis for legitimate government remains; the governed have to agree to be governed. Theorists of an original contract faced a dilemma. The government of

[10] But compare Nancy Hirschmann (1990: 172) who writes that my discussion of prostitution and "surrogate" motherhood "are the most deconstructive readings in the book, as Pateman takes as her 'texts' the actual, contractual practices."

[11] This seems to be taken for granted in a recent survey of contract theory, which includes Diana Coole's (1994) discussion of feminist interpretations; see Boucher and Kelly (1994b).

the modern state must be based (or must be said to be based) on agreement but, at the same time, the necessity of agreement could be used to challenge power structures, not least that of marriage, that they had no wish to disturb. *The Sexual Contract* can be read as an exploration of the stratagems adopted by the theorists of an original contract to limit the extent of their arguments and of the way in which those limits were embodied in subsequent political theory, law, social custom, and central institutions. Yet the radical implications of the starting-point are always there – feminist political theorists had begun to pursue them by the late seventeenth century – so that propping up relations of subordination in the modern world is a continuing theoretical, as well as a practical, task.

Moreover, my understanding of theories of an original contract is very different from that of the contemporary political philosophers who rely on what Charles Mills calls an ideal contract. Both he and I analyze "the nonideal contract . . . not to ratify it but to use it to explain and expose the inequities of the actual nonideal polity and help us see through the theories and moral justifications offered in defense of them" (Mills 1997: 5). Contemporary contract theorists typically assume that, while there may be a need for some distributive adjustment to achieve a more just society, no institutional or structural change is required.

Thus, *The Sexual Contract* and *The Racial Contract* are set apart from Rawlsian contract theory. The latter is about the principles that should govern a just society and contract becomes "a conceptual device to elicit our intuitions about justice" (Mills 1997: 5). Furthermore, Rawlsian contract theory has developed from Rawls's adherence to the Kantian view that the original contract is an idea of reason and not a portrayal of a (hypothetical or actual) social order, and so the notion of a contract becomes otiose. The focus of Rawlsian argument is moral reasoning. The consequence is made explicit in Hampton's (2001) feminist defense of "Kantian contractarianism." She treats contract as a mere image or metaphor that is useful for effective moral reasoning, yet the reasoning could take place without any reference to contract. As she says, the real work in this mode of argument is done by a conception of the person and equal worth of the person, not the notion of contract, which is not "in any sense foundational, or even necessary" (2001: 357).

In contrast, theories of original contracts were not merely potentially dispensable, heuristic devices to aid moral argument, but *political* theories devised to throw light onto societies of the time and to justify a particular form of political order, a modern "civil society." Their subject matter is human characteristics and relations, social institutions and practices. These theories are part of the "great transformation" (Polanyi 1944), the move from premodern or traditional societies to the modern state, a transformation encapsulated in formulations such as the shift from *Gemeinschaft* to *Gesellschaft*, from ascription to achievement, from status to contract, or from the state of nature to civil society.[12]

Standard interpretations of the texts of the theorists of an original contract treat the latter transformation as a move from patriarchy to contract. In *The Sexual Contract* I argued that, while traditional and classic (paternal) patriarchy were defeated, a new modern, fraternal form was created through and constituted by contract. The logic of this theoretical form then helps us understand the structure of central institutions (those maintained through contracts about property in the person) in modern Anglo-American societies. A crucial aspect of this logic is that, as I put it in one formulation, there are no feudal relics in civil society. A society is created *de novo* through the original pact; the state of nature is no more.

Fraser denies that this is my argument. She states that in *The Sexual Contract* what "appears to be a major historical transformation in the mode of domination is actually the same old wine of 'male sex-right' in new, contractual, bottles" (1997a: 227). In a similar vein, other critics argue that I present contract theory as the development of "legitimating ideology" to disguise old patriarchal relations (Coole 1990: 26; also Hegarty 1999). But this line of criticism ignores what is conveyed in my conception of *civil subordination*. Old forms of subordination are legitimated by God's word, nature, tradition, and ascription. The new form requires the agreement of the governed and free acts by individuals – a major historical transformation. Hence it has to be constituted through contract within institutions (held to be) constituted by free relations. Civil subordination is generated through contracts about property in the person within a context of juridical and civil freedom and equality.

II Contract, Property in the Person, and Feminism

A number of critics have charged that I seriously underestimate the usefulness of contract theory and the practice of contract for women and feminism. For example, Okin contends that "Pateman gives up too easily on the potential uses of contract for feminism" (1990: 666). Dickenson argues that "[w]hat is *right* with contractarian *theory* is that it insists on women's property in the person, thereby enhancing their moral and political agency" (1997: 77).[13]

---

[12] The stories of the overthrow of an "original" matriarchy by patriarchs that I discuss in chapter 2 of my book (Pateman 1988) are stories of an event that precedes the transformation of traditional and classic patriarchy into its modern, contractual, or civil form.

[13] Dickenson also objects to my "insistence that contract is to blame for women's subjection" (1997: 74). In *The Sexual Contract* I was not concerned with blame. It is

The denial that wives (women) owned the property in their persons was central to coverture, so it is easy to suppose that the demand that women should be owners and participate in freedom of contract fosters their freedom. Certainly, it was unjust for wives to be unable, for instance, to obtain credit without their husband's signature until the 1970s. But to argue for freedom of contract in the sense that wives should be able to enter into commercial transactions in their own right is by no means the same as arguing that members of both sexes ("individuals") should be conceived of as owners of property in the person.

Dickenson follows Waldron's (1988) reading of Locke and separates property in the person from property in the body.[14] The "person," she argues, refers to the moral person, not the body, and so talk of property in the person is a way of referring to agency, to individuals as creators of their own actions, as initiators of events in the world (Dickenson 1997: 179). To interpret "property in the person" in this way parallels recent discussions of self-ownership which treat the concept as merely a way of talking about moral autonomy (see Pateman 2002). In both cases, the political value and force of the fiction of property in the person vanishes.

The Sexual Contract is about political freedom not moral agency; the latter was presupposed in my argument (1988: 205). The idea of property in the person is a political fiction precisely because in practice "agency," "services," or "labor power" – property in the person – are inseparable from the body. But the fiction that what is available as a commodity for sale or rent in the market is merely a piece of property, just like any other, is necessary if such contracts are to be said to constitute free relations. The owner, exercising freedom or agency, rents out property (in the person) for use by another. But if the property is to be used as required, the body of the owner has to be available too. An abstract moral capacity to initiate actions, or an abstract service, is of no use in itself. Nor can these abstractions be rented out; necessarily, the body has to go along too. To be of use, the owner has to act as directed by the party who has acquired right of usage or the contract is

---

pointless to look for someone or some practice to blame for three centuries of political development.

[14] Her criticisms of *The Sexual Contract* are part of a wider argument about women and property. While I can agree with much of her argument about a Hegelian conception of property, such a conception is incompatible with the idea of property in the person. Waldron's discussion is about the problem of how Locke justifies the original appropriation of private property in the state of nature. I discuss the importance of ownership rather than performance in this part of Locke's story of origins in Pateman (2002: 24–5).

pointless. Thus, e.g., an employer acquires right of command over the use of the body of a worker, over his movements, capacities, skills, expertise, labor, and agency.[15]

To make the decision to rent out property in the person is an exercise of freedom, but the consequence of making that decision and entering into a contract is that the individual is subordinated. Anderson (1990: 1804–5) objects that, in the case of employment, not all labor contracts create relations of subordination. She mentions plumbers, actors, and professionals, but my interest was in the institution of employment, not in individual contracts between professionals or tradespeople hired by clients. The latter relationship differs from that between employer and worker, and a full account of labor contracts would need to explore these differences. I agree with Anderson that employment does not require "an unqualified" possessive conception of contract if that means there are no limits to the demands an employer can place on employees. Trade unions have always struggled to have such limits imposed. Yet if an employer does not have (limited) right of command over workers, if "workers" are not subordinates, then he is not an "employer." How, for instance, can what is now euphemistically called downsizing take place without workers' consent if there is no subordination?

To focus on moral agency distracts attention from the political significance of the idea of a "person." The person is a legal and political, not just a moral, term and, significantly, it includes corporations which have rights under the Fourteenth Amendment in the United States. Historically, women and nonwhites were seen as lacking in all kinds of agency and thus excluded from the legal and political standing of "persons," an exclusion that is part of the history of the practice of contract. At the extreme, slaves were property not persons. Under coverture, married women were held to be absorbed into the person of their husbands, and women were barred from professions and the franchise on the grounds that they were not persons. But it does not follow that to become a legal, political, and civil "person" requires that individuals (women or men) be seen as owners of property in the person. A "person" who is a citizen in a democracy can be conceptualized in other ways.

A second prong of the criticism that I underestimate the usefulness of contract for women is that I confuse "all of liberal contract theory with libertarianism" (Okin 1990: 666; see also, e.g., Anderson 1990:

---

[15] In an example of the frequent careless reading of *The Sexual Contract* by critics, Shannon Bell states that "Pateman equalizes the prostitute and worker on the grounds that neither own property in their persons" (1994: 78). My argument is precisely the opposite. *Only if* workers or prostitutes are seen as "individuals" who own the property in their person can wage labor be seen as free labor, or prostitution be defended on the grounds that prostitutes are renting out a "service," not a body for use.

1808). Perhaps I should have spelt out my argument more fully on this point. I was certainly not suggesting that all the theorists of an original contract, or all contemporary contract theorists, are contractarians (as, e.g., Kymlicka charges (1990: 461)). The importance of contractarianism (as I call libertarianism), the standpoint of contract, is that it reveals the full logic of contract argument. This is why it is essential to read the radical individualist Hobbes, who foreshadowed contemporary contractarianism.

Only by investigating how contractarian arguments work is it possible to understand the vital contemporary political potency of the fiction of property in the person, and to appreciate how individuals can be conceptualized *as if* they can rent out this property without involving themselves. Taking contract seriously as a way of ordering social life – contracts all the way down, or social life as an endless series of discrete "origins" – throws light onto trends that have gained pace rapidly since I wrote *The Sexual Contract*.

The doctrine that all parts of social life and individuals can and should be seen as private property and thus as open to commodification in the market now has global reach. Prevailing domestic and international policy proclaims that everything should be alienable for private profit, from individuals' "agency," to health care, water supplies, and transport; from animals, seeds, and plant life to genetic materials (and there is a flourishing underground trade in bodily organs).[16] All relations should be seen through the lens of contract and private property, so teachers make contracts with pupils, social workers with clients, and governments treat their citizens as consumers of public services rather than citizens who share in decisions about, and have a *right* to, those services.

As these trends illustrate, the belief that the practice of contract *is* freedom is now more widespread than when I wrote *The Sexual Contract*. Anderson claims that I see all contract as a self-interested exchange of private property. Indeed, that is the standpoint of contract, although, as I have stressed, relationships not exchanges are at issue. A contract, she argues, "is just a freely established agreement creating obligations between consenting adults" (1990: 1808; see also, e.g., Jaquette 1998: 218). To make contract appear as the exemplification of freedom is the brilliance of the theoretical tradition I was analyzing. Contract is one way of creating an agreement, but, despite the widely held assumption among political theorists and philosophers as well as neoliberal ideologues, it is not the only way.

---

[16] For some brief comments on property in the person and alienability, see Pateman (2002: 26–7).

This is a point about which I should have said more in *The Sexual Contract*. Underlying my argument about the sexual contract is a view, albeit undeveloped, of freedom. It is too often taken for granted that contract exhausts the ways of entering into free agreements or constituting free relations. I challenged this assumption in *The Problem of Political Obligation*.[17] In *The Sexual Contract* I made a similar challenge to the claim that marriage and employment embodied free relations because they "originate" in a contract. I did not spell out an argument about contract and free agreement in any detail and only noted that there "are other forms of free agreement through which women and men can constitute political relations" (1988: 232). I assumed, once more in an overly optimistic fashion, that my discussion as a whole made it clear that more work was needed on developing alternative conceptions of freedom, conceptions that abandon the political fiction of property in the person.

III Hobbes, Locke, and Freud

My interpretation of the classic texts, in particular Hobbes and Locke, has come under fire and critics have also taken issue with what I have to say about Freud.[18] I was alerted to the relevance of Freud's argument, as I noted, by Phillip Rieff and Norman O. Brown, who see Freud as providing a version of the story of an original contract; Freud states that the pact made by the brothers is "a sort of social contract" (Pateman 1988: 103). He is in my book because he offers a version of the story that comes from another theoretical tradition. This helps highlight, for example, that marriage and, more generally, the private sphere, is created through the original contract and so is a political contrivance not a natural fact.[19]

---

[17] In *The Problem of Political Obligation* I took promising to provide an alternative to contract as a practice of free agreement and a way to create new relationships. In that book I was concerned with freedom as voluntarily assumed political obligation, and I argued that a democratic theory and practice of political (self-assumed) obligation would not take the form of contract.

[18] My discussion of the early modern theorists built on my analysis in *The Problem of Political Obligation*. For different readings of Rousseau, see, e.g., Lange (2002) and Wingrove (2000). Mary Severance (2000: 509 n91) writes of my acceptance of a "conflation between Hobbes and Locke." In both books I take pains to emphasize the *difference* between the theoretical assumptions (not least over women's natural freedom) and views of the state of nature and civil society of Hobbes and Locke.

[19] That the early modern theorists, save Hobbes, present "the family" as natural makes it all the more difficult to see the sexual contract. Theorists then have no need to tell a story about origins of marriage, whereas private property must be justified (the "original" holdings are communal) and so must the modern state. The theoretical waters are muddied further by conjectural histories that tell how patriarchal families become political entities.

Okin (1990: 661–2) argues that I misread Freud by ignoring his statement that a matriarchate followed the incest taboo. Freud also talks about the overthrow of mother-right and the institution of patriarchy (Pateman 1988: 103), but he does not tell a story about it in the manner of the other theorists I discussed. I took Freud's account of the establishment of patriarchy, when the sons built on the new rules established after the parricide, as the equivalent of the creation of civil society and I interpreted his remarks about the origin of the incest taboo and the laws of exogamy ("kinship") as a story about the origin of civil society and (modern) marriage.[20] Freud's story is complicated in being brief and not just about the origins of morality and society, as are the classic accounts of an original contract (see Boucher and Kelly 1994b: ch. 1), but about the origin of religion, an aspect I did not discuss.

In "Mere Auxiliaries to the Commonwealth," Teresa Brennan and I (1979) were, I believe, the first to notice the embarrassment that wives posed for Hobbes and Locke. The same problem lies at the heart of *The Sexual Contract*. Theories of an original contract involve an endemic problem about marriage. Both Hobbes and Locke broke with the idea of a natural hierarchy in favor of convention and then faced the difficulty that their premise of natural freedom and equality provides no basis for women's subjection other than free agreement on their part. Yet that premise also makes it impossible to find a good reason why all free and equal women should voluntarily subordinate themselves to men within marriage. Many of the theorists' maneuverings to get round this knotty theoretical problem can be found in their conjectural histories of the development of the state of nature, but my critics pay little attention to this side of their argument.

The problem was particularly acute for Hobbes. He is the only theorist of an original contract who begins, quite explicitly, from the very radical assumption that both sexes are free and equal in the state of nature. Women share all of the characteristics of men, including the ability to kill other men and women if they (are perceived to) become enemies. Unless Hobbes was to disregard his own method of reconstituting his entities in perpetual motion into human figures, he could not differentiate between women and men in the natural condition – except in one respect, or they would not have been human. Women, but not men, can bear children. And this leads him to an even more radical conclusion; in the state of nature it is mothers who exercise dominion,

---

[20] Okin objects that Freud's stories are about "primitive or ancient people," not civil society. In *The Sexual Contract* I focus on the early modern theorists as tellers of stories of the origin of civil society, but as recent discussions of Locke have shown (e.g., Tully 1993b) they were also concerned with "primitive" people, especially in America. See also my discussion of Locke in chapter 2 in the present volume.

they are lords.[21] As Gabriella Slomp notes, Hobbes's assumption of maternal dominion "destroys the entire basis for natural patriarchy" (2000: 102).

But what of civil patriarchy? It is here that there is a large gap in Hobbes's otherwise rigorous logic. Men's conjugal power in civil society is based neither on nature nor custom; it is conventional, created by Leviathan, by the state and its civil laws. Hobbes provides no answer to the question of how and why women, who are free, equal, and lords as mothers, agree to subjection to their husbands after the original pact has been concluded. Thus, I offered a logical conjecture to fill this gap; namely, that if free women were to become "wives" (i.e. civil subordinates) men would have had to obtain power over them before the original contract was concluded. Theories of an original contract are full of conjectural histories about the origins of political society; Hobbes's demonstration of the necessity of Leviathan, for example, is accompanied by his own conjectural history of how families form kingdoms in the state of nature, so it seemed only appropriate to suggest another.

Wright accuses me of presenting an account of Hobbes that rests on "a general lack of historical and textual specificity," and "bears only a tangential relationship to Hobbes's texts" (2004: 110, 116). She asserts, for instance, that I produce no "satisfactory evidence from Hobbes's texts, or from [my] reconstructive exercise, to substantiate [my] claim or to show how the transformation" from women's freedom in the state of nature to their subordination as wives occurs (2004: 115). But – of course – there is no evidence from Hobbes's texts; if such evidence were available there would be no logical gap in Hobbes's argument and my little exercise in conjectural history would have been unnecessary![22]

My discussion of Hobbes drew, first, on my work with Teresa Brennan, in which we drew attention to the oddity of Hobbes's descriptions of the family where, except for his account in the *Elements of Law*,

---

[21] In the state of nature there are no matrimonial laws so there is no certain way of designating paternity. Therefore, the child belongs to the mother and because it is in her power she makes the decision whether or not to rear it. The infant, like any human faced with a choice between life or death, "consents" to her dominion to preserve itself: "every man is supposed to promise obedience, to him [or her], in whose power it is to save, or destroy him" (Hobbes 1996: 140).

[22] She takes my earlier analysis of the public and the private (Pateman 1983) and declares that it is "inapplicable to Hobbes" (Wright 2004: 109) – but I did not "apply" this to Hobbes. Wright makes no mention of my actual point; namely, that since there are no matrimonial laws in his natural condition, he shows very clearly that the "private" has to be created along with the rest of the modern civil order through the original contract, and that the patriarchal relationship between husbands and wives is thus a *political* construct. Nor do I make any claims about Hobbes's own view of his theory.

the inhabitants are entirely male. Second, I drew on my reading of his radical individualism in *The Problem of Political Obligation*. In 1989, I published an extended version of my reading of Hobbes, including discussion of commentaries presenting him as a patriarchalist – notwithstanding that he turned Filmer's universe of natural relations upside down into an entirely conventional world – which I believe I was the first to analyze. These commentaries ignored his proclamation of sexual equality in the natural condition, so no attention was paid to his endorsement of the subordination of wives in civil society and thus the logical gap remained unnoticed (Pateman 1989b).

Wright, the most strident of the critics who insist that *The Sexual Contract* is itself a story of origins, proclaims that moved by my "political desire" and despite my own intention in filling "Hobbes's textual silences," I produced "An Origin Story of [My] Own" (2004: 105–6, 122; see also J. Boucher 2003). According to Gatens, for example, my motivation was a "desire to know . . . the 'prime mover' of history," so that instead of writing a critical history "in the service of the future," I sought "to *discover* origins" (Gatens 1996: 40, 42–3). If I were interested in a prime mover I would not be a political theorist but a theologian. I was analyzing texts that contain stories of origins – what else are theories of an original contract? – but that does not mean that I, any more than the political theorists who have contributed to the voluminous literature on contract theory since the early 1970s, followed the same path. In fact, I stated explicitly that I was not interested in producing another account of origins (Pateman 1988: 18, 220, 232). However, my own statements are either ignored or acknowledged only to be dismissed (Miriam 2005 is one exception).

Wright's failure to engage with my conceptual framework allows her to claim to uncover the real reason why I wrote *The Sexual Contract*. I wanted to "prove conquest," and this is the theme of my book (Wright 2004: 122, 125).[23] There is, however, a major problem with this "discovery." Far from being about conquest, my argument is about contract (agreement). I attempted to show why even *voluntary* contracts about property in the person create relations of subordination. Such a travesty of my argument is possible because, like some other critics, Wright makes the strange assertion that I am really writing about Freud, not Hobbes or Locke. Okin was the first to claim that I "superimpose"

---

[23] For an argument about Hobbes and conquest see Lott (2002). Joanne Boucher (2003: 31) makes the same claim about my reading of Locke. My argument, she asserts, is that Locke disguises a *"specific secret,"* namely "conquest." But when I state that conjugal right is hidden in Locke (Pateman 1988: 92–3) I am *not* discussing conquest but writing about Locke's conjectural history and how the subjection of wives vanishes as he separates the "paternal" sphere from the political sphere.

Freud's account back onto the classic theories. Not surprisingly, she finds this puzzling – as I would do myself were I to encounter such a procedure. But others have repeated this; Drucilla Cornell, for example, writes that my "ultimate argument" is that we should "understand the social pact through Freud's account in *Moses and Monotheism*" (1992: 74). Wright announces that, via Freud's primal scene, *The Sexual Contract* is "a story about primal rape" (2004: 115).

Critics introduced rape very early. The first review that I saw of *The Sexual Contract* was depressing in its misunderstandings.[24] Linda Zerilli (1989) wrote that "Pateman tells us, in the beginning there was rape," and she suggests that this is part of my account of history. Okin (1990: 661) also argued that I offered "a very unusual interpretation" of Freud's primal scene as rape. On the contrary, my point about the primal scene is that it is inherently ambiguous. The young boy is usually taken to be making a mistake about what he sees. But, given the power accorded to husbands by law and views about sexual difference when Freud was writing, it is not possible to know whether the boy observed a loving act of conjugal intercourse or a husband (lawfully) exercising what used to be called conjugal rights when his wife was unwilling.

I introduced the primal scene to fill another logical gap.[25] All the classic theorists assume that the fathers already exist and there is no story of how they became patriarchs: "All the stories lack a political book of genesis" (Pateman 1988: 105). Given the power attributed to the fathers – Filmer's *patria potestas*, Locke's father-monarchs, Freud's ruler of the horde – they were, logically, unlikely to be much bothered with the niceties of a woman's consent once they had decided they needed a son. My reference to the "true origin" of political right (1988: 105) when introducing the primal scene, and my subsequent references, were ironical. Perhaps I was too early in this, irony only became fashionable later in the 1990s. When I was writing my book I thought it amusing to fill in that particular logical absence by using Freud's primal scene. It did not occur to me that anyone would think I was so stupid as to make "conquest" or "primal rape" the basis of a book in which I argued that contracts about property in the person, a form *of voluntary agreement*, were the mechanism of modern civil subordination.

---

[24] I do not know if this was the first review published, but it was a very early one – with the title "In the Beginning, Rape." For the record, Joan Acker wrote a letter critical of the review to the editor of the *Women's Review of Books*, but her letter was not published.

[25] Gatens (1996: 42), in another bizarre assertion about the primal scene, argues that it provides the missing link between my reading of the texts and my discussion of institutions. Her belief that such a link is required derives from her claim that I am searching for "origins."

Okin's view is that I come "very close" to proclaiming that "marital sexual intercourse is typically, if not always, rape" (1990: 660, 662). She argues that "presumably" my reading of the classic texts means that we must "accept that all their theories depend, and cannot but depend, on rape" and that Hobbes and Locke are "legitimizers of marital rape on a day-to-day basis" (1990: 663).[26] Odd though it is to have to do so, let me state explicitly that neither such a view of marital sexual relations nor of Hobbes or Locke is part of my argument. Okin is making the mistake of assuming that the behavior of individuals can be inferred from the existence of a law (coverture), the absence of a law (about rape within marriage), and an analysis of the structure of an institution (marriage). My argument implies nothing about how often husbands took advantage of their power over wives, or, come to that, how often wives initiated sexual relations.

One reason for this peculiar vein of criticism is the determination of some commentators to force my book into a container labeled "radical feminism." According to Wright, for example, "in turning to a feminist origin story, Pateman is repeating a pattern laid out by radical feminists in the late 1960s and early 1970s" (2004: 123).[27] After *The Problem of*

---

[26] Of the theorists I discuss, Rousseau comes closest to justifying rape; see *Emile* (Rousseau 1979: bk V, 558–60); and Wingrove (2000: ch. 6) on the story of Le Lévite d'Ephraim. I have published an article about consent that deals with rape: Pateman (1980). To avoid further misunderstanding, let me stress that my comments here do not mean that rape is irrelevant to my argument, or that a construction of sexual difference in which masculinity and femininity are identified respectively with freedom (as mastery) and subjection is not central to the struggle that has had to be waged to place enforced sexual submission, whether in or out of marriage, on the same criminal footing as other forms of assault, but this is not the subject matter of my book. Rape remains an enormous problem for girls and women, from infancy to old age. Since I wrote *The Sexual Contract* public awareness of the problem has grown, including the very high incidence of organized rape in warfare and newer forms such as "date rape" facilitated by drugs. But increased concern and publicity does not, in itself, lead to remedies, and rape is a crime easy to get away with. In Britain, for example, the conviction rate for rape dropped from 25% in 1985 to 5.5% in 2004–5. In 2006 it was revealed that some convicted rapists merely receive a caution. In a discussion of (more) legal reforms it has been seen as necessary to emphasize that consent is to be deemed absent where a woman is unconscious (Travis 2002). However, the question of why men would want sexual intercourse with an unconscious woman and what that tells us about "masculinity" and ideas about sexuality is rarely asked. Many of the beliefs and attitudes (held by both men and women) that I discussed in my 1980 article, and are part of the political construction of sexual difference I emphasize in my book, are still very much with us.

[27] She even makes the ludicrous assertion that "[t]he underlying assumption of . . . Pateman and others, is that without a dramatic story of victimization – original rape, mass slaughter of witches, or a worldwide historical conquest of women – feminism is not justified" (Wright 2004: 152).

Political Obligation I "was increasingly influenced by radical feminism," and she refers in a footnote to the preface of *The Sexual Contract* (Wright 2004: 122). I wrote that some of my arguments were "prompted by writers customarily labeled radical feminist" (Pateman 1988: x), but this was not to signal my adherence to a school of argument. Rather, I wanted to indicate that I had been alerted to the political significance of questions ignored in mainstream political theory, about marriage, the subordination of wives, and sexual relations, by writers called radical feminists, and I appropriated Rich's term "the law of male sex right." Anyone with some knowledge of the intellectual history of the left knows the provenance of a concern with subordination, but reading these writers set me thinking in new ways, and thus helped me formulate both a feminist perspective on theories of original contracts and some criticisms of socialist arguments. Unfortunately, seeing the words "radical feminism" in my preface sparked off a set of associations on the part of some critics that has nothing to do with my actual argument.[28]

Indeed, since I have always found the common classification of feminist theory into "radical," "liberal," etc. of very little help in understanding what is distinctive about feminist argument – and very misleading about the history of feminist political theory – there was no reason for me to place myself in a particular camp. Over the years, it has seemed to me that my book has been criticized from so many different directions precisely because it cannot be neatly slotted into the conventional classifications of either feminist theory or political theory. With hindsight, I can see that I made a mistake in not also stating that the way in which my argument in *The Sexual Contract* was developed was greatly influenced by the new techniques of theoretical analysis that were being used by deconstructionists and postmodernists in the 1980s.

Be that as it may, I now want to say something about criticism of my interpretation of Locke. Several critics argue that I am far too unsympathetic to Locke. For example, according to Dickenson, I "handicap" women "by ignoring the emancipatory aspects of Locke's theory"

---

[28] I did not know when I was writing *The Sexual Contract* that so much animosity would come to be directed toward "radical feminism" or I might not have used the words! Wright's book exemplifies how *The Sexual Contract* is sometimes criticized through a process of guilt by association. The two writers most prominently linked to radical feminism (and the focus of a good deal of hostile criticism) are Catharine MacKinnon and Andrea Dworkin, and their names are sometimes raised in discussions of my book. Gatens (1996: 32–3), for instance, brings in MacKinnon and Dworkin and "forcible violation of women" *before* turning to my book. For my views of MacKinnon's *Feminism Unmodified* (1987), see Pateman (1990c); for a very different view of MacKinnon than the stereotypical "radical feminist" see Laden (2003). And, let me confess here, I have never been able to read more than a few pages of Dworkin's work.

(1997: 70) and Kate Nash (1998) claims that I recognize, but repress, the ambiguities in Locke's argument and so ignore the "undecidability" of women in his text.[29]

I drew attention (Pateman 1988: 52) to Locke's insistence that a mother has authority over her children, that a wife can own property, and that he contemplates the possibility of divorce. He also states that "Community of Goods, and the Power over them, mutual Assistance, and Maintenance, and other things belonging to *Conjugal Society*, might be varied and regulated by that Contract, which unites Man and Wife" (*Second Treatise*, henceforth II, §83; 1988: 322). Such passages suggest that Locke extended his arguments about individual freedom and equality to women as well as men. The question is how far to emphasize this emancipatory side of Locke. My view remains that in the context of his theory as a whole, including his conjectural history of the state of nature and his division of social life between the "paternal" private sphere and the political realm, these passages, while certainly noteworthy, are outweighed by the other Locke.

He not only writes of the natural foundation for a wife's subjection to her husband, but he begins the *Second Treatise* (II, §1; 1988: 267–8) by setting down, in the context of a summary of his conclusions in the *First Treatise*, "what I take to be Political Power." He separates "the Power of a *Magistrate* over a subject" from four other examples of power (which could all be in the hands of one man), one of which is "a *Husband* over his Wife." Therefore, even before Locke has begun his argument in the *Second Treatise*, he lays down as a premise that a husband has power over his wife. Indeed, he had already established this point in the *First Treatise* (henceforth I, §48; 1988: 174). Despite his remark about the possibility of varying the terms of the marriage contract, Locke's point is not that conjugal power should be questioned or negotiated but that it is not *political* power.

Dickenson's picture of Locke as the enemy of (conjugal) patriarchy relies on a move that parallels her attempt to separate the mechanism of contract from its content. The problem about marriage, she argues, lies not within Locke's theory but within the legal doctrine of coverture. Contract does not disadvantage women, but, rather, the problem is "liberalism's *failure* to extend contract far enough" (1997: 87). Women are disadvantaged because marriage "is *exempt* from the contractual way

[29] Nash focuses on my earlier work although she obviously means her criticisms to apply to *The Sexual Contract* as well. The few references to my book appear to have been added after her main argument was written, which leads her to remark, for example, that I do not mention Mill's argument that whichever spouse brings home the means of support will have more voice; I refer to it on p. 162.

of looking at the world." The intensification of coverture after Locke's time should be seen as a backlash against the "triumphal progress" of liberalism (1997: 76, 88).[30]

To try and detach contract and Locke from coverture is to do what Dickenson accuses me of doing; namely, to give no weight to one side of Locke's argument. The practice of contract does not exist in a vacuum, but is regulated by law. In a series of cases in the seventeenth and eighteen centuries it was admitted that a wife was a legal individual, but in the early nineteenth century the unity of spouses was reaffirmed (see Todd 1998). The legal position of wives was at its nadir in the nineteenth century, which is why the marriage contract and coverture were central to the women's movement from the 1860s. As I discussed in *The Sexual Contract*, many feminists have argued, like Dickenson, that the solution was for the marriage contract to be more like other contracts. But that route runs into the problem of the idea of property in the person and subordination. Moreover, even with all its peculiarities and limitations on who could enter it, marriage was within the practice of contract.[31] I took my lead from the authority of Blackstone who stated that "our law considers marriage in no other light than as a civil contract" (1899: 154).

For Locke, a husband exercises a limited, civil power, but that is not to say that the glimpses he gives of a wife's freedom are irrelevant. A crucial plank of my analysis of the texts is that the meaning of "women" is not "decided" at all. The classic theorists use the language of nature, but they are constructing a political argument about a civil society that is (held to be) an order of freedom. This means that all inhabitants must participate in some fashion in the practice, contract, that signifies freedom (a point that also casts doubt on Dickenson's argument that marriage stood outside contract). Women cannot be left

---

[30] Dickenson also claims that "[i]nvoluntarily, through an improper jump from the marriage 'contract' under coverture to *all* contract, Pateman has given aid and comfort to the enemy" (1997: 70). But far from generalizing from the marriage contract, I spend a good deal of time in *The Sexual Contract* spelling out why the marriage contract is such an odd "contract," and I discuss, e.g., how it differs from the employment contract.

[31] Dickenson (1997: 88) argues that after the Hardwicke Marriage Act of 1753 "there was no such thing as contractual marriage," although the term "marriage contract" persisted in popular usage. I am uncertain of her point here. The 1753 Act concerned clandestine marriages and "contract marriage" in which the two parties said "I take you John/Jane to be my husband/wife." In church law this verbal exchange constituted a valid marriage, but in common law such a contract had no standing and gave the husband no rights. However, these marriages were usually elopements, i.e. clandestine, and so have relatively little importance for the marriage contract more generally. I am grateful to Molly Shanley for clarifying this for me.

in the state of nature or be involuntary participants in the civil order, or universal freedom is too obviously compromised.[32] Women are not parties to the original contract but they are parties to a civil contract, namely, the marriage contract. To enter into a contract women must retain their natural freedom. But once having entered the marriage contract (under coverture) their freedom is denied; they are "wives." Thus, as I emphasized, the freedom of women is at one and the same time *denied and affirmed*.

According to Anderson, this line of argument leads to the conclusion that contract theory is a tool for attacking patriarchy. She draws attention to the fact that if heads of households are the parties to the original contract they are disposing of natural liberties of household members, but these liberties are not rightfully theirs. Heads of households, she argues, do not exercise political power (necessary if they are to transfer the liberties of others) in the state of nature (1990: 1799–800). In Locke's theory, however, this problem is solved in his conjectural history of the state of nature.[33] The conjectural history sets out the process through which fathers become monarchs and so exercise political power in their households – yet somehow they lose *political* power as husbands in civil society but still retain *conjugal* power. But, even if women retain their natural liberties, it does not follow that contract is the enemy of patriarchy. This is, once again, to identify freedom with contract.

IV Marriage and Prostitution

Mary Lyndon Shanley (1979) showed a long time ago that marriage occupied a crucial place in political argument in the seventeenth century. The analogy between government in marriage and government in the state was the stock-in-trade of political battles. Since the early modern period, the institution of marriage has not only shaped wives' economic and political standing, but "other women have lived in the *shadow of marriage*, regulated by marriage's normative framework even as they have inhabited terrain outside of its formal boundaries" (Dubler 2003: 1646). In a recent study of the United States, Nancy Cott has shown how the "laws of marriage . . . sculpt the body politic" (2000: 5). A report in 1996 from the US General Accounting Office showed that

[32] Boucher (2003: 25), in another example of careless reading of my book, writes that I conceptualize women "as belonging to and remaining in a natural, pre-political world as men enter civil society," a view I explicitly reject.
[33] I first discussed the conjectural history in Pateman (1975); see also Brennan and Pateman (1979).

there are more than "*one thousand* places in the corpus of federal law where legal marriage conferred a distinctive status, right, or benefit." Cott concludes that "the traditional marriage bargain survived in skeleton form to the end of the twentieth century" (2000: 2, 210).

Yet critics of my book suggest that I should have been writing not about marriage but about the family. This criticism overlooks a crucial conceptual point in my analysis. My argument rests upon a *distinction* between marriage and family. "Marriage," the union of a man and woman, is not the same as a "family" or "household," but all too often they are conflated, as they are by many of my critics. *The Sexual Contract* is about marriage and so is about relationships between adults. The family is constituted by relations between parents and children as well as between the adult spouses and these are different forms of relationships. A child eventually becomes a political equal along with his or her parents but there is no similar path of growth and change of political status among adults.

Okin (followed, for example, by Kymlicka (1990) and Fraser (1997a)) claims that I pay insufficient attention to the division of labor between the sexes and so fail to appreciate that it is the fact that women undertake most of the unpaid work in the household, especially childcare, that accounts for the continuation of patriarchal power. Children, she states, "are virtually absent" from my argument. They do not even appear when I discuss the domestic division of labor or so-called surrogate mothering; "the fact that women have been and continue to be primary parents is inseparable from their subordination" (Okin 1990: 665).[34] I would not disagree but I was not concerned with parental responsibilities, so children rarely appear explicitly (but they are part of my argument on pp. 91–2 and pp. 182–3).

Focus on the family diverts attention from the standing of wives and makes it easier for political theorists to ignore the interconnections between marriage, employment, and citizenship. That neglect, in turn, reinforces the disappearance of marriage into the family. To be sure, until recently the only legitimate way for a family to be formed was through (heterosexual) marriage. The "family" arose as a consequence of marriage – the marriage contract was the "origin" of the family – and, in the past, a household commonly contained not just the spouses and their children but other relatives, servants, apprentices and, in the American South, slaves. The sexual division of labor within the family, including the care of children, *followed* from marriage. I discussed the private and public sexual division of labor in chapter 5, which is devoted

[34] In *Justice, Gender, and the Family* (1989), Okin discusses "vulnerability through marriage."

to slaves, servants, wives, and workers.[35] I explored how performance of household tasks, without pay, was part of what being a "wife" meant, with the corollary that to be a "husband" was to be the "breadwinner" or a "good provider"; that is to say, I looked at the connection between the institutions of marriage and employment.

I argued in *The Sexual Contract* that the story of an original contract made it possible to see how marriage provided all men with legitimate and orderly access to the labor and bodies of wives. Access to women's bodies is also available through prostitution, and my analysis of the latter aimed to raise some neglected questions about the ideas and beliefs required for the market in women's bodies to be seen as, and during the 1980s come to be defended as, part of a free social order and part of women's autonomy.

As I emphasized above in chapter 5, the global sex industry has grown dramatically since the early 1990s. In the past, prostitution was excused as a necessary evil; the new departure was that in the 1980s it began to be justified in terms of women's freedom and defended by contractarian arguments. More recently, the defense has been extended by some feminists who claim that prostitution is "transgressive," that it is empowering for women and provides an example of women's agency. It is presented "as though it can represent a form of resistance to [social] inequalities" (Davidson 2002: 87).[36] The focus of much recent discussion is about the experiences of prostitutes – but whose experiences are to be treated as authoritative: those, say, of a high-end call girl in New York, of a woman brought into France with her passport retained by her trafficker, of a woman in a refugee camp, or of a young girl in an Indian or Thai brothel? The assumption has also gained ground that to support improvements in working conditions, decriminalization, or the extension to prostitutes of rights accorded to other workers necessarily implies that nothing is wrong with prostitution (e.g. B. Sullivan 1995, 1997).

That is to say, it is being assumed that no distinction can be made between discussion of women who work as prostitutes and prostitution; the *institution* of prostitution, which was my subject, is placed beyond

---

[35] Boucher (2003: 33) accuses me of ignoring "the central significance of the servant in the patriarchal family of the era and in Locke's theory." I do not discuss servants in my analysis of Locke but in chapter 5; my book was not designed to be read as a series of discrete chapters.

[36] Feminists are now deeply divided over prostitution. Davidson (2002) provides a recent account of the controversies. Curiously, prostitution still seems to be taken to be about women (the supply), with few questions asked about the demand from men, apart from the resurrection of old claims about human needs and the provision of a valuable service to the disabled, etc.

question (cf. Overall 1992: 708). Criticism of prostitution is then (invalidly) taken to be criticism of, or to show contempt for, prostitutes. So Sullivan invokes the slippery slope and claims that "arguments about the inherent 'wrongness' of prostitution lead *inevitably* to arguments about the 'wrongness' of sex workers" (1995: 194; my emphasis).[37] I am said to argue that all prostitutes are mere victims, lacking agency, but, to repeat a point I have already made, criticism of an institution is not the same as criticism of individuals or their agency. My argument presupposed moral agency; it presupposed that individuals, including prostitutes, have the "agency" to enter contracts. I took it for granted that all humans have a capacity for freedom, but whether or not, and how far, they can exercise it (whether or not they are coerced victims or prostitutes by choice) depends on their circumstances. That is an empirical matter.

Barbara Sullivan contends that I "oppose" calling prostitution "sex work" because "in [Pateman's] view, it is not work but sexual slavery" (1997: 239). Let me take the point about slavery first. Earlier she claimed that I argued that prostitution only appears like sexual slavery (Sullivan 1995: 189). More recently, Ruth Sample has made a similar move from the statement that I argued that the "purchase of a woman's body, even only for a time, is in this case just like slavery," to the statement that I argued that "prostitution is essentially slavery" (2003b: 203, 208). I argued no such thing. I tried to put prostitution into some historical and cultural context to make clear that I was interested only in a form that has been defended as the voluntary sale of an abstract service, i.e. sale of property in the person. Only then can prostitution be presented as an example of women's freedom. I was not concerned with prostitutes who were coerced into the trade or held as slaves (for an example of the latter, see Bales 2002). My analysis was of prostitution as part of the wider trade in property in the person, a trade that rests on juridical and civil freedom and equality.

My argument was not that prostitution is slavery but that it is an example of civil subordination. Sample, like most other critics, has not examined my notion of civil subordination and (incorrectly) translates it as "slavery." She does so because she follows a familiar path on the left, a path from which I explicitly diverged in *The Sexual Contract*, and argues that what is wrong with prostitution is that it involves exploitation. She sees only two alternatives: exploitation or slavery. I am not

---

[37] Such statements fail to address the point that I made in *The Sexual Contract* that socialists and trade unionists who criticized capitalism did not hold workers in contempt; on the contrary they were their advocates. In recent discussions of prostitution the equivalent of their critique is missing, and only working conditions are criticized.

aware of any critic who has discussed my departure from the prevailing wisdom that exploitation is the major issue or my argument that exploitation follows from civil subordination.

As an example of civil subordination, prostitution is like employment. Thus (to come to Sullivan's other point) it, too, is "work." I did not use the term "sex work" because it is a general term, encompassing a wide range of activities in the global sex industry, and I used "prostitution" in a specific sense (Pateman 1988: 199–200). I also discussed how prostitution differs from employment. I argued that both involve use of persons, not abstract services, but in prostitution a woman's body is used differently from individuals' bodies in employment. A prostitute's body becomes a commodity for sale in the market for different reasons than labor power. No doubt my answer to the question of what is wrong with prostitution can be improved upon, but my analysis cannot be dismissed, as critics seem to suppose, without engaging with my concepts of property in the person and civil subordination.

Another problem with my analysis, according to Sample (2003b: 206, 202), is that I "have a tremendously flat-footed understanding of sexuality." This is because, she claims, I argued "that the need for sexual relations is not a genuine need." But I was not questioning that all human beings need contact with others, including sexual relations. My actual argument was twofold: first, that, unlike, e.g., the need for food, the need for sexual relations can go unmet for lengthy periods (even a lifetime!) without the death of the individual concerned; second, that how human needs are met can vary, and that, again unlike the need for food, individuals can themselves always assuage their sexual pangs (cost-free) – and here Sample flat-footedly misses my joke about "hand relief" (Pateman 1988: 259 n32). The serious point was that commodification of hand relief in the sex industry surely tells us something about prevailing conceptions of masculinity and femininity.

I noted in *The Sexual Contract* that many feminists have seen marriage as merely a legal form of the exchange of sex for subsistence but with one man instead of many men. Bell (1994: 79) takes me to task for suggesting that marriage could be reformed but that prostitution is inseparable from the subordination of women. Similarly, Sullivan writes that I am "explicit in [my] condemnation of prostitution and considerably less forthright about the institution of marriage" (1995: 190). I am not sure how much more forthright I could have been, given the many pages I devoted to coverture and the power of husbands. But possibilities for changing marriage are much greater than for prostitution. Prostitution could be reformed in the sense that it could be made more like any other occupation in its conditions, the status of the workers, the way it is regulated and so on. However, "prostitution" would remain payment for unilateral use of a woman's body without any desire or erotic attraction on her part. In contrast, unless the term "marriage" refers only to patriarchal forms, the possibility exists for intimate association to become a free relationship between two equals, based on mutual desire, mutual respect, and the well-being of both partners.

V No Way Out?

I have been criticized for not providing details of an alternative to contract, and doing little more than gesturing toward a noncontractual social order. My response is that I did what I set out to do. To the best of my knowledge I was breaking new ground; no one else had discussed the original contract, the sexual contract, and the institutions that I analyzed from the perspective I adopted. It was very hard work and I had done enough, I thought, for one book.

One line of criticism, however, suggests that it would have been impossible for me to provide such an alternative. This is the criticism that has surprised me the most and that I have found the most difficult to understand. The message of *The Sexual Contract*, it is held, is that nothing can be changed. Some critics write of my tone of "despair," "fatalism," or "pessimism" (e.g., Dean 1992; Dickenson 1997), and Schochet argues that my assessment is that patriarchal structures "*necessarily* sustain a sexual oppression that cannot be overcome" (1998: 241; see also I. Shapiro 1999: 113; Cornell 1992: 75). This was certainly not my view, or the conclusion that I expected readers to reach. I am puzzled why critics suppose that I would have bothered to undertake my analysis if I had thought that social and political transformation was out of the question.

This reading of my argument is connected to the preoccupation with essentialism in the 1990s. For example, critics of my reading of Locke have claimed that it was essentialist. Nash argues that I treat "liberalism," exemplified by Locke, as "*essentially* masculinist" and "necessarily . . . exclusionary of women's claims" (1998: 35). Similarly, Dickenson writes that I "risk essentialism" by mistaking a particular form of property holding for "universal and inevitable subordination" (1997: 80). Gatens states that *The Sexual Contract* is "far too complex to be consistently characterised as essentialist" (1996: 34), but, nevertheless, she goes on to play the essentialist card.

"Essentialism" has a number of meanings (see Martin 1994), but my critics seem to have two senses in mind. The first is that I treated the sexual contract as an historically necessary and inevitable development that cannot be undone, and it therefore follows that women's subjection cannot be changed. I argued that the sexual contract was integral to the historical changes that led to the consolidation of the modern state and its institutions. But nothing in my argument implied that such a development was necessary or inevitable or that we are stuck with it. I argued that modern patriarchy is historically and culturally specific, not universal. I took it for granted that because all political orders are created by humans during particular time periods, in particular places and oul tures, they are not unchanging features of the world. They are historical and social, not natural, entities. They can be refashioned – and they all have been and will be.[38] Indeed, I noted explicitly that the underpinnings of the patriarchal structures I had traced were already beginning to crumble (Pateman 1988: 233). I wrote my book because I believed that men's power could be undermined. My analysis of the logic of contractual argument was designed to show that an understanding of interconnecting, but neglected, ideas and political structures was central to any democratic transformation.

The second sense in which I am taken to be an "essentialist" is that I hold a biological, and hence unchangeable, view of sexual difference. Sullivan, for example, argues that my analysis of prostitution rests on a conception of masculine identity as "fixed and given" (1995: 190), Chantal Mouffe states that I "postulat[e] the existence of some kind of essence corresponding to women *as* women" (1993: 81),[39] and Severance asserts that I assume "that the sexed individuals who are covered by the social contract pre-exist the social order" it creates (2000: 479). I learned many years ago from C. B. Macpherson (1962) that Hobbes and Locke were dealing in social constructs, and contract is a conventional device. These theorists used the "essentialist" language of nature, but they set up a conventional *political* division between the sexes as the difference between freedom and subordination.[40] Some critics seem unable to distinguish a discussion of the logical requirements of arguments of political theorists, or an analysis of the conception of masculinity and femininity required by coverture, from (supposed) views held by the writer. Gatens comments that there are

[38] A theme of *The Problem of Political Obligation* was that political theorists tend to treat the modern state as a natural feature of the world rather than a political creation that might be changed. "The market" is now widely treated as if it were a natural object rather than a political construction, as is "marriage" by fundamentalists of all stripes.

[39] She continues that I identify "women *as* women with motherhood," whereas other critics, as I indicated above, complain that I ignore mothers and children.

[40] According to Laqueur (1990: ch. 5), "sex" in the sense of an incommensurable difference between men and women was invented, out of an interpretation of new scientific discoveries, during the period in which theorists of an original contract were at work. He writes: "Anatomy, and nature as we know it more generally, is . . . a richly complicated construction based not only on observation, and on a variety of social and cultural constraints on the practice of science, but on an aesthetics of representation as well" (1990: 163–4).

"points in her text" where I seem to be describing the views of others about sexual difference rather than providing my view "of natural and immutable sexual difference" (1996: 35). Quite so. I was analyzing a tradition of political theory, not offering a litany of my own opinions.

A related criticism is that I believe that "nothing can be salvaged from the liberal tradition" (Phillips 1989: 40). In *The Sexual Contract*, I wrote that "to move outside the structure of oppositions established through the story of the original contract . . . would not diminish the importance of juridical freedom" (1988: 231), a statement which hardly dismisses out of hand "the liberal tradition" (however that is understood). My distinction between *emancipation* from the old structures of subordination and freedom as *autonomy* (1988: 228–9) is a version of the familiar point that civil and political freedoms are necessary but not sufficient for democratization, a point accepted by some theorists who call themselves "liberals."

Finally, it has been claimed that I reject the possibility that women could "empower themselves by defining reality in their own terms" (Hirschmann 1990: 173). On the contrary, one reason for moving away from civil subordination toward a more robust democracy is to open up more possibilities for women to act autonomously. I argued that in the theories I analyzed the freedom of women must always simultaneously be denied and affirmed. This means that individual freedom is (to use a different idiom) always already present, and so the potential for women to use that freedom to bring about change is always there too. Since the seventeenth century, feminist political theorists have criticized the champions of natural freedom who denied that freedom to women, and have used theoretical weapons provided by those same theorists. For four centuries women have empowered themselves and been active in politics, including in the women's movement where they fought against the ideas and structures I discussed. I was not telling their story but looking at the context in which their activities took place. Nevertheless, without being able to draw on their legacy I could not have written *The Sexual Contract*.

8

Reply to Critics

Charles W. Mills

Criticism of *The Racial Contract* (Mills 1997) in the ten years since its original publication has come overwhelmingly from fellow political progressives who are, variously, dubious about my engagement with contract theory, critical of my neglect of Marxism, skeptical of the project of adapting Enlightenment liberalism for racial liberation (or, in some cases, conversely, skeptical that any modification of Enlightenment liberalism is necessary), but all in agreement with the importance of the goal itself, and in complete sympathy with my indictment of Western racism and its legacy. So these have basically been disagreements among friends as against enemies. For the most part, the political right has ignored it, if it even came to their attention in the first place (but see David Gordon 1998). Since the book is a short one – an "extended essay," in the words of more than one reviewer – that sacrifices detail for range and velocity, in many places the argument could have benefited from being developed more. So I will try here to provide more argumentation on certain crucial points. I have also explored some of its central ideas at greater length elsewhere,[1] so interested

---

[1] For a more explicit rationale for how I am using contract theory in the book, descriptively and prescriptively, see Mills (2000, 2003c); for my diagnosis of the problems with Rawlsian "ideal theory," see Mills (2005a), and for Rawls's inadequacies on race in particular, see Mills (2006c); for the idea of racial exploitation, see Mills (2004); for the "radical Enlightenment," see Mills (2003a); for the "epistemology of ignorance," see Mills (2007); for "subpersons," see Mills (1998b, 2006b); for white supremacy, both local and global, see Mills (1998d, 2003e, 2003f); for the deficiencies of Marxism on race, see Mills (2003b); and for a more detailed discussion of Kant and race, see Mills (2005b). Two symposia on *The Racial Contract*, with my replies, are (1) Lewis Gordon (1998), Bogues (1998), Hutton (1998), and Mills (1998c), and (2) Nagel (2003), Schmitt (2003),

readers should consult these pieces also, which, together with the present reply, provide a more comprehensive account than in the book itself.

The breakdown of topics is as follows: (I) The Contract as Descriptive/Explanatory Framework; (II) The Contract as Normative Framework; (III) White Contract Theorists and Race; (IV) Race and Political Economy.

I The Contract as Descriptive/Explanatory Framework

Reviving and revising the descriptive contract

In Thomas McCarthy's very generous review in *Ethics*, he characterizes *The Racial Contract* as being "in the tradition of radical Enlightenment critique . . .This is the ongoing, unfinished project of rethinking and reshaping [liberal-democratic] ideas to include all that, in their corrupted historical forms, they have unjustly excluded" (1999: 453–4). I am happy to endorse this reading. As against an "externalist" anti-Enlightenment, antiliberal, anticontractual critique, then, the book should be regarded as a critique of the white Enlightenment in the name of the nonwhite Enlightenment, a critique of racial liberalism in the name of nonracial liberalism, and a critique of the white-supremacist contract in the name of the racially egalitarian contract. (See also Mills 2003a; Bronner 2004.)

The starting-point of this critique is an alternative *factual* picture of the societies and polities created by modernity and, correspondingly, an alternative *modeling* of them. Whereas contemporary contract theory, following John Rawls (1999h), is (nominally) purely prescriptive, I argued in the book, following Jean Hampton (1990, 1993), for the revival of the descriptive side that was present in at least some of the classic contract theorists. So for me, then, the contract has two dimensions, the descriptive/explanatory and the normative/prescriptive. But it must immediately be emphasized that "explanation" here is *not* meant in the social scientific sense. One of the failings of the book is that I did not make sufficiently clear that I was using the term in the weaker and more abstract sense appropriate to the conceptual universe of contract theory, as updated by Hampton. So it is not, as some critics have misinterpreted me, that I am claiming that the origins of white racism and white supremacy can be traced to a literal contract among whites, and that this is an "explanation" superior to standard accounts in the social

Zack (2003), and Mills (2003d). In my opinion, the best critique so far is Garcia (2001); for my reply, see Mills (2003c).

scientific literature on the history of racism. Rather, the point being made is Rousseau's original simple but far-reaching claim in *Discourse on Inequality*: that many of what we take to be natural human inequalities are actually created by humans, and are thus non-natural and political. As he writes: "I conceive of two sorts of inequality in the human Species; one which I call natural or Physical, because it is established by Nature. . . . The other, which may be called moral, or political inequality, because it depends on a sort of convention, and is established, or at least authorized by Men's consent" (1997a: 131).

What Rousseau claimed for class, and Pateman claimed for gender, I am claiming for race. Racial inequality no less than class and gender inequality is artificial, conventional, *political*. But the "consent" is, of course, restricted to the privileged group, who are the real "contractors." So whereas the neutral state, the impartial legal system, and a codified universalist set of rights and freedoms are brought into existence by human activity in the (nominally classless, genderless, and raceless) mainstream contract, their real-life discriminatory class, gendered, and racialized versions (and class, gender, and race themselves) are brought into existence respectively by rich, male, and white humans in the class, sexual, and racial contracts. It is in this sense that they are "explained." Racial domination as a sociopolitical system, and indeed race itself, are human creations, and ones that have been sufficiently central to modern polities that we should think of them – to use Rawlsian language – as part of these polities' "basic structure."

But what is the overall point of trying to revive contract's descriptive side, given the shift to the (nominally) purely prescriptive and hypothetical in Rawls? And aren't I just misunderstanding the goals of the contemporary version of the contract, which is focused on the adjudication of matters of social justice? Tom McCarthy writes that my claim that the "racial contract" "is superior to the [social contract] both descriptively-explanatorily and prescriptively-normatively" is "doubtful" (1999: 453). After all, "the social contract tradition has largely ceded such matters to empirical, historical, and social inquiry and retreated to the purely normative domain of ideal theory." But that is precisely my point – and that's why, not just in Rawls but in the two generations of political philosophers inspired by Rawls, the results have been so problematic. The whole burden of my suggested rethinking of the contract tradition is that it should be reoriented to deal with *non-ideal* moral theory. And this necessarily requires, on several different levels, the advertence to rather than the ignoring of factual matters.

The contrast can be simply put as follows. For ideal theory, the project is, starting from ground zero, to map an ideally just society. For non-ideal theory, the project is, starting from an already-existent non-ideal unjust society, to prescribe what ideally would be required in the way of rectificatory justice to make it more just. But such a correction requires a factual characterization of past and present injustices, that is, a description. And the point of framing it in terms of a "contract" among the privileged is to register the crucial claim that *these injustices were (and are) embedded in the basic structures of these societies, not anomalies within a structure essentially just.*

So the concept of the "racial contract," or, more generally, the domination contract is not merely challenging the mainstream focus on ideal theory. It is also challenging the representation of the non-ideal *as* a minor deviation from this norm. As such, it is seeking to overturn idealizing assumptions embedded in the contractual apparatus at levels far deeper than the obvious ones. Rawls says explicitly in *A Theory of Justice* that he is going to work within ideal theory, mapping a "well-ordered society" with no history of injustice: "[F]or the most part I examine the principles of justice that would regulate a well-ordered society. . . . what a perfectly just society would be like. Thus I consider primarily what I call strict compliance as opposed to partial compliance theory" (1999h: 7–8). So this is the overtly announced idealization, with all its primary and secondary ramifications, that shapes his writing. But there is also what one could term a kind of "stealth" idealization that is the legacy of the supposedly repudiated descriptive side of the original contract, and that has not received enough theoretical attention. Rawls begins the book with the claim that "a society is a cooperative venture for mutual advantage," governed by rules "designed to advance the good of those taking part in it" (1999h: 4; see also 109). Not society *should be* – which everyone could agree with – but society *is*. This pivotal assumption is not itself identified as part of the idealizing apparatus. Yet it arguably is such in a deeper sense than anything else Rawls says. For once you have predicated the modeling of society on such a foundation, you are *already* assuming a consensual non-exploitative sociopolitical system that is completely antithetical to the way the modern world was actually created.

Moreover, this tacit idealization is carried further in a picture of history that generally abstracts away from social oppression and its consequences. Note that this also is a logically separate level of idealization from the explicit "ideal theory" announcement, since one could seek to paint an ideally just society in the light of – that is, while self-consciously cognizant of – the lessons we have learned from the past history of unjust societies. But Rawls idealizes here also. We are supposed to know "the general facts about human society" behind the veil – this knowledge is not stripped from us (1999h: 119). Yet if one were to put together the original Marxist critiques of Rawls from the 1970s (with their points about the historic role of class power in the functioning of the state and the legal system), the feminist critiques from the 1980s onward (with their points about the ubiquity of gender domination in human society, and the pernicious effects of the drawing of the public/private distinction), and the more recent critiques on race (with their points about the centrality of white racial domination to modern global history), then obviously Rawls's abstracting away from the aggregative total of these facts – *all of which, as emphasized, we are supposed to know* – represents a massive evasion of the actual history of the human race.

So that is why I have emphasized the "nominal" character of the supposed Rawlsian shift to the purely prescriptive. Though his updated contractual apparatus is supposed to be purely normative, its denial of the history and consequences of social oppression in his characterization of the social order is a *factual* claim and one that serves to orient his justice focus and priorities. Rawls is making crucial factual/descriptive assumptions about how societies work in the framing of his normative enterprise, and these assumptions are profoundly misleading ones. Moreover, it is a descriptive foundation that arguably derives precisely from the original contract's descriptive account of political society's consensual founding. This founding is not represented as a process of oppression in the original contract theorists' work (except in Rousseau), and its attenuated version in Rawls does not represent it as such either. So there is a *multiple* idealization: the explicit, acknowledged idealization of focusing on a perfectly just society, leaving discussion of non-ideal theory to some other time (a time that, 30-plus years later, has yet to arrive, and which we have no reason to think ever will), and the implicit, unacknowledged idealizations – in a sense more pernicious precisely for their embedded and covert character – manifest in the initial representation of political society as essentially a consensual non-exploitative creation, with no advertence to the long history of gender, class, and (more recent) racial domination that would expose how absurd and risible this framing is.[2]

In sum, then:

Mainstream contract theory is saying: political society is basically consensual and reciprocally beneficial; cases of class, gender, and racial exclusion are anomalies, since the contract (the sociopolitical order) was meant to include everybody with equal consideration.

---

[2] In *Justice as Fairness*, Rawls warns that "political philosophy is always in danger of being used corruptly as a defense of an unjust and unworthy status quo, and thus of being ideological in Marx's sense. From time to time we must ask whether justice as fairness . . . is ideological in this way . . .? Are the very basic ideas it uses ideological?" (2001: 4 n4). I would suggest that in these key respects, and especially where gender and race are concerned, it has indeed been ideological from the start. (Thanks to Michael Gray for bringing this footnote to my attention.)

Radical (or "alternative" or "revisionist" or "subversive") contract theory is saying: political society is basically coercive and exploitative; cases of class, gender, and racial exclusion are not anomalies, since the contract (the sociopolitical order) was not meant to include everybody but (cumulatively, in its different guises) to exclude the majority from equal consideration.

It can be appreciated, then, how radical the challenge of alternative contract theory is. Picking up on the original Rousseauean demystification of a supposedly "consensual" social order as actually an inequitable class society, it is extending the claim to gender and race, and alerting us to the ubiquity of structures of sociopolitical exclusion, and their manifestation in the juridical, state, economic, cultural, ideational, moral, and psychological realms. Thus its mission is a startlingly and unsettlingly far-reaching democratic one. By self-consciously developing non-ideal theory within this revisionist framework, alternative contractualism forces on to the agenda a whole range of topics never discussed by the mainstream contract.

Not social science explanation

So my claims about "explanation" were expressly intended as political-philosophical in nature (Mills 1997: 5–6). However, because of these ambiguities about the racial contract's "explaining" white racial domination, numerous critics have interpreted me to be putting forward an account meant to compete with, and to be theoretically superior to, the standard list of candidates in the social science literature: for example, racism as the result of European ethnocentrism writ large, or militant Christianity, or unconscious psychosexual drives, or white/black color symbolism, or rational-choice power politics, or the political economy of imperialism, and so forth. Critics identify the obvious weaknesses in a literally contractual account and then put forward their own superior candidate instead.

For example, in David Theo Goldberg's book *The Racial State* (2002), he criticizes the idea of a literal racial contract for its oversimplicity,[3]

---

[3] Goldberg also gets Pateman wrong (Goldberg 2002: 41), attributing to her the belief in a literal sexual contract when the opening paragraph of her book makes it quite plain that the contract for her is a "story," an "explanation" based on "treating our society *as if* it had originated in a contract [my emphasis]" (Pateman 1988: 1). Or, in the words of her concluding chapter, "The original contract is merely a story, a political fiction" (1988: 219), a formulation no different from Goldberg's own characterization (2002: 38), "The social contract tradition, far from being a realist(ic) account, then, is more aptly conceived as the prevailing modern story or narrative form."

advocating in its stead the Foucauldian discursive account of race he has developed elsewhere (Goldberg 1993):

> Mills takes at face value the realist interpretation of social contract theory. . . . Mills accordingly assumes that social contract theory accounts for an actual contractual arrangement. . . . Simplicity may be the mark of a certain sort of social science and philosophy. But while simplicity is a theoretical value worth pursuing, complex social phenomena require a more complex theoretical account than offered here. Racially configuring discourse did not follow from a social contract but emerged coterminous with modern state formation. . . . White supremacy accordingly emerges not out of some imaginary "racial contract" but as a complex product of this discursive diffusion. (Goldberg 2002: 37–8; see also 41, 47, 49–50)

Writing from a Marxist perspective, Philip Cohen (1999: 103) also takes me to be offering a social-scientific explanation. He chides me, accordingly, for not considering "one reasonable counter-explanation, that the world is 'essentially dominated' by *capital*," and calls for the "greater level of granularity" provided by Marxist political economy. Similarly, Robert Young dismisses my "materialist" pretensions (see, for example, Mills 1997: 129–30): "Mills removes the possibility of connecting white supremacy, a political-cultural structure, to its underlying economic base. Mills's empiricist framework mystifies our understanding of race. . . . [W]hat is needed is an explanation of this racial formation" (Young 2006: 36). Anthony Bogues strikes a similar note of complaint: "[T]he racial contract, while being more historically accurate [than the social contract], is not able to adequately explain the complexities of racial formation. . . . Its power lies in describing, not theorizing, racial domination" (2001: 269). Likewise, while as seen earlier Tom McCarthy is enthusiastic about the book, he is dubious about the claims to descriptive superiority: "[T]he racial contract is at best a highly condensed and stylized model of the endlessly variegated and shifting reality of centuries of liberal political practice," much less detailed than Marxist political economy, "which has itself proven to be undercomplex." Thus "explanatorily the 'racial contract' might better be thought of as an (adjustable) conceptual model useful for orienting empirical research into the politics of race and for representing its accumulating results" (1999: 453).

On the basis of the above clarification, then, it should now be obvious why these criticisms are misguided, if perfectly understandable. I did not intend the "descriptive/explanatory" claims to be thought of as attempted social science explanation, in terms of an actual literal agreement, but rather as located on the more abstract level distinctive of classic social contract theory, as updated and glossed by Jean Hampton.

Though I am, as Barry Wilkins (1999: 53) correctly guesses from my emphasis on "the global expansion of European capitalism," most sympathetic to Marxist social science explanations of racism, I don't see that I have to take a position on these controversial questions *for the purposes of engaging with and revising social contract theory.* We can agree that white racial domination has been central to the making of the modern world without having to agree on its exact causes; these are matters to be settled in some other forum and settling them is not a prerequisite for tackling social justice questions. The philosophical imperative is to register the fact of this domination in the contract apparatus.

But if the "contract" doesn't explain anything at the social science level, then what work is it actually doing? Andrew Valls is unsure what the point of the contractual framework is:

> Those skeptical of contractarianism's justificatory power may be skeptical of its force as a critique as well. . . . [O]ne must ask what is gained by speaking in terms of agreement and contract. Of course, the atrocities and racist policies that Mills cites occurred, and no doubt their legacies continue to shape our society and the world. But what is added to the account by the contractarian framework? It seems to raise more questions than it answers. . . . All this seems to obscure rather than clarify the important normative issues raised by the racist history of our society and, therefore, undermines rather than advances Mills's project. (1998: 692)

The point is not just to correct the whitewashed history of modernity standard in mainstream political philosophy (and elsewhere), a *factual/conceptual* revision, but also to provide a way of translating this suppressed history and alternative conceptual framework into the discourse now most influential in mainstream political philosophy, social contract theory, and thus a *theoretical* revision. And the goal is to assist our theorizing about justice. The main use of social contract theory today, post-Rawls, is not, of course, explanation but normative inquiry. So the point of working with a "racial contract" is to use it as a tool for dramatizing and making cognitively vivid the history of racial injustice, and then to facilitate – within a contractual framework – the discussion of matters of non-ideal rectificatory theory. I did not actually draw out the implications of this revisionist approach in *The Racial Contract*, but I am trying to do so here. Given that I did not in the book provide an example of the positive reconstructive use I had in mind, it is perhaps unsurprising that to many it came off largely as a completely negative trashing of the tradition. My hope is that the present book will correct this mistaken impression.

In a discussion of the usefulness or not for progressives of the idea of a domination contract, Sally Haslanger raises many good points, including the question of whether there might not be crucial asymmetries between gender and racial domination (2000: 1–2). She discusses weak and strong interpretations of the contract idea, and contrasts teleological and causal explanation:

[A]s I read the domination/exclusivist contract there is something of a dilemma: either we see it as giving us a substantive model of how group domination works across the board, but one which is not entirely plausible as an analysis of all cases and seems to over-generalize from the example of race; or we see it as giving us a kind of metaphorical (quasi-teleological) model of group domination, which is illuminating, but doesn't give us the kind of substantive analysis we need in order to understand how "social causation" works. (2000: 5)

I think this is a very clear statement of the different senses of explanation that could be involved. And as we have seen, the answer is that there is no actual dilemma since I was not trying to provide a "substantive model of how group domination works." So the weaker "as if"/"quasi-teleological" sense is all that I need for my purposes. As Haslanger herself goes on to write: "A very plausible interpretation would be [that Mills] is offering a 'picture' or 'iconography' that when applied to the actual situation highlights its morally relevant features. . . . [I]ts point is to illuminate the actual structure of society in such a way that our normative model can get a grip on it" (2000: 5). Exactly.

Problems in application

Let me turn now to criticisms about details of my application of the contract idea, rather than criticisms of the contract as would-be social science.

Stephen Ferguson (2004: 80) takes me to be saying in an endnote (Mills 1997: 137–8 n3) that "race functions as a transcendental category which overrides gender and class." And he really does mean *transcendental*, that is, in the Kantian sense (Ferguson 2004: 11, 116, 207). But the claim that race generally trumps gender and class as a social division (what sides people generally choose to line up on) is sociological, not metaphysical (except perhaps in the "social ontology" sense). In the United States, for example, as Donald Kinder and Lynn Sanders have shown in a comprehensive survey and analysis of numerous attitudinal studies of whites and blacks, racial division eclipses all others: "Political differences such as these [i.e. on race] are simply without peer: differences by class or gender or religion or any other social characteristic are diminutive by comparison" (1996: 287). That's not Kantian apriorism – that's a posteriori empirical sociology. So when Robert Young (2006: 36–7) claims I am implying in the endnote "some kind of [white] metaphysical alliance," this doesn't follow at all. The fact that I don't attempt to give a social science explanation myself doesn't mean that I think there is none. Nor is it true that I'm thereby "suppress[ing] other forms of oppression, such as gender and class oppression." I'm not denying that they exist; I'm just not focusing on them in the book.

That would also be my response to David Theo Goldberg's criticism that "while the concept of a 'racial contract' predicates itself on power *between* racially conceived groups, its presumption of voluntarism completely denies the constitution of power and its effects *within* such groups" (2002: 39). The "racial contract" is a simplifying abstraction that abstracts away from gender and class power, thereby making generalizations that have to be qualified (as I concede at the start in the same endnote: Mills 1997: 137–8 n3). But I was completely cognizant – how could I not be, when I explicitly acknowledge my debt to Carole Pateman's "sexual contract"? – that a comprehensive account would have to integrate gender and class also, and their intraracial effects. In chapter 6, as seen, I make a tentative start on this task.

Goldberg (2002: 36–7) also claims that a reference I make to "the social contract's application to non-Europe, where it becomes the Racial Contract" (Mills 1997: 42) implies I believe "that the social contracts that supposedly established European states historically formed are not racial." To begin with, as clarified above, I never meant to imply that European states were literally founded on a contract. Second, it needs to be borne in mind that to the extent that contract theory is a useful way, a metaphor, for thinking about states and political obligation, it goes back to the *premodern*, medieval period. Modern European states certainly are racialized from their inception, and it is the modern state that is Goldberg's subject in his book. But is Goldberg claiming that the premodern European contract theorists cited by Michael Lessnoff (1986: ch. 2) in his history of the tradition, such as Manegold of Lautenbach (writing around 1080) and Engelbert of Volkersdorf (writing around 1310), were advocating a racial contract? At a time when most experts in the field would deny that race had even come into existence as a concept and social reality? Presumably not.

Kenneth Warren (1997) is concerned that I am conflating varieties of nonwhite racial subordination with significant differences among them, and, correspondingly, in the nonwhite oppositional theory addressing them: "Mills's positing the transparency of the racial contract to its victims . . . prevents him from addressing nuances within nonwhite political thought. In the night cast by the racial contract," he says wittily, "all nonwhite political cats are gray." Warren goes on to cite the long list of nonwhite oppositional political thinkers I mention (Mills 1997: 111–13), from Sitting Bull to Aimé Césaire, and suggests that "If together these thinkers attest to 'the reality of racial subordination. . ..', their differences from each other may point to the limits of the kind of inquiry that Mills has attempted here" (Warren 1997: 46).

But the distinctive mission of political philosophy needs to be remembered and appreciated. Political philosophy deals with abstractions – if it did not, it would not be political philosophy, but something else. And by definition, abstractions abstract away from particulars to get at key commonalities. Certainly Warren is correct that there are all kinds of differences between, say, Native American expropriation, Jim Crow, and European colonial rule. Nonetheless, what they all have in common is that they are different kinds of racial subordination, in this case, white-over-nonwhite racial subordination, white supremacy. So just as the abstractions *aristocracy, democracy, absolutism, fascism, socialism, patriarchy* apply to a wide range of political systems, with many differences among them, they are, nonetheless, seen as crucial terms in the discipline's theoretical vocabulary, insofar as they capture, at the high level of abstraction appropriate to the subject matter, key varieties of political rule. What the book argues, as well as my articles and chapters elsewhere, is that the term *white supremacy* needs to be added to this vocabulary, and that its absence from the standard lexicon has served to blind us to crucial political realities.

Warren, who is a Professor of American Literature at the University of Chicago, mentions in passing, as if it would be a minor accomplishment, the possibility that my book "may tell us how to put race back into the center of our accounts of Western societies," before going on to criticize me for the really important issue, my failure to tell us what to do about white supremacy (1997: 46). But he does not seem to realize – from his privileged disciplinary perspective, where these curricular battles were fought and won decades ago – what a remarkable and considerable accomplishment such a "centering" would be. Even in political science, more closely linked to the empirical, it has been hard to get race taken seriously as a global national reality (as against a local subject in, say, urban politics). In philosophy, it is far more difficult. It is routinely the case that anthologies on Western political philosophy are published that run to hundreds of pages or more with no mention of historic white domination and the political resistance to it. A good example is Steven Cahn's Oxford *Classics of Political and Moral Philosophy* (2002), which – in 1,200 pages from Plato to Martha Nussbaum – only manages to include work from one nonwhite thinker, Martin Luther King, Jr's "Letter from Birmingham Jail," and "The March on Washington Address," and not even in the main text at that but in the appendices. No

Douglass, no Du Bois, no James, no Fanon. I led off *The Racial Contract*, published ten years ago, by making this point about the whiteness of the subject, and its consequent contribution to a racially sanitized picture of modern global history. (No racial oppression, no political struggle against racial oppression, no political texts of the struggle against racial oppression.) Ten years later, this picture has hardly changed. So if the battle to get white supremacy recognized as a historic political reality like absolutism in the discipline's defining texts is not remotely close to being accomplished, then why worry about *nuances* when even this *gross* reality has not been acknowledged?

The contract as bourgeois ideology

The representation of social contract theory as a classic example of bourgeois ideology is a familiar and important indictment from the left. Stephen Ferguson's (2004) dissertation, a "Marxist-Leninist" critique of the theory of the racial contract, offers the most detailed version of this accusation. (But see also John McClendon 2002 and Robert Young 2006.) Ferguson lists what he sees as "five essential characteristics of contractarianism":

> (1) [S]ocial contract theorists offer [a] justification for political obligation that rest[s] upon the voluntary consent, assent, choice, agreement, and promises of individuals; (2) contract theorists start from the same reflective starting-point, namely, an original state or position; (3) methodological individualism which upholds an atomistic social ontology . . . the individual is seen as prior to and the ultimate constituent of society; (4) civil society is a human convention . . . (5) social contract theory functions as a form of bourgeois ideology which historically has justified a liberal democratic political philosophy. (2004: 20–1)

Even for mainstream social contract theory, of course, this characterization is inaccurate, since Hobbes's absolutist ideal and Rousseau's "general will" are hardly examples of "liberal democratic political philosophy." But the real point that needs to be emphasized is that this listing does *not* capture the key features of the revisionist contract theory – utilizing the "domination contract" – that I am advocating. Rousseau's "class contract," the progenitor of this hitherto unacknowledged alternative tradition of contract theory, (1) seeks to demystify as a scam, rather than to justify, political obligation, since its whole point is that the rich are conning the poor; (2) does not start from the state of nature, but from a pre-existing social stage; (3) does not – at least in the creation of class society – presuppose methodological individualism; and (5) represents a critique of the mainstream contract as a mystification of class inequality and plutocracy. The only thing they have in common, then, is (4), the portrayal of society as a human creation, which Ferguson is surely not going to deny. So while claiming to recognize that my version of the contract is an alternative to the conventional formulation, Ferguson nonetheless assimilates it to orthodoxy, when it is a critique of orthodoxy.

Similar points can be made in reply to John McClendon. In his freewheeling "Marxist-Leninist" polemic against an extensive list of African-American scholars, of whom I am just one, McClendon distinguishes "ideological critique," aimed at uncovering "fundamental presuppositions" of a worldview, and "internal criticism," whether "empirical" or "conceptual," that "shares the same ideological commitments" with the target of criticism (2002: 49). He sees me as pretending to do the former while actually doing the latter: "Charles W. Mills is a more recent exemplar of how internal criticism masquerades as ideological critique. . . . For Mills, the problem is not the fact that contractarianism is, more fundamentally, a form of bourgeois ideology; his concern is only that contractarianism has been corrupted by 'white contractarians'" (2002: 50). McClendon goes on to cite Marx's comments from the *Grundrisse* deriding "Robinsonades," that is, the absurd idea of starting one's theorizing from "the solitary and isolated hunter or fisherman," as in "Rousseau's *contrat social*, which brings naturally independent autonomous subjects into relations and connection by contract" (2002: 50).

But unlike Rousseau's *contrat social*, Rousseau's class contract (1997a) is *not* cited by Marx anywhere in his work, and, far from being a "Robinsonade," is in fact, a century beforehand, an anticipation of Marxism itself. Indeed, Christopher Brooke characterizes Marx as "Rousseau's great successor in the tradition of European radical democracy," while noting that "Nowhere, however, is Marx's debt to the spirit and substance of [*Discourse on Inequality*] properly acknowledged, though it remained both deep and lifelong" (2001: 117–18). Rousseau's striking theoretical innovation within contract theory is to begin not from isolated individuals in the state of nature but from the main groups (classes) of an *already-existent society*. So its methodological presumptions and social ontology are radically different since it recognizes and condemns class inequality as foundational to the modern world (while justifying, of course, gender inequality). As Michael Lessnoff writes:

> Here we have Rousseau's revolutionary version of the original contract of government – portrayed as the outcome of cunning and short-sightedness, and having as its result the stabilization of inequality and oppression. Such a contract, one might suppose, could provide no basis for the legitimation

of government, for it could have no legitimacy itself. Rather, it appears to portray the governments known to human history as mechanisms for institutionalizing the rule of the rich over the poor (a view which prefigures that of Karl Marx). (1986: 79)

So it seems to me that the "bourgeois ideology" criticism fails for multiple reasons. To begin with, the critique is irrelevant to the specific aims of the book, which was the focus on racial injustice. It was not pretending to be a comprehensive analysis of every kind of social injustice (which is not to say, of course, that I *don't* think they should be identified and eliminated). Even abstracting away from class, the achievement of a non-white-supremacist capitalism would indeed represent major moral progress, a great stride forward in justice, though other inequities remained. Second, the factual assumptions of the domination contract rest on a different social ontology from the traditional methodologically individualist one of orthodox contract theory, so it is hardly "bourgeois ideology" in that sense. And third, this separation of the normative apparatus of bourgeois liberalism from its original social ontology (that restricts its emancipatory potential) opens the door for a corresponding rethinking of its content. Rodney Peffer (1990) showed nearly 20 years ago how a Rawlsian apparatus could be used to develop a socialist critique, behind the veil, of class society.

II The Contract as Normative Framework

We come now to the uncontroversial side of contract theory that is, of course, the one central to its present incarnation: the normative.

Glenn Loury says he finds the book "provocative but in my view ultimately unpersuasive" (2002: 211 n1). But this, it turns out, is because he sees me as trying to replace liberal universalism with some other principle:

But here is the problem, and the source of my dissatisfaction with Mills's argument. . . . What are we to do? Overthrow Kantian ethics? And put what, exactly, in its place? . . . To recognize the flaws of the liberal tradition is one thing; to replace it with something workable is quite another. . . . Thus a historically oriented effort to expose the particularity at the core of universalistic arguments may be interesting, but it is not a refutation of the universalistic claims. (Loury 2002: 120–1)

As readers will by now appreciate, I am not in the least trying "to refute the universalistic claims." Rather, I am pointing out that they have not *been* universalistic. Instead, pseudo-universalism has masqueraded as genuine universalism, for example in a Kantian theory that has been represented in innumerable books and essays as proclaiming the equality of all "persons," while in reality arguably restricting full personhood to whites. Loury would surely applaud, rather than condemn, the "overthrow" of the principle that we should "Treat only whites with respect." Yet, if the argument of Emmanuel Eze (1997a), Robert Bernasooni (2001a, 2002), and myself (Mills 2005b) is correct, that is exactly what Kant's categorical imperative is *really* saying, since "person" is a term of art with racial prerequisites.

So the point of racially demystifying Kant's work, and the writings of other central liberal theorists, is (1) to reveal that the "universalistic" claims and arguments were not really universalistic at all; (2) to attain, in the process, a more realistic picture of recent global history and the work of leading Western ethicists and liberals in rationalizing white racial oppression (currently denied in the typical textbook and anthology); and (3) to raise the question of what the attainment of genuine universalism would require. We need to recognize the centrality of the history of racial exclusion, both in reality and in the concepts employed to map that reality, *so that we can correct for it*. And, as argued, I would claim that a crucial initial move is the transition from ideal to non-ideal theory, since the seeming universalism of the former orientation tacitly reinscribes the priorities of the white male experience of modernity at its moral core, thus contributing to the retention of the racial particularism still covertly remaining even after overtly racist restrictions have been dropped.

From the perspective of a feminism dubious about retrieving liberalism and contract theory, Laura Brace (2004) characterizes Pateman's book as doing a "devastating rather than reconstructive analysis," and expresses her wariness about theorists like Donna Dickenson (1997) and myself, who think contract can still be salvaged:

> Feminist theory, theory that takes women's experiences seriously and pays close attention to the impact of ideas and practices on women, is unlikely to want to reclaim a theory that relies on the idea that human beings are not the product of their social existence, and is built on the assumption that the fundamental motivations of human beings are presocial, nonsocial and fixed. It is at least questionable whether the social contract can be reconstructed in a feminist manner. . . . In the end, Mills's project is as liberal as Dickenson's, and they share the problematic goal of purging liberalism of its repressive elements. . . . I would argue that their approach is unsustainable because liberalism is much messier than contractarianism. (Brace 2004: 1, 3)

But to begin with, as I have emphasized throughout (and as I make clear in my chapter 3 above, on Pateman), the founding assumptions of my recommended "domination contract" revision of the tradition are radically different from orthodox contract theory, and quite antithetical to the idea of human beings as asocial creatures with fixed motivations. So it is putting liberal values on a different social ontology, as should have been clear to Brace from my "subperson" concept (which she applauds: Brace 2004: 3). I agree that liberalism is not coextensive with contract theory (for one thing, there is utilitarian liberalism). But with the resurgence of deontological liberalism, contractual liberalism is now the most important variety, and, I claim, can in this revisionist version accommodate the different "messy" varieties of "bondage" ushered in by modernity and denied or marginalized in Whiggish histories of liberalism. Finally, the adjudication of the normatively justified autonomy (and rights and freedoms) of the members of these interlocking groups will undeniably be a complex and challenging task, but what's the alternative? It can't be to leave things as they are, in regimes of systemic injustice. And what alternative theory has the resources and legitimacy of liberal democracy?

Another kind of principled antiliberal criticism I encountered draws on particular interpretations of the black radical tradition. In his contribution to a symposium on *The Racial Contract*, Lewis Gordon expresses misgivings about its strategy (or at least what he sees as its strategy):

> [I]t is clear that this work is designed specifically for *white* audiences. . . . It is asking whites to challenge white hegemony. Such a tactic is a familiar one in black protest literature – particularly black liberalism. . . . [B]lack progressive radicalism usually takes at least two forms: (1) demanding coalitions with poor whites and other people of color or (2) focusing on the means of racial transformation *in spite of whites*. The second radical perspective, although not separatist, is not white dependent. (1998: 173)

I certainly hoped that whites would form a significant part of my audience, but I was definitely not aiming exclusively at them. Insofar as the book provides a salutary précis of a history of racial domination and atrocity that has largely been covered up, then whites, as the privileged race, are particularly in need of its demystificatory illumination. But I also hoped that nonwhites would find it useful, and this has indeed proven to be the case, as attested to by its enthusiastic reception by students of color across the country in classes where the book has been assigned. However, apart from this educative role, the crucial point is that the purpose of the book is to facilitate discussions of racial injustice and its remediation. Now the simple challenge for Gordon is this: how does he think that racial justice in a white-majority and/or white-dominated society is going to come about except, in part, through dialogue with whites? Certainly one can pursue other kinds of subjects through an internal intrablack dialogue. But how can racial equality and racial justice be achieved "in spite of whites"? If an internal dialogue were all that was necessary, then we would have achieved it long ago!

So we will need to get these arguments outside of the academy and into engagement with the general public, with white public policy makers and legislators and shapers of public opinion. And to this end, intellectual tools will be needed. The most influential, the most widely accepted, such tool in contemporary political theory in the Western world is social contract theory. Why not see, then, whether these concerns can be translated into a contract framework? In such an enterprise, how could it *not* be a tremendous advantage to have them translated into an intellectual framework and a language with which whites will be familiar? How could it *not* be a tremendous advantage to appeal to the set of values that whites at least nominally accept?

In a more recent work by Gordon, *Disciplinary Decadence*, where I appear as the mysterious and somewhat obtuse "Mr. X," Gordon (2006: 111–17) argues that one should not (as, it is implied, I do) endorse a liberalism "which is, in the end, not a genuinely *political* theory at all since it has subordinated itself to the grammar of economics" and "relies on eliminating the *political* from political theory," by presenting theories "devoid of analyses of power" (2006: 115–16). But the concept of the domination contract makes power *central*, appropriating liberal values but rejecting liberalism's atomistic social ontology for an ontology of groups in relations of privilege and subordination. So it is a liberalism only in a qualified sense.

Finally, to point to the possible racism of leading white political philosophers, or of whites in general, as the primary obstacle to progressive change (Gordon 2006: 115) is, though Gordon does not seem to realize it, to abandon the claim that liberal values are the main problem. Rather, one would be appealing to familiar if controversial theses (to which, as a materialist, I am quite sympathetic) about the pivotal role of group interests in shaping group cognition and group motivation. But the obvious riposte here is that if such factors are indeed so important and determinative, then what reason is there to think that a *nonliberal* framework will be any the more successful? Is it that white group interests and white racism will somehow magically evaporate as material and ideological barriers once an alternative conceptual framework is invoked? Surely not. So unless the plan is to somehow sidestep vested white power in bringing about progressive antiracist social change (how?), it does not seem to me that a convincing anticontract case can rest on these grounds.

Anthony Bogues has developed a comparable line of argument, based on his reading of the black radical tradition. For Bogues, the basic problem I face is that I am trying to do a critique while remaining within a framework that limits that critique:

> Mills's critique of contract theory is an external one. His is not an interior criticism that explodes the contract theory at its deepest levels. . . . There is a basic tension in *The Racial Contract* between the historical construction of race in a set of exploitative power relations and a programme that is limited by the acceptance of the interior norms developed within social contract theory – namely, that of liberalism. (1998: 178)

What we need to do, then, is to transcend liberalism: "If the *practices* of liberalism reveal an inadequate emancipatory logic, then can it give social equality and therefore freedom to racially oppressed groups and others who are dominated? If not, then do we require another theory of emancipation?" (Bogues 1998: 179). And in such a theory, Bogues claims, "political values like the meanings of equality and freedom are themselves transformed" (2001: 270).

But as I have argued in greater detail elsewhere (Mills 2006a), the problem with Bogues' prescription is that it is ironically undercut by the positive account he himself provides in his book *Black Heretics, Black Prophets* (Bogues 2003) (a book which I recommend highly to anybody interested in these questions). Taking the ex-slave Quobna Cugoano (1999) as a paradigm representative of this black radical tradition that supposedly makes a clean break with European humanism, Bogues (2003: 35) gives a ten-point summary of the "major political ideas" of Cugoano's 1787 *Thoughts and Sentiments on the Evil of Slavery* from which it is immediately apparent that virtually all of them can be readily derived not merely from liberalism in general, but right-wing Lockean liberalism in particular, once deracialized. Liberal values have not been "transformed" in the work of this "black heretic," as Bogues claims, but extended to a black population normally excluded from their scope. And in fact, as Bogues (2003: 35) is forced to admit, Cugoano's *own* political characterization of himself is as a liberal. So a more accurate rendition of Cugoano's achievement would seem to be Bogues' gloss elsewhere in the text (somewhat in contradiction to his announced conclusion): "Cugoano sees natural rights as 'common rights,' and applies these rights to African slaves. *In doing this he universalizes natural rights in ways others did not*" (2003: 36; my emphasis). In other words, and contra Bogues, he sought to develop a black liberalism that was simultaneously a radicalism in its extension of values previously confined to whites. But the radicalism inheres not in the axiological newness of the values (unless their extension to blacks is, definitionally, taken to make them new, which trivializes the claim) but the "astonishing" insistence (Bogues 2003: 45), with all its world-overturning implications, that norms applicable to whites should indeed be applicable to blacks also. Once the realities of racial subordination are acknowledged and incorporated into the contract apparatus, as the "racial contract" tries to do, white liberal norms generate black radical prescriptions – indeed heretical ones.

III White Contract Theorists and Race

In *The Racial Contract*, as part of my general critique of social contract theory, I characterize various contract philosophers as actually or incipiently racist, or at least as neglecting the issue of race in their work. Since I do not go into much detail, some of these characterizations have been challenged by commentators and critics. So let me now try to back up my claims (or, in some cases, make a partial retreat from them).

Thomas Hobbes

It is clear that there is a dichotomization between the civilized and Native American "savages" in Hobbes's *Leviathan* (see, for example: Macpherson 1968: 41; Ashcraft 1972). It might be, though, that I do "racialize" it to a greater extent than is warranted, as Tommy Lott (2002) contends in his important essay on gender and race in Hobbes. Lott makes various points against my reading: (1) Hobbes's (1996: 459) reference later in *Leviathan* to the "ancient Philosophers" of India, Persia, Chaldaea, and Egypt shows that he was not committed to European superiority (Lott 2002: 72). (2) Elsewhere in his writings Hobbes includes the ancient Germans as "savages." (3) Hobbes "does not use racial concepts, or terms such as 'Negro' and 'African,' in a negative fashion to imply inferiority" (2002: 72). (4) Hobbes explains the difference between Native Americans and Europeans "in terms of social development and environmental influences rather than in terms of greater intelligence," and insists that "although Native Americans are not philosophers, they have a basic capacity to reason," but because of lack of "leisure" have not been able to develop it (2002: 72). (Hobbes: "*Leisure* is the mother of *Philosophy*" (1996: 459).)

I concede that there is merit to some of Lott's criticisms, and that my claims about "a tacit racial logic in the text [*Leviathan*]" (Mills 1997: 66) might be a bit overstated. Nonetheless, there are points worth making in reply.[4]

(1) My claim was not that for the racial contract in general, or for the discussion of Hobbes in particular, *all* nonwhites were to be characterized

---

[4] The following points largely repeat what I said in my reply to Lott in Mills (2006b: 247–8 n10).

as "savages" still in the state of nature. Rather, early in the book I explicitly distinguish between the racial contract's characterization of "savages" still in the state of nature and "barbarians" in existing, though inferior and deficient, societies (1997: 13). It is not incompatible with certain "evolutionist" (and devolutionist) varieties of racism that particular non-whites are conceded to have had viable civilizations in the ancient past.

(2) Similarly, the fact that particular groups of Europeans were also characterized as once, in ancient times, having been "savage" does not undercut their superiority if, in the present epoch, they are long past that stage. And surely it must remain significant that a group of nonwhites are the only examples given of people *presently* in the state of nature.

(3) My discussion in the book of Hobbes on race is limited to Native Americans; I do not generalize to other groups who would now count as "nonwhite" for us. (I say "the *literal* state of nature is reserved for nonwhites" (1997: 66), not that "all nonwhites are in the literal state of nature." So being nonwhite is at least necessary (if this reading is correct), even if it is not sufficient, for being in the state of nature.) And I do contrast Hobbes's relative "racial egalitarianism" with John Stuart Mill's more clear-cut racial "ontological dichotomization" two hundred years later (1997: 66, 149 n57).

(4) However, perhaps my most fundamental difference with Lott is over the significance of "savage" as a term applied to a *contemporary* group of human beings, and, relatedly, the causes and import for Hobbes of Native American "savagery." I would claim that when used about people in the *modern* period, "savage" *is* indeed either incipiently racialized, or at least (perhaps the same thing) a very close conceptual precursor to race. In her discussion of "English Ethnocentrism and the Idea of the Savage," Audrey Smedley (1993) points out that the category first crystallized in mass English consciousness as a result of the sixteenth-century/seventeenth-century conflicts with the Irish, whom some theorists (for example Allen 1994) have seen as the first systematically racialized group in history – "incapable of being civilized" and "something less than human":

> To document and confirm the growing beliefs about the unsuitability of Irishmen for civilization, many of the Englishmen pointed to the experiences of the Spanish with New World natives. They cited Spanish practices of exterminating Indians . . . as justification for policies of killing Irish men, women, and children. . . . In the English collective consciousness, "the savage" was thus a kind of composite of these streams of negative ideas and images. . . . The savage came to embody all of those repulsive characteristics that were contrary and opposed to English beliefs, habits, laws, and values. . . . [S]uch attitudes were more strongly felt by Englishmen and were instrumental in molding the English's cognitive

perceptions of other conquered peoples in the New World as well as later in the Middle East, India, Burma, South Asia, and Africa. They became important subthemes to the ideology of race and in the characterization of racial differences. (Smedley 1993: 60–1)

Surely Hobbes, writing in the mid-seventeenth century, would have been strongly influenced by such perceptions and associations in his decision to use the term. So I would suggest that we have at least proto-racialization here, if not actual racialization.

Correspondingly, in response to Lott's claim that Hobbes sees Native Americans as different only because of "social development and environmental influences," not intrinsic inferiority, I would raise the simple challenge: why, then, are they still in the state of nature? Why have they *not* developed a society that would give them the necessary leisure to become "philosophers"? The horrible "environment" of the state of war described in *Leviathan*, chapter 13, is the consequence of human behavior, not extrahuman factors. So since all humans are (supposedly) mentally equal, why have *these* particular humans not been able to pursue the prudential, natural law-mandated imperative to create a sovereign and end the state of war? They may have a "basic capacity to reason," but it would seem that it does not attain the threshold level necessary for leaving the state of nature.

So when Lott writes "only those groups free from the necessities of survival will undergo the process of social evolution to make the transition to civil society," and "[cultural advancement] is made possible by having greater leisure time" (2002: 73), I would suggest that this reply only defers the question to another level: what is peculiar to *Native American* development (or lack thereof) that has made them, unlike Europeans, unable to find this leisure time? Mental equality is, Hobbes tells us, even greater than equality of strength: "For Prudence, is but Experience; which equall time, equally bestowes on all men, in those things they equally apply themselves unto" (1996: 87). Yet the "Savage people of America" are later singled out again in *Leviathan* as the paradigm example of those peoples unable to build a lasting house (a figure for a lasting commonwealth) and mistakenly inferring from their own architectural incompetence that the "Principles of Reason" for such a task do not exist (1996: 232). What explains this unique distinction if not their inferiority? And if they are indeed inferior for Hobbes, why is this not appropriately designated as racism?[5]

---

[5] Barbara Hall agrees that "the fact remains that Hobbes thought Europeans were superior. This view may not reflect a racist ideology, but it does smack of an uncomfortable bias" (2005: 48). After reviewing various passages in Hobbes, she concludes that Hobbes "can justifiably be termed a racist" (2005: 54).

John Locke

David Theo Goldberg's second major criticism of me (the first being his mistaken literalist reading of the racial contract) pertains to a distinction he draws in *The Racial State* (2002) between what he sees as two importantly different strains of racism, "naturalist" and "historicist" (p. 43). (The "naturalist" variety involves "the claim of inherent racial inferiority," the "historicist" involves "claims of historical immaturity" (p. 74).) Goldberg categorizes Locke as a historicist, and says that in my discussion of Locke in particular (pp. 43–4, 54 n5), but also more generally (pp. 97 n6, 136 n6), I only recognize the former (naturalist) kind.

Let me begin with the general claim. Whether or not Goldberg is right about the significance of his distinction, the matter can obviously not be resolved here – it will have to be evaluated by historians of racism. But even if he turns out to be right, it is false that I only recognize naturalist varieties of racism, though undoubtedly I lay far greater emphasis on them. (For example, my initial formulation of the racial contract (Mills 1997: 11) explicitly glosses the "racial" as including the "cultural," so it is clearly supposed to be broader than the "natural," and as such could, I claim, readily accommodate the "historicist" strain Goldberg is differentiating.) Goldberg offers as evidence (2002: 54 n5) a passage from my second book, *Blackness Visible*, where I say that, over its existence, "race has paradigmatically been thought of as 'natural'" (1998a: xiii). But this claim is not, as he mistakenly infers, incompatible with recognizing that there are other varieties of racism. The paradigmatic form need not be the only form. And I think that, especially on the level of mass consciousness as against the academic level, I *am* right about naturalism historically being the dominant form.

Another passage from *Blackness Visible* that he cites rests on a confusion on his part about natural law. I stated there that "for these beings [subpersons], a different set of normative rules applies; natural law speaks differently" (Mills 1998a: 188; original emphasis removed). Goldberg (2002: 136–7 n6) reads this as further evidence for my "naturalism," and it is true that what I subsequently go on to say again emphasizes the naturalist version. But natural law in the philosophical sense is quite different from *descriptive* laws (of physics, chemistry, biology). Natural law is the set of *normative* principles that are supposed to morally regulate human behavior, the natural moral law of a God-created universe. As such, its (alleged) prescriptions for the differential and inferior treatment of nonwhites need not rest on their biological inferiority, but could be justified by their cultural inferiority also – as my reference to Cicero's views of non-Roman barbarians on the same page (Mills 1998a: 188) makes clear. (Not to mention the obvious point that

Locke himself was a natural law theorist, so that even if Goldberg's "historicist" reading of him is correct, it would be because *of* natural law that differential treatment of such "immature" adult humans would for Locke be justified.)

I think part of the problem is that his literalism (failing to see that I am giving a "contractual" rather than social scientific account of racism) leads him to misread my later remarks about the less-than-humanness of subpersons (for example, in what I say about Locke's views (Mills 1997: 68)). He is taking these as (always being) *biological* claims about nonwhites rather than *normative philosophical* judgments about their "contractual" moral inferiority (which can have more than one foundation, including the cultural [see, for example, 1997: 56]). Subpersonhood need not imply literal subhumanity. Finally, he mistakes my gloss of Jennifer Welchman's (1995) controversial article on Locke as a statement of my own position, when I was just citing it as one possible way of addressing the problem hereditary enslavement of Africans poses for the principles articulated in the *Second Treatise*. Even if Locke, through some feat of rationalization and self-deception, was somehow able to convince himself that African slaves had been captured in a just war (Goldberg 2002: 44), how could he possibly have justified the enslavement of their wives and children, when chapter 16 of the *Second Treatise* explicitly prohibits such a policy? At least Welchman tries to answer this question ("Children born to non-persons are neither the children of men nor entitled to claim rights natural to men": Welchman 1995: 80); Goldberg does not.

Jean-Jacques Rousseau

Rousseau is obviously the classical contract theorist most crucial for my revisionist contract theory, and in *The Racial Contract* (1997: 68–9) I praised the environmentalist historical account of the *Discourse on Inequality* (Rousseau 1997a). Nonetheless, I did also make accusations about what I saw as racial differentiations in his writing, some of which I now concede might be too strongly phrased. For example, I had read his claim about the ignorance of metallurgy and agriculture of the "Savages of America" (Rousseau 1997a: 168) as applying generally to the two continents, and thus as flagrantly contradicted by the great Aztec and Inca empires (Mills 1997: 69). But in a passage I've subsequently noticed in the "Essay on the Origin of Languages," Rousseau (1997c: 258) refers to the "Mexicans" as "a civilized people," making clear that the reference to American "savages" was more geographically limited than I realized. It is still false, of course, that no native peoples in the territory we now call the United States practiced metallurgy and agriculture, but the degree of "historical amnesia and factual misrepresentation" (Mills 1997: 69) involved is somewhat less than I originally thought.

On the negative side, however, I should mention a point made by some other critics of Rousseau that I neglected to cite in *The Racial Contract*. Barry Wilkins says of my critique that "Rousseau's condemnation of slavery" is given "insufficient consideration" (1999: 52). And it is true that *The Social Contract* is famous for its supposedly principled and unequivocal condemnation of slavery (bk I, chs 1–4). But the question is this: Why – in the midst of the endless references to ancient Greece and Rome, long dead and buried – does Rousseau not take the opportunity anywhere in the book to condemn the *contemporary* enslavement of live and suffering Africans by the country in which he was writing, especially since in the French *Code Noir* it had its most infamous and explicit codification? If his principles were really meant to apply transracially, why omit this flagrant contemporary violation of them? Textual silence can speak volumes, especially when the subject has been broached by the author himself. Moreover, in a passage contrasting the freedoms of the ancients and the moderns, Rousseau characterizes the Spartan citizen as one who "can be perfectly free only if the slave is utterly enslaved" (1997d: 115), while judging the situation of his contemporaries to be quite different: "As for you, modern peoples, you have no slaves." That's a bizarre claim, if his reference class is transracial, as most readers have assumed.

In his stinging indictment of the hypocrisy (if that's the word) of Enlightenment thinkers such as Condorcet, Diderot, Montesquieu, and Rousseau, political philosopher Louis Sala-Molins[6] points out that despite "the definitive passage where [Rousseau] condemns the four possible forms of slavery examined by Grotius" (2006: 73), he falls strangely silent on the Atlantic slave trade:

> Rousseau, who resolutely condemned classical slavery, did not notice that the slave trade and the ordeal of Negroes in the Caribbean raised a philosophical problem. . . . I challenge anyone to find and show me the smallest little line where Rousseau condemns the kidnapping of Africans and their enslavement in the Antilles. It does not exist. . . . The Greek or Roman slave can serve as a term of comparison, and reference is frequently made to him. So can the European serf. . . . The Negro slave, the Negro, naturally a slave, does not fit the criteria of the comparable either on the grounds of universalism, as it is defined, or of accomplishment as it is perceived. The question asked is not "Who is the Negro?" It is most often framed differently as "What is the Negro?" (2006: 49, 73, 74–5)

---

[6] I thank Tony Bogues for bringing this book to my attention.

So I suggest that if the class inequality of white men is clearly for Rousseau unnatural, conventional, political, racial inequality is, at the very least, somewhat more ambiguous.

Immanuel Kant

Both in *The Racial Contract* (Mills 1997: 71) and in my second book, *Blackness Visible* (Mills 1998a: 188), I assert that Kant "mapped a natural racial hierarchy" in which Native Americans are at the bottom, with blacks one rung above. But again David Theo Goldberg corrects me: "[N]othing Kant says bears this ordering out" (2002: 136–7 n6). Rather, it is blacks who are unequivocally at the bottom.

Well, here are two such things Kant said:

> In the hot countries the human being matures earlier in all ways but does not reach the perfection of the temperate zones. Humanity exists in its greatest perfection in the white race. The yellow Indians have a smaller amount of Talent. The Negroes are lower and the lowest are a part of the American peoples. (Cited in Eze 1997a: 118)

> That their [Native Americans'] natural disposition has not yet reached a *complete* fitness for any climate provides a test that can hardly offer another explanation why this race, too weak for hard labor, too phlegmatic for diligence, and unfit for any culture, still stands . . . far below the Negro, who undoubtedly holds the lowest of all remaining levels by which we designate the different races. (Cited in Bernasconi 2002: 148)

That seems to "bear this ordering out" pretty definitively.

As he did with Rousseau, Barry Wilkins taxes me for not taking into account "other, countervailing features" of Kant's thought, specifically his "condemnation of colonial conquest and enslavement" (1999: 52). But as I have argued in an essay on Kant (Mills 2005b), it is not altogether clear whether his condemnation of colonialism is a condemnation in principle or a condemnation of "abuses." And based on his examination of the texts, Robert Bernasconi claims that in fact "there is *no* record of [Kant's] having expressly opposed [African chattel slavery]" (2002: 149; my emphasis).

John Rawls

We come now to the most famous modern contract theorist, John Rawls. I did not accuse Rawls of racism but race-evasiveness, making the point that in his *A Theory of Justice* (1999h), a book written by an American in the late twentieth century, "not a single reference to American slavery and its legacy can be found" (Mills 1997: 77). Rawls's work, and that of his disciples, does not confront the fact, with all its implications for the need to rethink American political philosophy, that the United States has been a white-supremacist polity, and that the Western democracies which are now his key reference class (the earlier transhistorical and transnational interpretations of *Theory* having been declared to be mistaken) were almost all imperialist states whose wealth was based in part on slavery and colonial expropriation. Rather, in such post-*Theory* work as *Political Liberalism* (1996) and *Justice as Fairness* (2001), Rawls says explicitly that these issues of race are matters of non-ideal theory, and so not to be appropriately dealt with in his framework, which is concerned with ideal theory. So as I pointed out in *The Racial Contract*, and have subsequently argued in greater detail elsewhere (2005a, 2006c), as well as in my previous chapters in this book, the framework itself militates against the consideration of these matters.

However, Ajume Wingo thinks I am being unfair to Rawls:

> Charles Mills objects that John Rawls's theory of justice is impoverished because it fails to take particular, historically contingent conditions (such as the lasting effects of slavery and racism) into consideration. . . . [Mills] maintains that they are relevant to political considerations in ways that are easily overlooked if we focus too closely on persons conceived in a completely abstract and general way. To be fair to Rawls, however, Mills's is a rather myopic snapshot of Rawls. A closer reading of Rawls tells us another story, a historically contingent story about Western liberal democracy in which the development of liberal democracy turns crucially on events that led first to a modus vivendi and then matured into the modern liberal value of tolerance. In other words, the contingent historical events in the West prepared people for liberal democracy. (2003: 31–2)

Wingo goes on to cite from Rawls's "Kantian Constructivism in Moral Theory" (Rawls 1999f: 305–7):

> [W]e are not trying to find a conception of justice suitable for all societies regardless of their particular social or historical circumstances. . . . What justifies a conception of justice is not its being true to an order antecedent to and given to us, but . . . our realization that, *given our history and the traditions embedded in our public life, it is the most reasonable doctrine for us*. (Cited in Wingo 2003: 32; Wingo's emphasis)

But it seems to me that this quote actually buttresses my own rather than Wingo's case, both with respect to Rawls's own position and Wingo's defense of Rawls. For it comes from one of Rawls's crucial 1980s essays signaling his shift from traditional contract theory, with its pretensions to be giving a cognitively "Archimedean" perspective on matters of justice, valid for all societies and all times, to a more situated and "contingent" viewpoint (a shift widely seen, though Rawls himself denied it, as a response to communitarian criticisms like those of Michael Sandel (1998)). But if justice is no longer to be conceived of in transhistorical terms, but rather as rooted in and responsive to local historical circumstances and distinctive national traditions, *then the case for the inclusion of racial justice as a central imperative becomes all the stronger*. As various theorists (outside of philosophy, of course!) have pointed out, the United States, along with apartheid South Africa, is virtually unique in the thoroughness with which white supremacy as a central organizing principle was incorporated into its "basic structure" (Fredrickson 1981; Horsman 1986; Saxton 2003; R. Smith 1997; A. Marx 1998). It follows, then, that a theory of justice sensitized to local conditions, *Sittlichkeit* rather than *Moralität*, must make the dismantling of white supremacy and remedying of racial injustice a priority. For it is nonwhite racial subordination that has "historically" been seen as the "most reasonable doctrine for us [whites]," and the "tradition" most deeply "embedded in our public life."[7]

Moreover, Wingo takes Rawlsian liberal democracy at its word, and speaks about its evolution from a modus vivendi to "tolerance." But insofar as this is supposed to apply to race it's doubly wrong. A modus vivendi is a compromise based on a standoff between adversaries with roughly comparable power. How could that possibly be an appropriate characterization of the white settler expropriation of Native Americans, and the white enslavement and subsequent segregation of blacks, of white power and nonwhite subordination? This is white *oppression* gradually alleviated through changing socioeconomic circumstances and concessions forced by nonwhite political struggles. Nor is it, as Wingo phrases it, a matter of "tolerance" – that's the wrong category to begin with – but of the moral imperative (which continues to be ignored) of the racial state's living up to its obligations to guarantee for nonwhite citizens equal opportunity, compensate for the past lack of such equality, implement measures to undermine white majoritarianism in the electoral arena, take steps against segregation, and so forth.

Tommie Shelby is also dubious that any fundamental rethinking of a Rawlsian framework is necessary. Thus in a recent symposium on Rawls, with a special section on race and ethnicity, he acknowledges the

---

[7] Actually, an alternative response – even more damaging for Wingo's defense of Rawls – would be that the moral relativism many ethicists have argued is inevitably associated with *Sittlichkeit* rules out any principled condemnation of racism, given this very "embeddedness" in US traditions.

undeniable, that Rawls has very little to say about race, while contending that the Rawlsian framework, unmodified, can still be used to tackle issues of the remediation of racial injustice (Shelby 2004). Shelby asserts that "it is a mistake to think, as some have [and here he cites to me], that abstraction from the social realities of race within the contractarian model is necessarily a way of obfuscating or denying the centrality of racial domination to the historical development of modern societies" (2004: 1700 n16). As he goes on to make clear, however, Shelby is really talking about the Rawlsian normative contract, whereas my claim was primarily meant about the descriptive contract. Obviously "modern societies" like the United States and the European colonial nations evolved in the modern period as white-supremacist states, so to the extent that mainstream contract theory ignores this crucial fact about them, it does indeed "obfuscate" a central social reality. Moreover, this mystification *does* survive in Rawls, in that he talks about "modern democratic societies" as his reference group while ignoring that they were (are) *racist* societies. And as just argued in reply to Wingo, and also at the start of the chapter, I would make the further claim that the evasion of race in the account of the original descriptive contract continues to haunt the framing of the normative contract also, in that issues of racial justice are methodologically marginalized.

Thus what Shelby says in his opening paragraph (and here we really do dramatically disagree) seems to me utterly wrong, a complete inversion of reality: "When liberal thinkers make this complaint [re the nondiscussion of racial justice in Rawls] they generally do not mean to deny what is no doubt obvious to anyone who has studied Rawls's work, namely, that he was concerned about racial problems and that this concern influenced how he constructed and defended his theory" (2004: 1697). With all due respect to Shelby, I find this statement quite astonishing. Where is there the textual evidence, in a career that spanned 50 years,[8] that Rawls was "concerned about racial problems," apart from the occasional pro forma platitude about the wrongness of racial discrimination? Where in Rawls's corpus over these five decades is there a single essay, or even a section of an essay – let alone a book – that addresses such problems (as against passages explaining why he is *not* addressing them!), as such concern would presumably motivate? If a white philosopher with strong antiracist commitments does not reveal them in his writing because he works in an area of philosophy remote from such issues, there is nothing surprising about such reticence. But how can this silence be explained when the issue is absolutely central to your field and you are *the* leading theorist of social justice in the United States?

[8] Rawls got his Ph.D. in 1950, and he died in 2002.

Shelby concedes that Rawls's remarks about racism are "sparse," but it is worthwhile underlining how truly exiguous they really are. If you add together *A Theory of Justice* (Rawls 1999h), *Political Liberalism* (Rawls 1996), the *Collected Papers* (Rawls 1999a), *The Law of Peoples* (Rawls 1999g), and *Justice as Fairness: A Restatement* (Rawls 2001), you get over 2,000 pages. If you add together every sentence about racism in these five books, you might get three or four pages, if that much. Indeed, so far as I can tell from an illuminating textual search I conducted one day, even the *phrase* "racial justice" never appears in Rawls's writing. If he was so concerned about racial problems, this was an odd way of showing it.[9] What was preventing him from addressing them? Fear of not getting tenure? Hope of landing a job at an institution more prestigious than the obscure liberal arts college in the boondocks at which, frustrated and unrecognized, he was forced to labor for so many unrewarding decades? Irony aside, to me, as earlier indicated, it's almost the exact opposite: that the theory was constructed to *evade* these problems. Shelby goes on to admit that "many of the most vexing and urgent questions of racial justice fall within the domain of partial compliance theory," and are thus located "outside the purview of [Rawls's] main theoretical concerns" (2004: 1698). But he does not draw the obvious conclusion, that this methodological decision *itself* demonstrates Rawls's lack of concern. And it's not just Rawls himself, but, as emphasized in chapter 4, the secondary literature also. I think Shelby needs to ask himself why it has been so easy for white philosophers in this tradition working on justice to evade racial questions, and what it says about the apparatus.

So it does not seem to me that Shelby is facing the implications of Rawls's explicit theoretical declarations about the limited scope of his principles. In *Theory* Rawls had written: "We must ascertain how the ideal conception of justice applies, *if indeed it applies at all*, to cases where . . . we are confronted with injustice" (1999h: 309; my emphasis). Thomas Nagel's essay in the *Cambridge Companion to Rawls* has an endnote – one of the few sentences on race in the entire collection – that makes this limitation explicit. Nagel points out there that as "corrective justice," "Affirmative action therefore does not form a part of what Rawls would call 'strict compliance theory' or ideal theory, which is what the two principles of justice are supposed to describe" (2003: 84 n3).

Affirmative action, preferential treatment, reparations, and so forth – all those topics which have preoccupied black moral philosophers like

---

[9] In his 1998 interview with George Yancy (1998: 294), Laurence Thomas also makes the useful point that nowhere in his work up to that time had Rawls ever cited a black philosopher. Nor would he do so subsequently.

Bernard Boxill (1992) and Howard McGary (1999) for decades – are not called for from the original position because they presume a history of racial injustice that is outside the ambit of Rawls's book. And that's why white philosophers following in Rawls's footsteps don't have to talk about them. But where there *has* been such a history – where the "basic structure" has been fundamentally shaped by Native American expropriation, African slavery, and then Jim Crow – ideal theory is clearly inappropriate, since measures are called for *to deal with* that history. What do we do *now* to correct for the multidimensional legacy of white supremacy in the forms of the non-ideal functioning of the state and the legal system, dominant tendentious interpretations of the Constitution, grossly inequitable racial distributions of income and wealth, residential segregation, the racial division of labor, color-coded education, white voting patterns, biases in the criminal justice system, white privilege, white moral psychology, white denial of the past (and present), and so forth? What "device of representation" is appropriate for adjudicating the normative questions generated by these issues?

By its very nature (the focus on ideal theory) Rawls's work gives no answer to these questions. One can, of course, appeal to antidiscrimination as a principle, which Rawls does explicitly endorse. But antidiscrimination as a guiding tenet is going to be of limited use, since it does not tell us how we should regard corrective policies which, as the white backlash against affirmative action confirms, will typically be seen by most whites today as *"reverse"* discrimination. Instead one will need a justification that refers to the workings of systemic and cumulative illicit racial advantage that will often manifest themselves *without* discrete acts of individual "discrimination" guided by conscious "intent" (which tends to be the gold standard in antidiscrimination law). As Rawls himself says explicitly in *Justice as Fairness*: "The idea of a well-ordered society is plainly a very considerable idealization. . . . Justice as fairness is a political conception of justice for the special case of the basic structure of a modern democratic society" (2001: 9, 14), and "a democratic society . . . *excludes* . . . *a racist one*" (2001: 21; my emphasis). By definition, a white-supremacist society is not a "well-ordered society," so the requirements for transforming it into a just society, or at least a less unjust one, are necessarily going to be different in key respects from the requirements for ensuring that racism does not enter into the basic structure of an ideally just society. These are two different kinds of enterprise. So though Shelby (2004) makes a gallant and ingenious attempt to extract racial justice prescriptions from Rawls's statements, it seems to me that he is underestimating the changes that (by Rawls's *own* admission) would need to be made in his framework.

IV Race and Political Economy

Finally, to repeat my earlier clarification about the kind of "explanation" I am invoking in the book, I do not (contra my left-wing critics) see the "racial contract" as competing with classical political economy approaches but rather, in a theoretical division of labor, as operating in a different conceptual space than they do. Explanation in this "philosophical," distinctively contract-theoretical sense thus has different goals than social science explanation, and is obviously compatible with a range of contenders in the field, including at least some Marxist ones.

But what kind of Marxism? Insofar as claims about "racial exploitation," "white supremacy," and "white" racial causality are central to my argument, a class-reductionist "white" Marxism will be hostile to some of my crucial assumptions (see Mills 2003b). So I have to admit that the "racial contract" is to a certain extent theoretically committed on the social science level also, ruling out theories that deny the social reality of race.

Steve Ferguson, for example, takes issue with what I say in the book about exploitation: "Although racism and national oppression are instances of white supremacy, class exploitation cannot be subsumed under and made identical to white supremacy, as Mills would have it" (2004: 99). But nowhere do I claim that it can; I am not talking in the book about "class exploitation" but *racial* exploitation (Mills 2004). For Ferguson, however – imprisoned as he is in the walls of orthodoxy – exploitation is by definition class exploitation. (How, one wonders, would he conceptualize the sexual exploitation of women? As an example of the transfer of surplus carnal value?) This concept has to be debated on its own merits; it can't be declared inconsistent with Marxism and *ipso facto* therefore invalid.

Robert Young offers a related challenge: "From Mills's logic, it seems that all whites (materially) benefit from the Racial Contract, but if this is true, then how does he account for the class structure within the white community?" (2006: 37). Quite easily: there is no inconsistency between racial group R1 benefiting from the exploitation of racial group R2 and the proceeds of this exploitation being distributed unequally among the members of racial group R1. Nor, indeed, does it rule out the possibility that other kinds of exploitation exist. Nowhere do I claim that racial exploitation is the only kind of exploitation. Though Ferguson and Young both obviously have difficulty grasping the idea, it is possible for someone, as a member of one group, to be a beneficiary of one kind of exploitation, while simultaneously, as a member of another group, to be a victim of another kind of exploitation – as with white women, for example.

Let me now say something about the term I use in *The Racial Contract*, "global white supremacy," a transgressive political concept which has a long history in the black radical tradition. (See, for example, W. E. B. Du Bois (1995) and Malcolm X (1989).) Philip Cohen expresses an orthodox left skepticism about such a notion, in keeping with a white left tradition (see, for example, Lenin 1996) that fails to recognize the ways in which European imperialism brings race into existence as a global reality:

> One may imagine a "common identity based on the transcontinental exploitation of the non-European world" ([Mills 1997:] 35) after the fact, but such an alignment is not clearly in evidence in history, beyond the machinations of a tiny group of rulers. . . . Mills does little to argue against at least one reasonable counter-explanation, that the world is "essentially dominated" by *capital*. (1999: 103)

In other words, the real movers and shakers are the (colorless) ruling classes, not the white population as such.

I see this as a class-reductionist Marxism that has historically been very prevalent on the white left, that is deeply wrong, and that has, tragically, blocked a recognition on the part of its proponents of what Howard Winant (2001: xiv) aptly calls the "world-historical" significance of race. While, as emphasized, I am sympathetic to the claim that white supremacy – and indeed race itself – are brought into existence by capitalism in its early imperialist phase, and that causality within the white population needs to be disaggregated, I do want to insist that, once created, *race achieves a causal efficacy of its own*. Europeans at home and abroad come to think of themselves *as* white, and this self-conception shapes their perceptions, their emotions, their motivations, and their actions. As David Roediger (1999) classically points out, the white working class make themselves as white, and are not just puppets of bourgeois agency.

Cohen needs to look at fellow sociologist Winant's recent powerful *The World Is a Ghetto* (2001), which explains the "immense planetary metamorphosis" (p. 21) that leads to the establishment of a "world racial system" (p. 3) in which race becomes "a corporealizing means of human identification and classification that informed everyday life and culture" (p. 112). Or he could look at British sociologist Frank Füredi's analysis of race as "a central element in the composition of Western identity," underpinning a "Western racial imagination" for which "racial thinking was an accepted part of the intellectual climate" (1998: 1, 5), with the growing international white conviction by the start of the twentieth century that racial conflict would take the form of "a racial threat posed by people of color against the white race" (1998: 1–2). Or the vast "whiteness" literature, for example sociologists Ashley Doane and Eduardo Bonilla-Silva's important recent anthology, *White Out* (2003) (interest disclosed: I am a contributor). Race is an emergent social structure with a real causality of its own, not to be reduced to class. And imperial domination, correspondingly, is in part racial domination, with whites across the world thinking of themselves as such, and in opposition to nonwhite "natives" everywhere.

Cohen says "such an alignment is not clearly evident in history." He should read historian Thomas Borstelmann's recent *The Cold War and the Color Line* (2001). Borstelmann himself refers to "the era of global white supremacy," "the international character of white rule over people of color," "the truly international sweep of white authority" (pp. 14–15). His prologue describes how "In the twentieth century the global movement toward racial equality and self-determination gathered speed and finally broke upon the bulwarks of white supremacy with irresistible force," so that "With the democratic elections of 1994 in South Africa, the long era of legalized white rule over people of color – much, much longer than the period of competition between Communism and capitalism – came finally to an end" (pp. 1, 6).

So these iconoclastic and seemingly outrageous concepts, pioneered with great intellectual courage by Du Bois and other mapmakers of the alternative black radical political cartography, are at last coming in from the cold, achieving the respectability they deserve. Contra Cohen and other like-minded white Marxists (or, for that matter, black Marxist-Leninists: see McClendon and Ferguson), white supremacy is more than just bourgeois rule, white workers are actively involved as well as the white ruling classes, and it was originally international in character. A political economy of race is indeed desirable, but it must be a nonreductionist one that recognizes the theoretical failures of white left orthodoxy.

And that brings me finally back to Steve Ferguson. I want to close by addressing what I think is his best and most important point: the question of white benefit from white supremacy (Ferguson 2004: ch. 3; see also Young 2006). This is a topic obviously of interest both in its own right and as one way of cashing out a version of "tacit consent" to the racial contract. (Not simply in the Lockean fact of benefits, though, since even white "nonsignatories" trying to undermine white supremacy will continue to benefit from their whiteness. Rather it is tacit consent as manifested in deliberate actions aimed at securing those benefits, and maintaining the structure that generates them.)

Ferguson writes: "Mills' racialist ideology – to put it bluntly – exaggerates the material significance of white privilege" (2004: 108). For Ferguson, despite the large amount of recent literature on the subject,

"White privilege is little more than a psychological sense of entitlement" (2004: 99). So the only "benefits" are illusory psychological ones. "Once we make a class analysis of white supremacy, we can see that white supremacy does not advance the objective material interests of the white working-class. . . . [T]he white working-class in no way benefits from the Black proletariat being exploited" (2004: 102–7). He cites as evidence work by the economist Michael Reich, glossing his argument as concluding that "the income share of middle-income and high-income families increases with an increase in racial inequality. . . . Since the income differences *among* whites [increase] with racial inequality, capitalist[s] gain and white workers lose" (2004: 103–4).

I want to make three points in reply, having to do with logic, scope, and methodology.

First, a simple logical point. If an individual, or a group (say, white workers), would benefit more under system S2 than system S1, it does not follow that they do *not* benefit under system S1, only that they benefit less. Nor does the fact that another group in system S1 (say, white capitalists) benefit far more than they do prove that they themselves do not benefit. And in terms of motivation, if S2 seems uncertain, while S1 is already here, beneficial, and entrenched, and the transition costs of moving from S1 to S2 loom high, one's "objective material interests" may well seem to be better served by remaining in S1 rather than risking trying for S2.

Second, the scope of my claims about racial exploitation was self-consciously global, including crucially the long-standing argument of various theorists that African slavery and colonial plunder were pivotal to the development of the West, and its economic dominance in the world (Mills 1997: 31–7). This thesis has, of course, always been a controversial one. But if the case can in fact be convincingly made for it, how would this not be a clear-cut instance of transcontinental racial exploitation that benefits Europeans in general, given the huge differences in living standards between "the West and the Rest"? Moreover, even within particular countries, such as white settler states like the United States, Australia, and South Africa, one also has to take account of benefits derived from land and resource expropriation from the indigenous population which white Marxists focused just on an abstract "capitalism" and "wage labor" tend to ignore. If working-class European immigrants to the United States, say, are better off than they would have been had they stayed in Europe, why should this not be the appropriate baseline of comparison, considering that the opportunities opened up for them in the United States have been made possible by the killing and expropriation – the racial exploitation, whether Ferguson wants to admit it or not – of Native Americans? Limiting the

debate to wage labor, the main kind of exploitation admitted by traditional Marxists, is illegitimate, since the point of the concept ("racial
exploitation") is in part precisely to *contest* this one-dimensional
conceptualization.

But finally, the crucial methodological problem with Ferguson's argument is that Reich's work was published more than a quarter-century
ago (Ferguson cites essays from 1978 and 1981), and the debate has
moved on considerably since then. At least since Melvin Oliver and
Thomas Shapiro's prizewinning 1995 *Black Wealth/White Wealth*, it has
been recognized in the literature that *wealth* is a far more significant
determinant of racial inequality than income. So Reich's assumptions
are dated insofar as he is using black/white median income ratios as "the
principal measure of racial inequality" (Ferguson). Wealth represents a
past cumulative history of discriminatory advantage and disadvantage
in multiple spheres that tends to reproduce itself intergenerationally. In
the words of Thomas Shapiro: "[W]ealth motivates much of what
Americans do, grounds their life chances, and provides enduring advantages and disadvantages across generations. Wealth ownership is the
single dimension on which whites and blacks are most persistently
unequal" (2004: 33). And as mentioned in chapter 4, as of 2004 the
white to black ratio in median net worth stands at ten to one and in
financial wealth at over a hundred to one, the reason being that the
sources of wealth are themselves racially differentiated in ways more
complex than income variation. So the natural inference one might
make of a straightforward correlation between income and wealth is
quite wrong, since "wealth discloses the consequences of the racial patterning of opportunities" (Shapiro 2004: 35–6). Instead one has to cast
one's theoretical net much more broadly, looking for example at
differential past and present chances of getting a mortgage, and so
being able to build wealth through home ownership; at segregation in
housing, and restricted access to the greater appreciation in property
values of the white suburbs; at inferior education, and what it means for
competitiveness on the labor market; at the racialized distribution of
transfer payments from the state, such as the postwar implementation
of the GI Bill; and so forth. Racial exploitation in this sense is multidimensional. And the point is that at *all* class levels whites do much better.

To illustrate this pattern, we only need to look at figures on wealth
distribution, broken down by quintiles for the white and black population, which show that "white households in *every income quintile* have
significantly higher median wealth than similar-earning black households" (Shapiro 2004: 49; my emphasis). For our purposes (since
Ferguson's claim is that the white working class do not benefit from
white supremacy) the crucial category is obviously "the lowest fifth

median." As Carole Pateman pointed out above in chapter 5 (I am using her more recent figures, from L. Williams 2004: 684, rather than Shapiro's), the figures for these bottom quintiles are as follows: whites (median net worth) $24,000; blacks (median net worth) $57. The ratio of difference is actually *greatest* at the lowest levels (over 400:1). In Shapiro's conclusion: "No matter how much or how little you make, then, wealth is dramatically higher for white households" (2004: 50).

This huge differential in the bottom quintile – greater than at any other level – is *prima facie* evidence of the reality of transclass racial exploitation, and of white working-class benefit from it, and a refutation of Ferguson's claim that "white privilege is little more than a psychological sense of entitlement." Moreover, the reality of this privilege – to return one last time to the "contract" framework – does indeed provide the motivation for whites to continue being "signatories" to the racial contract. It is not a matter, as Ferguson misunderstands me, of claiming that all whites are racist, but rather of recognizing how white group interest in maintaining their "competitive advantage" for themselves and their children, in Shapiro's phrase, encourages them to make certain kinds of decisions: "Recent surveys have shown repeatedly that nearly every social choice that white people make about where they live, what schools their children attend, what careers they pursue, and what policies they endorse is shaped by considerations involving race. . . . The incentives, rewards, patterns, expectations – indeed, the structure – [lead one's] family into an all-white world, rational decision by rational decision" (2004: 102, 143).

What clearer empirical confirmation could one want of the reality of an ongoing, rational, white "tacit consent" to the existing racial contract-founded racial polity?

I hope, then, that this reply will have clarified my position where it was fuzzy, and made it more convincing to those who were skeptical. The point, as emphasized throughout, is to reorient contract theory to deal with issues of racial justice and issues of non-ideal theory more generally – surely a worthwhile goal, indeed a goal that John Rawls himself declared his support for, even if he never got round to doing anything about it himself. Social contract theory provides us with an illuminating metaphor for thinking about the creation of society and the egalitarian values that should guide its construction. But if modern societies were not actually constructed on egalitarian lines, then we need to adjust social contract theory so as to model and address these inequities. Social contract theory claims to be including all adults as contractors, descriptively and prescriptively. But if only white men were originally part of the contract, both in theory and in practice, then obviously we need to rethink the contract to include, in a substantive way, white women and people of color. What could be controversial about any of that?

In our opening book epigraph, the worthy John Adams warns that the "tribes" of Native Americans, blacks, and white females are, bizarrely, actually assuming that the revolutionary liberal challenge to the "bands of government" should include them also. For the several hundred years since its inception, liberalism has restricted its egalitarian promise to a white male minority. If contemporary white male contract theorists continue to ignore gender and racial oppression in their prescriptions for a just society, even while disavowing that they are "masters," why should they too not be seen as simply carrying out two hundred years later, on the battlefront of political theory, the same "fight" against the "repeal" of the masculine and white-supremacist systems that Adams was confident "General Washington and all our brave heroes" would lead?

References

Ackerley, Brooke, et al. 2006. Symposium: John Rawls and the Study of Justice: Legacies of Inquiry. *Perspectives on Politics*, 4, no. 1: 75–133.

Alcoff, Linda Martín. 2002. Philosophy and Racial Identity. In Osborne and Sandford (2002).

Alcoff, Linda Martín, ed. 2003. *Singing in the Fire: Stories of Women in Philosophy*. Lanham: Rowman & Littlefield.

Allen, Theodore W. 1994. *The Invention of the White Race*, vol. 1: *Racial Oppression and Social Control*. New York: Verso.

Allen, Theodore W. 1997. *The Invention of the White Race*, vol. 2: *The Origin of Racial Oppression in Anglo-America*. New York: Verso.

America, Richard F., ed. 1990. *The Wealth of Races: The Present Value of Benefits from Past Injustices*. New York: Greenwood Press.

Amos, Valerie, and Pratibha Parmar. 2001 [1984]. Challenging Imperial Feminism. In Bhavnani (2001b).

Anderson, Elizabeth S. 1990. Women and Contracts: No New Deal. *Michigan Law Review*, 88, no. 6: 1792–810.

Antony, Louise M., and Charlotte E. Witt, eds. 2001. *A Mind of One's Own: Feminist Essays on Reason and Objectivity*. Rev. 2nd edn. (Orig. edn 1993.) Boulder: Westview Press.

Anzaldúa, Gloria. 2001 [1987]. *La Conciencia de la Mestiza*: Towards a New Consciousness. In Bhavnani (2001b).

Appiah, Anthony. 2000. The Uncompleted Argument: Du Bois and the Illusion of Race. In Bernasconi and Lott (2000).

Arendt, Hannah. 1973 [1963]. *On Revolution*. Harmondsworth: Penguin Books.

Armitage, David. 2004. John Locke, Carolina, and the *Two Treatises of Government*. *Political Theory*, 32, no. 5: 602–27.

Arneil, Barbara. 1996. *John Locke and America: The Defence of English Colonialism*. Oxford: Clarendon Press.

Asch, Michael, ed. 1997. *Aboriginal and Treaty Rights in Canada: Essays on Law, Equality, and Respect for Difference*. Vancouver: University of British Columbia Press.

Ashcraft, Richard. 1972. Leviathan Triumphant: Thomas Hobbes and the Politics of Wild Men. In Dudley and Novak (1972).

Asturias, Laura E., and Virginia del Águila. 2005. Unrelenting Danger. *Amnesty International*, Fall: 14–19.

Attwood, Bain, ed. 1996. *The Age of Mabo: History, Aborigines, and Australia*. Sydney: Allen & Unwin.

Bacon, Francis. 1909 [1625]. On Plantations. In *Essays, Civil and Moral: and The New Atlantis*. New York: P. F. Collier & Son.

Baker, Houston A., Jr, Manthia Diawara, and Ruth H. Lindeborg, eds. 1996. *Black British Cultural Studies: A Reader*. Chicago: University of Chicago Press.

Bales, Kevin. 2002. Because She Looks Like a Child. In Ehrenreich and Hochschild (2002).

Bancel, Nicolas, Pascal Blanchard, and Sandrine Lemaire. 2000. Human Zoos. Trans. Barry Smerin. *Le Monde Diplomatique* (English language edition), Aug., pp. 8–9.

Banchetti-Robino, Marina Paola, and Clevis Ronald Headley, eds. 2006. *Shifting the Geography of Reason: Gender, Science and Religion*. Cambridge: Cambridge Scholars Press.

Banner, Stuart. 2005. Why *Terra Nullius*? Anthropology and Property Law in Early Australia. *Law and History Review*, 23, no. 1: 95–132.

Barry, Brian. 2005. *Why Social Justice Matters*. Cambridge: Polity.

Barry, Kathleen. 1984. *Female Sexual Slavery*. New York: New York University Press.

Barthélémy, Françoise. 2004. Peru: The Scandal of Forced Sterilisation. Trans. Julie Stoker. *Le Monde Diplomatique* (English language edition), May, pp. 8–9.

Bartlett, Richard. 1993. *Mabo*: Another Triumph for the Common Law. *Sydney Law Review*, 15, no. 2: 178–86.

Bell, Shannon. 1994. *Reading, Writing, and Re-writing the Prostitute Body*. Bloomington and Indianapolis: Indiana University Press.

Benn, S. I., and G. F. Gaus, eds. 1983. *Public and Private in Social Life*. New York: St Martin's Press.

Bernasconi, Robert. 2001a. Who Invented the Concept of Race? Kant's Role in the Enlightenment Construction of Race. In Bernasconi (2001b).

Bernasconi, Robert, ed. 2001b. *Race*. Malden: Blackwell.

Bernasconi, Robert. 2002. Kant as an Unfamiliar Source of Racism. In Ward and Lott (2002).

Bernasconi, Robert, and Tommy L. Lott, eds. 2000. *The Idea of Race*. Indianapolis: Hackett.

Bhavnani, Kum-Kum. 2001a. Introduction. In Bhavnani (2001b).

Bhavnani, Kum-Kum, ed. 2001b. *Feminism and "Race"*. New York: Oxford University Press.

Blackstone, Sir William. 1899. *Commentaries on the Laws of England*, vol. 1. 4th edn. Chicago: Callaghan.

Blue, Gregory, Martin Bunton, and Ralph Croizier, eds. 2002. *Colonialism and the Modern World: Selected Studies*. Armonk: M. E. Sharpe.

Bogues, Anthony. 1998. Race and Revising Liberalism. *Small Axe: A Journal of Criticism*, no. 4: 175–82.

Bogues, Anthony. 2001. Review of *The Racial Contract*, by Charles W. Mills. *Constellations*, 8, no. 2: 267–72.

Bogues, Anthony. 2003. *Black Heretics, Black Prophets: Radical Political Intellectuals*. New York: Routledge.

Boose, Lynda E. 1994. "The Getting of a Lawful Race": Racial Discourse and the Unrepresentable Black Woman. In Hendricks and Parker (1994).

Borrows John. 1997. Wampum at Niagara: The Royal Proclamation, Canadian Legal History, and Self-Government. In Asch (1997).

Borrows John. 1999. Sovereignty's Alchemy: An Analysis of *Delgamuukw v. British Columbia*. *Osgoode Hall Law Journal*, 37: 537–96.

Borstelmann, Thomas. 2001. *The Cold War and the Color Line: American Race Relations in the Global Arena*. Cambridge: Harvard University Press.

Boucher, David, and Paul Kelly. 1994a. The Social Contract and Its Critics: An Overview. In Boucher and Kelly (1994b).

Boucher, David, and Paul Kelly, eds. 1994b. *The Social Contract from Hobbes to Rawls*. New York: Routledge.

Boucher, David, and Paul Kelly, eds. 2003. *Political Thinkers: From Socrates to the Present*. New York: Oxford University Press.

Boucher, Joanne. 2003. Male Power and Contract Theory: Hobbes and Locke in Carole Pateman's *The Sexual Contract*. *Canadian Journal of Political Science*, 36, no. 1: 23–38.

Bowe, John. 2003. A Shameful Harvest. *American Prospect* (July–Aug.): 38–9.

Boxill, Bernard R. 1992. *Blacks and Social Justice*. Rev. edn. (Orig. edn 1984.) Lanham: Rowman & Littlefield.

Boxill, Bernard R., ed. 2001. *Race and Racism*. New York: Oxford University Press.

Boxill, Bernard R. 2003. A Lockean Argument for Black Reparations. *Journal of Ethics*, Special Issue: Race, Racism, and Reparations, 7, no. 1: 63–91.

Brace, Laura. 2004. How Is It that All Women Are Born Slaves? Feminism and the Social Contract. Paper presented at a conference at the University of Huddersfield, 2004. Just Something for the Girls: The Impact of Feminism on Political Concepts and Debates.

Breines, Winnifred. 2006. *The Trouble between Us: An Uneasy History of White and Black Women in the Feminist Movement.* New York: Oxford University Press.

Brennan, Frank. 1998. *The Wik Debate: Its Impact on Aborigines, Pastoralists and Miners.* Sydney: University of New South Wales Press.

Brennan, Samantha, ed. 2003. *Feminist Moral Philosophy.* Calgary: University of Calgary Press.

Brennan, Teresa. 2003. *Globalization and Its Terrors: Daily Life in the West.* New York: Routledge.

Brennan, Teresa, and Carole Pateman. 1979. "Mere Auxiliaries to the Commonwealth": Women and the Origins of Liberalism. *Political Studies*, 27, no. 2: 183–200. Reprinted in *Feminist Interpretations of Locke*, ed. Nancy J. Hirschmann and Kirstie M. McClure, University Park: Pennsylvania State University Press, 2007.

Bronner, Stephen Eric. 2004. *Reclaiming the Enlightenment: Toward a Politics of Radical Engagement.* New York: Columbia University Press.

Brooke, Christopher. 2001. Rousseau's Political Philosophy: Stoic and Augustinian Origins. In Riley (2001b).

Brooks, Roy, L., ed. 1999. *When Sorry Isn't Enough: The Controversy over Apologies and Reparations for Human Injustice.* New York: New York University Press.

Broome, Richard. 1995. Victoria. In McGrath (1995).

Brown, Michael K., Martin Carnoy, Elliott Currie, Troy Duster, David B. Oppenheimer, Marjorie M. Shultz, and David Wellman. 2003. *Whitewashing Race: The Myth of a Color-Blind Society.* Berkeley and Los Angeles: University of California Press.

Brown, Wendy. 1995. *States of Injury: Power and Freedom in Late Modernity.* Princeton: Princeton University Press.

Burnham, Margaret A. 1992. The Supreme Court Appointment Process and the Politics of Race and Sex. In Morrison (1992).

Burton, Antoinette M. 1992. The White Woman's Burden: British Feminists and "The Indian Woman," 1865–1915. In Chaudhuri and Strobel (1992).

Cahn, Steven M., ed. 2002. *Classics of Political and Moral Philosophy.* New York: Oxford University Press.

Caine, Barbara, and Rosemary Pringle, eds. 1995. *Transitions: New Australian Feminisms*. New York: St Martin's Press.

Capistrano, Tricia. 2006. Emil's Big Chance Leaves Me Uneasy. *Newsweek*, June 19, p. 14.

Carby, Hazel V. 1987. *Reconstructing Womanhood: The Emergence of the Afro-American Woman Novelist*. New York: Oxford University Press.

Carby, Hazel V. 1996 [1982]. White Woman Listen! Black Feminism and the Boundaries of Sisterhood. In Baker, Jr, Diawara, and Lindeborg (1996).

Caton, Hiram. 1990. Gendering the Social Contract: Comment on Carole Pateman's *The Sexual Contract*. *Political Theory Newsletter*, 2: 64–8.

Chaudhuri, Nupur, and Margaret Strobel, eds. 1992. *Western Women and Imperialism: Complicity and Resistance*. Bloomington and Indianapolis: Indiana University Press.

Chesterman, John, and Brian Galligan. 1997. *Citizens without Rights: Aborigines and Australian Citizenship*. New York: Cambridge University Press.

Clark, Lorenne M. G., and Lynda Lange, eds. 1979. *The Sexism of Social and Political Theory: Women and Reproduction from Plato to Nietzsche*. Toronto: University of Toronto Press.

Clément, Carine. 2003. Russia: The Default Option. Trans. Barry Smerin. *Le Monde Diplomatique* (English language edition), Feb., pp. 10–11.

Clément, Carine, and Denis Paillard. 2005. Snapshots of Russia Now. Trans. Barbara Wilson. *Le Monde Diplomatique* (English language edition), Nov., pp. 6–7.

Coates, Ken. 1999. The Gentle Occupation: The Settlement of Canada and the Dispossession of the First Nations. In Havemann (1999).

Cohen, Philip N. 1999. Review of *The Racial Contract*, by Charles W. Mills. *Review of Radical Political Economics*, 31, no. 2: 102–5.

Cohen, Stanley. 2001. *States of Denial: Knowing about Atrocities and Suffering*. Cambridge: Polity.

Coleman, Jules. 1983. Moral Theories of Torts: Their Scope and Limits, Part II. *Law and Philosophy*, 2, no. 1: 5–36.

Colley, Linda. 2002. *Captives: Britain, Empire and the World, 1600–1850*. London: Jonathan Cape.

Combahee River Collective. 2000 [1977]. A Black Feminist Statement. In James and Sharpley-Whiting (2000).

Commager, Henry Steele, ed. 1968. *Documents of American History*. 8th edn. New York: Appleton-Century-Crofts.

Conley, Dalton. 1999. *Being Black, Living in the Red: Race, Wealth, and Social Policy in America*. Berkeley and Los Angeles: University of California Press.

Connor, Michael. 2003. Error Nullius. *The Book Bulletin*, Aug. 26, pp. 76–8.

Coole, Diana. 1990. Patriarchy and Contract: Reading Pateman. *Politics*, 10, no. 1: 25–9.

Coole, Diana. 1994. Women, Gender and Contract: Feminist Interpretations. In Boucher and Kelly (1994b).

Cooper, Anna Julia. 1998. *The Voice of Anna Julia Cooper: Including "A Voice from the South" and Other Important Essays, Papers, and Letters*, ed. Charles Lemert and Esme Blah. Lanham: Rowman & Littlefield.

Corlett, J. Angelo. 2003. *Race, Racism, and Reparations*. Ithaca: Cornell University Press.

Cornell, Drucilla. 1992. The Philosophy of the Limit: Systems Theory and Feminist Legal Reform. In Cornell, Rosenfeld, and Carlson (1992).

Cornell, Drucilla, Michel Rosenfeld, and David Gray Carlson, eds. 1992. *Deconstruction and the Possibility of Justice*. New York: Routledge.

Cott, Nancy F. 2000. *Public Vows: A History of Marriage and the Nation*. Cambridge: Harvard University Press.

Crenshaw, Kimberlé. 1992. Whose Story Is It, Anyway? Feminist and Antiracist Appropriations of Anita Hill. In Morrison (1992).

Crenshaw, Kimberlé. 2000 [1989]. Demarginalizing the Intersection of Race and Sex: A Black Feminist Critique of Antidiscrimination Doctrine, Feminist Theory, and Antiracist Politics. In James and Sharpley-Whiting (2000).

Cudd, Ann. 2003. Contractarianism. In *The Stanford Encyclopedia of Philosophy*, Spring 2003 edn, ed. Edward N. Zalta. At http://plato. Stanford.edu/archives/spr 2003/entries/contractarianism/.

Cugoano, Quobna. 1999. *Thoughts and Sentiments on the Evil of Slavery* (1787 version), ed. Vincent Carretta. London: Penguin.

Darwall, Stephen, ed. 2003. *Contractarianism/Contractualism*. Malden: Blackwell.

Davidson, Julia O'Connell. 2002. The Rights and Wrongs of Prostitution. *Hypatia*, 17, no. 2: 84–98.

Davis, Angela. 1981. *Women, Race, and Class*. New York: Random House.

Davis, Angela. 2003. Racism, Birth Control and Reproductive Rights. In Lewis and Mills (2003).

Day, David. 2001. *Claiming a Continent: A New History of Australia*. Rev. edn. (Orig. edn 1996.) Sydney: HarperCollins.

Dean, Mitchell. 1992. Pateman's Dilemma: Women and Citizenship. *Theory and Society*, 21, no. 1: 121–30.

Dench, Geoff, ed. 1997. *Rewriting the Sexual Contract*. London: Institute of Community Studies.

De Tocqueville, Alexis. 2000 [1835–40]. *Democracy in America*. Chicago: University of Chicago Press.

Dickenson, Donna. 1997. *Property, Women, and Politics: Subjects or Objects?* New Brunswick: Rutgers University Press.

Di Stefano, Christine. 1991. *Configurations of Masculinity: A Feminist Perspective on Modern Political Theory*. Ithaca: Cornell University Press.

Doane, Ashley W., and Eduardo Bonilla-Silva, eds. 2003. *White Out: The Continuing Significance of Racism*. New York: Routledge.

Dubler, Ariela. 2003. In the Shadow of Marriage: Single Women and the Legal Construction of the Family and the State. *Yale Law Journal*, 112, no. 7: 1641–715.

DuBois, Ellen Carol. 1978. *Feminism and Suffrage: The Emergence of an Independent Women's Movement in America, 1848–1869*. Ithaca: Cornell University Press.

Du Bois, W. E. B. 1995 [1920]. The Souls of White Folk. In D. Lewis (1995).

Dudley, Edward, and Maximillian E. Novak, eds. 1972. *The Wild Man Within: An Image in Western Thought from the Renaissance to Romanticism*. Pittsburgh: University of Pittsburgh Press.

DWP (Department for Work and Pensions, UK). 2004. *Households Below Average Income 1994/95–2003/04*. London: DWP. At www.dwp.gov.uk/asd/hbai/hbai2004/contents.asp.

Dyer, Richard. 1997. *White*. New York: Routledge.

Edgeworth, Maria. 2003 [1804]. The Grateful Negro. In *The Novels and Selected Works of Maria Edgeworth*, vol. 12, ed. Elizabeth Eger, Clíona ÓGallchoir, and Marilyn Butler. London: Pickering & Chatto.

Edwards, Laura. 1996. "The Marriage Covenant Is at the Foundation of All Our Rights": The Politics of Slave Marriages in North Carolina after Emancipation. *Law and History Review*, 14, no. 1: 81–124.

Edwards, Paul, ed. 1967. *The Encyclopedia of Philosophy*. 8 vols. New York: Macmillan and Free Press.

Ehrenreich, Barbara, and Arlie Russell Hochschild, eds. 2002. *Global Woman: Nannies, Maids, and Sex Workers in the New Economy*. New York: Metropolitan Books.

Eisenberg, Avigail, and Jeff Spinner-Halev, eds. 2004. *Minorities within Minorities: Equality, Rights and Diversity*. New York: Cambridge University Press.

Ellerman, David. 2005. *Translatio* versus *Concessio*: Retrieving the Debate about Contracts of Alienation with an Application to Today's Employment Contract. *Politics and Society*, 33, no. 3: 440–80.

Ertman, Martha. 2001. Marriage as a Trade: Bridging the Private/Private Distinction. *Harvard Civil Rights-Civil Liberties Review*, 36,

Eze, Emmanuel Chukwudi. 1997a [1995]. The Color of Reason: The Idea of "Race" in Kant's Anthropology. In Eze (1997b).

Eze, Emmanuel Chukwudi, ed. 1997b. *Postcolonial African Philosophy: A Critical Reader.* Cambridge: Blackwell.

Eze, Emmanuel Chukwudi, ed. 1997c. *Race and the Enlightenment: A Reader*. Cambridge: Blackwell.

Ferguson, Moira. 1992. *Subject to Others: British Women Writers and Colonial Slavery, 1670–1834.* New York: Routledge.

Ferguson, Stephen C., II. 2004. Racial Contract Theory: A Critical Introduction. Ph.D. diss., University of Kansas.

Finan, Khadija. 2006. Western Sahara Impasse. *Le Monde Diplomatique* (English language edition), Jan., p. 14.

Forde, Steven. 1998. Hugo Grotius on Ethics and War. *American Political Science Review*, 92, no. 3: 639–48.

Forsyth, Murray. 1994. Hobbes's Contractarianism: A Comparative Analysis. In Boucher and Kelly (1994b).

Frankenberg, Ruth. 1993. *White Women, Race Matters: The Social Construction of Whiteness*. Minneapolis: University of Minnesota Press.

Fraser, Nancy. 1997a. Beyond the Master/Subject Model: On Carole Pateman's *The Sexual Contract*. In Fraser (1997b).

Fraser, Nancy. 1997b. *Justice Interruptus: Critical Reflections on the "Postsocialist" Condition.* New York: Routledge.

Fredrickson, George. 1981. *White Supremacy: A Comparative Study in American and South African History.* New York: Oxford University Press.

Freeman, Samuel, ed. 2003. *The Cambridge Companion to Rawls*. New York: Cambridge University Press.

French, Peter A., Theodore E. Uehling, Jr, and Howard K. Wettstein, eds. 1990. *Midwest Studies in Philosophy: The Philosophy of the Human Sciences.* Notre Dame: University of Notre Dame Press.

Frost, Alan. 1981. New South Wales as Terra Nullius: The British Denial of Aboriginal Land Rights. *Historical Studies*, 19, no. 77: 513–23.

Frye, Marilyn. 1983. *The Politics of Reality: Essays in Feminist Theory*. Freedom: Crossing Press.

Füredi, Frank. 1998. *The Silent War: Imperialism and the Changing Perception of Race*. New Brunswick: Rutgers University Press.

Galton, Sir Francis. 1978 [1869]. *Hereditary Genius: An Inquiry into Its Laws and Consequences*. New York: St Martin's Press.

Galton, Sir Francis. 2000 [1909]. Eugenics: Its Definition, Scope and Aims. In Bernasconi and Lott (2000).

Garcia, Jorge. 2001. The Racial Contract Hypothesis. *Philosophia Africana*, 4, no. 1: 27–42.

Gatens, Moira. 1996. Sex, Contract and Genealogy. *Journal of Political Philosophy*, 4, no. 1: 29–44.

Gates, Henry Louis, Jr, ed. 1986. *"Race," Writing, and Difference*. Chicago: University of Chicago Press.

Gauthier, David P. 1986. *Morals by Agreement*. New York: Clarendon Press.

Gauthier, David P. 1997 [1977]. The Social Contract as Ideology. In Goodin and Pettit (1997).

Gentili, Alberico. 1933 [1612]. *De Iure Belli Libri Tres*, vol. 2, trans. John C. Rolfe. Oxford: Clarendon Press.

Geras, Norman. 1998. *The Contract of Mutual Indifference: Political Philosophy after the Holocaust*. New York: Verso.

Giddings, Paula. 1984. *When and Where I Enter: The Impact of Black Women on Race and Sex in America*. New York: Bantam Books.

Gilens, Martin. 1999. *Why Americans Hate Welfare: Race, Media, and the Politics of Antipoverty Policy*. Chicago: University of Chicago Press.

Gilliam, Angela. 1991. Women's Equality and National Liberation. In Mohanty, Russo, and Torres (1991).

Gilman, Charlotte Perkins. 1908. A Suggestion on the Negro Problem. *American Journal of Sociology*, 14, no. 1: 78–85.

Gilman, Charlotte Perkins. 1966 [1898]. *Women and Economics: A Study of the Economic Relation between Men and Women as a Factor in Social Evolution*, ed. Carl N. Degler. New York: Harper & Row.

Gilman, Sander L. 1986. Black Bodies, White Bodies: Toward an Iconography of Female Sexuality in Late Nineteenth-Century Art, Medicine, and Literature. In Gates, Jr (1986).

Gilroy, Paul. 1993. *The Black Atlantic: Modernity and Double Consciousness*. Cambridge: Harvard University Press.

Gilroy, Paul. 2000. *Against Race: Imagining Political Culture beyond the Color Line*. Cambridge: Harvard University Press.

Glenn, Evelyn Nakano. 2002. *Unequal Freedom: How Race and Gender Shaped American Citizenship and Labor*. Cambridge: Harvard University Press.

Goldberg, David Theo. 1993. *Racist Culture: Philosophy and the Politics of Meaning*. Cambridge: Blackwell.

Goldberg, David Theo. 2002. *The Racial State.* Malden: Blackwell.

Goodin, Robert E., and Philip Pettit, eds. 1993. *A Companion to Contemporary Political Philosophy.* Oxford: Blackwell Reference.

Goodin, Robert E., and Philip Pettit, eds. 1997. *Contemporary Political Philosophy: An Anthology.* Malden: Blackwell.

Gordon, David. 1998. Single-Issue Scholarship. *Mises Review* (Summer 1998): 1–3.

Gordon, Lewis R. 1998. Contracting White Normativity. *Small Axe: A Journal of Criticism*, no. 4: 166–74.

Gordon, Lewis R. 2006. *Disciplinary Decadence: Living Thought in Trying Times.* Boulder: Paradigm.

Gordon, Linda. 1990. *Woman's Body, Woman's Right: Birth Control in America.* Rev. edn. (Orig. edn 1976.) New York: Penguin Books.

Gough, J. W. 1978. *The Social Contract: A Critical Study of its Development.* 2nd edn. (Orig. edn 1936.) Westport: Greenwood Press.

Grinde, Donald A., Jr, and Bruce E. Johansen. 1991. *Exemplar of Liberty: Native America and the Evolution of Democracy.* Los Angeles: American Indian Studies Center, University of California, Los Angeles.

Grotius, Hugo. 1925 [1646 edn]. *De Jure Belli Ac Pacis Libri Tres*, vol. 2, trans. F. W. Kelsey. Oxford: Clarendon Press.

Grotius, Hugo. 1983. The Freedom of the Seas or the Right which Belongs to the Dutch to take part in the East Indian Trade. In *The Grotius Reader*, ed. L. E. Van Holk and D. G. Roeflofsen. The Hague: T. M. C. Asser Instituut.

Guinier, Lani. 1994. *The Tyranny of the Majority: Fundamental Fairness in Representative Democracy.* New York: The Free Press.

Guy-Sheftall, Beverly, ed. 1995. *Words of Fire: An Anthology of African-American Feminist Thought.* New York: New Press.

Haggis, Jane. 2003. White Women and Colonialism: Towards a Non-Recuperative History. In Lewis and Mills (2003).

Hall, Barbara. 2005. Race in Hobbes. In Valls (2005).

Hampton, Jean. 1990. The Contractarian Explanation of the State. In French, Uehling, Jr, and Wettstein (1990).

Hampton, Jean. 1993. Contract and Consent. In Goodin and Pettit (1993).

Hampton, Jean. 1997. *Political Philosophy.* Boulder: Westview Press.

Hampton, Jean. 2001. Feminist Contractarianism. In Antony and Witt (2001).

Haney López, Ian F. 1996. *White by Law: The Legal Construction of Race.* New York: New York University Press.

Haney López, Ian F. 2005. Race on the 2010 Census: Hispanics and the Shrinking White Majority. *Daedalus*, 134, no. 1: 42–52.

Harris, Angela P. 2000 [1990]. Race and Essentialism in Feminist Legal Theory. In Montmarquet and Hardy (2000).

Harris, Cheryl I. 1993. Whiteness as Property. *Harvard Law Review*, 106, no. 8: 1709–91.

Haskell, Thomas L. 1985. Capitalism and the Origins of the Humanitarian Sensibility, Part 2. *American Historical Review*, 90, no. 3: 547–66.

Haslanger, Sally. 2000. Comments on Charles Mills' "Race and the Social Contract Tradition." Comments presented at the annual meeting of the Central Division, American Philosophical Association, 2000.

Havemann, Paul, ed. 1999. *Indigenous Peoples' Rights in Australia, Canada and New Zealand*. New York: Oxford University Press.

Hegarty, Paul. 1999. Doubling Legitimacy: Reading Rousseau's *Contrat Social* after Pateman's *Sexual Contract*. *French Studies*, 53, no. 3: 292–306.

Hegel, Georg Wilhelm Friedrich. 1956 [1830–1]. *The Philosophy of History*, trans. J. Sibree. New York: Dover.

Held, David, Anthony McGrew, David Goldblatt, and Jonathan Perraton. 1999. *Global Transformations: Politics, Economics and Culture*. Cambridge: Polity.

Hendricks, Margo, and Patricia Parker, eds. 1994. *Women, "Race," and Writing in the Early Modern Period*. New York: Routledge.

Heyrick, Elizabeth. 1824. *Immediate, not Gradual Abolition: or, An Inquiry into the Shortest, Safest, and Most Effectual Means of Getting Rid of West Indian Slavery*. 3rd edn. London: Hatchard.

Hill, Anita Faye. 1995. Marriage and Patronage in the Empowerment and Disempowerment of African American Women. In Hill and Jordan (1995).

Hill, Anita Faye, and Emma Coleman Jordan, eds. 1995. *Race, Gender, and Power in America: The Legacy of the Hill-Thomas Hearings*. New York: Oxford University Press.

Hill, Thomas E., Jr, and Bernard Boxill. 2001. Kant and Race. In Boxill (2001).

Hirsch, James S. 2002. *Riot and Remembrance: The Tulsa Race War and Its Legacy*. New York: Houghton Mifflin.

Hirschmann, Nancy J. 1990. Review of *The Sexual Contract*, by Carole Pateman. *Political Theory*, 18, no. 1: 170–4.

Hirshman, Linda R., and Jane E. Larson. 1998. *Hard Bargains: The Politics of Sex*. New York: Oxford University Press.

Hobbes, Thomas. 1981 [1651]. *Leviathan*. New York: Penguin.

Hobbes, Thomas. 1996 [1651]. *Leviathan*. Rev. student edn, ed. Richard Tuck. (Orig. edn 1991.) New York: Cambridge University Press.

Hochschild, Jennifer L. 2005. Looking Ahead: Racial Trends in the United States. *Dædalus*, 134, no. 1: 70–81.

Hocking, Barbara. 1993. Aboriginal Law Does Now Run in Australia. *Sydney Law Review*, 15, no. 2: 187–205.

Hoetink, Harmannus. 1967. *Caribbean Race Relations: A Study of Two Variants*, trans. Eva M. Hooykaas. New York: Oxford University Press.

Holder, Cindy. 2004. Self-Determination as a Basic Human Right: The Draft UN Declaration on the Rights of Indigenous Peoples. In Eisenberg and Spinner-Halev (2004).

Hollinger, David A. 2005. The One Drop Rule and the One Hate Rule. *Dædalus*, 134, no. 1 (Winter): 18–28.

Holmes, Rachel. 2007. *African Queen: The Real Life of the Hottentot Venus*. New York: Random House.

Honderich, Ted, ed. 1995. *The Oxford Companion to Philosophy*. New York: Oxford University Press.

hooks, bell. 2000 [1984]. Black Women: Shaping Feminist Theory. In James and Sharpley-Whiting (2000).

Hope, Donna P. 2006. *Inna di Dancehall: Popular Culture and the Politics of Identity in Jamaica*. Mona, Kingston: University of the West Indies Press.

Horne, Thomas A. 1990. *Property Rights and Poverty: Political Argument in Britain, 1605–1834*. Chapel Hill: University of North Carolina Press.

Horsman, Reginald. 1986 [1981]. *Race and Manifest Destiny: Origins of American Racial Anglo-Saxonism*. Cambridge: Harvard University Press.

Hughes, Cheryl, ed. 2003. *Social Philosophy Today: Truth and Objectivity in Social Ethics*, vol. 18. Charlottesville: Philosophy Documentation Center.

Hull, Gloria T., Patricia Bell Scott, and Barbara Smith, eds. 1982. *All the Women Are White, All the Blacks Are Men, but Some of Us Are Brave: Black Women's Studies*. New York: Feminist Press.

Hulliung, Mark. 2001. Rousseau, Voltaire, and the Revenge of Pascal. In Riley (2001b).

Hulme, Peter. 1990. The Spontaneous Hand of Nature: Savagery, Colonialism, and the Enlightenment. In Hulme and Jordanova (1990).

Hulme, Peter, and Ludmilla Jordanova, eds. 1990. *The Enlightenment and Its Shadows*. New York: Routledge.

Hund, Wulf D. 2006. *Negative Vergesellschaftung: Dimensionen der Rassismusanalyse*. Münster: Verlag Westfälisches Dampfboot.

Hunter, Rosemary. 1996. Aboriginal Histories, Australian Histories, and the Law. In Attwood (1996).

Hutton, Clinton. 1998. Opening up the Intellectual Closet of Modern Western Political Philosophy. *Small Axe: A Journal of Criticism*, no. 4: 183–90.

Ishiguru, Kazuo. 2005. *Never Let Me Go*. New York: Alfred A. Knopf.

Ivison, Duncan, Paul Patton, and Will Sanders, eds. 2000. *Political Theory and the Rights of Indigenous Peoples*. New York: Cambridge University Press.

Jacobs, Harriet. 1969 [1861]. *Incidents in the Life of a Slave Girl: Written by Herself*, ed. L. Maria Child. Reprint. Miami: Mnemosyne.

Jacobson, Matthew Frye. 1998. *Whiteness of a Different Color: European Immigrants and the Alchemy of Race*. Cambridge: Harvard University Press.

James, Joy, and T. Denean Sharpley-Whiting, eds. 2000. *The Black Feminist Reader*. Malden: Blackwell.

Jaquette, Jane S. 1998. Contract and Coercion: Power and Gender in *Leviathan*. In H. Smith (1998).

Jennings, Francis. 1971. Virgin Land and Savage People. *American Quarterly*, 23, no. 4: 519–41.

Joseph, Gloria, and Jill Lewis. 1981. *Common Differences: Conflicts in Black and White Feminist Perspectives*. New York: Anchor Press/ Doubleday.

Kant, Immanuel. 1965 [1764]. *Observations on the Feeling of the Beautiful and Sublime*, trans. John T. Goldthwait. Berkeley and Los Angeles: University of California Press.

Kant, Immanuel. 1978 [1798]. *Anthropology from a Pragmatic Point of View*, trans. Victor Lyle Dowdell. Carbondale: Southern Illinois University Press.

Kant, Immanuel. 1991a [1786]. Conjectures on the Beginning of Human History. In Kant (1991b).

Kant, Immanuel. 1991b. *Political Writings*. 2nd edn, ed. Hans Reiss, trans. H. B. Nisbet. (Orig. edn 1970.) New York: Cambridge University Press.

Kant, Immanuel. 1997 [17–]. Physical Geography (extract). Trans. Katherine M. Faull and Emmanuel C. Eze. In Eze (1997c).

Kant, Immanuel. 1999 [1798]. *Metaphysical Elements of Justice*, part I of *The Metaphysics of Morals*. 2nd edn, trans. John Ladd (orig. edn 1965). Indianapolis: Hackett.

Kant, Immanuel. 2000 [1777]. Of the Different Human Races. Trans. Jon Mark Mikkelsen. In Bernasconi and Lott (2000).

Kant, Immanuel. 2001 [1788]. On the Use of Teleological Principles in Philosophy. Trans. Jon Mark Mikkelsen. In Bernasconi (2001b).

Katznelson, Ira. 2005. *When Affirmative Action Was White: An Untold History of Racial Inequality in Twentieth-Century America*. New York: W. W. Norton.

Keene, Edward. 2002. *Beyond the Anarchical Society: Grotius, Colonialism and Order in World Politics.* New York: Cambridge University Press.

Kerber, Linda K. 1998. *No Constitutional Right to be Ladies: Women and the Obligations of Citizenship.* New York: Hill & Wang.

Kercher, Bruce. 2002. Native Title in the Shadows: The Origins of the Myth of *Terra Nullius* in Early New South Wales Courts. In Blue, Bunton, and Croizier (2002).

Kinder, Donald R., and Lynn M. Sanders. 1996. *Divided by Color: Racial Politics and Democratic Ideals.* Chicago: University of Chicago Press.

King, Deborah K. 1995 [1988]. Multiple Jeopardy, Multiple Consciousness: The Context of a Black Feminist Ideology. In Guy-Sheftall (1995).

King, Desmond. 2005. *The Liberty of Strangers: Making the American Nation.* New York: Oxford University Press.

King, Reyahn, Sukhdev Sandhu, James Walvin, and Jane Girdham. 1997. *Ignatius Sancho: An African Man of Letters.* London: National Portrait Gallery Publications.

King, Robert. 1986. Terra Australius: Terra Nullius aut Terra Aboriginum? *Journal of the Royal Australian Historical Society*, 72: 75–91.

Klausen, Susanne. 2002. The Imperial Mother of Birth Control: Marie Stopes and the South African Birth-Control Movement, 1930–1950. In Blue, Bunton, and Croizier (2002).

Korman, Sharon. 1996. *The Right of Conquest: The Acquisition of Territory by Force in International Law and Practice.* New York: Clarendon Press.

Krysan, Maria, and Amanda E. Lewis, eds. 2004. *The Changing Terrain of Race and Ethnicity.* New York: Russell Sage Foundation.

Kulchyski, Peter, ed. 1994. *Unjust Relations: Aboriginal Rights in Canadian Courts.* New York: Oxford University Press.

Kymlicka, Will. 1990. Review of *The Sexual Contract*, by Carole Pateman. *Canadian Philosophical Reviews*, 10, no. 9: 461–4.

Kymlicka, Will. 1991. The Social Contract Tradition. In Singer (1991).

Kymlicka, Will. 1995. *Multicultural Citizenship: A Liberal Theory of Minority Rights.* New York: Oxford University Press.

Ladd, John. 1999. Translator's Introduction to Kant's *Metaphysical Elements of Justice.* In Kant (1999).

Laden, Anthony. 2003. Radical Liberals, Reasonable Feminists: Reason, Power and Objectivity in MacKinnon and Rawls. *Journal of Political Philosophy*, 11, no. 2: 133–52.

Lange, Lynda, ed. 2002. *Feminist Interpretations of Jean-Jacques Rousseau.* University Park: Pennsylvania State University Press.

Laqueur, Thomas Walter. 1990. *Making Sex: Body and Gender from the Greeks to Freud.* Cambridge: Harvard University Press.

Laslett, Peter. 1967. Social Contract. In P. Edwards (1967), vol. 7.

Lenin, Vladimir I. 1996 [1916]. *Imperialism: The Highest Stage of Capitalism.* Chicago: Pluto Press.

Lessnoff, Michael. 1986. *Social Contract.* Atlantic Highlands: Humanities Press.

Levy, Jacob T. 2000. *The Multiculturalism of Fear.* New York: Oxford University Press.

Lewis, David Levering, ed. 1995. *W. E. B. Du Bois: A Reader.* New York: Henry Holt.

Lewis, Reina, and Sara Mills, eds. 2003. *Feminist Postcolonial Theory: A Reader.* New York: Routledge.

Lipsitz, George. 1998. *The Possessive Investment in Whiteness: How White People Profit from Identity Politics.* Philadelphia: Temple University Press.

Litwack, Leon F. 1998. *Trouble in Mind: Black Southerners in the Age of Jim Crow.* New York: Alfred Knopf.

Locke, John. 1988 [1690]. *Two Treatises of Government.* Student edn, ed. Peter Laslett. (Orig. edn 1960.) New York: Cambridge University Press.

Lorde, Audre. 2002 [1979]. The Master's Tools Will Never Dismantle the Master's House. In Moraga and Anzaldúa (2002).

Lott, Tommy L. 2002. Patriarchy and Slavery in Hobbes's Political Philosophy. In Ward and Lott (2002).

Loury, Glenn C. 2002. *The Anatomy of Racial Inequality.* Cambridge: Harvard University Press.

Lumb, R. D. 1993. The *Mabo* Case: Public Law Aspects. In Stephenson and Ratnapala (1993).

MacKinnon, Catharine A. 1987. *Feminism Unmodified: Discourses on Life and Law.* Cambridge: Harvard University Press.

MacKinnon, Catharine A. 1989. *Toward a Feminist Theory of the State.* Cambridge: Harvard University Press.

MacKinnon, Catharine A. 2005. Genocide's Sexuality. In M. Williams and Macedo (2005).

Macpherson, C. B. 1962. *The Political Theory of Possessive Individualism.* Oxford: Clarendon Press.

Macpherson, C. B. 1968. Introduction. In Thomas Hobbes, *Leviathan.* New York: Penguin.

Markus, Andrew. 1994. *Australian Race Relations, 1788–1993.* St Leonards, New South Wales: Allen & Unwin.

Markus, Andrew. 1996. Between Mabo and a Hard Place: Race and the Contradictions of Conservatism. In Attwood (1996).

Marr, David. 1999. *The High Price of Heaven*. Sydney: Allen & Unwin.

Marshall, John. 1987. *The Writings of John Marshall on the Constitution*. Littleton: Fred B. Rothman.

Martin, Jane Roland. 1994. Methodological Essentialism, False Difference, and Other Dangerous Traps. *Signs*, 19, no. 3: 630–57.

Marx, Anthony W. 1998. *Making Race and Nation: A Comparison of the United States, South Africa, and Brazil*. New York: Cambridge University Press.

Massey, Douglas S., and Nancy A. Denton. 1993. *American Apartheid: Segregation and the Making of the Underclass*. Cambridge: Harvard University Press.

Maynard, Mary. 2001 [1994]. "Race," Gender and the Concept of "Difference" in Feminist Thought. In Bhavnani (2001b).

McCarthy, Thomas. 1999. Review of *The Racial Contract*, by Charles W. Mills. *Ethics*, 109, no. 2: 451–4.

McCarthy, Thomas. 2002. *Vergangenheitsbewältigung* in the USA: On the Politics of the Memory of Slavery, Part I. *Political Theory*, 30, no. 5: 623–48.

McCarthy, Thomas. 2004. Coming to Terms with Our Past: On the Morality and Politics of Reparations for Slavery, Part II. *Political Theory*, 32, no. 6: 750–72.

McClendon, John H., III. 2002. Black and White contra Left and Right? The Dialectics of Ideological Critique in African American Studies. *APA Newsletter on Philosophy and the Black Experience*, 02, no. 1: 47–56.

McClintock, Anne. 1995. *Imperial Leather: Race, Gender and Sexuality in the Colonial Context*. New York: Routledge.

McEachern, Allan. 1991. *Reasons for Judgment of the Honorable Chief Justice (Delgamuukw v. British Columbia)*. Vancouver: Smithers Registry No. 0843.

McGary, Howard. 1999. *Race and Social Justice*. Malden: Blackwell.

McGary, Howard, ed. (forthcoming). *Reparations for African-Americans: Arguments For and Against*. Lanham: Rowman & Littlefield.

McGrath, Ann, ed. 1995. *Contested Ground: Australian Aborigines under the British Crown*. Sydney: Allen & Unwin.

McHugh, P. G. 2004. *Aboriginal Societies and the Common Law: A History of Sovereignty, Status, and Self-Determination*. New York: Oxford University Press.

McNeil, Kent. 1997. The Meaning of Aboriginal Title. In Asch (1997).

Mehta, Uday Singh. 1999. *Liberalism and Empire: A Study in Nineteenth-Century British Liberal Thought*. Chicago: University of Chicago Press.

Meir, Golda. 1969. Golda Meir: 'Who Can Blame Israel?' *Sunday Times*, June 15.

Midgley, Clare. 1992. *Women against Slavery: The British Campaigns, 1780–1870.* New York: Routledge.

Mill, John Stuart. 1989 [1869]. *The Subjection of Women.* In *On Liberty; with the Subjection of Women; and Chapters on Socialism*, ed. Stefan Collini. New York: Cambridge University Press.

Millett, Kate. 1969. *Sexual Politics.* New York: Ballantine.

Milliken, Robert. 1986. *No Conceivable Injury: The Story of Britain and Australia's Atomic Cover-Up.* New York: Penguin Books.

Mills, Charles W. 1997. *The Racial Contract.* Ithaca: Cornell University Press.

Mills, Charles W. 1998a. *Blackness Visible: Essays on Philosophy and Race.* Ithaca: Cornell University Press.

Mills, Charles W. 1998b. Non-Cartesian *Sum*s: Philosophy and the African-American Experience. In Mills (1998a).

Mills, Charles W. 1998c. Reply to Critics. *Small Axe: A Journal of Criticism*, no. 4: 191–201.

Mills, Charles W. 1998d. Revisionist Ontologies: Theorizing White Supremacy. In Mills (1998a).

Mills, Charles W. 2000. Race and the Social Contract Tradition. *Social Identities: Journal for the Study of Race, Nation and Culture*, 6, no. 4: 441–62.

Mills, Charles W. 2003a. Defending the Radical Enlightenment. In Hughes (2003).

Mills, Charles W. 2003b. *From Class to Race: Essays in White Marxism and Black Radicalism.* Lanham: Rowman & Littlefield.

Mills, Charles W. 2003c. The "Racial Contract" as Methodology. In Mills (2003b).

Mills, Charles W. 2003d. Reply to My Critics. In Stokes and Meléndez (2003).

Mills, Charles W. 2003e. White Supremacy and Racial Justice. In Mills (2003b).

Mills, Charles W. 2003f. White Supremacy as Socio-Political System. In Mills (2003b).

Mills, Charles W. 2004. Racial Exploitation and the Wages of Whiteness. In Krysan and Lewis (2004).

Mills, Charles W. 2005a. "Ideal Theory" as Ideology. *Hypatia: A Journal of Feminist Philosophy*, 20, no. 3: 165–84.

Mills, Charles W. 2005b. Kant's *Untermenschen*. In Valls (2005).

Mills, Charles W. 2006a. Comments on Anthony Bogues' *Black Heretics, Black Prophets*. Paper presented on an Author Meets Critics panel at the American Philosophical Association Central Division annual meeting, 2006.

Mills, Charles W. 2006b. Modernity, Persons, and Subpersons. In J. Young and Braziel (2006).

Mills, Charles W. 2006c. Rawls on Race. In Banchetti-Robino and Headley (2006).

Mills, Charles W. 2007. White Ignorance. In Sullivan and Tuana (2007).

Miriam, Kathy. 2005. Getting Pateman "Right": How to Read and Not Read *The Sexual Contract*. *Philosophy Today*, 49, no. 3: 274–86.

Mishel, Lawrence R., Jared Bernstein, and Sylvia Allegretto. 2006. *The State of Working America 2006/2007*. Ithaca: ILR Press/Cornell University Press.

Modood, Tariq. 1998. Anti-Essentialism, Multiculturalism and the "Recognition" of Religious Groups. *Journal of Political Philosophy*, 6, no. 4: 378–99.

Moens, Gabriel. 1993. Mabo and Political Policy-Making by the High Court. In Stephenson and Ratnapala (1993).

Mohanty, Chandra Talpade. 1991. Cartographies of Struggle: Third World Women and the Politics of Feminism. In Mohanty, Russo, and Torres (1991).

Mohanty, Chandra Talpade, Ann Russo, and Lourdes Torres, eds. 1991. *Third World Women and the Politics of Feminism*. Bloomington and Indianapolis: Indiana University Press.

Monbiot, George. 2005. Africa's New Best Friends. *Guardian Weekly*, July 15–21, p. 4.

Montmarquet, James A., and William H. Hardy, eds. 2000. *Reflections: An Anthology of African American Philosophy*. Belmont: Wadsworth/Thomson Learning.

Moraga, Cherríe L., and Gloria E. Anzaldúa, eds. 2002. *This Bridge Called My Back: Writings by Radical Women of Color*. Expanded and rev. 3rd edn. (Orig. edn 1981.) Berkeley: Third Woman Press.

More, Thomas. 1965 [1516]. *Utopia*. Harmondsworth: Penguin Classics.

Morris, Christopher. 1999a. Introduction. In Morris (1999b).

Morris, Christopher, ed. 1999b. *The Social Contract Theorists: Critical Essays on Hobbes, Locke, and Rousseau*. Lanham: Rowman & Littlefield.

Morrison, Toni, ed. 1992. *Race-ing Justice, En-Gendering Power: Essays on Anita Hill, Clarence Thomas, and the Construction of Social Reality*. New York: Pantheon Books.

Morrison, Toni. 2000a [1970]. *The Bluest Eye*. New York: Penguin USA.

Morrison, Toni. 2000b [1989]. Unspeakable Things Unspoken: The Afro-American Presence in American Literature. In James and Sharpley-Whiting (2000).

Mouffe, Chantal. 1993. *The Return of the Political*. New York: Verso.

Mulgan, Richard. 1998. Citizenship and Legitimacy in a Post-Colonial Australia. In Peterson and Sanders (1998).

Murphy, Michael. 2001. Culture and the Courts: A New Direction in Canadian Jurisprudence on Aboriginal Rights? *Canadian Journal of Political Science*, 24, no. 1: 109–29.

Murray, Pauli. 1995 [1970]. The Liberation of Black Women. In Guy-Sheftall (1995).

Nagel, Mechthild E. 2003. Reforming the Contract? In Stokes and Meléndez (2003).

Nagel, Thomas. 2003. Rawls and Liberalism. In Freeman (2003).

Narayan, Uma. 2003. What's a Brown Girl like You Doing in the Ivory Tower? Or, How I Became a Feminist Philosopher. In Alcoff (2003).

Nash, Kate. 1998. *Universal Difference: Feminism and the Liberal Undecideability of "Women"*. New York: St Martin's Press.

Nelson, Jill. 1997. *Straight, No Chaser: How I Became a Grown-up Black Woman*. New York: G. P. Putnam's Sons.

Newman, Louise Michele. 1999. *White Women's Rights: The Racial Origins of Feminism in the United States*. New York: Oxford University Press.

Nichols, Robert Lee. 2005. Realizing the Social Contract: The Case of Colonialism and Indigenous Peoples. *Contemporary Political Theory*, 4, no. 1: 42–62

Nozick, Robert. 1974. *Anarchy, State, and Utopia*. New York: Basic Books.

Nussbaum, Martha. 2003. Rawls and Feminism. In Freeman (2003).

Nussbaum, Martha C., and Amartya Sen, eds. 1993. *The Quality of Life*. New York: Clarendon Press.

Okin, Susan Moller. 1989. *Justice, Gender, and the Family*. New York: Basic Books.

Okin, Susan Moller. 1990. Feminism, the Individual, and Contract Theory. *Ethics*, 100, no. 3: 658–69.

Okin, Susan Moller. 1992. *Women in Western Political Thought*, with a new afterword. (Orig. edn 1979.) Princeton: Princeton University Press.

Oliver, Melvin L., and Thomas M. Shapiro. 1995. *Black Wealth/ White Wealth: A New Perspective on Racial Inequality*. New York: Routledge.

Omolade, Barbara. 1995 [1983]. Hearts of Darkness. In Guy-Sheftall (1995).

O'Neill, Onora. 1993. Justice, Gender, and International Boundaries. In Nussbaum and Sen (1993).

Osborne, Peter, and Stella Sandford, eds. 2002. *Philosophies of Race and Ethnicity*. New York: Continuum.

Outlaw, Lucius T., Jr. 1996. *On Race and Philosophy*. New York: Routledge.

Overall, Christine. 1992. What's Wrong with Prostitution? Evaluating Sex Work. *Signs*, 17, no. 4: 705–24.

Pagden, Anthony. 1995. *Lords of All the World: Ideologies of Empire in Spain, Britain, and France, c.1500–c.1800*. New Haven: Yale University Press.

Pancevski, Bojan. 2005. German Zoo Sparks Outrage by Parading Africans Next to Baboons. *Daily Telegraph*, June 12, p. 29.

Pateman, Carole. 1970. *Participation and Democratic Theory*. Cambridge: Cambridge University Press.

Pateman, Carole. 1975. Sublimation and Reification: Locke, Wolin, and the Liberal-Democratic Conception of the Political. *Politics and Society*, 5, no. 4: 441–67. Reprinted in Pateman (1989a).

Pateman, Carole. 1980. Women and Consent. *Political Theory*, 7, no. 2: 149–68. Reprinted in Pateman (1989a).

Pateman, Carole. 1983. Feminist Critiques of the Public/Private Dichotomy. In Benn and Gaus (1983). Reprinted in Pateman (1989a).

Pateman, Carole. 1985. *The Problem of Political Obligation: A Critical Analysis of Liberal Theory*. 2nd edn. (Orig. edn 1979.) Cambridge: Polity.

Pateman, Carole. 1988. *The Sexual Contract*. Stanford: Stanford University Press.

Pateman, Carole. 1989a. *The Disorder of Women: Democracy, Feminism and Political Theory*. Stanford: Stanford University Press.

Pateman, Carole. 1989b. "God Hath Ordained to Man a Helper": Hobbes, Patriarchy and Conjugal Right. *British Journal of Political Science*, 19, no. 4: 445–63. Reprinted in *Feminist Interpretations and Political Theory*, ed. Mary Lyndon Shanley and Carole Pateman, University Park: Pennsylvania State University Press, 1991.

Pateman, Carole. 1990a. Contract and Ideology: A Reply to Coole. *Politics*, 10, no. 1: 32.

Pateman, Carole. 1990b. Reply to Reviews of *The Sexual Contract*. *Political Theory Newsletter*, 2: 78–82.

Pateman, Carole. 1990c. Sex and Power. *Ethics*, 100, no. 2: 398–407.

Pateman, Carole. 1996. The Sexual Contract and the Animals. *Journal of Social Philosophy*, 27, no. 1: 65–80.

Pateman, Carole. 1997. Beyond *The Sexual Contract*? In Dench (1997).

Pateman, Carole. 1998. Women's Writing, Women's Standing: Theory and Politics in the Early Modern Period. In H. Smith (1998).

Pateman, Carole. 2002. Self-Ownership and Property in the Person: Democratization and a Tale of Two Concepts. *Journal of Political Philosophy*, 10, no. 1: 20–53.

Pateman, Carole. 2003. Mary Wollstonecraft. In Boucher and Kelly (2003).

Pateman, Carole, and Elizabeth Gross, eds. 1997 [1987]. *Feminist Challenges: Social and Political Theory*. Boston: Northeastern University Press.

Paul, Diane. 1984. Eugenics and the Left. *Journal of the History of Ideas*, 45, no. 4: 567–90.

Peffer, R. G. 1990. *Marxism, Morality, and Social Justice*. Princeton: Princeton University Press.

Peterson, Nicolas, and Will Sanders, eds. 1998. *Citizenship and Indigenous Australians: Changing Conceptions and Possibilities*. New York: Cambridge University Press.

Phillips, Anne. 1989. The Original Contract? *Radical Philosophy*, no. 52: 38–40.

Pogge, Thomas W. 2002. *World Poverty and Human Rights: Cosmopolitan Responsibilities and Reforms*. Cambridge: Polity.

Polanyi, Karl. 1944. *The Great Transformation*. New York: Farrar & Rinehart.

Prewitt, Kenneth. 2005. Racial Classification in America: Where Do We Go from Here? *Dædalus*, 134, no. 1: 5–17.

Prince, Mary. 2000 [1831]. *The History of Mary Prince: A West Indian Slave*, ed. Sara Salih. New York: Penguin Books.

Procida, Mary A. 2002. All in the Family: Marriage, Gender, and the Family Business of Imperialism in British India. In Blue, Bunton, and Croizier (2002).

Pufendorf, Samuel. 1934. *On the Law of Nature*, trans. C.H. Oldfather and W.A. Oldfather. Oxford: Oxford University Press.

Puwar, Nirmal. 2004. *Space Invaders: Race, Gender, and Bodies Out of Place*. New York: Berg.

Rawls, John. 1996. *Political Liberalism*. Expanded paperback edn. (Orig. edn 1993.) New York: Columbia University Press.

Rawls, John. 1999a. *Collected Papers*, ed. Samuel Freeman. Cambridge: Harvard University Press.

Rawls, John. 1999b [1987]. The Idea of an Overlapping Consensus. In Rawls (1999a).

Rawls, John. 1999c [1997]. The Idea of Public Reason Revisited. In Rawls (1999a).

Rawls, John. 1999d [1985]. Justice as Fairness: Political Not Metaphysical. In Rawls (1999a).

Rawls, John. 1999e [1975]. A Kantian Conception of Equality. In Rawls (1999a).

Rawls, John. 1999f [1980]. Kantian Constructivism in Moral Theory. In Rawls (1999a).

Rawls, John. 1999g. *The Law of Peoples, with "The Idea of Public Reason Revisited."* Cambridge: Harvard University Press.

Rawls, John. 1999h. *A Theory of Justice,* Rev. edn. (Orig edn 1971.) Cambridge: Harvard University Press.

Rawls, John. 2001. *Justice as Fairness: A Restatement*, ed. Erin Kelly. Cambridge: Harvard University Press.

Resnik, Judith. 1995. From the Senate Judiciary Committee to the Country Courthouse: The Relevance of Gender, Race, and Ethnicity to Adjudication. In Hill and Jordan (1995).

Reynolds, Henry. 1982. *The Other Side of the Frontier: Aboriginal Resistance to the European Invasion of Australia*. Ringwood: Penguin Books Australia.

Reynolds, Henry. 1987. *The Law of the Land*. Ringwood: Penguin Books Australia.

Reynolds, Henry, ed. 1989. *Dispossession: Black Australians and White Invaders*. Sydney: Allen & Unwin.

Reynolds, Henry. 1993. Native Title and Pastoral Leases. In Stephenson and Ratnapala (1993).

Reynolds, Henry. 1996. *Aboriginal Sovereignty: Three Nations, One Australia?* Sydney: Allen & Unwin.

Riley, Patrick. 1982. *Will and Political Legitimacy: A Critical Exposition of Social Contract Theory in Hobbes, Locke, Rousseau, Kant, and Hegel.* Cambridge: Harvard University Press.

Riley, Patrick. 2001a. Introduction: Life and Works of Jean-Jacques Rousseau (1712–1778). In Riley (2001b).

Riley, Patrick, ed. 2001b. *The Cambridge Companion to Rousseau.* New York: Cambridge University Press.

Roberts, Dorothy. 1999 [1997]. *Killing the Black Body: Race, Reproduction, and the Meaning of Liberty.* New York: Vintage Books.

Roberts, Rodney C. 2002a. Introduction. In Roberts (2002b).

Roberts, Rodney C., ed. 2002b. *Injustice and Rectification.* New York: Peter Lang.

Roberts-Wray, Sir Kenneth. 1966. *Commonwealth and Colonial Law.* New York: Praeger.

Roediger, David R. 1999. *The Wages of Whiteness: Race and the Making of the American Working Class.* Rev. edn. (Orig. edn 1991.) New York: Verso.

Roth, Benita. 2004. *Separate Roads to Feminism: Black, Chicana, and White Feminist Movements in America's Second Wave.* New York: Cambridge University Press.

Rousseau, Jean-Jacques. 1968 [1762]. *The Social Contract*, trans. Maurice Cranston. New York: Penguin.

Rousseau, Jean-Jacques. 1979 [1762]. *Emile:* or *On Education*, trans. and introd. Allan Bloom. New York: Basic Books.

Rousseau, Jean-Jacques. 1984 [1755]. *A Discourse on Inequality*, trans. Maurice Cranston. New York: Penguin.

Rousseau, Jean-Jacques. 1997a [1755]. *Discourse on the Origin and the Foundations of Inequality among Men,* or *Second Discourse*. In Rousseau (1997b).

Rousseau, Jean-Jacques. 1997b. *The "Discourses" and Other Early Political Writings*, ed. and trans. Victor Gourevitch. New York: Cambridge University Press.

Rousseau, Jean-Jacques. 1997c. Essay on the Origin of Languages. In Rousseau (1997b).

Rousseau, Jean-Jacques. 1997d [1762]. *Of the Social Contract*. In Rousseau (1997e).

Rousseau, Jean-Jacques. 1997e. *"The Social Contract" and Other Later Political Writings*, ed. and trans. Victor Gourevitch. New York: Cambridge University Press.

Ruiz, Vicki L., and Ellen Carol DuBois. 2000a. Introduction to the Third Edition. In Ruiz and DuBois (2000b).

Ruiz, Vicki L., and Ellen Carol DuBois, eds. 2000b. *Unequal Sisters: A Multicultural Reader in US Women's History*. 3rd edn. (Orig. edn 1990.) New York: Routledge.

Rydell, Robert W. 2002. Science in the Service of Empire; Empire in the Service of Science. In Blue, Bunton, and Croizier (2002).

Sala-Molins, Louis. 2006. *Dark Side of the Light: Slavery and the French Enlightenment*, trans. John Conteh-Morgan. Minneapolis: University of Minnesota Press.

Salih, Sara. 2000. Introduction to *The History of Mary Prince*. In Prince (2000).

Salter, John. 2001. Property and Consent. *Political Theory*, 29, no. 4: 537–55.

Salzberger, Ronald P., and Mary C. Turck, eds. 2004. *Reparations for Slavery: A Reader*. Lanham: Rowman & Littlefield.

Sample, Ruth J. 2003a. *Exploitation: What It Is and Why It's Wrong*. Lanham: Rowman & Littlefield.

Sample, Ruth J. 2003b. Sexual Exploitation and the Social Contract. In S. Brennan (2003).

Sandel, Michael J. 1998. *Liberalism and the Limits of Justice*. 2nd edn. (Orig. edn 1982.) New York: Cambridge University Press.

Saxton, Alexander. 2003 [1990]. *The Rise and Fall of the White Republic: Class Politics and Mass Culture in Nineteenth-Century America*. New York: Verso.

Schloesser, Pauline. 2002. *The Fair Sex: White Women and Racial Patriarchy in the Early American Republic*. New York: New York University Press.

Schmitt, Richard. 2003. Liberalism and Racism. In Stokes and Meléndez (2003).

Schochet, Gordon. 1998. The Significant Sounds of Silence: The Absence of Women from the Political Thought of Sir Robert Filmer and John Locke (or, "Why Can't a Woman Be More Like a Man?"). In H. Smith (1998).

Schott, Robin May, ed. 1997. *Feminist Interpretations of Immanuel Kant*. University Park: Pennsylvania State University Press.

Schröder, Hannelore. 1997. Kant's Patriarchal Order. Trans. Rita Gircour. In Schott (1997).

Seager, Joni. 2003. *The Penguin Atlas of Women in the World*. Rev. and updated edn (orig. edn 1997). New York: Penguin.

Sen, Amartya. 1990. More than 100 Million Women Are Missing. *New York Review of Books*, Dec. 20, pp. 61–6.

Severance, Mary Laura. 2000. Sex and the Social Contract. *English Literary History*, 67, no. 2: 453–513.

Shanley, Mary Lyndon. 1979. Marriage Contract and Social Contract in Seventeenth Century English Political Thought. *Western Political Quarterly*, 32, no. 1: 79–91.

Shapiro, Ian. 1999. *Democratic Justice*. New Haven: Yale University Press.

Shapiro, Thomas M. 2004. *The Hidden Cost of Being African American: How Wealth Perpetuates Inequality*. New York: Oxford University Press.

Shaw, Malcolm. 1978. The Western Sahara Case. *British Yearbook of International Law*, 119: 127–34

Shaw, Malcolm. 1986. *Title to Territory in Africa: International Legal Issues*. New York: Oxford University Press.

Shelby, Tommie. 2004. Race and Social Justice: Rawlsian Considerations. *Fordham Law Review*, 72: 1697–714.

Shelley, Toby. 2004. *Endgame in the Western Sahara: What Future for Africa's Last Colony?* London: Zed Books.

Shipler, David K. 2004. *The Working Poor: Invisible in America*. New York: Alfred A. Knopf.

Shklar, Judith N. 2001 [1991]. *American Citizenship: The Quest for Inclusion*. Cambridge: Harvard University Press.

Singer, Peter, ed. 1991. *A Companion to Ethics*. Cambridge: Blackwell Reference.

Slomp, Gabriella. 2000. *Thomas Hobbes and the Political Philosophy of Glory*. New York: St Martin's Press.

Smedley, Audrey. 1993. *Race in North America: Origin and Evolution of a Worldview*. Boulder: Westview Press.

Smith, Barbara. 2000a [1983]. Introduction. In B. Smith (2000c).

Smith, Barbara. 2000b. Preface to the Rutgers University Press Edition. In B. Smith (2000c).

Smith, Barbara, ed. 2000c [1983]. *Home Girls: A Black Feminist Anthology*. New Brunswick: Rutgers University Press.

Smith, Hilda L., ed. 1998. *Women Writers and the Early Modern British Political Tradition*. New York: Cambridge University Press.

Smith, Rogers M. 1997. *Civic Ideals: Conflicting Visions of Citizenship in US History*. New Haven: Yale University Press.

Spelman, Elizabeth V. 2001 [1988]. Gender & Race: The Ampersand Problem in Feminist Thought. In Bhavnani (2001b).

Squadrito, Kathy. 2002. Locke and the Dispossession of the American Indian. In Ward and Lott (2002).

Stanley, Amy Dru. 1996. Home Life and the Reality of the Market. In Stokes and Conway (1996).

Stephenson, M. A., and Suri Ratnapala, eds. 1993. *Mabo: A Judicial Revolution: The Aboriginal Land Rights Decision and Its Impact on Australian Law*. St Lucia: University of Queensland Press.

Stevens, Jacqueline. 2003. On the Morals of Genealogy. *Political Theory*, 31, no. 4: 558–88.

Stokes, Curtis, and Theresa Meléndez, eds. 2003. *Racial Liberalism and the Politics of Urban America*. East Lansing: Michigan State University Press.

Stokes, Melvyn, and Stephen Conway, eds. 1996. *The Market Revolution in America: Social, Political, and Religious Expressions, 1800–1880*. Charlottesville: University Press of Virginia.

Strobel, Margaret. 2002. Women's History, Gender History, and European Colonialism. In Blue, Bunton, and Croizier (2002).

Sullivan, Barbara Ann. 1995. Re-thinking Prostitution. In Caine and Pringle (1995).

Sullivan, Barbara Ann. 1997. *The Politics of Sex: Prostitution and Pornography in Australia since 1945*. New York: Cambridge University Press.

Sullivan, Shannon, and Nancy Tuana, eds. 2007. *Race and Epistemologies of Ignorance*. Albany: SUNY Press.

Swain, Carol. 1992. Double Standard, Double Bind: African-American Leadership after the Thomas Debacle. In Morrison (1992).

Tamang, Seira. 2002. Dis-embedding the Sexual/Social Contract: Citizenship and Gender in Nepal. *Citizenship Studies*, 6, no. 3: 309–24.

Thompson, Janna. 2002. *Taking Responsibility for the Past: Reparation and Historical Injustice*. Cambridge: Polity.

Todd, Barbara J. 1998. "To Be Some Body": Married Women and *The Hardships of the English Laws*. In H. Smith (1998).

Travis, Alan. 2002. Overhaul of Victorian Sex Laws Wins Cross-Party Support. *Guardian Weekly*, Nov 28–Dec. 4.

Truth, Sojourner. 1995. When Woman Gets Her Rights Man Will Be Right. In Guy-Sheftall (1995).

Tuck, Richard. 1994. Rights and Pluralism. In Tully with Weinstock (1994).

Tuck, Richard. 1999. *The Rights of War and Peace: Political Thought and the International Order from Grotius to Kant*. New York: Oxford University Press.

Tully, James. 1993a. *An Approach to Political Philosophy: Locke in Contexts*. New York: Cambridge University Press.

Tully, James. 1993b. Rediscovering America: The *Two Treatises* and Aboriginal Rights. In Tully (1993a).

Tully, James. 1994. Aboriginal Property and Western Theory: Recovering a Middle Ground. *Social Philosophy and Policy*, 11, no. 2: 153–80.

Tully, James. 1995. *Strange Multiplicity: Constitutionalism in an Age of Diversity*. New York: Cambridge University Press.

Tully, James. 2000. The Struggles of Indigenous Peoples for and of Freedom. In Ivison, Patton, and Sanders (2000).

Tully, James, with the assistance of Daniel M. Weinstock, ed. 1994. *Philosophy in an Age of Pluralism: The Philosophy of Charles Taylor in Question*. New York: Cambridge University Press.

Turner, Frederick. 1994. The Significance of the Frontier in American History. In *Rereading Frederick Jackson Turner: "The Significance of the Frontier in American History" and Other Essays*, ed. and with comments by John Mack Faragher. New York: Henry Holt.

UNDP (United Nations Development Programme). 2005. *Human Development Report 2005*. New York: UNDP. At http://hdr.undp.org/reports/global/2005/.

Uzgalis, William. 2002. "An Inconsistency Not to Be Excused": On Locke and Racism. In Ward and Lott (2002).

Valls, Andrew. 1998. Review of *The Racial Contract*, by Charles W. Mills. *American Political Science Review*, 92, no. 3: 691–2.

Valls, Andrew, ed. 2005. *Race and Racism in Modern Philosophy*. Ithaca: Cornell University Press.

Van Holk, L. E., and D. G. Roeflofsen, eds. 1983. *The Grotius Reader*. The Hague: T. M. C. Asser Instituut.

Van Krieken, Robert. 2000. From *Milirrpum* (1) to *Mabo* (2): The High Court, Terra Nullius and Moral Entrepreneurship. *University of New South Wales Law Journal*, 23, no. 1: 63–77

Vattel, Emer de. 1982 [1758]. *The Law of Nations*. New York: AMS Press.

Vulliamy, Ed. 2005. Streets of Despair. *Amnesty International*, 31, no. 4: 12–16.

Waldron, Jeremy. 1988. *The Right to Private Property*. New York: Oxford University Press.

Waldron, Jeremy. 1994. John Locke: Social Contract versus Political Anthropology. In Boucher and Kelly (1994b).

Wallace, Michele. 1995 [1975]. Anger in Isolation: A Black Feminist's Search for Sisterhood. In Guy-Sheftall (1995).

Walzer, Michael. 1995. Contract, Social. In Honderich (1995).

Ward, Julie K., and Tommy L. Lott, eds. 2002. *Philosophers on Race: Critical Essays*. Malden: Blackwell.

Ware, Vron. 1992. *Beyond the Pale: White Women, Racism and History*. New York: Verso.

Warren, Kenneth. 1997. Constructing Subpersons. *The Nation*, 265, no. 14: 44–5.

Washington, Mary Helen, ed. 1975. *Black-Eyed Susans*. New York: Anchor Books.

Washington, Mary Helen. 1982. Teaching *Black-Eyed Susans*: An Approach to the Study of Black Women Writers. In Hull, Scott, and Smith (1982).

Webber, Jeremy. 2000. Beyond Regret: *Mabo*'s Implications for Australian Constitutionalism. In Ivison, Patton, and Sanders (2000).

Welchman, Jennifer. 1995. Locke on Slavery and Inalienable Rights. *Canadian Journal of Philosophy*, 25, no. 1: 67–81.

Wells-Barnett, Ida B. 1995. Lynch Law in America. In Guy-Sheftall (1995).

Wells-Barnett, Ida B. 2002 [1892–1900]. *On Lynchings*. Amherst: Humanity Books.

Wertheimer, Alan. 1996. *Exploitation*. Princeton: Princeton University Press.

Westlake, John. 1894. *Chapters on the Principles of International Law*. Cambridge: Cambridge University Press.

Wilkins, Barry. 1999. See: Review of *The Racial Contract* and *Blackness Visible: Essays on Philosophy and Race*, by Charles W. Mills. *Radical Philosophy*, no. 95: 51–3.

Williams, Glyndwr. 1981. "Far More Happier Than We Europeans": Reactions to the Australian Aborigines on Cook's Voyage. *Australian Historical Studies*, 19, no. 77: 499–513.

Williams, Linda Faye. 2003. *The Constraint of Race: Legacies of White Skin Privilege in America*. University Park: Pennsylvania State University Press.

Williams, Linda Faye. 2004. The Issue of Our Time: Economic Inequality and Political Power in America. *Perspectives on Politics*, 2, no. 4: 683–9.

Williams, Melissa S., and Stephen Macedo, eds. 2005. *Political Exclusion and Domination. Nomos*, 46. New York: New York University Press.

Williams, Robert A. Jr. 1990. *The American Indian in Western Legal Thought: The Discourses of Conquest*. New York: Oxford University Press.

Winant, Howard. 2001. *The World Is a Ghetto: Race and Democracy Since World War II*. New York: Basic Books.

Winbush, Raymond A., ed. 2003. *Should America Pay? Slavery and the Raging Debate on Reparations*. New York: Amistad/ HarperCollins.

Wing, Adrien Katherine, ed. 2003. *Critical Race Feminism: A Reader*. 2nd edn. (Orig. edn 1997.) New York: New York University Press.

Wingo, Ajume. 2003. *Veil Politics in Liberal Democratic States*. New York: Cambridge University Press.

Wingrove, Elizabeth Rose. 2000. *Rousseau's Republican Romance*. Princeton: Princeton University Press.

Wright, Joanne H. 2004. *Origin Stories in Political Thought: Discourses on Gender, Power, and Citizenship*. Toronto: University of Toronto Press.

X, Malcolm. 1989 [1971]. *The End of White World Supremacy: Four Speeches by Malcolm X*, ed. Imam Benjamin Karim. New York: Arcade Books.

Yancy, George, ed. 1998. *African-American Philosophers: 17 Conversations*. New York: Routledge.

Yancy, George. 2004a. A Foucauldian (Genealogical) Reading of Whiteness: The Production of the Black Body/Self and the Racial Deformation of Pecola Breedlove in Toni Morrison's *The Bluest Eye*. In Yancy (2004b).

Yancy, George, ed. 2004b. *What White Looks Like: African-American Philosophers on the Whiteness Question*. New York: Routledge.

Young, Iris Marion. 1990. *Justice and the Politics of Difference*. Princeton: Princeton University Press.

Young, Joseph, and Jana Evans Braziel, eds. 2006. *Race and the Foundations of Knowledge: Cultural Amnesia in the Academy*. Urbana and Chicago: University of Illinois Press.

Young, Robert. 2006. Putting Materialism Back into Race Theory: Toward a Transformative Theory of Race. In Young and Braziel (2006).

Yuval-Davis, Nira. 1997. *Gender and Nation*. London and Thousand Oaks: Sage.

Zack, Naomi. 1997a. The American Sexualization of Race. In Zack (1997b).

Zack, Naomi, ed. 1997b. *Race/Sex: Their Sameness, Difference, and Interplay.* New York: Routledge.

Zack, Naomi, ed. 2000. *Women of Color and Philosophy.* Malden: Blackwell.

Zack, Naomi. 2003. The Racial Contract according to Charles Mills. In Stokes and Meléndez (2003).

Zerilli, Linda. 1989. In the Beginning, Rape. *Women's Review of Books,* 6: 6.

Index